Between Give and Take

A Clinical Guide to Contextual Therapy

D0169092

Between Give and Take

A Clinical Guide to Contextual Therapy

By

Ivan Boszormenyi-Nagy, M.D.

Professor and Chief of Family Therapy Section,
Department of Mental Health Sciences,
Hahnemann University, Philadelphia, Pennsylvania;
Director, Institute for Contextual Growth,
Ambler, Pennsylvania

and

Barbara R. Krasner, Ph.D.

Clinical Assistant Professor, Department of
Mental Health Sciences, Hahnemann University;
Adjunct Professor, Graduate Religion Department,
LaSalle University, Philadelphia, Pennsylvania; and
Director, Center for Contextual Family Therapy
and Allied Studies, King of Prussia, Pennsylvania

BRUNNER/MAZEL Publishers • NEW YORK

Library of Congress Cataloging-in-Publication Data

Boszormenyi-Nagy, Ivan, 1920–
  Between give and take.

  Bibliography: p.
  1. Family psychotherapy. I. Krasner, Barbara R.,
1933–   . II. Title. III. Title: Contextual
therapy. [DNLM: 1. Family therapy. WM 430.5.F2 B7476]
RC488.5.B549 1986   616.89'156   86-2219
ISBN 0-87630-418-8

Copyright © 1986 by Ivan Boszormenyi-Nagy and Barbara R. Krasner

Published by
BRUNNER/MAZEL, INC.
19 Union Square West
New York, New York 10003

Contents

Preface

This book is addressed to therapists of all schools, modalities and convictions. It incorporates experience with both psychodynamic individual therapy and systemic-classical family therapy, but aims to transcend them. Summarizations and critical reviews of these approaches are helpful, introductory reading to the subject matter of contextual therapy.

The authors' long-term dialogue started with a common interest in Martin Buber's writings. It dates back to the time when the manuscript for Invisible Loyalties was completed (1971). This dialogue was the source of our book.

As the basic architect of the contextual approach it was Ivan Boszormenyi-Nagy's responsibility to designate its building stones and compose the first version of the manuscript. He was expected to define the design for an up-to-date textbook and clinical guide for the approach that reflects his current view of the premises of therapy rooted in the reality of human relationship. In this, the book represents the outcome of his 40 years of reflections on the essence of effective therapy and prevention. The actual writing of the book was dialogic.

As a codeveloper of the contextual approach, it was Barbara Krasner's task to contribute new formulations, fresh perspectives and extensive illustrations. She recast the new version of the writing and strove to make its complexities and language more accessible to the reader. In this, the book also represents an integration of her 20 years' involvement in social, political and religious concerns, her work with social agencies and her clinical experience.

This collaboration between Boszormenyi-Nagy and Krasner was based on a 15-year cooperative effort at formulating a cohesive, convincing and communicable system of therapeutic approach. In the end both authors collaborated on a final, finished manuscript.

Our acknowledgments are due to numerous colleagues who have over the years contributed through the exchange of thought, and clinical experiences. Geraldine Spark was Ivan Boszormenyi-Nagy's co-author of *Invisible Loyalties*, the first major formulation of the approach. Special recognition is due to Margaret Cotroneo whose critical and creative thinking through discussion, teaching and co-authorship has helped to develop the contextual approach. Beneficial input was obtained through clinical, conceptual and social service exchanges with many colleagues, especially Judith Grunebaum, David Ulrich, J. Bruce Grisi and Suzanne Noble.

Ammy van Heusden (Amsterdam, Holland), Catherine Ducommun (Lausanne, Switzerland) and Siri Rinnyng (Vikersund, Norway), themselves teachers of the approach in Europe, have been generous readers and critics of the manuscript.

We are grateful to Doris Duncan and Shirley Medley for their steady readiness to type.

David Krasner lent himself to the lengthy writing process as sounding board, critic and source of courage. We are grateful to our families for providing us with experience, support, patience, and understanding without which this book could not have been written.

Prologue

THE AUTHORS' PATHS TOWARD CONTEXTUAL THERAPY

Ivan Boszormenyi-Nagy

Contextual therapy, a preventive and healing mode of intervention that is both a method and a set of premises, was founded and initially developed by Ivan Boszormenyi-Nagy. As a set of premises, it informs both personal and professional relationships. As a method, it introduces a new, ethical dimension of relational leverages and determinants. Contextual therapy was an offshoot of dialectical intergenerational therapy (Boszormenyi-Nagy, 1972; Boszormenyi-Nagy & Spark, 1973) which itself evolved out of early attempts at intensive family therapy with schizophrenics (Boszormenyi-Nagy, 1960, 1962, 1965a).

Ivan Boszormenyi-Nagy was one of the originators of what became the family therapy "movement" in the United States. He was the founding director of what became the Department of Family Psychiatry of Eastern Pennsylvania Psychiatric Institute of Philadelphia (1957), one of the earliest and most active exploratory and training centers in family therapy. Many well known early family therapists developed through affiliation with the Department (Margaret Cotroneo, James L. Framo, Philip Friedman, Geraldine Lincoln-Grossman, Leon Robinson, David Rubinstein, Geraldine Spark, Oscar Weiner, Gerald H. Zuk, and others).

Unlike psychoanalysis, family therapy evolved from several conceptual frameworks. Boszormenyi-Nagy's interest centered on both the development of a broad-based family relational theory and a live exchange with the leaders of other schools of thought. Some of the early nationwide conferences in family therapy (1964, 1967) were sponsored by the Department of Family Psychiatry. With Geraldine M. Spark and Alfred Friedman, Nagy initiated the Family Institute of Philadelphia in 1963, and with Gerald Berenson and Geraldine M. Spark the American Family Therapy Association in the late 1970s. Live contact with the development of the family therapy field was inseparable from the evolution of contextual therapy. Boszormenyi-Nagy and two of his associates (David Rubinstein and Gerald Zuk) had an early input into family therapy development in Europe through a three-month nationwide training program in Leyden (1967) which, along with the contributions of Ammy Van Heusden and others, launched the Netherlands as the first active country in family therapy outside the United States.

The late 1930s witnessed progress in the understanding of the biochemical basis of enzymatic function, the elements of cellular physiology. Intellectually, during the same period continental Europe witnessed the development of existential thought. As a psychiatric resident at the University of Budapest, Boszormenyi-Nagy decided to complete formal, chemical training at the University of Budapest (1944-1948). At the same time he was eager to learn about the existential and psychological dynamics of schizophrenia. In this endeavor Kalman Gyarfas was his initial guide. Later, in Chicago, Gyarfas became Virginia Satir's mentor (Jackson & Weakland, 1961).

However, the implications of his research at the University of Illinois on the enzymatic properties of the blood cells of psychotics convinced Boszormenyi-Nagy that the contemporary tools of enzyme biochemistry were no closer to the understanding of psychosis than previous efforts at neurohistology had been. Nor did the fascinating development of psychopharmacology in the mid 1950s appear to be capable of producing the answer.

Since 1955 Boszormenyi-Nagy has endeavored to focus on the exploration of the connections between depth psychology and close relationships. This was further facilitated by two new influences. One was Martin Buber's writings which pointed to a relationally-based existential understanding of human life. Another came through the writings of Ronald Fairbairn, the founder of the object relations school of psychoanalysis. It was his intention to apply these frameworks to the treatment of schizophrenics that caused Boszormenyi-Nagy to accept the offer of the Board of Eastern Pennsylvania Psychiatric Institute to set up a research-therapeutic department in 1957. The Department of Family Psychiatry continued its therapeutic training and research work until 1980 when the Pennsylvania Department of Welfare terminated the programs of this distinguished academic institute.

As director of the Department, Boszormenyi-Nagy was administratively free to design therapeutic strategy. During a period of concentration on intensive individual therapy with schizophrenics, he had ample opportunity for useful exchanges with leaders of Chestnut Lodge Sanatorium in Rockville, Maryland, perhaps the most significant of the centers for the therapy of psychosis. Over time, he became convinced of the crucial therapeutic role of trustworthiness, a conviction that was confirmed by the work and writings of Harold Searles, Otto Will, Donald Burnham, and others who worked in the outstanding tradition of Frieda Fromm-Reichman and Harry Stack Sullivan.

Another early methodological influence on Boszormenyi-Nagy came from Maxwell Jones' brief visit to the Family Psychiatry Department in 1958. It was then that Nagy was inspired to institute several procedures practiced at Jones' "therapeutic community" in London.

Yet only one of Jones' innovations had a lasting impact on the program of the Department of Family Psychiatry. That was a joint meeting of staff, patients and their relatives on a weekly basis. These meetings corroborated Nagy's and Kalman Gyarfas' earlier convictions about the importance of the patient-parent treatment context. It became increasingly evident that in the context of their families the otherwise withdrawn and bizarre psychotics were suddenly transformed into different people. Often taking leadership roles among their family members, they remained controversial but appeared to be authentic. By 1958, Nagy and his associates were seeing psychotic in-patients with their families. Before long the individual therapy sessions were discontinued. Within a few years Nagy extended the work from schizophrenics to all types of conditions and the inpatient program yielded to an outpatient one. During this period Nagy was also interested in the early work of Murray Bowen, Lyman Wynne, Nathan Ackerman, Carl Whitaker, and Don Jackson.

By the mid 1960s the Department had become a training facility, teaching hundreds of professionals annually and initiating the family therapy training programs of all five medical schools of Philadelphia. It established a family-day program based on multiple family treatment and it consulted with churches, schools, courts, city housing projects, community leaders of deprived neighborhoods, community mental health centers, mental hospitals, institutions for the mentally deficient, etc. This enabled the project to become one of the first known family therapy programs (Jackson & Weakland, 1961).

The family approach to schizophrenia at first and later to all forms of psychiatric problems enabled Nagy and his associates to see improved results in their work with the identified patient and now with the rest of the family. Instead of engendering therapist burn-out, workers at this state-supported research therapeutic program were able to share their enthusiasm with colleagues in the field. This led to organizing early nation-wide conferences in 1964 and 1967 and to subsequent "integrative" publications (Boszormenyi-Nagy & Framo, 1965, Zuk & Boszormenyi-Nagy, 1967).

The early development of the contextual approach was inseparable from Nagy's concern about contributing to the field of family therapy. Conceptually, the initial emphasis on individually-based, existential-psychodynamic understanding yielded to systemic transactional formulations and, under the influence of Martin Buber's writings, to the focus on the ethical dimension.

Barbara R. Krasner

Contextual therapy was in its second decade when Barbara Krasner first encountered it. Its focus on the justice dynamics of human relationships converged with her involvements in social justice movements, including civil rights, the peace movement, and the women's movement. Its linkages to the work of Martin Buber converged with her studies in religion and psychotherapy. Her work in Jewish-Christian relations and in Arab-Israeli relations was profoundly influenced by Buber's emphasis on "healing through meeting." This emphasis also provided her work with a bridge to therapeutic theory and practice.

Essentially a way of knowing and living, the notion of healing through meeting became a cornerstone of her emphasis in the contextual approach, i.e., healing occurs most fully when relating partners can bring themselves and their terms for relationship to each other for dialogue, mutual consideration, acknowledgment and negotiation. Through its unapologetic affirmation of the validity of many-sidedness (multilaterality), contextual therapy also embraced Buber's realm of "the Between." This realm is more familiarly known as the "meeting place of an 'I' and a 'Thou'."

Purely as a therapeutic modality, contextual therapy was developed by Boszormenyi-Nagy, and expanded by him and other clinicians. As a way, however, the contextual paradigm with its dynamics of loyalty, justice and trustworthiness are intrinsic to the philosophical anthropology of Martin Buber. They are also the basis of Jewish mysticism and the prophetic tradition. Krasner's (1975) Ph.D. dissertation was an attempt to integrate the wisdom of the therapeutic and religious communities. For her, the seed core of religious wisdom is transdenominational and consists of every generation's obligation to help its members find a balance between personal freedom and interpersonal responsibility.

Krasner was also influenced by people from the American religious community whose faith, stance and life work were essentially dialogic. Unabashedly rooted in the particularity of their own personal, ethnic, and communal legacies, they were graced with a capacity to be universally empathic. Anchored in time-honored traditions of learning and wisdom, they retained a capacity for impassioned commitment and action. Among them were Lillian Miller, Howard Moody, Abraham Heschel, Maurice Friedman, Charlotte Meacham, Alexander Shapiro, Marjorie Penney, Paul Chapman, and Martin Luther King.

In 1970 Krasner began to train at the Department of Family Psychiatry, EPPI, where she was invited to join the staff. Later she became associate director for community outreach. In this capacity she began to use contextual methodologies in varied milieus, including social, legal, and religious agencies. Contextual therapy began to inform her intragroup and intergroup work. In many of these efforts and projects, she was joined by Margaret Cotroneo, and worked and wrote in close collegiality with her. Krasner currently directs the Center for Contextual Family Therapy and Allied Studies, whose emphases are clinical, social and spiritual.

Between Give and Take

A Clinical Guide to Contextual Therapy

I. PREMISES

CHAPTER 1

An Orientation to Contextual Therapy

Psychotherapy today is only one branch of a huge healing industry that seems to have an insatiable market. The public's search for help and guidance has grown to the point where countless schools of healing exist. Many of these schools and modalities are, of course, legitimate. Others are bereft of proven knowledge, reason and training. The public's press for human services occasionally gives rise to cultism and other ephemeral forms of change artistry that convey a promise of secular salvation.

It is easy to criticize the current state of affairs, but inherent difficulties exist in any attempt to critique the quality of the wares offered in a busy marketplace. The social and fiscal accountability of psychotherapy and the related healing arts themselves have come under increasingly close scrutiny and comment. To be sure, psychotherapy is derived from the field of medicine. The intuitive genius of Sigmund Freud, as well as the boundless input of many others, have produced truths that can be mutually validated among practitioners, and between practitioners and their clients. Even so, psychotherapy cannot claim a causally founded, scientific basis.

From the early nineteenth century on, *medicine* has depended on its practitioners' capacity to establish scientific causality. Here the patient typically functions as the monitor of the subjective signs of physical breakdown or illness. These signs function as indicators of the fact that a person's bodily integrity is under "objective" attack by bacteria, by tumor, by allergies, or by the processes of autoimmunity, among other possibilities. Beginning with the client's symptom or complaint, physicians proceed on the hypothesis that they can uncover the biological regulations that underlie and determine scientific truth. Scientific medicine may often fall short of its ideal goals but, at the very least, causality is intrinsic to its design.

By comparison, psychotherapy has never reached the stage of a truly causal science. From its beginnings, *classical psychotherapy* stressed its own truth. Emerging out of a biological background, psychotherapy acknowledged causality as well as it could. At base, however, Freud's focus was on the degree of consonance between a patient's ''reality principle'' and his or her neurotic denial of it. Had the patient failed to become master of his existential options and limitations? Freud wanted to make his patients accountable for the mature planning that leads to reasonable enjoyment of life's potential—and to do it essentially from the patient's own vantage point. This goal included scrutiny of the patient's capacity for relationships: that is, from his own unilateral perspective, how was he to secure benefits attached to mature relationships with people. In brief, a person's capacity to consider the implications of short-term pleasure and satisfactions for his or her long-term goals and life consequences constitutes the essence of Freud's principle of reality.

It is psychology rather than biology that became the medium of intervention for psychoanalysis. Nevertheless, traditional psychotherapy retained the medical model of contracting with one ''patient.'' The patient's complaints or symptoms continued to be viewed as subjective indicators of *his* objective illness. By contrast, from the start, *classical family therapy* expanded its contract to include the interests of the patient's family members. Revolutionary in its impact and implications, in our view family therapy represented a shift to a multipersonal contract, rather than a change to a new method or new theory of pathology.

From its inception, family therapy was essentially unrelated to marriage counseling. Developing out of its own basis in the fifties, the *family movement* was chiefly the creation of therapists who treated psychotics: Theodore Lidz, Stephen Fleck, Alice Cornelison, Murray Bowen, Lyman Wynne, Don Jackson, Ivan Boszormenyi-Nagy, Virginia Satir, the latter two inspired by Kalman Gyarfas. Carl Whitaker and their associates had long evinced interest in psychotics and their development from within their families of origin. Though an outsider to the psychotherapy professions, Gregory Bateson, a scientist, was primarily interested in the familial roots of schizophrenia. Nathan Ackerman and Warren Brodey were among the few therapists who came from therapy with children and their families. So, too, it seems, was the case with John Bell.

It may be that the underlying common denominator unifying these early pioneers was the courage to struggle with challenges of *parent-child relating*, a realm of uniquely powerful characteristics, dynamics and motivations. The primary interests of these early family workers offered a sharp contrast to the central concerns of marriage counselors whose goals were geared to peer relating. A focus on the peer relationships of mates is founded on symmetrical options for reworking skewed balances between them, and on options for terminating the relationship and finding replacements when required. No such options exist for parents and children whose relatedness holds global consequences for each other, regardless of the status of their current intimacy or estrangement. In sum, the newly emerging family field was reaching into the theoretical abyss of *multipersonal* and *intergenerational* relationships. Its practitioners had come to conclusions that forced them to expand the scope of their therapeutic contract. At the same time, they were being overwhelmed by the inherent incompatibility that exists between a unilateral, individual viewpoint, and the systemic-transactional realm of phenomena with its latent risk of depersonalizing the individual.

The rationale of *group therapy* is unable to cover the essentials of parent-child relationships. Still, the assumptions of group therapy constituted at least a partial prototype for the systemic-structural thinking that became the mainstay of classical family therapy. Classical family therapy shifted its focus from the unique realities of the differentiating individual to the systemic realities whose constituent elements could be identified in any group. These included the here-and-now interactions and communications that took place in the therapy room, transactional patterns that were embedded in the family group, family structures, interpersonal boundaries, role assignments, and power alliances among other factors. Nonetheless, the early family movement did not establish links with group therapy or organizational association with marriage counseling. Instead, it developed its special emphasis on a systems point of view, typically emphasizing parent-child relationships.

CONTEXTUAL THERAPY AS AN INTEGRATIVE STANCE

An outgrowth of both individual and classical family therapy, contextual therapy takes an *integrative stance*. It argues that a truly comprehensive grasp of human existence is inevitably composed of both individual and relational realities. It also contends that, as usually applied, systems theory tends to surrender personal depth and scope to address the complexities of parent-child relations. These have more to do with equity of responsibility than with family structure and transactional patterns. At base, contextual therapy means to reintroduce the truth of personal uniqueness into systemic therapy, and to bridge with individual therapy through relational linkages and balances.

In this approach, *relational reality* may be viewed as a large container that surrounds and includes the fundamental dimensions of individual uniqueness or personhood. These dimensions are fourfold, involving biology, psychology, transactional patterns, and responsibility. That is, biologically determined, each person as a self is responsible for facing his or her own life options. These options occur and must be identified in a milieu that is burdened with transactional patternings that ricochet from person to person, and from generation to generation. In the process specific *consequences* evolve and, in their flow from one life to another, impinge on the futures of people who are still unborn. In its design, the *contextual approach* may be defined as more than a therapeutic modality, given the organismic base of biology, psychology, transactional patterns, and responsibility, and how they intertwine. Its basic stance is inseparable from the primary prevention that must be implied whenever adults take responsibility for the welfare and well-being of posterity.

CONSEQUENCES: A KEY TO THE CONTEXT

The fundamental design for contextual interventions is based on two convictions: 1) That the *consequences* of one person's decisions and actions can affect the lives of all the people who are significantly related to him, and 2) that *satisfactory relating* for one person is inseparable from the responsible consideration of consequences for all of the people to whom he or she is in significant relationship. As we use the term, context implies consequences that flow from person to person, from generation to generation, and from one system to its successive system. The term "context," then, is used by the authors to convey a highly specific meaning: the dynamic and ethical interconnectedness—past, present and future—that exists among people whose very being has significance for each other.

In our view the consequential nature of relationships is ontological, based on the very fact of *being*. Family relationships are empowered by the fact that the members *are* connected to each other by birth. They are empowered only secondarily by what family members *do* for each other. Simply put, relationships draw their significance from *being* itself. Unrivalled in its closeness, the relationship between a mother and her fetus best demonstrates our point. The weightiness of their connections is rooted in begetting, in becoming, in being, and in deserving. Despite what they may eventually do to and for each other, in the first instance the significance they hold for each other is invested in their being. Communications and transactions will inevitably contribute to the quality of their lives together. However, it is the connectedness *per se* that proves to be the factor of greatest consequence. The unwavering assumption that connectedness continues to exist, even among those close relatives who may cut themselves off from contact and communication, is a therapeutic resource by itself.

Given the pull of close attachments, the younger the person is, the more dependent he will be on the integrity of his adult world. The more dependent, the more likely he will be to suffer from the destructive consequences of exploitative adult behavior whose input may engender lasting negative character traits. Obviously, then, infants and children are highly vulnerable to destructive consequences.

In any case, individual, e.g., psychological and transactional characteristics, tend to be derived from the consequences of past relationships, and hold consequences for future relationships. It should be noted here that the process of transmission is an open-ended one whose *forward thrust* offers new options for healing and growth. In our experience, the consequences of successive generations never form a closed feedback system. Consequences of the past are decisively influential, perhaps even irreversible, but not rigidly *predetermining*, circular, or homeostatic.

As we use it then, the term "context" implies a given "order of being." It implies the inescapability of intergenerational consequences. It implies that no one is exempt from the good or bad consequences of relationship. It also implies that there are intrinsic opportunities in significant relationships for transforming existing consequences—through discovering new options for relating, and making fresh inputs into stagnant relationships. Context is shaped by the openness of people's realities and by the malleability of people's fates.

An enabling whole, context recognizes the limiting aspects of thinking in terms of family "pathology." Instead, it emphasizes the existence of *resources* in significant relationships that, once actualized, can rechannel hatred into closeness, felt injustice into balances of fairness, and mistrust into trust. In this sense context is inductively defined by the process and flow of relational consequences. Contextual interventions are never solely defined by a set of premises about the causes of the family members' pathology nor by a set of methodologies on how to rework pathology. In the first instance, contextual therapists respond to empirical evidence that suggests that, at any time, partners have options for responsibly acting on the relational consequences affecting themselves and each other.

In part, there is an overlap between *context* and *system*. The difference between them is substantial, however, and chiefly has to do with their logical processes. As already indicated, context implies a realm of relationship defined and characterized by the dynamics inherent in the prospect of vital give and take between significantly interconnected partners. Its methodologies are linked to people's responsible readiness to investigate the consequences to every partner to these relationships, and how to alter them for the purposes of healing. On the other hand, system implies a descriptive realm of relationship that is held together by certain functional rules. The system is encompassed within specific deductive criteria, i.e., accepted conclusions drawn from a set of premises, whose truth is based only on the formal or functional unison of the constituents. Systemic conclusions are defined by categorical descriptions like role definitions, coalitions, networks, recursive or homeostatic sequences of behavior, social organization, and subsystems among others.

Systemic epistemology organizes family relationships into behavioral categories. It then posits that pathology can be righted by therapeutic interventions that focus on enmeshment, rigid coalitions, generational boundaries, or role reversals, for example. By contrast, context implies an existential openness that belongs to the totality of the consequences and influences that impinge on the welfare of relating parties now and later. Thus, any behavioral, structural description of relationship is not viewed as inherently "good" or "bad" for the family. Instead, structural descriptions of relationship are seen as additional sources of consequences, whether helpful or detrimental. Relational *consequences* have widespread implications for all relating partners, for future generations, and for posterity as a whole. Inevitably these consequences will affect a conflicted young couple and their prospective children alike—whatever the systemic characteristics. To consider the isolated therapy of a parental couple as a subsystem, unrelated to the fate of their young children, is noncontextual.

In summary, context is an ontological realm. It consists of pre-ethical reality, i.e., the fact of personal accountability for relational consequences. Its criteria for validity rest on an ethical choice: assuming or refusing to assume responsibility for the consequences of current relationships that are bound to affect others. The *willingness to care* about consequences is not synonymous with predictive knowledge about all future prospects of past and present behaviors. This, of course, would be a humanly impossible task.

A young adult may suffer from painful and disturbing shortcomings in his daily life without realizing that his problems hinge on stagnation in his formative relationships. The shadow of abandoned relationship with members of one's family of origin can fall on a person's most important peer relationships. The linkage between the two relationships is often completely obscured by avoidance, forgetting or a genuine lack of awareness. *Contextual therapy aims at interventions based on the understanding of the fundamental connections between formative and all later relationships.* The most important therapeutic resources stem from facing the responsibility for these consequential linkages.

A young woman has given up seeking closeness with her allegedly distant and coldly rejecting parents. She has had years of marital difficulties. Her moods and evasion of a frustrating sexual life have discouraged her husband and filled her with feelings of guilt. It seems that resentment and disappointment have blocked any moves toward her parents.

The contextual therapist's repeated efforts to prod this woman to reconnect with her parents were met with evasiveness and arguments on the uselessness of all attempts. She argued that her parents were rigid and unchangeable. The therapist recognized that the woman was entitled to attention focused on her own suffering, and so offered a moratorium: He would initially attend to her marital and mothering concerns and only periodically return to the theme of how her "cutoff" from her parents was functioning as a festering wound.

Over the months, however, attention was repeatedly directed at the prospect of how her parents might respond to her, or what her own reaction might be if she tried to approach them. The therapist suggested that some of the family members' detached behavior might itself amount to them "screaming out" to each other. Eventually the young woman recalled an occasion at which she literally screamed out to her mother while she was in the house by herself. This recollection helped convince her that she too had a deep need to connect with them and soon she was able to go to lunch with her mother. Their conversation was promising and new excitement and interest entered into all of the aspects of this young woman's life.

The Role of Responsibility

Responsibility for consequences as a relational reality is a demanding notion that is sometimes viewed as retrogressive and even countercultural. It seems to fly in the face of the ordinary wisdom of life that offers more expedient routes, e.g., the readiness to appease people's self-oriented claims and alleged rights, provided that no one seems to get hurt. "Please people and make no enemies!" is an appealing position if it can be done. But it is rarely possible. Moreover, such a position is essentially unrealistic and unethical; it entices people into the false hope that they can live their lives free of the need to be responsible for the consequences of relating.

It is easy to overlook the fact that children are obliged to pay the price of adult freedom from responsibility. It is children who will inherit the costs of poor parenting, indifferent education, hypocritical values, vindictive intergroup traditions, alienation, and a lack of trustworthiness and stability in failing nuclear families and their alternatives—to say nothing of the costs for our children of issues like air and water pollution, and the terrifying specter of the ultimate radioactive contamination of the environment. In our view, few caring parents would deliberately ignore the consequences of overt behavior like eating all of the food in the house while their children went hungry. Sadly, in terms of less overt or immediate forms of responsibility, it seems less costly for adults to take what they can get, and let their children fend for themselves.

One of the fundamental guiding principles of contextual therapy is based on its recognition that children are captive legatees of past and present behavior. Given this reality, contextual work, like other therapies, is geared to helping people first find short-term, immediate interventions to their problems and their pain. Its work is also geared towards helping adults incorporate responsibility for the *consequences* for posterity. Moreover, contextual workers argue that there is ample evidence to prove that a person's responsible investment in posterity *ipso facto* constitutes therapeutic intervention. A divorcing parent may want her freedom. By providing her child with continuity of parenting from both her ex-husband and herself, she is likely to win her freedom as well as incremental degrees of healing.

To put it in other terms, the contextual approach asks its therapists to help clients order their life's priorities. The task of ordering personal and interpersonal priorities is, of course, a demanding one, for it occurs in the midst of relationships between family members that are both intensely ambivalent and irrevocably interdependent. Nonetheless, *contextual priorities* are inseparable from responsibility for prospective consequences, especially for posterity.

RESOURCES AND RELATIONAL REALITY

The contextual approach's fundamental value bias is a universal one— that it is costly for a person to deny the basic existential realities of his or her own life: "Where do I come from? Who am I? And where am I going?" The therapist is no exception to this rule. He cannot be oblivious to the task of pursuing his own point of view on life's major relational priorities. By exploring his own key relationships from other people's sides, a therapist gains a multilateral perspective on the consequences of relationships. A multilateral dialogue helps a person assert his own claims and consider the due claims of others. A person learns to discern her own identity or self through this dialogue. She also validates the worth of this self through due care for the other. Without a multilateral perspective, a therapist cannot guide clients toward viable relating that is based on the trustworthiness of fair give-and-take.

Given the complexity and intensity of the interpersonal field that he or she is about to enter, the beginning therapist may well be struggling with his own insecurities and defensiveness. On the other hand, if he has done contextual work with his own family and friends, he is likely to be buoyed by a direct knowledge of resources that can continue to exist even among seriously warring family members.

The contextual approach offers new options for discovering the residual *resources* in close relationships, regardless of their state of disrepair. Its concepts and experience guide people towards untapped, sometimes previously unidentified, reservoirs of trustworthiness, often at exactly those times when long periods of mistrust persist and seem to belie the worth of any new effort on the part of a family member. Contextual therapists operate out of an empirically derived conviction that there is a universally valid reality in the order of existence.

Obviously, it is in the just order of things for adults to care for their helpless infants. It is also in the just order of things to earn the rewards that are dynamically linked to offering due care. The most fundamental of these rewards is the enhanced personal freedom that derives from what we have termed *entitlement*. Entitlement, earned through offering due care, flows from the resolve to accept active and personal responsibility for the consequences of relational reality. It is not to be confused with the "shoulds" or "oughts" of idealism and moralism. Contextual ethical priorities are based in universal human reality, not in value priorities of particular groups or cultures. The reality, for example, that the future is more vulnerable to consequences than the past is a universally valid fact rather than a value.

Contextual therapists are guided by operating principles that begin with their capacity to integrate a family's own definition of its problems into a therapeutic plan. The therapist has to have the eyes to see and the ears to hear family members *on their own terms*. Conveyed through behavior and words, people define their interpersonal conflicts and describe the existential and psychological sources of their pain. In the process, they require a measure of acknowledgment from their listener, a legitimation of the validity of their past and present suffering.

From her side, the therapist is bound to be respectful of what is proffered, a task more easily said than done. A therapist's capacities to be respectful are often jarred, especially by people's universal urge to blame. Prudence and convenience dictate that people urge each other to correct their faults and change their ways; it is considerably more difficult to begin therapy with the kinds of disclosures that are self-incriminating.

A therapist's capacity for eliciting multilateral acknowledgement of people's suffering is to be sharply differentiated from "strategically" *joining or colluding with one family member against another*. Not only is such collusion a hopeless position from the perspective of the deep loyalties that bind family members to each other and keep strangers and therapists out; it is also countertherapeutic. Sometimes the temptations can be overwhelming, for example, in cases of child abuse in which there seems to be little question of who is victimizing and who is victimized. But who is to say whether the victimizer was once victimized and, if so, what is to be done about it? Are there still avenues through which he might acquire redress or, at least, fair acknowledgment of his wounds? From a contextual perspective, a therapist can ill afford to join family members in disqualifying each other through the manipulative mechanism of assigning blame.

The leverages of contextual therapy emerge from the polar opposite of mutual blame: a mutuality of commitment and reciprocal accountability on the part of the family members. "Now that you and I are in this mess, what if anything, can each of us do to turn it around?" Here the basic hypothesis is no longer one of simply trying to please someone. In all probability that route has already been tried. What is at work instead is a fresh option for freeing one's self from jointly held despair. "I may not think you merit my goodwill, given all you've done to me, but unless I take some action, whether you do or not, my situation will get worse."

Contextual therapy aims to support attitudes and behaviors that actively contribute to the well-being of all relating parties, whether or not they are present in the therapy room. It operates out of a contract that offers *therapeutic accountability* that family members can *offer* each other. Accountability to the other requires that one define and assert one's own side too. The martyr does not really contribute anything to the person who is held on a string of guilt. On the other hand, reciprocal giving and benefiting between partners form the ethical basis of relationship viewed as *dialogue*.

In every family, diffuse and nameless "pathologies" exist in and among individuals who often function as each other's antagonists. In addition, beyond specific symptoms and frequently in place of them, family members suffer from other shortcomings: family disintegration, estrangement and alienation, fear of the future, fear of competition, fear of the community, an inability to commit themselves or apply themselves usefully, an overly materialistic grasp of life, and escalating degradation through mutually dehumanizing processes and mechanisms.

A family's renewed concern for a *redistribution of burdens and benefits* among its members may be comprehended as "change," or as restoration of viable continuity of relationship, a major resource from a contextual perspective. Self-sustaining continuity of relationship is a more valid and specific goal of therapeutic intervention than is the simpler goal of change. In the first instance, the process of restoring viable relationships in the midst of injustices and mistrust requires a measure of intergenerational integrity. The ability to define one's own fundamental truths and entitlements is the beginning of such integrity. It is also tantamount to improving the quality of life itself. Moving from a random struggle for the survival of the fittest is one step towards attaining a gain in the quality of human life. Another step has to do with the willingness to disclose one's terms of relationship. Such active self-disclosure is in itself an offer of care that can enhance the giver's personal freedom and enable interpersonal justice.

Loyalty and Its Implications for Fairness

One of the main concepts of familial dynamics, loyalty, was introduced into therapeutic literature as a contrast to psychodynamic considerations (Boszormenyi-Nagy, 1972). In this sense loyalty is almost synonymous with the essential irrefutability of family ties. No matter how successfully a person displaces or transfers his or her filial attachment to therapist, boss or partner, the primary commitment basis of family loyalty remains untouched. On what is this commitment based?

Loyalty in contextual therapy is not based on a "sense" of loyalty or on the psychology of attachment or attraction. Nor is it based on power-inspired dependence or submission of the weaker person, as in feudal loyalty to king or high nobility. Loyalty in our sense is a preferential commitment to a relationship, based on indebtedness born of earned merit. Parents beget offspring and become obligated to their survival and nurturance. Parents also earn their child's commitment in return for mother's and father's unique, unrepayable contribution. Spouses commit their lifetime and life options to a common venture; to that extent, they merit loyal commitment from each other.

Still another function of the justice criteria of the human context has to do with the phenomenon of unresolved *loyalty conflicts*. A person's commitments to his family of origin on the one hand and his peer commitments on the other hand often collide and conflict in terms of priority. Thus, loyalty conflicts seem to be ubiquitous causes of marital and partnership incompatibilities. Of central interest to contextual therapists, loyalty conflicts can be a major deterrent to individual freedom and interpersonal fairness among peers.

This dynamic is especially important to explore in situations where avoidance clouds people's ambivalence towards their parents. Adolescents and adults often profess a high priority for working on their peer relationships and shun concern about parent-child relating. In clinical experience, however, it is precisely those people who "protest too much" who are often unable to commit themselves to peers or individuate in any age-appropriate way. Paradoxically, rather than being a source of persistent bondage under parental authority, due consideration of parental needs is a liberating resource.

Even very small children are sensitive barometers; they *know* when their parents are overburdened with anxiety, guilt and mistrust. Moreover, they want to do something about it. Clinical observation of families gives ample indications of how enormously giving and caring very young offspring want to be toward their massively needy parents. It is precisely this reality that lies at the core of later, adult-age loyalty conflict: "By what right can I enjoy other relationships if my parents are always suffering?"

It is easy to confuse filial loyalty and its implicit conflicts with fixated dependency needs that persist from childhood. Loyalty conflict also lies in the parents' needy condition, not just in the child's needs. It is more legitimate, therefore, to identify just how significant children are as relational resources to their parents.

Contextual therapy resists the tendency to regard children merely as the end products of adult pathology. Dealing with relational reality requires a multilateral concern about every relating member's merits, credits, benefits and burdens. It becomes increasingly evident to contextual practitioners just how often the "royal road" to self-mastery weaves through the complex maze of a person's indirectly self-victimizing, invisible loyalties to his or her family of origin. Liberation from loyalty conflict through direct rather than invisible loyalty contributions leads to the freedom to enjoy commitment to peers, partners or spouse.

How can *therapists help family members* reclaim new degrees of wholeness and satisfaction in the midst of dissatisfying and fragmented existences? At some point clients try to turn towards directions that can lead them to something "better", something "more." How can therapists help people learn that,

- Strong family members can gain from concerning themselves with weak, helpless and handicapped family members;
- Individual freedom is most effectively won through a consideration of balances of fairness between the self and all of the significant others with whom the self is in relationship.
- Grown-ups will find a more peaceful resolve in their own lives if they can claim their own just due at the same time that they are actively involved and invested in caring for posterity.

In sum, how can therapeutic effectiveness be grounded in the resources that rely on the foundations and consequences of the truths of relational reality?

A Clinical Illustration of the Resource Orientation

The following situation is meant to illustrate the *relational* truths that are linked to a presenting symptom or complaint, in this case a marital crisis. The reader will note, however, that neither marriage nor the disappointments attached to it begin to define all of the significant and long-festering sources of the young couple's struggle and pain:

Jessie, 25, is a lively, outspoken young woman, and Kevin, 24, a shy, somewhat sad-looking young man. They had lived together, unmarried, for over two years. At first they had gotten along well; sex, they said, was great. They liked each other and felt that their styles of life meshed. It also appeared that they were allies against their respective families of origin. Before they met, Kevin drank heavily. After they started living together, he gradually reduced his drinking to a few beers a night. Jessie occasionally smoked marijuana. Kevin started to work at a steady job and made it possible for Jessie to work part time.

Neither of them minded when Jessie got pregnant. In fact, the idea of a family seemed appealing to them. It was then that they decided to get married. They went to City Hall where they had a "no ceremony" wedding. Kevin was able to share the news of his marriage and expected baby with his mother. He had long ago lost track of his father who had been an alcoholic.

As the pregnancy progressed, tensions between the couple began to grow. Their sexual relations diminished and became almost non-existent. On the evening that Jessie experienced her first labor pains, Kevin walked out. He stayed away, drinking at a bar all night long. Jessie was brokenhearted; her disappointments built up to near murderous rage. She felt she had been abandoned at precisely the point in life when she most needed to be loved. It was hard to believe that this was happening to her. She concluded that Kevin was callously indifferent to both her and his own unborn child.

Jessie had to go to the hospital alone. On the taxi ride there, she decided that there was no one in this world to rely on but herself and her child to be. She presumed that she would have to raise the baby without benefit of father just as her mother had had to do with her. She felt sad at the prospect but also reassured. In her fantasy she saw the baby-child as a strong grownup man. Unlike other men, he would be deeply devoted to Jessie, his mother.

In the meantime Kevin felt enormously guilty and worthless. He felt that he did not deserve to be a parent, nor was he ready for all it implied. He felt a sudden flow of warmth for his father who had never wrenched free from a sense of failure. Did his dad use alcohol to help him handle his self-deprecation? Kevin's thoughts went from his father to Ellen, a woman with whom he worked. From the time he started at the store, she had shown an interest in him. Ellen was divorced and raising a four-year-old by herself. She relied heavily on help from her mother, who was outspoken and tough. Ellen was having a hard time just like Kevin.* He had never realized how scary life could be. He suddenly realized how lost he felt in a frightening world. If that's how it really is, he thought, there seemed to be little purpose to struggling.

---

*Kevin's thoughts of Ellen were typical of an attempt to escape from relational accountability. A loving partner, of course, is more than a caring neighbor. For his part, in the presence of unfaced responsibility for parental obligations, Kevin was tempted to take an all too familiar escape from the difficulty of a known relationship to an unknown one.

Representative of a large segment of human experience in current society, Jessie's and Kevin's situation evokes fundamental therapeutic questions: What is the symptom and whose is the pathology? Is pathology confined to the hidden realms of one person's unconscious? It hardly seems
to lie in the rigidity of any dominating, recalcitrant family system, as alleged by some advocates of classical family therapy. Or might pathology
also lie in the failure of these young people to mobilize and actualize
resources that are *already there* for them in their families of origin?

Who is to be identified here as the object in need of help? Does Jessie
need therapy so she can rid herself of an immature, unreliable man? Is
it Kevin who requires help, given his proclivity towards a heavy use of
alcohol? In his present state, he may even be a candidate for suicide. From
the beginning, Kevin's and Jessie's parents mistrusted the marriage and
competed with their child-in-law. Should therapy be offered to them? The
tiny baby who arrived on the day that his parents split up stands a high
chance of being maltreated. A symbol of his parents' pain, he may eventually have reason to wreak retribution on a world which views him as
a low priority. Is it the newborn baby for whose sake intervention should
be made, and how should that occur? Or are there ways to help all of the
members of this context, this inherently related set, learn how to help one
another as well as help themselves? Still more, what are the sources of
this help?

A caring neighbor, an attentive bartender or beautician, a family physician or lawyer can all offer empathic listening and good common-sense
advice. A show of any kind of friendly interest undoubtedly helps. Why
then professional intervention? And at what point? What is the role of
therapeutic training and skill? What options and leverages are specific to
therapy? And what kind of therapeutic intervention makes sense? Countless books have been published to guide confused consumers in learning how to distinguish the characteristics of the wide range of available
choices, among them individual psychotherapy, client-centered therapy,
group dynamics, encounters, network therapy, gestalt therapy, systems
therapy, and restructuring or strategic intervention to name just a few.

Contextual work utilizes all of the resources at hand, including the effective "techniques" of all reliable therapeutic modalities. Even more
significantly, it is geared toward using all of the available resources of the
family network. Almost needless to say, any comparative generalization
of one family member's problems over and against others would be useless. On the other hand, it is a steadfast rule of contextual theory and practice that therapists regard and treat family members as prospective sources
of reserve relational energy, even those whose behavior warrants a desig-
nation as unruly "monster." Successful parenting, a family's major ethical
task, requires stable relating among adults who are capable of identify-

ing their own resources as well as their problems. These resources may be among the family members themselves or in the extended family.

Contextual therapy tries to help people discover and construct multilaterally responsible solutions in the very situations in which their impulses drive them in opposite directions. Akin to classical Greek drama, a victory based on disregard for significant people in an individual's life weaves tragic consequences into the fabric of the future. Conversely, therapeutic help that considers the consequences of one person's reality on another person (centrifugal), as well as the legitimacy of self-concern and regard (centripetal), is of benefit to all.

The methodological resources of contextual therapy are composed of the fundamental assets and truths of each family member's being and relating. Such truths inevitably have negative as well as positive characteristics and consequences. The *negative* aspects of relating include exploitativeness, symbiotic possessiveness, narcissistic self-confinement and blame, and refused responsibility for consequences, among others. The *positive* characteristics and consequences of relationship include fair availability, need-complementarity, trustworthiness, well-founded loyalty, exoneration, and the autonomy that is gained through the process of earning merit or entitlement.

At issue here is not whether parents and children, among other significantly relating parties, have done each other harm. Injuries and pain are inescapable aspects of all relating and are ever likely to be so. For us the central question has to do with whether, in a misplaced longing to avoid further "hurt," people settle for too little, too late. To what extent are family members caught in a negative definition of life's characteristics and consequences to the unintended exclusion of any positive side? To what degree does a consistently negative definition of being and relating induce families to a failure to identify, mobilize and utilize the relational resources that underlie their subjective experiences of injustice and mistrust?

The therapeutic methods of contextual therapy are chiefly based on eliciting an active, assertive and responsible position-taking on every family member's part. The therapist turns to every member with the expectation that each will state his or her side. The purpose is to evoke not a therapist-client dialogue but eventually an intermember dialogue of genuine spontaneity and "self-delineation" (Boszormenyi-Nagy, 1962, 1966). In that dialogue, based on responsibility and a capacity to respond, every participant is reinvesting new trust. The therapist can help them rework interpersonal patterns distorted by repetitious reliance on any one person's internal relating pattern. Its elicitory rather than prescriptive or structuring methodological approach makes contextual therapy an *activating* rather than a merely *active* procedure.

Trust in the therapist-client relationship leads to a helpful spontaneity in the client's work. Only through trusting can the client bring the genuine, nondefensive manifestations of his behavior and his relationships to the therapist for exploration. Trust enables the client not only to reveal the true reality of his life manifestations but also to follow the therapist's guidance with genuine spontaneity. Initially people's feelings of trust can follow the fulfillment of emotional satisfaction. Here, however, the importance of emotional resonance is secondary to more solid bases for trust that include people's due concern for each other. A mutually responsible relationship benefits the self at the same time that it benefits the other. Contextual therapy is based on the healing evoked through due concern, a refinement of "healing through meeting."

In sum, contextual therapy is concerned with the comprehension of causal factors in human behavior. Causal factors as sources of relational consequences and their therapeutic ramifications, in our view, can best be grasped through an integrative effort. Therapeutic intervention can be most effective if it can penetrate the crucial existential criteria in every person's world. This possibility is most likely to occur through a consideration of a rightful synthesis of facts, individual motives, transactional systems and a dialectical perspective of fair relating.

CHAPTER 2

The Challenge of the Therapy of Psychotics: Background of the Contextual Approach

ORIGINS OF CONTEXTUAL THERAPY

Like its predecessor, classical family therapy, contextual therapy has grown out of a desire to overcome the limitations of classical individual psychotherapy. Although there have been attempts at modifying Freudian psychoanalysis to fit the requirements of the treatment of more severely disturbed patients, much remains to be accomplished. Having spent considerable time and energy on searching for biochemical clues in the mid 1950s, Boszormenyi-Nagy's interest soon focused on the behavioral and psychological phenomena of schizophrenia. What therapeutic options have remained unutilized after pooling all available knowledge about serious mental conditions? How can the knowledge of human relationships contribute to a more effective therapeutic design?

Throughout history, efforts have been made to uncover causal clues to the problem of *psychosis*. Striking unreason in human behavior has always called for an explanation. Many approaches have been taken toward the challenge of explaining and curing madness: Religion, magic, exorcism, have been employed for ages. More recently, early environmental conditioning, neuropathology, inherited brain damage, and disordered biochemistry have been advanced among other explanations but have resulted in no conclusive causative clues.

The hardest test of therapeutic endeavors has been presented by psychosis and what has been diagnosed as personality disorders of severe types. Many therapists have tended to avoid the continuing and unyielding existence of hard, recalcitrant symptomatologies. Paranoia, psychosis and psychopathic character traits, among other like manifestations, have traditionally been described as inaccessible to ordinary, corrective logic. People afflicted with these conditions seem to maintain an enduring commitment to a rigidly-held inner, distorted logic. Consequently, the "patient" repetitiously falls into the same conflictual social situation. For all of his great charisma and competence in solving fundamental puzzles of "psychopathology," Freud resigned himself to the unanalyzability of these recalcitrant, ego-deformed patients. Basically, he joined Kraepelin and perhaps the majority of humanity in a pessimistic despair over the curability of insane forms of irrational, antisocial behavior.

If human beings tend towards a despair over their possibilities, they are also reluctant to accept real limits of their reasoning power. Attempts at healing irrationality have been as obdurate as the conditions they were intended to remedy. In the past, efforts were made to literally shake desperately insane people out of their social or even physical contexts. Regarded as obsessed by witches or the devil, they were frequently threatened with inhuman torture or with execution. At other times they were exposed to the shock of cold water, rotation, and, more recently, to insulin, metrazol or electrical shocks. For a while, hypnotic-suggestive approaches gained credence. In the middle of the twentieth century, tranquilizing medication was added to these efforts. And currently, behavioral restructuring and paradoxical "unsettling" of family relationships are on the ascendency.

Part of the difficulty may lie with the fact that it is difficult to generalize when it comes to psychotics. One potentially universal trait may have to do with their massive failure to process social behavior. This failure seems to occur to such a blatant extreme that even—or perhaps particularly—the closest family relationships seem to overburden the psychotic's adaptational capacities.

If it is true that family situations require a lower degree of adaptational skills than other, less familiar social situations, what dooms psychotics to failure in their own family relationships? Is there a massive "pathology" that underwrites their failure? What are the *latent factors* that initially predispose certain people to becoming psychotic? And why does it typically occur in their late teens or early adulthood? What necessitates the suspicious withdrawals and the "paranoid" misinterpretations of people's motivations that estrange psychotics from others? Why the enormity of rhapsodic mood swings in which near murderous rage can be evoked by apparently trivial disagreement or conflict? What causes their oscillation between the extremes of dependent love and vindictive rage? What underlies a mode of thinking that is so distorted and constricted that it leads to a delusional misinterpretation of reality?

Answers to these questions have been sought in a variety of directions, including genetic causation, ethology, unconscious motivation, object relations theory, and psychosocial developmental stages. Each of these factors is likely to be a partial ingredient in the blend of pathogenic determinants and each deserves at least passing reference here.

Genetic Causation

In our view, there is no reason to question the role of genetic causation. It is logical to assume that in all life situations, inborn, *gene-dependent* regulations are co-determinant in their effect with *environmental* influences. These two sets of factors consistently combine to shape a person's behavioral patterns. Genetic preprogramming is obviously an element of psychotic development. So, too, is personality formation. No reasonable argument seems to exist that would preclude the significance of both developmental structuring and personal experience in the formation of human personality. To this point, however, our accrued information on the long range "mechanisms" of human environmental influences on the growing child is rudimentary. It is to be hoped that, over time, therapeutic knowledge will evolve that can offer guidelines for preventive interventions.

Ethology

This is one such attempt to increase our knowledge of the roots of human behavior. The scientific study of animal and human development is a relatively new field. One of its most compelling concepts has to do with the irreversible processes of early conditioning, i.e., with "imprinting." Independent of external reinforcement, imprinting requires a suitable, critical period of susceptibility that occurs over a specific and specifiable length of time. Its manifestations in animals are typically long-delayed.

It is clear that ethology's study of the inborn and learned roots of animal behavior (Lorenz, 1981) holds obvious implications for human beings. But there is a higher degree of complexity in human ethology. It is decisively more difficult to study causal factors and their impact on human social environments. To date human ethology is still relatively virgin territory. Its theories are intriguing but await solid data.

Nevertheless, ethology's basic concerns have to be linked to contextual concerns over relational consequences. The family therapy setting may provide an arena in which to study if and how ethological and contextual data and premises converge and combine. Hopefully and inevitably, our knowledge of the developmental input of adult relationships will increase. Whatever its promise for the future understanding of character formation, ethology remains a recent development whose implications are still untested.

Unconscious Motivation

The Freudian perspective of unconscious motivation, on the other hand, is by now an almost universally accepted element in contemporary thought about the roots of human behavior. In fact, it is difficult to estimate the degree of the impact that the concept of unconscious determinants has had on Western culture. In this view, lasting character traits are inevitably influenced and shaped by unconscious motives as well as by consciously realistic goals. Here, inherited and imprinted components in an individual converge with still another component of human programming: the conscious and unconscious requirements of personal satisfaction. Certain environmental circumstances, for example, can condition sadistic, destructive patterns of satisfaction in a person. These patterns eventually become a habitual outlet through which to channel the natural human need to relate.

The formation of individual identity involves the entire spectrum of psychic development. Psychoanalysis has introduced concepts that describe how identifications evolve out of a state of undifferentiation. Parental interactions provide the background to identification even while primary identifications are still embedded in psychic fusion.

In defining his concept of "reality testing," Freud emphasized the fact that a person's healthy life interests are served by her efforts to extricate herself from pet distortions of this nature. His argument was based on an implicit relational premise for therapy. Thus, the patient's best prospect for reworking her faulty personality formation lies in a useful therapeutic regression and a struggle with resistances to relinquishing "neurotic" patterns of inner attachments. In turn, these inner attachments lead to a transferred dependence on the therapist and, finally, to the relinquishment of that dependence both on the therapist and on the pattern.

In point of fact, success in systematic elimination of pathology has always been secondary to psychotherapy's efforts to help people mobilize their resources. Freud's discovery of unconscious motivations, for example, lent itself to a therapeutic process that relied on the degree to which a person could mobilize his ego strength. It was not simply a function of the therapist's surfacing secrets unknown even to the patient himself, and then curing him through conscious, insightful explanations. Freud's methods were not recommended in cases of psychoses or certain character disorders. In these situations, people tended to lack the resources that the ego requires to endure the process of therapy. The transference, set in motion by the impact of the therapeutic relationship, obviously imposes huge demands. Chief among them is a person's capacity to live with the therapeutic resurgence of old hatreds, fears, suspicions, pains, shame, and cravings.

Contextual therapy also requires its clients to endure the trauma of facing old injuries and reworking hateful and painful realities. Here, however, transference is additionally viewed as an indication of potential ethical disengagement. A complete reliance on the notion of transference-based cure is predicated on an implicit, relative undervaluation of actual family relationships. Contextual therapy is concerned about the prospective disloyalty connotations of therapeutic alliances and of transference. (Boszormenyi-Nagy, 1972). The intensity of contextual therapy is thus linked less to the relationship between therapist and client and more to every individual's capacity to work through the ongoing relational context of his just or unjust human order. All of this is helped by the therapist's expert elicitation of relational resources.

Over time, therapeutic thinking has gradually began to shift from an individual to a *relational understanding* of human behavior. Hypotheses about the pathogenic nature of parental behavior began to emerge out of this shift, all of them unidirectional. It was assumed that the child, when he suffered, did so because of his mother's shortcomings. For example, the concept of the "schizophrenogenic mother" emerged. Here the parent's vicarious need gratification through her child was described as an unconscious, implicitly exploitative parental attitude (Johnson & Szurek, 1952).

Object Relations Theory

Defined by Fairbairn (1952, 1954) and later Guntrip (1961), object relations theory made important contributions to the development of new therapeutic methods. It was assumed that, from its beginnings, the mind's dynamics are essentially rooted in structurally implicit dialogue between the self (ego) and the other (internal object). This assumption provides a helpful explanation of the human tendency to misperceive relationships: The patterns that program distortions in interpersonal relationships are themselves relational. The basic need for both good and bad internal others (objects) colors our use of significant relationships (projective identification). Conversely, a person may adapt his own inclinations to oblige his relating partner's needs for a "bad" counterpart. Consideration of relational phenomena like these is crucial for an understanding of concepts like projection, displacement, and therapeutic transference.

Freud's insistence on the individual's need for (object) relationships retained its obvious validity. By itself, however, it stopped short of a concern for the relational benefits and burdens for the "object." Simply put, it failed to examine the "centrifugal," other-directed consequences of a person's concern and needs for his partner. As such, it lent itself to relational implications that could prospectively become exploitative and trust-diminishing. The phenomenon of transference implies that relationships, apparently operating out of interpersonal and reciprocal criteria, are also patterned in part by each relating partner's inner mental set. Thus, each person in a relationship relies on a generalized internal relational formula whose roots may be inborn, imprinted, or simply reinforced.

From this perspective, particular, current "real" interactions between people are used to compete with, substitute for, or document the existence of each person's internally valid mental formula or set. This set is presumably guided by a gyroscope of subjective and unconscious agendas, as in: "Why aren't you acting as I wish my father would have acted? Haven't I extended you the privilege of getting closer to me than my father ever was?" In other words, "I want you to behave in ways that can address my earlier inner needs, without consideration of what you want or need to do." From the vantage point of contextual therapy, one can even be indirectly loyal to one's parents via blaming current relationships.

Unfortunately, as a relationship gets more intense and involved, the need for making one's partner fit the internal relational format can intensify. At the same time, the balance of the relationship becomes unfair and exploitative. The dialogue takes on an I-It format instead of the mutually responsible I-Thou pattern described by Buber in his seminal work (1958). It is this fateful internal drive toward passionately possessing the other as a recreated replica of the "internal object" rather than a mere instrumental "use" of the other that represents the greatest source of unfairness in close relationships.

Object relations theory describes a ubiquitous human tendency that deserves serious consideration. Fairbairn, for example, went so far as to define the human mind as a relationally constructed entity from its outset. For him, primary, psychological need-configurations presuppose matching ego and internal object components. To us, his psychological view of individual depth dynamics seems to be analogous to and compatible with Buber's existential-ethical view of dialogue as the foundation of human being and becoming. Both perspectives can help therapists better understand the *relativistic basis* of the human mind as well as of human relatedness. The parallel between the two frameworks served as an early foundation for contextual therapy (Boszormenyi-Nagy, 1965a).

The integration of the Fairbairn-Guntrip view of internal object relations theory with Buber's notion of genuine dialogue can powerfully characterize the futility of many "close" relationships. We usually pick relationships on the basis of their emotional meaningfulness to us. Freud observed that a man may seek to find a woman whom he can squeeze into the image of his maternal introject. Yet this is only partially true. In part, the man is also reacting to his attraction to the "real" characteristics of a particular woman. In the sense of Fairbairn and Guntrip there is a rivalry between the requirements of the internal and the external or interpersonal relationship. Contextually, the more one squeezes the partner into an internally desirable image, the more one is likely to be unfair and exploitative.

Psychosocial Development Stages

Fairbairn's (1952) object relations constructs about the basic dynamics of the mind might be linked to and aligned with Erikson's (1959) foundation of psychosocial (instead of simply psychological) notions of development. Basic trust versus mistrust characterizes Erikson's first stage of psychosocial development; however, it also remains that lasting foundation for all of a person's later stages. In this regard, Erikson's optimism is matched by Kohut's (1977) hopes for "empathic" therapeutic parenting. In Kohut's view, the young child who fails to receive the empathic parenting that he needs (deserves?) turns out to be a narcissistic person who suffers from an injured "self-psychology."

From a Freudian perspective, Erikson's emphasis on basic trust versus mistrust and Kohut's emphasis on empathic parenting can be viewed as pointing to a large-scale, global "fixation." This kind of fixation afflicts people who appear compelled, at least symbolically, to return to early patterns of relating, and to desperately test whether basic trust or empathy can belatedly be found in the world.

On the other hand, from a contextual perspective, Kohut's rationale of "restoration of self" represents a welcome stance, but one that requires still further integration. For no individually-oriented model is sufficient to grasp the interpersonal balances of the relational context. What is called for here is an *integration of individual models* of psychic restoration with a *supra-individual regulatory force*, that is, what Buber termed the "justice of the human order."

In our terms, this supra-individual regulatory force may also be called "the context of residual trustworthiness," a realm that plays a vital role in enabling self-sustaining trust. That is to say that self-sustaining trust is regulated by the degree of justice that a person has met in his own human order: Being injured can give rise to widely varying degrees of feeling injured, hurt, deprived, ripped off. There is a tragic truth to the fact that an individual's deep desire and willingness to test what residual trust still exists in his human order is inseparable from historically justified negative input into here-and-now relationships. Past injustices, unilaterally perceived, typically result in a currently vindictive input. As a person continues to press for his historically justified, unrequited "rights," he is likely to become even more alienated from the resources and possibilities of his present living context. Under the circumstances, he is likely to appear increasingly incorrigible, inappropriate and insane.

It was Martin Buber who first formulated the principles of therapy on the level of caring and just interhuman relationships (1948, 1957). He made a decisive distinction between healing through efforts at integrity in relationship and technical, often implicitly dehumanizing attempts at symptom change. In all likelihood, he contributed more to building the foundations of accountable human relating than any other thinker of our time. He sensitively defined the profound human issues of relationship and interpersonal suffering and witnessed to the proposition that, in the spirit of a responsible I-Thou dialogue, the self can gain merited reward. History will probably recognize Buber as a giant of twentieth-century thought. He was not a psychotherapist but a philosophical anthropologist. His contributions may be more fully acknowledged in philosophy, religion and disciplines linked to issues of community than in the field of psychotherapy. But Buber seems to have addressed people and society by references to therapy as well as through his other concerns. For us, his passion for realized justice in the human order has direct and immediate implications for a world in danger of abandoning its children.

The early, contextual realization that trust as a foundation of personality development and as a relational resource is different from trust as an experience led to the recognition of trustworthiness as a crucial requirement for viable, close relationships. The psychological criteria of the need for trust interlock with the ethical criteria of trustworthy relationship. It is at this juncture that Martin Buber's concept of genuine dialogue presents a unique opportunity for integration between the clinical foundations of individual and relational theory. The dialogic notion of responsible responding was an important underpinning of the first formulation of the intergenerational dialectic (Boszormenyi-Nagy & Spark, 1973).

Buber's concern for the "realm of the between" seemed to provide a conceptual approach that incorporated and extended Freud's theory of individual object need. His focus on the equitable validity of words that bridge (*dialogue*) offered a helpful guideline for trustworthy therapeutic interventions. It rightly implied that a genuinely trustworthy relationship requires relating partners to consider the validity of each other's interests, rights and needs as well as of their own. It also rightly implied that therapeutic interventions geared towards building merited trust required methodologies founded on *simultaneous consideration* of two or more relating partners. Since neurotic "distortion" of any kind diminishes the person's trustable relating capacity, successful individual therapy may or may not result in increased trustworthiness.

PERSPECTIVES ON CHANGE: FAMILY THERAPY

From the very beginnings of family therapy, there were warning signs that cautioned its practitioners against the lure of assuming easy or automatically lasting change. Anyone involved in the demanding attempts to help psychotics was put to an early test. Bateson et al. (1956) came to important conclusions about how double-binding communications contribute to the onset and development of schizophrenia. Significantly, however, most family therapists eventually abandoned their work with schizophrenics. The tedious process of helping people learn how to trust again seemed to become too trying. One way or another, the efforts of these early family therapists were likely to give them pause: Enlightened practitioners had to come face-to-face with implicit difficulties that—beyond psychosis—attend all human interchange. Short-term and long-term relational interventions could and would be conceived, tested and promulgated over the ensuing years. How many of them would lead to enduring individual and relational improvement was another issue.

With the advent of classical family therapy, motivational explanations were joined by the concept of inadvertently collusive, relational dynamics. Now the fluctuations of the identified patient's role and the "homeostatic" phenomena (Jackson, 1957) of family behavior required explanation. It seemed reasonable to assume that certain behavioral functions were regulated on a systemic level that transcended the individual. It was the system that was characterized by health or pathology rather than its members. Thus, the system was personified at the risk of depersonalizing people.

The newfound knowledge forced many initially individually-oriented therapists to reconsider how the relational understructure of life interfaces with personal motivations, rewards and benefits. On the other hand, the tendency of some therapists toward an impersonal, systemic "supraindividualism" led to a new kind of professional magic and, in our view, became a major impediment to the conceptual growth and development of the "family therapy movement." At the same time, however, Bowen's (1965) stress on undifferentiation in adults and even in entire families has significantly contributed to a more balanced systemic perspective. His therapy is aimed at the formation of differentiated selves for the identified patient and, eventually, for his or her family members as well.

In contextual therapy, it is abundantly clear that each individual's efforts to survive and thrive constitute the driving force of relationship. Surely nobody gains from a therapeutic dismissal of the resources implicit in knowledge about individual motivations. *Mutually interlocking individuation* is one definition of a relationship system.

By and large, to date, most family therapists have followed the path of *transactionally* anchored concepts and interventions, for very apparent reasons: 1) All relating partners collectively go through a "dance" of transactional sequences regardless of what other discrete criteria inform and shape their lives, and 2) transactional patterning is the most easily observable of any relational criteria. One might conjecture that even a Martian therapist, recently arrived atop the Empire State Building, could pick up formally valid patterns of human behavior by looking down during the morning and evening rush hours. He could describe which cars go in which direction and on what streets. Seeing the congestion, he might diagnose the problem and suggest an appropriate intervention. It would obviously be helpful to break up and restructure the "rigid," compulsive rules that keep humanoids in such a chronic jam. Yet the Martian does not know that it is not the direction or the congestion nor the flow that motivates the person desperately in search of a cab to get to his first appointment with an important prospective customer. He couldn't care less about whether the taxi that gets him to work in time fits a pattern of cars going north or south on a given street.

No understanding of the transactional pattern is complete without regard for coexisting multipersonal criteria. To deny the existence of the individual is a self-deceptive parsimony. Ignorance of the self-other or I-You dialectic tends to weaken rather then strengthen the therapist's spectrum of options.

Attempts to establish a *bridge between individual and relational motivational regulations* have been relatively rare: Traditional psychotherapies have based their rationales on the individual's motivations to be free of symptoms and complaints and to attain a successful life. A client is helped to move toward these goals through a variety of measures that include insight, an ability to express real emotion, recognizing transference attitudes, working through, internalizing, and a capacity to rework defenses. A person is hindered in these projects by the inertia of his former habits and by the limits imposed by his dynamically unconscious resistance. Throughout the struggle, it is the improvement of his own condition *per se* that is presumed to motivate and ultimately reward the patient for his efforts to heal.

From its inception, family therapy grasped the fact that some conditions that were disabling to people lay in relationship configurations. So did many resistances to change, as well as the capacity to improve. It has typically been assumed that effective individual reorganization in one or several family members can result from "changing" these debilitating behavioral configurations. This assumption was reinforced by the observation that one family member can induce and sustain self-damaging behaviors in another family member.

Proceeding on these hypotheses, family practitioners designed techniques to affect individual behavior through *changing transactional patterns*. What were the guidelines for change? At times a rationale was offered to justify why certain patterns needed to be altered and show how new patterns could be more efficacious. Sometimes change was defined in terms of needing to produce new patterns that would better correspond to cultural values than did old patterns. Other times, the need for change was defined in social science terms, e.g., power coalitions, boundaries, and role change. Frequently, any change was valued as a good one by comparison with patterns that had been rigidly held.

A significant cautionary note was lodged against indiscriminate destruction of the old in favor of anything new (Bateson, 1979). Yet it was especially rare to have anyone spell out the ways in which transactional changes were linked to genuinely favorable progress from everyone's vantage point. By and large, improvement was equated with the magic of changing people's invisible, here-and-now transactions with each other, often against their will. In some cases there seemed to be an almost curse-like representation of the rigid and repetitious sequences of visible interactions. Changes in transactional behavior are highly visible, of course, and at times can be novel and exciting. As a result, *change-making strategies* began to improve on themselves. They became bolder and even self-justifying, as if it were a disadvantage to know and care about one's clients as persons.

Some practitioners began to make impressive claims about the success rate of their interventions. Transactional, here-and-now changes occurring in the therapy room, they maintained, led not only to new and desirable patterns, but to change that was likely to endure outside of therapy sessions. At times, a commitment to the promises of transactional change tended to glorify what seemed to occur at the expense of a rightful regard for the nuances, consequences, and complexities of being itself. Developing schema and techniques that appear to produce short-term change, however, is a far cry from actually effecting healing interventions. Despite claims to the contrary (Selvini-Palazzoli, 1978; Hoffman, 1981), "seeming" simply cannot do the work of "being." Dell (1981) is only one of a growing number of authors in the family field who have begun to question the validity of the claims surrounding mere transactional change. He has also surfaced the implicit stumbling blocks involved in trying to effect transactional change regardless of cost. More recently Jacobson (1983) has offered some penetrating insights in his reexamination of short-term foci in the concepts and methods of classical, behavioral, marriage therapy.

CHAPTER 3

A Dialectic View of Relationship: The Development of the Contextual Approach

In our view, transactional patterning remains a formal and shallow therapeutic framework if it fails to allow for the *simultaneous coexistence of several individuals' rights and motives*. In point of fact, every relating person responds from the reality of his or her separate and distinct biological life. There is a discrete existential realm in which people are born by themselves, live for themselves, and, perforce, die by themselves. At certain specific levels there is simply no way in which one person's biology or psychology can contain all the same existential criteria as those that are part of another person's biology and psychology. How, then, can an understanding of relationships be designed that takes genuine, simultaneous consideration of the terms of the rights and needs of two or more partners? What useful assumptions might be made about relationships that can transcend both the psychological reductionism of an absolute ''psychic determinism'' and the sheer chaotic power confrontation that Sartre seems to imply (1956)? What are the most parsimonious requirements for a relational basis of programming? How can the therapist negotiate a contract in which he is an ally to two or more contending people simultaneously?

Contextual theory and practice offer an alternative to power-based strategic models: a *dialectical* perspective that incorporates individual and relational criteria alike. The dialectical theory of relationship (Boszormenyi-Nagy, 1965a) finds its validity in an inherent, antithetical relation with and a will to a viable reciprocity that exists between a self and his or her relating partner. This contrasts with linear, one-sided, self-motivated, psychological theories with their emphasis on individual needs for success, satisfaction and expediency. It also contrasts with circular, cybernetic models of relationships with their emphasis on system, transaction, control and structure.

Contextual therapy holds that real progress lies in the genuine integration of all valid knowledge about both mind and system. A "system" cannot be made responsible if no participating person is willing to act responsibly. A dialectical view of relating considers each partner's vantage point on selfishness and altruism, but in fact transcends them. Most significantly, it operates out of the empirically-rooted conviction that the self and his or her relating partner create a personalized human order in the realm that exists *between an "I" and a "Thou"* (Buber, 1948, 1957).

Martin Buber's grasp of the relationship which he termed "I and Thou (You)" pointed to a paradigm for healing that comes from connectedness itself. Each person's presence, directness and immediacy characterize the moment in which two people genuinely care about each other's side. Buber presumed a kind of asymmetry when he included the possibilities of a profoundly healing connection between a teacher and a pupil, a therapist and a patient, a person and an animal, a person and history, and even between a person and an inanimate object like a rock. Translated into our terms, he, too, seemed to imply that the chief predeterminants of relationship were contextual rather than merely psychological or transactional.

Buber grasped the demand and difficulties that are involved in genuine dialogue even while his every effort exhorted people toward it. He grieved over the human tendency to settle for so little when genuine dialogue (which he called speech-with-meaning), conceived, thought and spoken with the whole of one's being (1966, p. 107), subdues chaos and gives order to community. Overall, however, his emphasis fell on the symmetrical—that is, peers have an equal prospect for balanced give-and-take. Mates, lovers, friends, and even strangers are each entitled to expect an approximately equal return on their investments and contributions. Each of them is entitled to be able to rely on an eventually just return.

It has long been recognized (Boszormenyi-Nagy, 1965a) that the dialectical model of thesis, antithesis, synthesis is eminently suitable for the understanding of relational dynamics. It is clear that the organizing and programming principles of any relationship have to include a *multiplicity of the existential criteria* of two or more people. Less clear are answers to the question of which organizing and programming principles offer the most efficacious route to therapeutic intervention.

FROM CLINICAL EXPLANATION TO
CONCEPTUAL FRAMEWORK

The guideline for the evolution of the specifics of what is now called the Contextual Approach developed out of a quarter-century of search for the explanation of therapeutic effects. The approach has been guided by and constantly tested through its clinical effectiveness. Each of the afore-mentioned historical and theoretical sources was applied to its limit of applicability and bumped into boundaries of explanation. The push then went on for new ways of raising questions to determine if clinical data and therapeutic effectiveness could provide an answer. The early ways of raising questions, of course, were based on simultaneously multiple, individual dynamics, soon to be followed by systemic constructs of an evolving classical family therapy framework.

The notion of *need-complementarity* evolved from early therapeutic attempts at bridge-building between individual, systemic, and multipersonal entities (Boszormenyi-Nagy, 1962). It provided the first step toward designing a model that could define a pattern of interlocking motivations "based on fitting reciprocity rather than on identical sharing" (p. 106). The question at hand was how does need-complementarity come about between two or more relating persons. An answer began to offer itself in the model of the chance dovetailing between the needs of partners involved in well-matched sexuality. Each anticipates mutually satisfying prospects of simultaneous satisfaction. Over time, however, in order to be satisfied, each has to offer availability, tolerance, consideration, and room for his or her needs to be gratified.

In this paradigm, reciprocity is motivated by an individual (centripetal) concern for self-gratification. There are obviously innumerable times in a person's life when his own need to be satisfied motivates him to incorporate a concern for a relating partner who also has needs to satisfy. The satisfying relationship thus synthesized the antithetical prospects of my self-serving needs and your self-serving requirements. In a pathological need complementarity, the parents' "need for symbiotically retaining their child as a quasi-parental object" was assumed to dovetail with the child's "willingness to surrender his autonomous life goals" (Boszormenyi-Nagy, 1962, p. 109).

The concept of need-complementarity was closely linked to the concept of the *counterautonomous superego* (Boszormenyi-Nagy, 1962). The parental inducement of a counterautonomous superego describes a personality formation that will automatically censure and reject a person's urges toward his own individuation, engagement with peers, or assumption of adequate adult roles. In a prototypical process of need-complementarity between generations, parents offer care, consideration and freedom through which their child might grow. In exchange, they are likely to receive the satisfaction that comes of seeing the development of healthy and differentiated offspring. A further problem is introduced into the process, however, when parental neediness overrides a child's right to autonomy. The more needy the parent, the more likely she is to try to possess her child. The more parentified the child, the more likely it is for his anxiously possessive parents to exploit his sacrificially devoted availability and compliant readiness to please them. Parental input into the development of a counter-autonomous superego (Boszormenyi-Nagy, 1962) is the contextual formulation that was initially used to describe this motivational dynamic.

A mother who told her 15-year-old daughter "You can go out and do anything, as long as you tell me all about it" offers freedom to ignore conventional moral constraints in exchange for total sharing, i.e., the daughter thus remains a child vis-à-vis her.

Each member's contributions through his or her own counter-autonomous superego constituted an early attempt at a multi-personal, if systemic, formulation of family behavior. In its totality, this formulation was a precursor of the notion of *invisible loyalties* (Boszormenyi-Nagy & Spark, 1973). What amounted to collusive transactional-systemic behavior from an observable clinical level was now also being interpreted from the perspective of each family member's personal motives and attitudes. It seemed increasingly clear that at its most counter-autonomous, the partners' symbiotic need-complementarity also utilized each family member's capacity to turn into a "not-self context . . . for the other" (Boszormenyi-Nagy, 1965a, p. 59). It became clear that the totality of relational reality was no more encompassed by a paradigm founded on the psychology of possessive need than it was captured by a model of transactional and communicational binds based on the epistemology of "conflicting definitions of a relationship" (Bateson et al., 1962). It has also become appropriate to raise the clinical utility of the concept of *loyalty* and its basic relational paradigm, *justice* (Boszormenyi-Nagy, 1962; Boszormenyi-Nagy & Spark, 1973).

In the meantime it became possible to fit "intersubjective fusion" (Boszormenyi-Nagy, 1965a) into the expanding perspective of relational dynamics. Such "coordinated role playing" was seen to be rooted in an "unconscious contract among members" (Boszormenyi-Nagy, 1965b, p. 67). Here it was assumed that: 1) Growth *per se* produces the experience of loss; 2) All family members strive to avoid the pain implicit in such loss; and 3) Each family member has a shared stake and mutually collusive investment in avoiding the painful implications of loss. What is gained from such collusion is the security that comes of "not rocking the boat" (p. 67). The concept of an implicit contract for mutual protection was still another obvious precursor to the later development in contextual therapy that describes the existence of shared invisible loyalties that remain operational years after family members physically separate.

The concepts of intersubjective fusion and being an object for the other

(Boszormenyi-Nagy, 1965a) are linked to the more specific formulation of the *"collusive postponement of mourning"* (Boszormenyi-Nagy, 1965b). The collusive tendency to postpone mourning alludes to situations in which relating partners engage in spontaneous offers of matching obligations. These offers are inadvertently made in the service of an "unconscious conspiracy to prevent each other's maturation." Here all family members are expected to become accomplices to each other in the task of avoiding the painful sense of loss that occurs to all through the trauma set in motion by the event of separation through growth. A direct correlation emerged between the degree of "pathogenicity" in a family and the degree to which "betrayed" family members exerted pressure on their "escaping" partner. Here was still further evidence of fusion and collusive stagnation; a new opportunity to point to relational sources of pathology in individuals.

Over the course of 20 years, the concept of need-complementarity was to lead to an equally significant and parallel, if complementary, explanatory notion, one that eventually was to be termed *entitlement*. It had already been clinically established that reciprocity in relationship was motivated by individual needs for self-gratification. The notion of need-complementarity and its implications were based on the observation that a person deferred or temporarily yielded his own satisfactions on the presumption that they could be most reliably met and filled through continued reliance on a relationship. Logically, this led to the conclusion that reciprocity is motivated by an individual's need for self-gratification. Both psychologically and ethically it follows that in a healthy, close relationship, an individual's capacity for self-gratification has to be complemented by his other-directed (centrifugal) concern: the need to reciprocate the care received from a closely relating party.

Put in other terms, earning entitlement means that a person wins the right and freedom to accept pleasure and enjoy life through offering a measure of care to people who have invested their care in him. Earning entitlement as a goal of contextual interventions will be discussed extensively in a later part of this book. Our point here is to establish the fact that through its relevance to trust the concept of need-complementarity provided a cornerstone to contextual bridge-building between individual, systemic and multipersonal theories on the causal factors in human behavior.

THE IMPLICATIONS OF TRUSTBUILDING FOR THE MANDATE OF THERAPY

It is easier to be lured into diagnosing pathology than it is to learn to formulate the premises of health. The contradiction, of course, lies in the fact that neither fusion nor stagnation nor any pathogenic manifestation is finally representative of all relational reality. To the contrary. Relationships are not molded by pathology alone. They are need-satisfying. Moreover, in their depth they are governed by *existentially ethical dynamics*. The ethical balance of give-and-take between relating partners implies a fair return, though it includes instances of exploitation too. The dynamic here has to do with the fact that people have been cared for and owe care in return. The *personalized human order* that relating partners form between them is composed of at least two equal and opposite parts: The one has to do with the consequences of having benefited from other people's care. The second has to do with the obligation to offer due consideration in return, and to posterity as well.

In our view, people's capacity to balance these two aspects of the human order constitutes relational justice and leads to interpersonal trust. Contextual theory and practice are based on the conviction that the prospect of trust among people is rooted in the degree of *interhuman justice* that exists between them (Boszormenyi-Nagy & Spark, 1973). A concern for the state of relational justice or fairness in a family provides a healthy basis for each and every member's regard for other people's interests as well as for her own. A chronic failure of concern for the balances of fairness among family members constitutes relational stagnation (Boszormenyi-Nagy & Spark, 1973). Since fair relating is anchored in trustworthy attitudes which then warrant trusting, trustbuilding has subsequently become a primary goal of contextual therapy (Boszormenyi-Nagy, 1979; Boszormenyi-Nagy & Krasner, 1980). "Rejunction," the term used to describe the process of restoring responsible concern for the balances of justice among family members (Boszormenyi-Nagy & Ulrich, 1981), has become a primary methodology.

Frequently, the goal of therapy is pictured after the medical model—removing pathology or "maladaptive" behavior. Family therapy has moved from an investigation of individual psychopathology to a search for "family pathology." Yet therapy, physical or behavioral, has to be based on more than a search for obstacles to healthy function. As an incessantly evolving process, life itself is chiefly a goal-oriented use of resources. Contextual therapy is resource- rather than pathology-oriented. The necessity for *balance* between creative assertion and relational integrity characterizes the trustability of all human relational systems, including family relatedness and therapy. The literature of psychotherapy as a whole has largely avoided explanations of an ethical nature. Yet the domain of *relational integrity* is inseparable from health or, in the parent-child relationship, from prevention. Concern about the criteria of relational integrity is one of the main dimensions of contextual therapy.

Traditional sociological concerns about a fair balance, a *quid pro quo* in relating, will be contextually expanded to include both the asymmetry of adult-child relationships and the self-serving, subtle, exploitative implications of each member's intrapsychic programming of the relationship. Classical family therapy (or social science) has been concerned with the systemic implications of the *equity of give-and-take* in transactions. However, parents as adults are unequally more effective and powerful partners. They are also able to shape their children's built-in relational programming and thereby manipulate the children's motivations. For example, children can be made to feel guilty while actually overgiving to their parents. To manipulate people to guilt through their points of sensitivity is the most powerful method of control in close relationships.

But why attempt to manipulate and control others? Social science provides models that address issues of economic and political advantage, such as the control of land or distribution of wealth. Contextual theory extends the areas in which people strive to manipulate one another for internal, psychological use. Without touching on the motivational programming within individuals, simply to base therapy on *power* considerations will prove insufficient in the long run. Therapy has to consider the built-in internal relational attitudes in each of us since they have ethical implications. The ledger of fairness or relational integrity between people is always partly shaped and distorted by each person's internal needs as he or she carries over displaced internalized justifications for presently inappropriate vindication even if such vindication is historically valid retrospectively. Invariably, then, the stability of every relationship depends on its *equilibrium between internal and interpersonal relational ledgers* of justifiability.

Here lies the dilemma between the goal of fair relational complementation on the one hand and the individual goal of autonomy on the other. If people remain too "enmeshed" (Jackson, 1961; Minuchin, 1974), undifferentiated (Bowen, 1965), or fused with relating partners, they fail the test of individuation in a world of inevitable competition for success and survival. *Individuation* is therefore a key goal of any therapy and the main theme of self-improvement guide books.

On the other hand, individuation at a cost to all trust in relating deprives even the self-serving actor. Many people are programmed to be unnecessarily *anti-cooperative* because of the trust-demolishing experiences in their past. From victims of manipulative abuse they turn into perpetrators of new injustices within their subsequent relationships. This is one of the foremost ways in which parents fail the test of accountable childrearing. They may contribute to an irreversible imprinting input in their children's personality formation, in their capacity for trust, and in their future ability to cope with mistrust.

While curious to assess the nature of damage to the offspring's future capacity to trust, contextual therapy focuses on *options for tapping trustworthy resources* in family relationships. The mandate of this kind of therapy is to enable the evolution of life's prospects rather than to diagnose and change what has been defined as pathology.

More recently (Boszormenyi-Nagy, 1983), the concept of the justice of the human order has been expanded to encompass the whole spectrum of the criteria for responsible relating. The issue at the center of this *intrinsic relational tribunal* is not intended to create controversy either between individualism and tribalism (Wilson, 1980) or between individual and systems-based thinking. Instead, its central notion is the vital significance of responsibility for relational consequences. Through the perspective of inclusive fairness, the essence of the tribunal extends the notion of the dyadic ledger of fairness into the criteria of retributive and distributive justice among all relating persons, especially as these criteria affect our descendants. The conceptual and clinical implications of the hypothetical tribunal will be explained in later sections of this book.

II. OUTLINES OF THE HUMAN CONTEXT

CHAPTER 4
The Four Dimensions of Relational Reality

An accountable therapeutic design requires consideration of an extensive *knowledge of human behavior*. The requirement for a comprehensive knowledge of complex phenomena applies to all rigorous disciplines, of course, but has lifesaving and life-damaging implications in the healing arts and sciences. Medical practitioners, for instance, cannot be defined as accountable unless they command an adequate, functioning grasp of all the branches of scientific knowledge about the human body, among them surgery, immunology, pharmacology, and their convergences. With the explosion of information in the computer age, the fundamental requirement for an accountable therapeutic design has placed imposing burdens on healing practitioners.

In the field of psychotherapy, the demand for an adequate working knowledge of complex behavioral phenomena has led to a periodic alternation of tendencies: Periods have fluctuated between inclinations towards simplistic unilateral reductionism on the one hand and empirical eclecticism on the other. At the turn of the century, Freud's claims of a "psychic determinism" competed with attempted explanations from the biological sciences that then composed scientific medicine. Prior to the emergence of the family therapy approach, psychotherapeutic theory and practice relied heavily on clues and explanations of a psychological universe. In the fifties, family therapists introduced new knowledge based on systemic and transactional processes and relational determinants of human behavior.

The current state of the art confronts its theorists and practitioners with the question of what can now pass for an accountable therapeutic design.

Therapists obviously choose individually and systemically oriented modalities that conform to their own personal and professional preferences. Given this fact, is there room for a *parsimonious integration* of convergent causal factors? In the midst of competing and conflicting claims, what currently constitutes adequate knowledge of the essential components of effective psychotherapy? In sum, where is the "narrow ridge" to be trod between the quicksand of encyclopedic all-inclusiveness and the thin ice of monolithic reductionism?

AN ORDERING OF RELATIONAL REALITIES

At one level, answers to these questions may take centuries to unfold. At another level, beginning steps are already in process. As a result of years of search for an inclusive and parsimonious categorization of the totality of the therapeutic spectrum, a fundamental *ordering of relational realities* has been proposed that in our view contains the seeds of an accountable therapeutic design (Boszormenyi-Nagy, 1979; Boszormenyi-Nagy & Krasner, 1980; Boszormenyi-Nagy & Ulrich, 1981). This proposal is meant to be an initial effort towards developing an economic integration or, at least, juxtaposition of the needs, characteristics, life interests, and relational configurations of all the members of a given family. These relational realities include four fundamental dimensions:

I. Objectifiable Facts;
II. Individual Psychology;
III. Systems of Transactional Patterns; and
IV. The Ethic of Due Consideration: Merited Trust.

A consideration of these fundamental realities in every person's and every family's life helps therapists address the options and resources for healing that are rooted in a transgenerational, multipersonal world.

The four dimensions represent relational paradigms. Each of the paradigms contains a valid realm of understanding and inquiry into relational reality. Knowledge of the basic premises of relational reality is a precondition to a therapist's ability to mobilize hidden relational resources, the core of contextual therapy.

This ordering bridges the gap that has traditionally existed in the therapeutic search for either individual or relational determinants. It provides guidelines for therapy that include a concern for:

Individuals and their relating partners;
The impact that their origins and transactions have had on them, their behavior and their relationships;

The real and potential consequences of each person's impact on posterity; and

The existential conflicts that are intrinsic to interpersonal relationship.

The Place of Intuition

In our view, ordering fundamental relational realities also offers an underpinning to what amounts to a current therapeutic obsession with developing unique and refined technologies. Refined therapeutic technologies obviously have important functions, among them a clarification of the rationales that underlie therapeutic goals and strategies. They also function to define the aims and justify the methods of specific therapeutic modalities.

It should be noted, however, that these benefits are not to be confused with the imponderable element of therapeutic intuition. In order to elicit a spontaneous choice of options in clients, the therapist needs free access to intuition. Subjective and indefinable though it may be, *therapeutic intuition is a product of comprehensive knowledge*. In fact, it may be the end result of a personal, hence professional, integration of complex psychotherapeutic and behavioral phenomena. In the following situation, for instance, it is the therapist's grasp of the human condition that paces the direction of his intervention. "Technology" helps of course—but only in balance with an intuition of where meaning lies in "every person's" life and relations.

Mr. and Mrs. Jones were seeking help for their marriage. The presenting problem had to do with Mrs. Jones' angry outbursts at her husband and mother. An intelligent and compulsively neat person, Mrs. Jones is resentful of the fact that her mother has humiliated and frustrated her. Their relationship, she claimed, was characterized by mistrust and manipulation. She handled her rage through long distance calls to her parents which inevitably resulted in tortuous arguments with her mother; or else she ignored them for prolonged periods of time.

His wife's hostile outbursts rendered Mr. Jones helpless. A hardworking, meticulously responsible salesman, he was deeply discouraged and never knew what he would face when he came home from work: On occasion, Mrs. Jones would try to ruin the garden equipment that he so highly prized. On other occasions, she would throw out his favorite books. On the other hand, there were times when their marriage seemed to be alright. For example, they could function as a team whenever members of their extended family were in real need. During their brief respites, they could enjoy each other and reported that their sexual relations were good.

However, the couple was often at war over their only child. Sheila, age 12, was chronically caught between them and lived in constant jeopardy of being split in her loyalties to them. Mrs. Jones would greet her husband at the door with complaints about their daughter. He resented being cast into the unfair role of referee and retaliated by forming a subversive alliance with Sheila. In therapy sessions, the couple finally consented to hear each other out. Together, the three of them began to work towards fairer ways of relating.

Mr. and Mrs. Jones and Sheila seemed comforted by the therapist's capacity to elicit the justifications of each of their sides (multidirected partiality). Yet, Mrs. Jones was openly annoyed at any attempts to offer fair consideration to her mother.

In the interim, things went better for the family. Until now Mrs. Jones had lacked the security to look for a job commensurate with her intelligence and ability. For a long time she invested her energies in compulsive housekeeping. Suddenly she found a job that she liked. Immediately, tensions eased as her world widened and opened up. Mr. Jones learned to distance himself from his wife when she regressed into outbursts of anger. And Mrs. Jones began to exchange letters with her mother and managed some pleasant visits with both of her parents.

On occasion, some of the vindictiveness previously channelled towards her parents was now transferred to the therapist. At one point, Mrs. Jones refused to accompany her husband to their therapy session, arguing that the therapist "didn't care" about her. Two weeks later, though, she left an emergency message with the answering service: Her mother had died suddenly, unexpectedly! Overcome by the intensity of her emotions, she expressed profound gratitude. What would have happened to her, she wondered, if the therapist had not enabled her to find a way to her mother? What if she had failed to repair their relationship before it was too late?

Obviously, all of the dimensions of relational reality are at play in this brief vignette. Most significantly, rather than focusing on change-making techniques within therapy sessions themselves, contextual therapy relies on the fundamental reality of each person's relational integrity and ethic of responsibility.

In other terms, Mrs. Jones' mother had a side of her own, regardless of anyone else's perceptions of how she had treated them. As a parent, she had made massive, if imperfect, investments in her children. At the very least, then, she was entitled to have them inquire into her side despite the many ways in which she may have done them harm. Moreover, knowing her mother's side was in Mrs. Jones' own vested interests: She could earn personal entitlement and, consequently, freedom through the simple act of offering her mother due consideration. She wanted that from her own daughter. Why would her mother not want that from her? By what justification would she withhold from her mother what she herself as a mother so desperately expected from her own child?

It was not simply a matter of doing still one more thing to please her parents. Had her mother died without Mrs. Jones moving toward her to rework where they were "stuck" (relational stagnation), it would have been Mrs. Jones who would have been bereft. On what basis could she hope to gain a more trustworthy level of relating with her husband and child if she had voluntarily eschewed that option with the person who had given her life? If Mrs. Jones had not been prodded to reengage with her mother while there was still life and time, she would have lost an irreplaceable dialogic chance to move beyond a continuing reliance on her own unjust and trust-demolishing relational operations, i.e., on punitive distancing and outbursts of rage.

In sum, the four dimensions of the relational context indicate that contextual therapy integrates rather than opposes the *spectrum of valid therapeutic approaches* and methods. Though its guiding consideration relies on Dimension 4—The Ethic of Due Consideration: Merited Trust, it accommodates considerations and methods based on the other three dimensions. For the same reason, it is neither simply individual nor family therapy *per se*—it encompasses both.

DIMENSION I. OBJECTIFIABLE FACTS

Preexisting Factors

A brief review of the proposed ordering of fundamental relational realities best begins with the dimension of objectifiable facts. This aspect of reality is anchored in the determinative leverage of the following *preexisting factors*: Genetic input, physical health and appearance, basic historical facts of one's developmental circumstances, and the occurrences and events in each person's life cycle. Hereditary diseases and other facts of inheritance belong in this dimension. So does relational happenstance. For example, parental divorce and remarriage reconstitute the factual basis of an offspring's reality: Parents have choices to make about how they view their ex-mate, how frequently they will visit their children or allow their ex-mate to visit, and the degree to which they encourage their children to ask hard questions about the circumstances of their parents' separation. Parents obviously have a variety of options from which to choose, some that work out well and others that work out poorly. Whether parental choices are good or bad is secondary in our consideration. The point is that parental choices convert into their offspring's objectifiable, factual reality, whatever the options or consequences.

Unavoidable Conflicts

Objectifiable facts also have to do with *unavoidable existential conflicts* among family members. The fundamental life interests of closely relating parties are often in inherent conflict with each other. Parents' investment in possessing their children, for example, potentially conflicts with children's evolving right to own their own lives.

Another example has to do with the fact that in childrearing, parents have to be prepared to give more to their children then they have a right to expect in return. Raising children to maturity holds many satisfactions, of course, but at the level of reciprocity, care offered to posterity amounts to an essentially unilateral, *asymmetrical* act. The era of the nuclear family has deprived parents of the company of other adults who might help with the children and offer concern and care to the parents themselves. The often bereft and abandoned situation of many single parents or over-burdened step-parents in nuclear or even in remarried families constitutes a conflict of interests for children who are expected to fill the breach. Children who are destructively parentified not only experience personal exploitation and depletion; however inadvertently, they are also robbed of the energy and resources to offer adequate care to the next generation.

Inherently existential conflicts among family members obviously cannot be changed. They are here to stay. People have to learn how to *cope* with them better. Yet people can offer care and concern about their actions whose consequences affect posterity. Divorced parents are unlikely to marry each other again. But they can treat their children in ways that protect them from subtle and destructive costs of a heritage of split loyalty. Children of divorce and of conflictual marriages like the Jones' are inevitably cast into a referee-like role. A youngster's struggle to keep his mistrusting parents together is automatically bound to parentify him. This specific circumstance aggravates the universal conflict that exists between a parent's possessive interests and tendencies and a child's need for autonomy and the space in which to grow.

Objectifiable facts help determine the course of therapy. Therapeutic moves are obliged to address a family's existing realities. For example, it became an important fact that Ms. Jones was able to approach her mother before the mother's death. The motivating significance of the prospect of a parent's anticipated death is an important trust-building, therapeutic reference point.

Consequences

The contextual therapist is interested in what turns relational exchanges into *consequences*, i.e., facts that unilaterally impact certain people. It often takes therapeutic intervention to convert the fact of consequences into relational exchanges. Psychosomatic conditions can be one illustration. A father's long-term, severe gastric ulcer remitted after he did serious work on the consequences of his earlier incestuous relationship with his daughter. A woman's long-standing frigidity disappeared after she started to constructively reengage with her ambivalently rejected mother.

From the individual's standpoint, what may appear to be a factual consequence may still amount to an unused relational option or contextual resource from the therapist's standpoint. Even an exploratory reactivation of stagnant relationships or facing the consequences of hidden relationships can offer a helpful mobilization of resources. As the therapeutic method of multidirected partiality swings into full gear, even more specific benefits can occur. In summary, turning a frozen world of factual consequences into a live commitment to responsible dialogue is the understructure of what, on the surface, might be called "revitalizing a frozen family system."

The extensive matter of medical and medicinal treatments also belongs to this dimension.

DIMENSION II. INDIVIDUAL PSYCHOLOGY

The world of objectifiable facts is a mixture of individual and relational realities. In contrast, the psychological integration of one human being's experience and motivations is clearly subjective. Individually based, it is located in the brain functions of each person and always refers to one individual as a discrete entity.

Therapeutically, individual psychology is one of the greatest potential resources of relational reality. In fact, relational therapy is hardly imaginable without a minimum requisite of psychological knowledge. Even simple common sense would require an understanding of each relating partner's personal *life goals and motivations*. For who can deny that everyone strives for recognition, love, "strokes," power, and pleasure? Everyone is motivated by some degree of aggression, exploitative expediency, dependent mastery, and ambivalence, among other similar characteristics. Everyone is governed by the character traits that result from his or her own developmental assets and handicaps.

The input of individual family members can also be partly understood in behavioral and learning terms. On a more sophisticated level, their motivations, unconscious defensiveness, and character structure can be explored. A case in point is the situation in which a lack of early empathic parenting can lead to narcissistic personality development in a child. This failure can potentially interfere with all of the child's later developmental stages.

The Contextual Approach

From a contextual vantage point, the functions of each person's mind are important data and valuable knowledge. As such, they are significant parts of a contextual code. The continuous experience of a unique self and the organization of its behavior are *subjectively programmed* in each person's mind. This programming encompasses the whole spectrum of stimulation, perception, satisfaction, dissatisfaction, attraction, pleasure, pain, intelligence, identification, instinctual drive, developmental imprinting, conditioning, learning, insight, distortion, defense mechanisms, dreams, scripts, archetypes, fantasies, memories, contents, gestalts, metaphors, suggestions, etc.

To illustrate, feelings of loyalty and a sense of entitlement can be interpreted as psychological phenomena. As such, though, they have to be differentiated from *the relational essence of loyalty and entitlement*. Nevertheless, contextual work cannot proceed on the simple basis of a one-person, individual orientation. One person's mind can never fully encompass either another's subjective vantage point or what Buber called the "realm of the between."

Empathic Siding

A plain multiplication of the psychological model cannot account for all the complexities of relationship. Early in the development of the family field, therapists concluded that they could not afford simple, simultaneous empathy with each person's side. For example, *unilateral,empathic* siding with one family member may throw a therapist into an adversarial role with another family member. Or empathic support of a family's current victim may serve to obscure far-reaching, systemic implications of that family's interpersonal balances and conflicts. Moreover, certain family members, e.g., a child-abusing parent, could very easily be seen as worthless "monsters."

The Individual Approach

If therapy proceeds on a *purely individual* basis, it hypothesizes that each family member is able to "change" his or her behaviors to fulfill the goal of therapy. To maintain such change, each of them will then have to develop insights and modify their *long-range motivations*. For example, if Mr. and Mrs. Jones could lessen the pressure that Sheila is experiencing from having to choose one of them over the other, each parent would have to find ways to cope with their own mistrust. To appreciate some of her husband's positive initiatives toward her, Mrs. Jones might have to face and cope with her own "narcissistic" character traits. In individual therapy, she would have occasion to micro-internalize the therapist's empathic concern (Kohut, 1977). In the process, she could become more capable of deriving satisfaction from mature heterosexuality, and from her evolving "generative" (Erikson, 1959) pattern of parenting. Through the processes of transference to her therapist, she could reexperience and modify some of her basic relational attitudes and thus become less defensively dependent on her husband and daughter. It is to be noted that the complexities of the psychoanalytic approach are omitted here.

For his part, Mr. Jones could be helped to become more of an assertive "*self*" (Bowen, 1965). He could learn how to cope more effectively with his aggression and anger as well as develop and assert some of his own need-satisfactions. As a consequence of "individuating" himself, Mr. Jones could begin to pace the family in establishing new transactional patterns. Sheila, too, could be helped to assert her own age-appropriate needs. As a girl in her preteens, she may be caught in some of the problems of her growing sexual identity. She may be struggling with the guilt of an oedipal rivalry with her mother as well as with a heightened sensitivity to intimacy with her father. At the very least, she could be helped to cope with her angry ambivalence towards her mother.

Anger and Aggression

Here a divergence is to be noted between a psychodynamic approach and a contextual approach to coping with anger and aggression. Psychodynamically, aggression can be defined as one of the basic drives of the mind. As such, it requires an understanding of aggression's emotional meaning. It also requires both endopsychic structuralization and "insight" to cope with it. From a contextual vantage point, aggression, like all other expressions of *affect*, constitutes a *relational indicator*. The angry person is more likely to have a creditor's claim on relationship and his guilt-laden partner is more likely to be on the debtor side.

To be sure, contextual therapists recognize that each member's own psychic configuration and "pathology" are also activated by the unavoidable conflicts of interests that are part of their family's life. Furthermore, new situations tend to be cloaked by the shadow of "old ghosts" which evokes unfaced feelings and preempts the possibilities of fresh and more trustworthy solutions.

A resolution of interpersonal conflicts requires that each of the relating parties claim his or her own due terms. The decision to assert one's own side tends to lead to an affect-laden confrontation which in itself is anxiety producing. If such confrontations can clear the way to a more constructive avenue for relating, however, healing will have taken place.

Multidirected Partiality

Contextual therapists, then, retain a concern for the psychological realities of each family member. But their therapeutic stance is shaped by a *multipersonal attitude of partiality* (Boszormenyi-Nagy, 1966). Competent contextual therapists can offer due partiality to a multitude of the family members' one-sided terms (multidirected partiality): Is Mrs. Jones' current behavior predicated on a felt sense of isolation and deprivation in her own parenting? Then she is entitled to therapeutic consideration that will help her assess her terms and make an effort to rework the balances of give-and-take that exist between her and the significant people in her life. Is Mr. Jones depressed by his wife's unreasonable and seemingly limitless demands on him? Then he is entitled to therapeutic concern that will help him assert his needs, and help him refuse to function as a surrogate parent to Mrs. Jones. Is Sheila exploited by her mother's and father's inability to act as a parenting team? Then she is entitled to therapeutic interventions that recognize and help her rework her invisible loyalties to her parents, and that help Mr. and Mrs. Jones acknowledge the height and breadth of Sheila's contributions to her family. Whether or not they are ever present in therapy sessions, are Mrs. Jones' parents confused and perplexed by their daughter's erratic and punitive behavior towards them? Then they are entitled to therapeutic interventions that forfend scapegoating and permanent estrangement through enabling Mrs. Jones to reassess old injuries through adult ears and eyes.

Multidirected partiality is the therapeutic attitude that protects the therapist from becoming unilaterally attached to one person via countertransference, or from turning into a fragmented referee who gets caught between the conflicting goals and aspirations of competing family members. The therapist becomes trustworthy through a honed ability to maintain her genuine interest in eliciting the mutually exclusive and incompatible interests and aspirations of each and every family member. She addresses an intrafamilial *intrinsic tribunal* that holds all family members implicitly accountable. Instead of passing judgment on the family members, the therapist elicits their active concern about everyone's terms for fairness.

Explanations for human behavior, whose orientation is historical, psychological and developmental, can be contrasted with explanations and linkages rooted in Dimension IV, the *merit dimension* of relationships. Sheila, for example, is a deprived, scapegoated and parentified child. As such, she failed to develop the basic trust that is the central ingredient of viable relationships. She is lacking self-esteem and security as well as empathic identifications. Her psychological development has clearly been impeded. An undisputed victim of unfair circumstances, over time, she is likely to become a victimizer too. Deprived of *justice* in her "human order," Sheila is *entitled, however destructively,* to press the world to compensate her for her loss. In a tragic correlation with her own victimization, she is likely to inflict unjust demands and impose unjust expectations on innocent third parties. If relational realities have psychic consequences, psychological realities also have relational consequences. Motivational psychology and relational ethics with its balance sheet of merits and credits intersect with each other and partially overlap.

The nongiving attitude of Mrs. Jones can be psychologically diagnosed as a narcissistic character pattern. She may be developmentally fixated on the level of "pre-object relating" mental patterns. Yet on an ethical level, deprived of empathic parenting herself, Mrs. Jones became destructively over-entitled, as well. In addition to not having learned how to relate in an effectively giving fashion, so to speak, she could also justify her vindictiveness toward a world that discriminated against her by not giving her every young child's due: "good enough" (Winnicott, 1965) parenting and nurturance.

On the other hand, when a vindictively overentitled person turns her historically justified grudge against an unsuspecting other, *her* position becomes unjustifiable. Even if she has a need for channelling her original hurt and anger through displacements in the psychological realm, the ethical validity of her vindictive claims cannot be justly transferred into the context of another relationship. It seems highly probable that as a fellow human being, the psychodynamic therapist cannot help but react to the clues of striking unfairness in his patient's relating, even if the therapist consciously restricts his method to exploring psychological connections and derivations.

Transference

Transference is a special case of displacement from one's parent figures to the therapist. Displaced or projective identification of the partner stems from one's inner needs and is a common occurrence between closely related people. "You seem to treat me as if I were your father and I act toward you in the way I act towards my mother." Convenient for the actor, such distorted identification is likely to victimize the other. In some way, this use of relating amounts to an intrinsic parentification of the other. The other is dependent on and implicitly asked to oblige the distorter. Yet the target of the distorter is unlikely to ever get any acknowledgement for his services.

The therapist is obliged to know about the manifestations of such distorted identifications of the partner. Many times only the end result, a deep helpless frustration and anger, is noticeable and then over some apparently banal issue. As we will describe, the therapeutic attitude of multidirected partiality is a helpful entry point toward sorting out "real" interpersonal conflicts from transferred, displaced or projective identifications between family members.

DIMENSION III. SYSTEMS OF TRANSACTIONAL PATTERNS

General Systems Theory

Multipersonal patterning of manifest transactions and communications is a realm apart from the dimensions of objectifiable facts and individual psychology. Obviously these three dimensions intersect and overlap with each other at many points. But at its beginning, classical family therapy was characterized by its claim that a *supraindividual level* of behavioral determination constituted an unnamable entity with dynamic forces of its own. General systems theory offered the name "system" for this entity whose regulatory mechanisms pointed beyond the fact of one person's imposing his will on others, of random coexistence of individuals or of commonly held rational goals and purposes. Attempts to describe this essential facet of relational phenomena relied heavily on terms borrowed from social science literature. Much useful development and growth in the family therapy field derives from elaborations on the systems notion.

Ever since its beginnings in the late 1950s, systemic conceptualizations of relationship have contributed brilliant intuitions and useful insights. Part of these insights pertained to effective, expedient, and competitive, if neurotically reinforced, goal orientations to human conduct, e.g., the "games people play" (Berne, 1964). The competitive efficiency of the person's conduct in worldly affairs has a long tradition in Western writing, that includes Baltasar Gracian's 17th century book on *The Wise Man's Guideline for Conduct at the Court and in Society* (*Oraculo Manual*).

Other aspects of systemic writing helped with the understanding of a complex supraindividual level of regulation of behavior, health and illness within families. Family homeostasis and enmeshment (Jackson, 1957), marital schism and skew (Lidz, Fleck and Cornelison, 1957), "family jigsaw puzzle of strengths and weaknesses" (Bowen, 1965), pseudomutuality (Wynne, 1958), double-bind (Bateson et al., 1956), complementarity of need templates and merger (Boszormenyi-Nagy, 1962) were among the early efforts at formulating systemic rather than individually-based principles of regulation. As the schools of family therapy evolved, no method has remained unaffected by some form of transactional systemic conceptualization.

Classical Family Therapy

Like sociology, classical family therapy tended to define its processes in essentially, if not overtly, *power-related terms*, such as: competition for control, collusion, confrontation, conflict resolution, manipulative influence, hierarchy, and the geography of being present or absent. Systemic formulations vary and include patterns, rules, games, sequences, structures, subsystems, homeostasis, control, power alignments, boundaries, cybernetic feedback, role distribution, and customs. In addition, this dimension includes processes and interventions like double-binding, triangulation, scapegoating, labeling, distorted communication, withholding, power competition, reframing, sculpting, restructuring, creating metaphors for prescribing and blocking change, and others.

As part of the context of relational reality, the systemic framework of transactional patterning represents a useful guideline for understanding and describing phenomena, and for defining technical steps in therapy. In contrast with classical family therapy, however, contextual therapy builds its main intervention design on Dimension IV though it utilizes Dimension III for tactical moves.

Limitations of Transactional Systems

It is important to note that essentially transactional systems are defined by the functional and geographical aspects of the transacting contexts themselves, e.g., by role assignments and other facets of manifest behavior. For example, all persons affected by scapegoating and contributing to it constitute a particular system. All children, as opposed to all adults, constitute a subsystem. So does a nuclear family of members living under the same roof, and so on.

In order to stress their unique insights, pure transactional-systemic formulations ostensibly omit both psychological and merit components of relational reality. Moreover, their emphasis on the notions of circularity and feedback can be unduly self-limiting: Systemic conceptualizations tend to ignore the *forward-thrusting, unidirectional consequences* of each generation's effect on subsequent generations.

Even more problematic, perhaps, is the reductionism that at times attaches itself to the dimension of transactional patterning. The undeniable validity of much of its knowledge is often vitiated by the inclination of certain classical family therapists to address the family system as if it were a personal entity, a systemic homunculus capable of thoughts, wishes, feelings and experience, e.g., "the family is ambivalent," "the family feels 'you have to fight the system,'" and so on. As the notion of system becomes more sophisticated and relativistic, its meaning tends to capture the short-term, ephemeral aspects of an ever-changing relational sphere and bypasses the context of consequences.

Family transactional patterns do impinge on each of the members' lives. If we return to the Jones family as an example, it is easy to see that some of their transactions could benefit from *behavioral restructuring*: Mr. and Mrs. Jones could behave with more adultlike responsibility. Sheila could assume more genuinely childlike roles. The parents could deal more directly with each other rather than "triangulating" their child, and keeping her in the middle. The repetitious sequences of Mrs. Jones' behavior could be interrupted and "changed." Moreover, the family members' behaviors can be cast into a framework of rules and metarules. For example, Mr. Jones' passive behavior is obviously a determining factor in the household, one that invites control by his wife. And indeed, it is true that the usually collusive, relational imbalance between a persistently passive partner and a persistently destructive partner requires change from both sides. Furthermore, from Sheila's point of view, the communication between her parents is often double-binding. Who can deny the advantages of encouraging a more straightforward style of communication in the family? Still, serious problems exist in thinking about family life as chiefly a behaviorally determined, metaphorical whole.

In structural or strategic (classical) family therapy, for example, the symptomatic behavior is assigned a control characteristic that is viewed as quasi-volitional. This assumption is then often used to formulate therapeutic prescriptions that are aimed at paradoxically undermining the symptom. Maintaining the symptom as the primary reference point for therapeutic work thus amounts to a form of "reverse psychology" that is applied to an invisible, *anthropomorphic agent*. The resulting behavioral change is then predictable and at times has been equated with essential cure.

Other similar technical devices, described by classical family therapists, manipulatively affect a family's visible, transactional structure. These include joining, tracking, accommodating, relabeling, blocking, reorganizing, prescribing, restraining, positioning, positive reinforcement, and positive connoting, among others.

Carried to its impersonal extreme, classical family therapy based on this dimension is often geared to *ephemeral changes of manifest behaviors*, an orientation that overlooks the relational resources in a family that are capable of improving the quality of each of its members' lives. In more reductionistic expressions, it tends to assume a relatively new, judgmental, "diagnostic" attitude whose target is the family. Carrying the notion of diagnosis from the individual to the family realm is questionable. However sophisticated the message, blaming "the family" for its members' faults can serve to diminish individual responsibility. It can also contribute to further fragmentation and abandonment of human relationships in an already fragmented world.

A systemically oriented diagnostic attitude tends to overlook the family members' resources for improving the quality of their relationships, and can undermine each individual's appropriately assuming responsibility for the consequences of his or her own behavior. Concomitantly, of course, the burden of responsibility for change has been shifted to the therapist. "Active" therapists are then expected to know how they want to "change" families. It is frequently assumed that therapists can substitute "normal" behavior patterns or feedback sequences for the *rigid repetitiveness* that causes a family's "pathology."

It is also often believed that changing patterns of a family's behavior in the therapy room is akin to lasting individual health and growth. If behavior causes behavior, the reasoning goes, then a therapist's task lies primarily in establishing "healthy" behavior patterns, i.e., based on the therapist's values of the criteria for a family's growth. It is then assumed that a family's capacity to meet these criteria will secure healing and enduring growth.

In our experience, however, it is not primarily the rigid unchangeability of the behaviors of its members that present families with their fundamental dilemma. In fact, rigid insistence on family "rules" tends to reveal itself as a defense against an underlying threat of unrelatedness. The most pervasive problem of today's family life has to do with its felt loss of resources and the imminent threats of abandonment and fragmentation.

DIMENSION IV. THE ETHIC OF DUE CONSIDERATION OR MERITED TRUST

The Justification Factor

In contextual work, Dimension IV encompasses and supersedes the previous ones. Ethics implies the criterion of earning merit. Merit on the other hand carries justification with it. Trying to understand people's motives for action, we consider the first three dimensions: material facts, psychological needs, and transactional "game plans." Yet, another often decisive factor remains: *justification*. Justification includes consideration of all three other dimensions but it adds a new, fourth social reality. An action may fulfill both the person's psychic needs and the requirements of a relational transactional system and yet not automatically qualify as justified.

Justifiable actions connote trustworthy actors. Exploitation of one partner by another is incompatible with trustable relationships. To the contrary. People's capacity to remain reasonably trustworthy keeps relationships sustainable over time.

One person's side may appear or be unjustifiable from the vantage point of the other. In a sense, Dimension IV pertains to a conflict of justifications. The justifiability of any act or attitude derives from the consideration of the merits of both sides. At the very least, contextual therapy aims at a modicum of bilateral consideration in addition to mutual assertiveness between partners. A consideration of the overall fairness (Dimension IV) of the interpersonal ledger requires weighing factual, psychological, and transactional circumstances from each partner's vantage point. The therapeutic guideline based on Dimension IV dialectically transcends the other three dimensions.

The Need for Trustworthy Relationships

If a person can expect no gain from continuing to invest in his relationship, then abandoning it becomes a reasonable option. After all, what advantages can accrue from a life situation in which relational burdens outweigh benefits, exploitation precludes acknowledgments of genuine care, and the consequences of basic life conflicts consistently overshadow new options for relating?

Concern for relational balances is the key to viable close relating and is the cornerstone of contextual work. Contextual therapists operate out of a conviction that all family members gain from trustworthy relationships, which are the outcome of 1) due crediting, 2) responsible responding, and 3) care about a fair distribution of relational burdens and benefits. It is the therapist's task to engender a search for the visible and invisible contributions of every family member. His capacity to help family members define for themselves how they can be fair to each other highlights the therapeutic relevance of the ethical dimension of relational reality.

The Ethical Aspect

The ethical dimension of relational reality is easily misunderstood. Obviously, merit as a motive flies in the face of assumptions that power motives and expediency constitute the only legitimate theoretical frameworks of relationship. It also resists the use of any therapeutic techniques that are implicitly discrediting or that tend to weaken one or several family members' competitive capacities in order to fit the therapist's criteria of how a family "should" act and be. Interventions that help needy people *discover resources* for actively wanting to aid each other are to be differentiated from successful exercises in manipulating them.

In a dialectical fashion, the dimension of merited trust also challenges traditionally polarized views of altruism and self-sacrifice. As far as we can tell, the paradigm of unrelieved, one-sided giving is an unrealistic and potentially destructive one that is fraught with the dangers of depletion and guilt-evoking control.

Due Crediting

Over the long haul, then, neither power nor altruism can do the work of merit which earns entitlement for the self through duly contributing to and crediting the other. *Due crediting* evolves from a person's convictions about the merit of a partner's contributions to his life. Offering credit, of course, is intrinsically connected with relational balances. In accordance with the goal of trust-building, contextual therapists support the process of mutual crediting and a fair redistribution of relational benefits and burdens. For example, a therapist may want to elicit parental acknowledgment of the fact that a destructively acting-out, parentified child is also a caring and considerate family member. While parents may be legitimately dismayed by their child's unacceptable behavior, they are equally obliged to come to grips with the fact that their youngster is also frequently available to meet the personal needs of both parents.

Hazards of Relabeling

It should be noted that progress toward due crediting is not to be confused with the technique of automatic, positive relabeling or reconnoting what can amount to irresponsibility on the part of a family member or, indeed, of any negative aspect of a person's behavior. At times transactional, e.g., strategic, therapists typically use false positive relabeling as a paradoxical prescription aimed at extinguishing symptomatic behavior.

In our view, even if symptomatic change does occur, *manipulative relabeling* hardly leads to a gain in trustworthiness. Implicit stumbling blocks exist in praising an essentially destructive trait in an insincere if effective manner. Manipulating people for their own good is, of course, a common function of therapy. But manipulation rightfully assumes the name of therapy only if it is based on a genuine consideration of each person with the intention of helping them. A genuine consideration of family members is rooted in their own spontaneous progress toward due crediting and *improved balances of fairness*. It does not lie in the notion that therapist knows best!

Obviously, everyone shares the need for a minimally trustworthy relational context. It is not just the infant's developmental considerations that are at stake here. All interpersonal relationships retain viability only insofar as they embody some degree of trust. Marriages become untenable if trust disappears. And, paradoxically perhaps, much of the desperate behavior of seemingly uncaring adolescents and young adults is rooted in an intrinsic need to test their world's residual trustworthiness. Under the circumstances, paradoxically reinforcing a delinquent youngster's behavior through feigning its alleged positive contributions seems unnecessarily Machiavellian, superficial and groundless. In contrast, acknowledging the *truth* of the genuinely positive core of such a child may extinguish his need for symptomatic behavior. Addressing deeper truths fosters hope, trust and resource-oriented relational patterns. Conversely, manipulating a child's feelings of trust is in itself untrustworthy.

Earned Entitlement

The dimension of merited trust or *earned entitlement* exists in diametric opposition to the dimension of *power-based expediency*, social superiority, successful exploitation, and winning against a weaker competitor, among other like characteristics. On a purely linear, material basis, the more one person can extract from another person, the better off he is. In contrast, benefits derived from earned merit are based on what one receives through the process of caring or giving.

Expedient power confrontations may and do describe most of the dynamics of give-and-take in business or in political life. It is obvious, however, that they cannot be applied to how adults relate to small children without incurring the risk of serious and lasting consequences to the formation of their trust. Nor can the relationship between man and woman remain trustable if it is simply based on power operations.

If the merit dimension of relational reality differs from transactional patterning, it also differs from the psychological dimension that focuses on narcissistic and arrogant claims to entitlement. That is to say that merited trust or earned entitlement differs from a mere claim or sense of entitlement. A deprived or exploited child may or may not *feel* entitled, but he certainly *is* entitled to be compensated for what he has lost. In a parallel vein, earned merit is not a function of the superego or of moral character formation. A mere sense of indebtedness or "neurotic" guilt originates from the conflicting intrapsychic trends of only one person's mind. In other terms, existential guilt is to be differentiated from superego guilt. Existential guilt is founded on a person's actual harm to the justice of the human order (Buber, 1948), and thus requires interpersonal repair. It is also the source of *due* remorse on the part of the perpetrator.

The merit dimension of relational reality is based on an *action* sphere that incorporates the individual but also transcends him. Operating in the realm of the "between," all parties in a significant relationship are presumed to be responsible for the consequences of how their individual actions affect each other. That is not to suggest that a person's willingness to accept such responsibility in relationship results in some idealized form of peaceful coexistence. The fact remains that two people, however dialogic their relationship, cannot finally avoid *genuine conflicts of interest* between them. What they can do is face into conflicts to see how they can be addressed and if they can be reworked. Sometimes a simple if painful acknowledgment of each person's entitlement to pursue his or her own interests and autonomy is freeing, hence healing, in itself.

On the other hand, this fourth dimension of relational reality should not be made synonymous with incessant scrutiny of who has more merit or of whether or not a person is acting responsibly in every or any given situation. It does not imply a tireless, compulsive preoccupation with relational failures and their accompanying feelings of guilt. It does imply that, even in deeply trying circumstances, attempts *to earn constructive entitlement* offer everybody untapped sources of genuine liberation.

Quality of Parenting

In the center of the healing movement of contextual therapy lies the dialectic of each person's choice to earn entitlement. This is the point at which the breach between self-directed versus other-directed concern is overcome: The self benefits from due caring offered to the other. Precious between peers, this healing event is crucial to the process of parenting young offspring. Whether or not they are capable of staying together in a viable union, father and mother owe it to their young children to offer some degree of enabling cooperation. The gift to the child of basic trust brings returns through each parent's gain of self-enhancing merit. Conversely, the threat of severe mistrust between the parents can crush the autonomous growth of the young adult who has to leave the "empty nest" behind. The key to the greatest source of earned entitlement lies in the quality of parenting and in the capacity to enable posterity to thrive and grow. In an analogy with physical nurturance as the biological key to survival, the capacity for entitlement through offering due care constitutes the core of contextual guidelines for good parenting.

Personal Accountability

The merit dimension of relational reality then, represents the chief source of individual freedom. It also forms the basis for contextual therapy's chief methodological guideline. As such, it functions as an umbrella that overarches the other three dimensions and all other methodological considerations. In our experience, personal accountability as a guideline for caring and *relational integrity* constitutes the foundation of trustworthiness and individual health. If this is so, it follows that an accountable therapeutic contract will retain a profound regard for the consequences of its interventions on everyone who is potentially affected by them. This contractual principle goes beyond family therapy, in our view, and applies to all forms of individual therapy as well. For unlike the consequences of physical medicine, the consequences of psychotherapeutic intervention, whatever the modality, never affect just one person's world.

In the case of the Jones family, the therapist would have been gravely irresponsible if he had chosen to function solely on the parents' original contract for couple therapy. Whether or not he literally incorporated Sheila into the therapy sessions, it is clear to us that his major ethical concern needed to focus on how the consequences of her parents' work in therapy inevitably affects Sheila. Otherwise, Sheila will suffer further losses of a trustworthy parenting context of relating that is her just and rightful due. In turn, Mr. and Mrs. Jones will be driven further away from their stated goal of personal autonomy, a goal that each of them regards as their just and rightful due.

Autonomy

Paradoxically, the individual's goal of *autonomy* is inextricably linked to his capacity for relational accountability. In fact, responsibility for the consequences of one's action on his relational partners may be the true test of autonomy. This contrasts with notions of personal growth that are either indifferent to how one person's progress affects his or her relationships or presume that each relating party will simply have to make his or her gains at the expense of others. In either case, relationships are reduced to a matter of secondary concern.

In contrast, contextual therapists maintain a close interest in processes of relating and in each family member's goal of genuine autonomy. It is these personal goals and aspirations that offer people hope. Abstract constructs of "normal" interactional patterns appropriate to given subcultures, in our view, are less likely to offer the human meaning and motivation that come from attaining personal goals. Self-gain and the survival of trust are the likely end results of individual autonomy earned through offering responsible concern. Under the circumstances, a multilateral assessment of consequences is an important part of the contextual process. Therapeutic accountability begins with helping family members take stock of all their relationships from the vantage point of each of their own sides.

The capacity to *earn entitlement* may be the most reliable and enduring form of autonomy. Trust-based in nature, this capacity gains its impetus from the existence of invisible resources that surface when a person offers another *due consideration*. As such, a person's capacity to earn entitlement is clearly akin to Erikson's concept of generativity (1959). In contextual terms, life's creativity, pleasure and promise flow from actualized trust. Trustworthy relating, however, is supported by a therapeutic willingness to nudge people towards trustbuilding options rather than away from them.

In the Jones case, if in the long run the therapist had colluded with Mrs. Jones' unequivocal condemnation of her mother, an irretrievable opportunity to establish trust would have been lost. If the therapist had been guided by his fear that any preferential siding with her mother stood to alienate Mrs. Jones from therapy, the therapeutic process would have suffered an incalculable and unnecessary loss of relational sources. These resources were still latent between mother and daughter even during the worst moments of their estrangement. In this situation, the therapist opted to help Mrs. Jones identify and mobilize the resources that still existed in the family. This process was begun through his reminding Mrs. Jones of the value and promise of a fair reassessment of her relationship with her mother. Responsible intermember coexistence and collaboration in the midst of interpersonal conflicts of interests are the guidelines of contextual therapy's resource orientation.

New Options

Mrs. Jones' reluctant decision to reassess her relationship with her mother raised *new options for relationship*: She created the opportunity to reconnect with her mother and rework old injuries and pain while there was still time. In the process, she became more fully entitled to attend to her own personal priorities, among them a career. Perhaps most significantly, she managed to free herself of the invisible loyalty to her parents which took the form of blaming her husband instead of them. Displacing negative attitudes towards parents onto a mate provides a common escape from the painful consequences of a person's filial ambivalence, resentment and contempt. Victimized as a child, Mrs. Jones was able to justify her retributive tendencies, at least for her.

The *destructively entitled* person is often blocked from experiencing remorse as a consequence of her unjust treatment of an innocent party. Operating from a purely psychological dimension of relational reality, it would be easy to assume that Mrs. Jones' childhood paved the way for the development of her patterns of relying on destructive entitlement. An individually-oriented therapist might help her rework these tendencies by capitalizing on her transference attitudes and helping Mrs. Jones gain insight into her displacements and distortions. For many classical family therapists operating from a dimension of pure transactional patterning, it might seem sufficient to change or restructure these patterns through relabeling interventions or through paradoxical injunctions.

From a contextual perspective, a more genuine individuation is attainable through the dimension of merited trust: In exchange for his offer of due consideration of her own childhood suffering and victimization, the contextual therapist expects Mrs. Jones to take a responsible stance towards the consequences of her input for all of her significantly relating partners. In this process, the therapist would enlist Mr. Jones as a partner in a team relationship. They would work together towards an ultimate improvement of Mrs. Jones' relationship with her parents. Of course, a thorough reorientation of relational goals and patterns needs time and space for change to be noticeable.

Summary: Merited Trust

In summary, then, the dimension of merited trust is founded on *ontic care* based on existential interdependence. It is about:

- The consequences of the past for the present and the future;
- The impact of these consequences for every affected party in a family regardless of their behavior;
- The development of relational resources, with a special bias towards family members who have paid or will pay the heaviest and most irreversible costs (usually young children);
- The prevention of further prospective injuries and damages in the present and in future generations.

The logic of the merit dimension leads to *ethical guidelines* for therapy. Given its cornerstone of ontic care, contextual intervention offers first priority to the well-being of infants and dependent children, and to those people whose suffering has made them destructively entitled or even insane. Given its *relational* nature, this ethic benefits both the initiator and the recipient of the act.

The significance of merited trust as a methodological principle is confined neither to a specific therapeutic technique nor to any particular kinds of behavior. A grasp of the fourth dimension of relational reality helps therapists move beyond symptoms and patterns of behavior. Here people are helped toward active consideration of the context of justice in the human order, and toward the *resources of residual trustworthiness*.

Thus, in the Jones family, the therapist will be free to offer care to Sheila regardless of parental blaming or reported symptoms or gross malfunction on her part. Even though it is her parents and their marriage that have been presented as the identified problems in the family, the simple fact of the context of Sheila's family position in itself requires therapeutic attention. The conclusion that Sheila and her prospective children are destined to be the main beneficiaries of therapy leads to a need for translation into action designs. Her parents may reasonably argue that they are staying together primarily to protect their child's interest. However, they are likely to be out of touch with their own exploitation of Sheila, that is, with the cumulative consequences of how each of them uses her as a captively available referee or an implicitly accountable parent.

Here it will become the therapist's task to help the Jones convert their positive inclinations into action. For example, can these parents find ways to acknowledge each other's positive traits and actual contributions to each other's lives in front of Sheila? Can they make the time to offer a listening ear to their daughter's problems and concerns? Can they *earn constructive entitlement* through offering her due attention, consideration, acknowledgment and care?

If the members of the Jones family are helped to convert their concern for each other into relational action, they will have entered into the process of redistributing the burdens and benefits among them. This process of redistribution, in which each family member takes personal responsibility for his or her own part and terms, can lead to new, *more freeing balances of relational justice* among them.

It must be noted here, though, that an impeccably just or fair distribution of advantages and burdens is an *idealized goal*. In its ideal form justice is unreachable. On the other hand, the human bent towards justice cannot be ignored indefinitely without exacting grievous tolls to the trustworthiness of a given relationship. Fair consideration among family members requires that no one be placed in the expected role of an absolutely just, trustworthy or reliable parent.

If the assignment of these kinds of traits are invariably unfair to adults, they are even more unfair to children. Adult attribution of idealized relational traits to their children amounts to a direct road toward their parentification and to their subsequent scapegoating as failures. For all of the danger implicit in *destructive idealization*, it is a common occurrence in families and is typically beamed at one designated child, often an adopted child.

Fair distribution of burdens and benefits in a family also requires that no member be adjudged an *absolute "monster."* It is easy to scapegoat a rotten egg, and it lends to satisfying feelings of self-righteousness. Upon scrutiny, however, even a hostile, exploitative grandparent, for example, can be found to have a valid side. The apparent victimizer eventually can be found to have been a victim of past generations for those who choose to look! Besides, to whom do we turn for signs of human integrity if the ghosts of our past are irrevocably strained? If members of the present generation are finally unable to discover ways to exonerate parents about whom they have hateful or contemptuous feelings, if adult children are indeed incapable of viewing their mother or father as worthy of human consideration, can they expect fair consideration as their own children grow up? Deep-seated resentments towards her mother had long inhibited Mrs. Jones' capacity for pleasure, growth and trust. For a long while, she remained refractory to therapeutic suggestions that considered her parent's side. Yet over time, her behavior confirmed the validity of the therapeutic goal of exonerating her mother.

On the other hand, *destructively entitled* people evoke chronic resentment and rage from those who are closest to them. A major souce of ongoing suffering and malfunctioning in families, the manifestations of destructive entitlement are a fundamental concern of experienced contextual therapists. The difficulty in addressing and reworking this relational burden lies in the fact that, in a self-contradictory manner, the perpetrator *is entitled* to be destructive. This "entitlement" allows him to cause new injuries while he remains essentially immune to the ordinarily self-corrective influence of remorse over harming an innocent third party.

Remarkable turnarounds sometimes occur for the person who has learned to rely on the "credits" of destructive entitlement. Now reaping the gains of earned constructive entitlement, a parent will be increasingly inclined to acknowledge her child's needs and entitlements. She will also be oriented to look for ways to exonerate her own parents. Equally significant, she will learn to *state her own terms,* claims and life priorities and to assert them instead of continuing to rely on the criteria of substitutive vindictiveness. If Mrs. Jones can trust the value of trying to make her mother hear her side, she can try to state her terms to her husband as well. But, if she fails to test the residual trust resources in *any* relationship, Mrs. Jones is likely to become increasingly retributive.

In summary, therapeutic goals consistent with Dimension IV focus on addressing a fairer, if still periodically inequitable, distribution of relational burdens and benefits. This goal is synonymous with each family member's vested interests, and with their free options for autonomous growth. In the case of a young child, his parents have to carry a disproportionate burden of responsibility for a longer period of time, that is, until the youngster is reasonably able to accept his share of accountability. In the process, parents do well to keep the child's long-range interests at heart, and not require as much of him as is being offered to him. No youngster should be exploited, for example, with a parent's unyielding possessiveness. Nor should he be instilled with the seeds of self-destructive, counterautonomous motivations (Boszormenyi-Nagy, 1962).

CHAPTER 5

Interpersonal Conflicts of Interests: A Four-Dimensional Perspective

Conflicts of interests between people are omnipresent and inevitable but not necessarily destructive, pathological or unfair. Interpersonal in nature, they can neither be reduced to intrapsychic conflicts between the forces of one mind nor to power conflicts between persons or systems. Conflicts of interests between relating parties are inherent in the fact of giving and receiving, in being and becoming, and in competitive struggles for the same object or territory. The give-and-take between parent and child represents a conflict of interests that is peculiar to unmatched partners, that is, to asymmetical options. In fact, while other sources of conflicts of interests are avoidable, asymmetry itself is unavoidable. As already indicated, if legitimate asymmetry is ignored and a child is expected to repay his parents in kind, conflicts of interests become enormous.

The basic personality makeup of parents constitutes still another source of conflict. The more a parent was deprived and bereft in his own parenting, the more likely are his or her offspring to suffer damaging, existential conflict.

Classical psychodynamic, individual therapy, and classical family therapy approaches alike have tended to overlook the therapeutic significance of interpersonal conflicts of interests. Insufficient consideration has been given to the notion that conflicts of interests encompass all four dimensions of relational reality: facts, psychology, transactions, and the ethic of due consideration. Early in his career Freud was interested in the ways in which young children are actually harmed by their parents. Eventually, he relegated these alleged, relational conflicts of interests to his patients' historic, formative past that had become important through its internalization. At the same time that he dropped his "seduction theory," Freud placed conflicting interests within the mind, viewing them as *intrapsychic conflicts*, a battle between evolving mental forces and structures. The additional elements of relational reality were thereby diminished, if not eradicated.

For its part, *classical systemic family therapy* mainly chose to emphasize the transactional and communicational patterns between subsystems. Interest in the "systemic" level of one person diminished. By including family members in conjoint sessions, classical family therapy shifted its focus from both the intrapsychic conflict and personal responsibility to transactional patterns of behavior whose underlying framework of process had yet to be defined.

As indicated earlier, a framework of transactional "pathology" started to evolve and included elements like triangles, collusions, schisms, power alliances, games, blurred generational boundaries, double bind, faulty role distributions, and scapegoating, among others. Classical family therapy borrowed language from the social sciences whose overriding models are based on power confrontations and struggle for control within systems. From a sociological perspective, for example, conflict is relegated to *power conflict*, a collision of identifiable forces between identifiable entities. In our view, however, conflicts of interests are also rooted in the polarizations between a self and another, between an I and a You—in their *contexts of consequence and merit*.

CONTEXTUAL THERAPY AND INTERPERSONAL CONFLICTS OF INTEREST

At base, contextual work is founded on the observations and conclusions that interpersonal conflict itself helps to define and sustain people and their relationships. Precious healing resources are obscured and lost through an exclusive focus on impersonal, transactional, behavioral patterns. A narrowly transactional approach not only deemphasizes legitimate concerns for each relating partner's psychic process, but may also overlook the creative implications of existential dialogues between people who, in their uniqueness and quest for wholeness, are more than component pieces of a transactional puzzle. It is far more parsimonious for the therapist to address the dimensions of individual psychology and trustworthy dialogue than to try to eclipse them.

Confusion over what is owed and what is deserved in relationships underlies a host of problems between parents and children, in friendships and marriage. Emotional cutoffs, adolescent rebelliousness, and marital struggles that lead to divorce all represent some degree of struggle on this level of fair give-and-take. Behaviorally, the outward manifestations of conflicts of interests that surface in the process of individuation cover a wide range of difficulties that include financially exploitative schemes, aggressive acts, and sexual problems. All of these manifestations may lead to a collision course which appears to be essentially avoidable and optional.

For contextual therapists, the measure of conflicting interests lies in the impact and duration of relational consequences rather than in the intensity of affect, effort or confrontation. Clearly then, the greatest of any potential conflicts of interests exists between the child and his or her adult world. The 14-year-old who daydreams about how much he and his imagined son will talk and touch and play together has angrily confronted his father from the time he was a tot. Father is confused over his son's lack of appreciation of how good life is for him. He is also stuck in a family loyalty in which boys were delegated to perform without consideration of the emotional cost. A gifted overachiever himself, father is still answering to his own father's admonition never to waste one's intellect. He is also answering to his mother's cloying overinvestment in him. In consequence, his son is paying for transgenerational failures to attain a sense of entitlement. The enduring persistence of relational deprivation, however subtle, can long outlast the lifespan of an adult or even of his child. Specific delegations (Stierlin, 1974) can aggravate the natural tendency for parent-child conflicts of interests and entitlements.

Obviously, relational deprivation exists in varying degree. A parent's selfish possessiveness of her child can, in fact, constitute violent or sexual abuse, abandonment and rejection. As such, it can cause lasting damage to the youngster's personality development as well as to her own prospects for becoming a caring parent. But potential existential conflicts between the generations can be explored even before a person commits himself to parenthood:

Recently married, a 40-year-old professional woman was eager to have a child before it was too late. Her husband was already the father of two teenagers, and objected to having another child. Edna was both surprised and relieved when she realized that her main struggle was with her child-to-be rather than with her reluctant husband. She was reassured by the recognition that giving life to an infant under current circumstances would not be fair to her child and might represent a conflict of enduring significance.

It is somewhat paradoxical that the therapist's appeal to her parenting accountability evoked Edna's willing cooperation to further explore the implications of her situation. Simultaneously, she reported an instant improvement in her chronic insomnia.

It is always tempting for therapists to invest themselves in the here-and-now aspects of interpersonal conflicts: Is it fair for a man to marry and deprive his wife of children? Is it right for a woman who has never had to change a diaper to impose her belated longings for a baby on her child-weary mate? Couldn't Edna invest her energy in writing a dissertation? Her husband is always gone anyhow; why not let her have a baby on which to spend her time? Answers to these questions will affect the current conflict between husband and wife for good and for bad. Should the answer result in a baby, however, he is likely to fall heir to a conflict not of his own making and beyond his purview. Some part of such conflicts is inevitable while another part can be aggravated by a lack of parental concern for the consequences for posterity.

The long-term consequences of current conflicts between people are difficult to assess. The therapist who helps people face their option to cause injustices in future generations accepts a high level of demand. Still, parental responsibility is always invested with long-term consequences which exist even if they are momentarily hidden. These consequences differ for each relating partner, of course. The very structure of relational conflicts of interests highlights how different they are for the self on the one hand, and for the partner on the other. Who can compare the loss of parenthood for Edna with the potential of a baby who was never given life? Still her decision has centripetal and centrifugal consequences from her vantage point and from the vantage points of each and every doer. In summary, important existential conflicts of interests involve trans-generational expectations, mandates, legacies and delegations. In a contextual orientation, psychological reactions in relating partners are treated as epiphenomena of existential consequences.

Predetermined Sources of Existential Conflicts

Existential sources of interpersonal conflicts are essentially *preattitudinal* and *inadvertent* as well as predetermined. Still other sources of conflict depend on the attitudes of one or several partners. For example, adoption creates a conflict of interests between one's biological origins and one's coexistence with adoptive family members. Being an unwanted child or a child of chronically mistrustful parents amounts to an inevitable source of existential conflict. Other predetermined sources of conflict are constituted by being born with congenital defects, being a child in a single-parent family, being an only child, or having to grow up in a stepfamily. Moreover, the gradual disappearance of the extended family in our age has added to the conflicts that exist between overburdened parents and their often overparentified children.

Attitudinal Sources of Conflicting Interests

Predetermined conflicts of interests can be aggravated by attitudinal sources of conflict. Examples include,

- Not wanting a child, harming or abandoning him, or a strangling possessiveness of him;
- Parentifying a child or not letting him individuate;
- Hypocritical parental values that induce confusion in a child;
- Pseudo-closeness, pseudo-separation, and scapegoating.

The Contextual Approach

Contextual therapists operate out of the conviction that conflicts of interests emerge from the factual, psychological, transactional and ethical dimensions of relational reality. They understand that initial symptomatology and family problems require a gradual *translation into cogent conflicts of interests* between family members. They know that as the level of trustworthiness begins to rise in therapy, they can begin to elicit each family member's terms and views of the conflict. They also understand that the capacity of family members to own their respective sides of a conflict can lead to bridges that eventually reconnect them with each other.

However, contextual therapists also know that a comprehensive therapeutic design rather than reductionistic reliance on any one of the four dimensions is required to mobilize constructive relational resources. For example, consider the family that consists of two divorced and remarried parents who have one shared child as well as the wife's two children from her previous marriage:

Here the *fact* of her former husband's irreplaceable parental significance has to be recognized. In our view, mother is obliged to explore how her continuing hostile involvement with the children's natural father (transactions) burdens the two older children with an ongoing predicament of split loyalty (ethics). Experienced therapists know that there is no more effective weapon with which one ex-spouse can hurt the other (transactions and psychology) than through implicit or implied blame for his or her destructive parenting (ethics).

In this situation the two older children are automatically expected to become their stepfather's allies (transactions). They are hostages (ethics) to his rivalrous role (transactions) as their mother's second husband, that is, as a man who replaced their father (fact). It is also true that these children need (psychology) and deserve (ethics) a

trustworthy family life (ethics) in which they can earn their own entitlement through offering each other some care (ethics).

Interventions that address the interests of the children's prospects for the
future—including their capacity to parent the next generation (facts, need,
transactions and ethics)—represent a strong and responsible therapeutic
design.

CHAPTER 6
Three Aspects of the Dialogue Between Persons

Close relationships are established by blood or by emotionally meaningful satisfaction. Over a long period of time the quality of close relationships depends on their trustable core, the genuine dialogue. In its essence the genuine dialogue depends on the reciprocity of responsible caring (Buber, 1923, 1958). In our sense it is the core of that relational reality that becomes the context of mature *individuation*. Disregard of these basic, functional principles of relatedness underlies much of what is considered pathology. For example, both hostile distance and fused enmeshment can reflect failure of genuine dialogue.

Therapists can, of course, focus either on the more visible manifestations of close relationships or on the deeper foundations that resemble the skeleton and tendons which firmly hold soft tissue together. In contextual work it is important to know about the characteristics of these deep, holding structures. The therapist has to be able to address not only behavior patterns, roles, systemic feedback, individual emotions, and motivations but also the ledgers of fairness that form the basis of trustworthy relationships.

There are three aspects of dialogue that represent inner guidelines for discovering the self-corrective *resources* in close relationships. They point to missed opportunities for sturdiness through mutuality of commitment. They also point to clues for therapeutic options. Presented here in summary form, they will be described in detail later in the chapter.

The first aspect of dialogue is the *polarization* between selves: The clue for differentiation versus fusion, merger and guilt-laden "enmeshment." Mutual delineation leads to a creative use of otherness. On the other hand, options for self-validation hold the clues for chances to earn entitlement. Polarization is also a key to constructive rather than destructive competition.

Symmetry versus asymmetry is the second aspect of dialogue. Here a person's responsible contribution to another is one of the criteria that determine the rules of equitable give-and-take. Equitability within asymmetry is the key to fair reciprocity, especially in intergenerational relationships.

Inclusive multilaterality is the third aspect of dialogue. It is another key to trustworthy mutuality of commitment. Inclusion of every present and future participant safeguards distributive and retributive ledgers of justice. It warrants an integrative perspective, or joint consideration of the spousal and the parental ledgers of a marriage.

It is of great practical, therapeutic significance to understand that the three aspects of dialogue are not simply behavioral patterns. They pertain to that core of living in which basic attitudes to relationships are formed and sustained. If parenting may be characterized by child neglect and exploitation, it may also replicate a three-generational pattern. In that case, therapy has to address the basic attitude of the parent's insensitivity to the child's welfare, not just the particular, presenting, behavioral, communicational or transactional patterns. Basic attitudes have more to do with long-term consequences running through generations than with here-and-now observable feedback. Therapeutic planning has to cover both.

Contextual therapy is concerned with the inner structure of close, trustworthy relationship, i.e., what Buber called genuine dialogue (1923/1958). From our vantage point such relationships are more fundamentally linked to the notion of ledger than to role. In other terms, the X-ray picture of role behaviors in close relationships shows an infrastructure based on balances of fairness. The ultimate regulation of the quality of close relationships depends on the dimension of relational ethics. If the therapist wants to deal with more than just surface manifestations of relating behavior, he will be greatly helped by understanding these three aspects of the criteria of relational trustability. For example, a child of divorced parents may lose a great source of self delineation and self validation in addition to losing the actual relationships with the noncustodial parent. Under the circumstances, he may also lose the option for genuine dialogue.

When a contextual therapist assesses the family's condition, he is curious about their resources, i.e., the quality of relationships. He will not be limited to evaluating pathologies, problems, symptoms or conflicts. He is also concerned about the "clinical" criteria of good relating, love, hope, and trust. Trustworthiness, the main resource of genuine dialogue, is the glue of viable relationships. Manifest problems represent only the tip of the iceberg. It is mistrust that unglues relationships.

POLARIZATION: THE DIALECTIC BETWEEN SELVES

This aspect of genuine dialogue offers two major options for individuation or personality formation through the mutual definition of otherness. One is self-delineation: *The use of relationships for defining one's self vis-à-vis the other as ground.* The other option is self-validation: *The validation of self-worth through entitlement earned by offering due care.*

Contextually, individuation is a relational process. Even the Freudian approach with its thorough understanding of individual, depth psychology is inseparable from its implicitly relational constructs. Conversely, relationships can be properly understood only if due recognition is offered to the significance of individual strivings. *Psychic and social development are essentially indivisible.* Two poles of human reality, they exist in dialectical relationship to each other. Infants survive and thrive in supportive, human community.

If individual psychology and relationship are integral parts of each other, so too are the present and the past. If people are participants in their current sets of relationships, they are also links in the chain of transgenerational consequences. In point of fact, birth itself is a basis of relationship, a consequence rather than a transaction, change, feedback, or other feature of relating behavior. From a contextual perspective, even the biological aspects of a person's becoming and unfolding are relational. Subsequent generations are in dialogue with one another even if the dialogue can never be a spoken one.

Self-Delineation

Individuation in a psychic sense is akin to survival in a biological sense. Somewhere between birth and death, people have to come to terms with the *delineation of a unique self*, one that is set apart from the world and from other selves. In the process, a person's life will develop personal meaning that is specifically his own.

Life's purpose and meaning are derived from many sources, of course. Struggle for survival is one such source. Significant relations are another. The chain of transgenerational consequences is still another. On the one hand, individual identity is a person's own unique, psychological product. On the other hand, personal identity is influenced by chance circumstances, like being born to loving, caring parents, as well as by one's gender, religion, race and ethnicity. A person's background lends itself to meaningful identity. So does the quality of his or her significant relationships. By virtue of their mutual availability, relating partners establish a foundation and ground for each other's meaning and identity. The formation of the self requires a dialectical antithesis with the existence of the other or non-self. Personal meaning intertwines with relational modes (Boszormenyi-Nagy, 1965a, 1967).

Polarization is an important, relational principle and therapeutic guideline. As an aspect of the process of dialogue, it means mutual individuation through the existence of otherness. But stereotyped notions of a discretely independent and autonomous self portray the self as if it were separable from the dialectic of relationship. Consequently, all aspects of close relatedness, e.g., fair concern and care, emotional interdependence, and sympathy, can then be regarded as interference with the freedom of individuation. They can be referred to in disparaging terms like enmeshment or "emotional system." As an exponent of this exclusively self-directed, centripetal view of individualism, Sartre has portrayed human relationships as boundlessly competitive and mutually and unceasingly exploitative.

The view of the individual as a sacrosanct and absolute, self-sustained entity characterizes certain trends of Western civilization. The philosophies of Nietzsche (Kaufmann, 1968) and especially of Stirner (1845/1913) went to extremes in claiming the rights and superiority of the socially unconcerned, callously self-serving individual. In our sense, these thinkers split the self-delineating use of others from the use of the relationship as an option for earning merit (self-validation). In their denial of social interdependence, advocates of absolute, nondialectical, individual autonomy appeal to the egocentric, narcissistic bent of human nature. "Let me do my own thing" leads to social philosophies that are apologia for exploitative, "rugged individualism," freedom from parenting responsibility, and unabated prejudice toward outgroups. Total disregard for the rights of others in the larger social field can lead to callous industrial exploitation of workers, intolerance toward political opposition, one-party dictatorship, slavery, and, at its extreme, genocide. In Martin Buber's terms, such callous disregard for the other represents an I-It relationship at best.

As one self becomes an antithesis to another, a relational dialectic requires implicit and explicit accounting of credits and debits. In the first instance, *individuation* between two or more people is characterized by an aspect of polarization between the self and the other. From a psychological perspective, the event of birth, experiences of separation, and individual growth converge into the self's being and becoming, and define its prospects for experiencing life's meaning. From a transactional perspective, the prospects of giving and receiving develop. From an ethical perspective, possibilities develop for fair dialogue and genuine care. In addition, as individual identity sets in, it becomes necessary for people to face up to their conflicts of interests.

The negative options of relatedness may take the form of an existential anxiety about becoming a person or about being *per se*. Individuation, the self's very becoming, is invariably coupled with feelings of loss. A partner's development and growth *ipso facto* induce fears of abandonment and implicit betrayal. Fears and anxieties about this loss may lead to phenomena that transactionally can be characterized as enmeshment. Or, on a somewhat deeper level, these phenomena may be viewed as an "undifferentiated ego mass" (Bowen, 1965) or as "pseudomutuality" (Wynne, 1958). As a result of the differentiation of a significant partner, people may be motivated to "collusively postponed mourning" (Boszormenyi-Nagy, 1965b).

Fears and anxieties over the loss and betrayal that are implicit in a partner's attempts to individuate are also manifested in indirect, invisible loyalties, a major source of pathogenesis in relationships (Boszormenyi-Nagy & Spark, 1973). Indirect, invisible loyalties to one relationship commonly show in the substitutive victimization of another relationship. Behaviorally, they also give rise to a whole range of self-destructive patterns like addiction and psychosomatic illness (Cotroneo & Krasner, 1977).

Psychotherapeutic literature considers individuation and autonomous maturation almost entirely from the vantage point of the self's (*centripetal*) interests. Here it is assumed that a client's mature insight and mastery of neurotic defensiveness, for example, will increase the efficacy and expediency by which she can satisfy her own needs. But contextual therapy adds a *centrifugal*, other-directed concern to its consideration of individuation. In our view, an equal if opposite criterion of genuine autonomy lies in a person's capacity to consider the consequences of a relationship from the partner's vantage point as well as from one's own. A centrifugal attitude is particularly appropriate if one's partner is vulnerable by reason of health, age, or social status, among other factors. Our psychological need to be generous may help us choose the option of self-validation by way of earning entitlement.

Self-Validation

We approach the process of self validation from both a psychological and existential-ethical perspective. In other words, by extending care to one's partner, people not only satisfy an existing psychic need but enhance their own worth and merit. Self-validation thus affects the balance of relational claims and obligations too. It enhances the justifiability of the self's claim toward the world.

Erik Erikson, Abraham Maslow and D. H. Winnicott stand among those conceptualizers whose psychological concerns were also oriented to consequences to others. Erikson included "generativity" among the criteria of psychosocial maturity in adults. Maslow included a concern for others among his criteria for the mature, self-actualizing personality (1954).

Although it is a requirement of individual maturation and growth, responsible parenting is the most obvious illustration of centrifugal, other-directed concern. Yet in our experience, the innate tendency to care about other people is characteristic of very young children rather than limited to parents or parenting figures. Family therapy demonstrates how caring and appropriately considerate three- or four-year-old children can be towards squabbling and mistrustful parents. Needy parents who fail to acknowledge their children's consideration of them inevitably aggravate the condition of parentification that usually exists in their children in any case. For their part, therapists require experience and skill to be able to identify and observe the subtle manifestations of a child's "adultlike" caring. Even more experience and skill is required of the therapist who means to help parents see what they receive from their children and learn how to acknowledge what is being offered.

The adult capacity to "love" small children has to include an automatic, blanket acknowledgment of the child's caring characteristics. Yet such caring is often locked up in a youngster's unexpressed attitudes, and consequently can be next to impossible to recognize. Under the circumstances, a global crediting of a youngster's intrinsic caring about the good of the family is frequently a parent's best option for both affirming his or her own personal worth and entitlement, and *encouraging the child's interest in earning entitlement*, i.e., in mature relating.

A child whose attitudes and contributions to his parents' well-being are recognized and acknowledged will learn to choose to earn constructive entitlement. He will grasp the rewarding characteristics of caring. Conversely, children whose naturally caring propensities are routinely manipulated and exploited suffer from the most destructive features of chronic parentification. An adult can misuse a child's care for him or her rather than be willing to pay the costs of contributing to the child's autonomous individuation.

The human psychological potential includes a need for caring about others. This fact facilitates a person's choice to opt for self-validation through offering care. On the other hand, without considering the terms of the other's needs and rights, people lack a reliable criterion for their just due in the context of their relational ledgers. A materially generous father may feel he has given his child his due when he compares his own toyless childhood with the flow of toys he offers. Yet the child may be yearning for the father's time, not toys.

A person's desire to use a relationship for self-validation is not reliable *per se*. Genuine care about the due needs and rights of others does contribute to one's own worth and entitlement. But an inauthentic use of a partner to enhance a person's own sense of worth is also possible. For example, I may offer my partner what *I* think he needs rather than what he thinks he needs. Or in the midst of using my partner's availability to me, I may not only fail to give her credit but also unfairly blame or scapegoat her. Dialogue invariably deteriorates when relating partners are manipulated into the role of culprit.

Recurrent tendencies to scapegoat "bad" family members constitute an exploitative and destructive use of relationships. At an ethical level, inauthentic attempts at self-justification actually diminish the self's ethical worth. In the first instance, the scapegoated member cannot help but oblige the scapegoaters through his sheer, if reluctant, availability during the time he is being attacked. In the process of scapegoating, family members obtain a favorable self-definition vis-à-vis the target of their attack. The scapegoat's contribution to their well-being is hardly credited, however. He is abandoned and depreciated.

Futhermore, blaming may protect the blamer from facing the nuances of his own accountability. Sometimes it is simply easier to project our own imperfections onto somebody, *anybody*, else. Regardless of the age of its target, scapegoating always suggests implicit parentification. The scapegoat is being unfairly forced to take responsibility for someone else's burdens or sins. For example, it is common for parents beleaguered by an untrustworthy world to place unrealistic expectations of perfect trustability on their child. Needless to say, no child can meet such idealized expectations, try as he may. In point of fact, no human being can fulfill another person's longings for him to neutralize the untrustability that characterizes the world. Over-idealization of a child is thus usually the precursor of his being targeted for blame.

The *predicament of split loyalty typically* represents an extreme in parental expectations of superhuman perfection. Covertly or insidiously, each parent expects his or her child to know how to be trustworthy *despite the fact* that parental mistrust is dominating the youngster's adult world. Parentified to the extreme the child, caught between two parents' conflicting demands, is rarely credited for his positive contributions to the family. He is more likely to be reproached for his failings. He may even be blamed as the cause of his parents' problems. More subtly still, he may suffer the brunt of his parents' wish for him to find ways to reconcile them. The tragic upshot of destructive parentification has as much to do with parental loss as with filial loss: Parents typically forfeit their options for self-validation through earned entitlement, and lose ground in the quest for their own autonomy. When they abandon their child to their own unrealistic longings, parents yield a chance to earn entitlement through offering due care to that child's priorities, interests and needs. On the other hand, the child, who has to "be the object" (Boszormenyi-Nagy, 1965a, 1967) loses an important option for active self-delineation. Still, parents can also grow:

> A young woman of 22 decided to retrieve her 2 year old daughter from a couple who were ready to adopt her. They had already cared for the baby for two years. Previously a careless, self-serving mother addicted to drugs, alcohol, and promiscuity, Joyce was now determined to seek ways to become a better mother to her child. She did alter many of her habits and devoted considerably more time and effort to raising Jane than ever before.

Parenthood is an exemplary opportunity for adults to validate their worth via relating. Energized by the child's obvious needs for nurturance, early parenting is the most typical life situation for a mature self-polarization of a young adult. The resultant definition of the self occurs via cognitive and behavioral differentiation between caretaker and helpless child. It also occurs through a person's capacity to assume mature responsibility.

> A simple therapeutic intervention may highlight the importance of evolving self-polarization. At the beginning of the first session to which Joyce and her mother came, the therapist asked: "Should I call you mother (to include her child who is absent) or Joyce, in which case I would address your mother as mother?" Joyce: "In my family I am the kid. No one calls me mother. I am used to that. But as I think about it, I would like you to call me mother. I would like to learn how to be a good mother." Through insisting that this young woman decide how she prefers to be addressed, the therapist elicits active, responsible self-definition and self-validation. This is in clear contrast to the therapeutic relabeling or positive connoting in accordance with the therapist's own choice of an identity for Joyce.

The same therapeutic objective was true for the entire course of this young woman's therapy. The formation of discrete, mature identity is a requirement of mature trustable relating as well.

The availability of the options of self-delineation and self-validation are important aspects of relational trustability. They are therefore touchstones for the quality of close relationships. Interference with either option lowers the quality of the dialogue of close relating. Self-delineation and self-validation also represent important therapeutic leverages and resources.

The practical implications of the notion of self-validation undergird the therapeutic theory of the contextual approach, i.e., the motivating force of the process of earning entitlement. In the first instance, there is obvious relief for the parent who has duly discharged his child-rearing accountability. From here the motivating force of the process ranges to the seemingly abstract act of exonerating one's deceased parent. On the other hand, why not let the offspring forget about his dead father and contribute his effort to some tangible, expedient undertaking?

Our answer is linked to the contextual emphasis on the integrity of close relationships. An act of integrity within the parent-child dialogue is not only desirable for its benefit to the recipient. Through his inner investment in self-validation the doer's act primarily benefits himself. The process of polarized selves starts out with mutual self-delineation and is completed through the dialectic of mutual self-gain. One of the most important contextual therapeutic leverages lies in the skillful utilization of these relational resources.

The process of self-gain that occurs through relational self-validation highlights the significance of the therapeutic value of caring for unresolved, unrequited close relationships. People are inevitably psychologically invested in the trustable integrity of formative and generative relationships. Here the test of integrity is more concrete and definable than in superficial relating. Close relationships also become the laboratory for the formation of the offspring's personality. The consequences of the parents' relational integrity or their lack of integrity profoundly affect posterity's chances for trust and for earning self-worth. A major clue here lies in working on unfinished family "business" that is steeped in significant resources. It is one of the foundations of a person's freedom to engage in future relationships.

LIABILITIES IN RELATIONSHIP: THEIR SYMMETRY VERSUS ASYMMETRY

Symmetrical and asymmetrical liabilities in relationship represent an inherent, factually based contextual limit to simple equality between partners. The more intrinsically asymmetrical a relationship, the more the balance of requirements is skewed and slanted. The same is true about the force of consequences of equitable give-and-take between partners. The tendency to overlook covert asymmetries in presumably symmetrical relationship is the frequent cause of relational confusion and despair.

The second aspect in the dialogic process of individuation has to do with the justifiability of what people owe each other. Put another way, it addresses the issue of one person's *inherent limits in accepting liability for another person's justifiable expectations.*

Most social interaction theories talk about exchanges between presumed equals who are entitled to equal expectations. Expectations can be viewed as gain as they pertain to grown-up, fully competent members of any human group. Any assumption of an inborn asymmetry between people would contradict the principle of equality proudly claimed by the American Constitution and French Revolution. The modern mind would ostensibly abhor the open legalization of slavery or of inborn feudal subservience. The search for an equitable balance between man's and woman's rights is pursued vigorously on today's political and social stage. Nevertheless, the question becomes vastly complex for many reasons, including the asymmetry in the personal contribution of women to the reproductive process.

Symmetrical relationships are intrinsically reciprocal. People of equal strength and station who give of themselves are entitled to a return of approximately equal measure. To keep their relationship trustworthy or fair, peers who receive from each other are expected to give back in approximately equal measure. By contrast, in the ethical dimension asymmetrical relationships are intrinsically limited in their reciprocity. Parents cannot expect to receive an approximately equal measure of return for what they give to their young children. In other words, intergenerational giving is not only of a different order of magnitude, it is also of a different quality. For example, it is obvious that parents have the option of giving their children life. Children do not have that option with their parents.

In sum, the symmetry or asymmetry in giving and receiving is essentially factual, preattitudinal and pretransactional. The sequence of the generations itself dictates and justifies the degree of direction of equity. If intrinsic asymmetry in a context is disregarded, the trustworthiness of the relationship is bound to suffer.

Compensatory Resources

The concepts of earned entitlement through the offer of due care and of transgenerational mandates and legacies can help illuminate compensatory resources in asymmetrical relationships. We have already made ample references to *earned entitlement*. Here we have an internal reward that, in essence, compensates a parent for doing her best by her child even when no visible acknowledgment or reciprocal care can be expected in return. Obviously some reciprocity is due from child to parent but that can only be partial. On the other hand, parental caretaking by itself is likely to bring emotional satisfaction to the parent. The option to earn entitlement mitigates against the asymmetrical nature of intergenerational balances of expectations of give-and-take.

As an illustration, for their own future entitlement children become obliged to fulfill some transgenerational mandates or legacy expectations.

Among the most poignant of these is the obligation to care about aging and ailing parents, or to care about the captive vulnerability of their own young and dependent offspring, including posterity as a whole. Expectations to repay one's parents are thus balanced and matched by delayed and indirect expectations to fulfill transgenerational mandates and legacies.

Periodic Assessment

It is not compulsive, instantaneous balancing but a reasonable responsibility for periodic assessments of fair repayment that is the *sine qua non* of trustworthy peer relationships. If one relating partner constantly fails to care or make that care manifest through new balances of give-and-take, a relationship is bound to lose its trustworthiness over time. In symmetrical, e.g., peer relationships, at a given point along the way, the exploited or uncared for partner may argue for his just due—and thereby confirm his continuing interest in sustaining the viability of the relationship. His protests may be met by his partner with surprise, denial, anger, gratitude, indignation, or relief. Whatever the response to it, an effort to restore fairness will have been made. New resources for the relationship may be discovered. New attitudes may emerge and new behaviors may result. On the other hand, efforts to restore just balances may fail; the relationship may become "pathogenic" for at least one partner in its progressive disintegration and subsequently it may decay.

The function of multilateral fairness is easily grasped in peer-to-peer relationships. A relative balance of give-and-take establishes a fair distribution of the burdens and benefits of each relating person. Given a symmetry of commitments, neither partner is likely to be captively victimized by the other except by an act of choice or ignorance. Each of them usually retains the option of terminating the relationship or of reworking its cost. On the other hand, when partners are "unmatched," it is always more difficult to assess the nature of equity.

Unmatched Partners

"What is just between partners?" is a fundamental question for contextual therapists (Boszormenyi-Nagy & Spark, 1973, Chap. 4). How are conflicting claims, interests and justifications to be balanced between two people when one of them cannot give back in equitable proportion to what he or she receives? *Justitia*, the allegorical figure of Roman justice, is typically pictured with a scale composed of equal and equidistant trays. This measure of balanced equity, however, cannot be made to apply to the very young or the very old. Still, it remains in everybody's benefit and best interests to develop the relational resources that they hold in common. It is exactly due consideration in asymmetrical relations that is most likely to yield the optimum degree of merited entitlement. Even when parents are palpably destructive, children benefit from efforts to exonerate them. Reaching for a broader basis of fair concern is always a more healing option than cutting off a parent or permanently viewing him or her as a hopeless "monster."

Obviously, the more trustworthy the parental investment in his or her offspring's context, the easier it is for the child to exonerate her parent. The more capable the parent is of fairness, the more likely his or her child is to be fair. The more accepting the parent is of the fact that children cannot repay parental investments in kind, the more likely are adult children to offer a partial return.

Despite the truth of these generalities, it is important to note that in all concrete situations, care must be taken to inquire into the specific criteria of parental giving. When does it turn into possessiveness and over-protectiveness? Or in cases in which parents are disinclined to give, as in the termination of an unwanted pregnancy, is theirs an act of care and giving or is it to be read as purely selfish and inconsiderate? Beyond judging the ethics of the parent's decision, however, the dependent child's prospective rights and benefits are the weightiest criteria of fair decision.

As in peer relationships, an equitable distribution of burdens and benefits between parents and children depends on two fundamental factors: (1) balances *between* the self-serving interests of the partners, and (2) the balance between selfishness and due consideration of the other *within* each relating individual. Chances to earn entitlement through offers of care tend to bridge the antithesis between self-service and self-validation through due consideration, especially when an adult is in relation to a helpless little child. The adult willingness to acknowledge a youngster's trust-seeking attitude can be manifested in many forms, from the simple act of caring for a hungry, wet and irritable baby to the complex and demanding effort to help a child relate to a parent who is also one's deeply resented ex-spouse. In neither case is the adult compensated by an equitable or direct return except through the reward of merited entitlement. Moreover, the freedom that evolves from duly earned entitlements is not only rewarding, but also self-sustaining. Once people grasp its benefit to their self-interest, they tend to enter an ascending "spiral" of repeatedly earned entitlement.

Intergenerational Relationships

In contrast to peer relationships, intergenerational relationships are fundamentally *asymmetrical*. There is no justification for reducing the parent-child relationship to one of simple friendship, lovers or pals. On the other hand, parent-child relationships do have symmetrical options too: Parents can behave in ways that their children like and enjoy. Children may develop interests, like theater, reading or sports, in which their parents may participate. Parents and children may work together or account for their time or absences in a definitively symmetrical way. Moreover, children can and do evaluate their parent's behavior—just as they would do with other people. Activities in common can create an illusion of peer camaraderie.

However, whether they reflect likes or dislikes, intense involvement or apparent indifference, the prospects of friendly relationship between child and parent are not to be confused with genuine symmetry. The adult who disregards this asymmetry of relational liability is crossing into the territory of parentification. In the final analysis, children cannot be equal sources of existential giving to their parents as their parents must often be to them. Asymmetry lies in the unevenness of the justifiability of the parties' respective expectations of each other. In asymmetrical relationships, it is as if the arms of the scale of justice have become unequal.

A person's motives for parenting incorporate but transcend the issues of just due. An adult's freedom to give to her child is as much influenced by the fact that she has chosen the option of being a parent as it is by how the child responds and behaves. After all, parents usually benefit from the emotional satisfactions derived from the parenting task.

The one-sided devotion of parenting is also governed by the prospect of consequences. It is a paradoxical fact that a parent's concern for the consequences of his behavior on his child's well-being leads to enhanced degrees of his own personal freedom. In matters of earned entitlement, however, it must be noted that constructive behavior and concern for consequences are not to be confused with moralistic judgments about being good or bad. For example, whether parents stay in a marriage to avoid being cast into the role of a "bad guy" in the eyes of their children is a different and secondary issue from the factual outcome of what happens to dependent young children as a consequence of their parents' marriage, emotional estrangement or divorce. Parent-child relationships frequently founder on the failure of an adequate consideration of asymmetry.

For example, after a year's indecisiveness over whether or not to divorce, a woman abruptly decided to end her marriage shortly before Christmas. Without preparation or concern for consequences —though they had been reviewed with her at her request by her therapist—she demanded that her husband leave the house and announced to the children that they could not spend any part of the holiday with their father. Father became violent and had to be calmed by the police; the 12-year-old son turned belligerent as he defended his father's right to stay; and the 14-year-old daughter withdrew and became even more tearful than she had already been over the past year. Mother not only insisted that her actions were in the best interests of the children but filed for "protection from abuse." The intent of such legal action is to protect a family from physical or decisive, emotional harm by one of its members. In effect, it forces the offending person or mate out of the house well before a divorce procedure can produce a settlement negotiated by law.

In this situation, clinical goals were eclipsed by legal expediency. Despite mother's avowal that her husband is a good father and that she would in no way ever act to deprive the children of him, once she decided to divorce him, she wanted to be done with him—quick! Her lawyer encouraged Ms. Mack "to help us incriminate him." The therapist was subpoenaed to testify to Mr. Mack's abusive tendencies but was quickly discounted as a helpful witness because, for her, all family members had a right to the therapist's pledge of privileged, multidirectional partiality.

Twelve months earlier it was Mr. Mack who sought therapy and Mrs. Mack who refused to come. Mrs. Mack's behavior seemed to be a collusive factor in provoking Mr. Mack's frustration in and out of the therapy room in the past six months. And if Mr. Mack had taken to traveling with his son's out-of-state junior high football games in an effort to secure his son's allegiance, Mrs. Mack had taken to sleeping in her daughter's bed rather than moving to a couch in another room. Thus, the children were being programmed into a predicament of split loyalties as a consequence of both parents' behavior. In addition, mother and her lawyers forced the children into a position of having to excuse their father for events that may in part have been falsely or unjustly imposed on him by a one-sided assignment of blame and abuse.

Given their captive position with their parents with its attendant dependence and relative helplessness, children are inherently entitled to asymmetrical consideration. They need to be able to count on a world in which their interests are given a built-in slant. Instead, as in this case, they are often inherently parentified by their parents' dependence on them.

No therapist can be spared from experiences in which a client reacts abruptly, irrationally and destructively to his or her child. It is hard to see such a parent turn insensitive to a youngster's vital interests and act in ways that may cause the parent considerable guilt reactions at a later point in time. The therapist's interest has to turn in the direction of the parent's apparent destructive entitlement. Even if the current irrational behavior cannot be changed, the therapist may be able to find ways in which to credit the parent's own childhood victimization and help the parent earn constructive entitlement via responsible caring.

Here considerations of Dimensions II and III naturally have to be incorporated. Whatever insight can be gained into the parent's behavior can help build more mature, responsible behavior. The therapist should be aware of the pitfalls of positive and negative transference reactions. She should notice when she is cast into the role of a boundless provider or untrustworthy scoundrel. From a transactional vantage point, it is important to review all the steps that the parent is taking regarding their consequences on others, especially the children. Finally, the therapist needs to maintain her attitude of multidirected partiality even if it costs her her popularity with the impulsively destructive parent. The therapist's commitment to fair multilaterality will reap eventual therapeutic benefits for the children.

The ontological hierarchy of parent-child relationships is fundamentally irreversible and can never be fully offset by compensatory behavior. The one-sided caring that ensues from this reality is not only based on power and the psychology of dependence. Equity accounting in asymmetrical relationships begins with the fact that an infant's captive position and helplessness endow him with intrinsic credit. Furthermore, his innate pliability makes the young child a vulnerable target for lasting developmental consequences.

On the other hand, years of one-sided nurturing and devotion earn his parents' credit. As parents age, it is their children who are faced with obligations for one-sided consideration. Like the very young child, the aging parents may be limited in their capacity to return their adult child's concern. Here is another instance in which a person's relative helplessness entitles him to a kind of giving that may bring little or no immediate gratification in return. The issue is made even more complex by the conflicts of interests carried by the adult child who wants to offer his sick or aging parent care: "My husband and I have spent our lifetimes doing for our children, our families, our church," said a woman who is well into her fifties. "Now we want to live a little, travel and have some fun. But my parents are in their eighties and I'm their only child. What do I owe me? What do I owe them?"

The questions that surface are based on conflicting justifications: For example, how do adult children differentiate between their parents' shifting but legitimate needs on the one hand, and their parents' unfair, long-term dependency and ingrained possessiveness on the other? How much of an extra allowance is owed to parents who have made heavy investments—or even just a lifegiving investment—in their children's existence and well-being? What kinds of sacrifices should an offspring and his or her mate and children have to endure in making allowances for a sick or aging parent's genuine needs? To what degree must a person's autonomous strivings be put away to address one-sided parental claims? In what measure do unfaced injuries from parent to child entitle an adult offspring to retributive behavior?

Conversely, in what measure do unaddressed injuries from child to parent predispose an adult child to guilt-laden efforts to gratify his parents' every wish or need? Moreover, what are people to do with a lifetime full of anger, resentment and guilt as one person's existential neediness makes inordinate demands on another person? In everyday practice, therapists are constantly faced with interpersonal conflicts whose understructure relies on complex issues of asymmetry.

Parentification

Every subjectively determined use, e.g., projective identification, infantilization, and possessive holding on implicitly means *parentification* of the partner even if it is not based on expecting the parentified one to act like a supernormal, executive-like performer. The very fact of the doer's possessive dependence creates the asymmetry, placing the target into a captive role. The more the partner is made to be helplessly captive, the more he becomes a predictable respondent who will chastise his captors like an angry parent.

This is one of the reasons why some of the ''can't live with—can't live without'' relationships prevail over a long period of time. This applies to destructively dependent marriages and also to the intrinsically parentified basis of a parent's relationship with a psychotic offspring.

In designing therapy, it is important to realize that the asymmetry of dependent possession is a deeper dynamic than the obvious, symmetrical reciprocity of angry, retaliatory feedback cycles. Parentification is the converse of fair acknowledgment of the partner's contributions. At its most destructive extreme, parentification deprives the child of his or her natural right to be a child. This is likely to occur if parentification is sustained and if it is reinforced by inappropriate blame of the child. Destructive parentification makes its victim destructively entitled.

INCLUSIVE FAIR MULTILATERALITY

This aspect of relationship, the extent of actualized, responsibly caring reciprocity indicates the *degree of trustworthiness* in the relational context. The term ''inclusive'' pertains to consideration of the justifications and liabilities of *all sides* in an ongoing, monitoring fashion. In fact, inclusiveness as a requirement postulates that no dyadic ledger can be involved in fair give-and-take without consideration given to all those who might be affected through consequences. Moreover, relatedness through consequences is just as valid a tie as relatedness through interactional feedback. In summary, the fairness of any ledger of give-and-take has to encompass the consideration of *connectedness through consequences* and *inclusion of all those who are to be affected*.

Contextual therapy moves from role and transaction to ledgers of merits, obligations and credits. Ledgers of justifiability are connected among themselves. For example, parents' fairness to each other builds marital trustability; but its main consequences show through their children's improved options for living. Contextually, marital relationships may often be in the focus of therapy, but never without regard for the inclusion of the prospects of the parent-child ledgers, or without responsible caring about consequences for posterity. Here lies the great clinical significance of the knowledge of this aspect of relationship.

Multilaterality and Family Therapy

To a significant extent the aspect of inclusive, fair multilaterality underlies the very notion of family therapy . The therapist's insistence on including all family members in her work, even those who are seemingly irrelevant or cut off, stems from the conviction that people benefit from responsibly facing their relationships. The elimination of avoidance and cutoffs is by itself therapeutic. The main methodological principle of contextual therapy, multidirected partiality, is explicitly built on the assumption of the mutual healing power of responsibility, assumed through facing every member's balances and ledgers of give-and-take and their consequences.

The need for partners to polarize is the basis of each individual's need to validate his or her relational worth. Thus the ledger of give-and-take between persons is one measure of their degree of earned entitlement or due obligation. As contextual therapy includes "centrifugal" consequences for others in its considerations, give-and-take obtains an added meaning. The criteria of justifiability of any act are not merely determined by the current context of relating but also by those to be unilaterally affected through consequences, i.e., posterity. The individual's ability to earn relational merit, or his chances to increase his self-validation, are codetermined by the degree to which consequences for posterity are justifiable. Rather than mere learning through the knowledge of preceding generations, it is this "ethical" consideration that constitutes the rationale for *any* intergenerational extension of family therapy.

The Self and the Other

In contextual work, close relationships are viewed from centripetal and centrifugal vantage points. Contextual therapy incorporates the more standard approaches to relationship that have characterized the literature of individual psychology and of classical family therapy. In the first instance, relationship is defined from the perspective of the self as the referent, with the partner serving as a potential source of gratification to the self's needs. In the second instance, relationship is defined from the perspective of the other as the referent, with the self or groups of selves seen as serving the purposes of the other or others.

Genuine dialogue, however, goes beyond these two obvious dynamics to the realm of "the between." Here two people are constantly involved in a reciprocity of self-aimed (centripetal) exchanges which we characterize as mutually self-delineating and self-validating. The context of self-validation, rooted in the quest for justice in the human order, addresses the relative legitimacy of each partner's claims *for himself but in consonance* with the terms of the other. Relational claims are predicated on each person's right to both distance and intimacy, i.e., to separate identities and assertions as well as to reciprocal accountability. The genuine human dialogue can be called the dialogue of claims for equitable justifiability.

Conflicting justifications pervade ordinary, day-to-day marital struggles and parent-child controversies.

A case in point is the man caught between the self-serving (centripetal) claims of his second wife, his daughter of a previous marriage, and his own-self-justifying needs and claims.

"I deserve some peace," he reasons. "I've sent my kid to the best psychologists from the time that her mother died. How long am I supposed to atone for my first wife's death? Why can't my 15-year-old step out of the past after all this time and worry about me for a change?" From the youngster's side, father's second wife is "just tired of this ongoing mess." 'He has two more children now," she complains, "but all he ever does is worry about his daughter. When I married him I didn't count on this. That kid is involved in emotional blackmail; she'll never have enough!"

His daughter, now living with her mother's only sister, doesn't understand why everyone is upset: "It's true that I hate his wife; she seems to be the only one who counts. And I'm not so keen on my stepbrother either. He not only has my own brother's name— he was killed with my mother—but he has also taken my place with my father. I guess that I'm really jealous of him. I took care of him a lot when he was born but I didn't get any credit for that either. My father only calls me when he has to. It seems more like duty than like love. We never talk about anything important when he calls anyway, or even twice a year when I visit. It's always awkward there anyhow. He let his wife throw me out of his house. He only mentioned the accident when a therapist said it was good for me. He knows the name of the woman who was in the car when my mother was killed but he's never shared it with me. I've never told him that

I want to meet her because I'm afraid he'll say "no." Besides, I might hurt him if I ask. I don't want to upset him but I'd like to meet her one day and find out what really happened. Her friend was the last one to see my mother alive. Why can't he understand that I really have to know?"

A parent may exploit a child in the process of unilaterally validating his own side. He is clearly entitled to ask her to see him as he delineates himself. Yet he is also obliged to consider her self-validating claims. On the other hand, father may resort to prejudicial labeling and thus attempt to inauthentically justify his stand. Still, his decision to exploit his daughter for the purpose of his own self-validation has long-term consequences that threaten to confine her to living in an untrustworthy world. Moreover, he cannot earn real entitlement at the expense of hurting his child's chances for life.

In a similar vein, progeny are often held accountable for their parents' faults. Obviously a husband may rightfully object to certain of his partner's behaviors but he is not justified in loading his objections with lifelong incriminations against "people who are unfair." Substitutive blaming is always a scapegoating act. At best it can amount to an invisible loyalty acted out to protect one's parents.

Conflicts of Interest

The self-delineating and self-validating aspects of a dialogue between people of significance to each other are obviously weighted in asymmetrical relationships. Conflicting justifications between adult children and their sick or aging parents are akin to the conflicts of interests between self-service and reciprocal accountability that exist in other asymmetrical relationships. For example, consider the poignancy of a situation in which a person is struggling to decide whether or not to try to salvage a crumbling marriage solely because of his or her child's need for an "intact" family. The parent's need for self-delineation may conflict with his chance for fair self-validation. An adult's right to autonomy *and* his or her obligation to offer children the best kind of care constitute a fundamental collision between centripetal and centrifugal interests and terms.

Implicit in this collision are basic questions of freedom and responsibility: To what degree must children be protected, and from what? To what degree are people obliged to sacrifice their justifiable strivings for personal satisfactions to the demands of parental (centrifugal) accountable? At what point is a parent entitled to meet his own terms instead of his children's terms? At what point does parental accountability translate into deprivation for the adult involved? At what point does parental deprivation, i.e., lack of consideration for the parenting adult, translate

into filial deprivation? When does parental accountability become an evasive and obsessive refusal to look at the option of living according to
autonomous terms? For that matter, to what degree is the struggling or
disintegrating marriage under consideration here a victim of an overinvestment in parenting that has allowed no energy or room for marital claims?

The Young Child's Entitlement

Contextual work obviously emphasizes the ethical priority of the young
child's inherent entitlement. This emphasis, however, is not meant to
deny the simultaneous legitimacy of the beneficial claims of adult peers.
It does mean to address the child's reality and to challenge views of adult
autonomy and marriage that would render children inconsequential. Lederer & Jackson (1968), for example, observed that the social pressure on
people to regard marriage as sacred almost functions as an actual third
relationship (p. 166). Vaguely defined, this third party may be embodied
by "society-at-large" or by specific family demands. "Once the legal
ceremony of marriage has taken place," they wrote, "the question may
arise at any point as to whether the spouses are together because they *must*
be." Yet the consequences of the marriage on the couple's offspring go
almost totally unaddressed here. The contextual therapist raises the question: Isn't the prospective offspring the real third party? In point of fact,
many approaches to marriage and marital therapy proceed as if children
and their entitlements are insignificant elements in the institution of marriage.

As we have already indicated, issues of trustworthiness and justice in
relationships depend on periodic assessments and reassessments of each
person's indebtedness and entitlements vis-à-vis his relating partner. This
process may be straightforward or circuitous, but it always has to do with
the balances between two people. On the other hand, asymmetrical relationships are always triadic; acting in the interests of the weaker partner
tends to involve the expectations of one's legacies. The legacy-based
expectation of relational fairness is analogous to the claims of a demanding third party.

Distributive Justice

Distributive justice is a principle of relational reality that commands a
higher degree of therapeutic perceptiveness than retributive justice. One
family member may carry an unequal burden out of his or her destiny
rather than from another member's acts. The fact of a brain-damaged child
places inevitable burdens on family members. They are all victimized by
circumstances for which no one can be blamed. Yet the fairness of the
distribution of bearing the burden *is* their responsibility.

The same obligation exists over who is to take care of a sick parent. Unevenness in the family members' willingness to share responsibility leads to the secondary issue of retributive justice that arises among them. Callous indifference by all of them will lead to indirect but actual exploitation of one member. If a person's capacity to offer care is not equitably shared, the implications of distributive injustice can earn high degrees of entitlement for the responsible member. This entitlement is not diminished by efforts to involve other members in an appropriate sharing of the burden.

Reciprocal Accountability

Lack of courage and discipline may make people reluctant to define their own terms for reciprocal accountability, much less inquire into the terms of others. The threat of loss and fear of abandonment between the generations *per se* are intense and are exacerbated by expectations of poor or negative response. Consequently, the process of defining reciprocal accountability in asymmetrical relations is always associated with at least two major groups of questions:

1) To what degree does return on our investments in a person have to originate from him or her? Can repayment come from a source other than the direct recipient of our care? To what extent does repayment occur from satisfying the terms of one's legacies? What if circumstances deprive people of the option to repay? What if we make an effort to return someone's care, and it is rejected or refused?
2) If we can offer a return of "care received" to people other than the ones who contributed to our well-being, what criteria can be used to measure the adequacy of the repayment? Who then are the invisible creditors, and how does the "bookkeeping" work?

Obviously, the give-and-take between the generations is not confined to parent-child relationships. People can validate themselves and earn entitlement through offering care in asymmetrical relationships, e.g., to incapacitated people, whether or not they are biologically related. A person who has offered care in responsibly continuing relationships can accept the gratification and pleasure to which he is entitled from people other than his own parent or child.

Moreover, posterity is always the hidden creditor of responsible continuity of care. Our own legacies, i.e., viable give-and-take, or contributions and injuries that have been our lot and have helped us sustain the relationships between us and the generations that went before, make up the best measure or guideline for discerning what we owe to future generations and what we want to take for ourselves. Whether we like them or would have chosen them or not, it is from the bedrock of our inherited legacies—and a fair understanding of them—that we translate our lives into mandates for posterity.

Expression of Self-Assertion

Inauthentic claims to self-validation tend to put one's partner on the defensive. Essentially non-dialogic, these claims may take unilaterally self-justifying forms: "Look how much I've suffered; I deserve better;" or "It's my business if I want to drink myself to death." Here is an implicit demand that the "world", i.e., any future partner, compensate its speaker for his misery, a stance that contains a retributive bent. At the other end of the spectrum stands the person whose unilateral giving posture leaves no room for self-delineation. Here is the "martyr" who compulsively gives of himself and technically asks nothing in return. Chronically refusing to receive anyone's contributions to his life or offers of care, he builds up a backlog of disappointments rooted in the fact that people rarely seem invested in meeting his unspoken claims. Inauthentic efforts at self-delineating manifest themselves through unyielding, unilateral efforts at attention-getting through overdependency, contrariness, possessiveness, exploitation, intimidation, power manipulation, and threats of destructive maneuvering, among other behaviors.

Other expressions of self-assertion include claimed attempts at individuation that are cast in terms of "absolute independence," running away, or total cutoffs. An inauthentic search for self-assertion and self-validation can also provide the basis for suicide, depression and psychosomatic illnesses. Under these circumstances, the self and the partner are punished at one and the same time. The destructive outcomes of a person's behavior are not only harmful to himself but often cast loved ones into helpless positions.

The Accounts of Young Children

The self-delineating justifications that adults "borrow" from the accounts of their young children are extremely insidious and exploitative in impact. At the very point of its conception or at the moment of its adoption, a child may be assigned the destructively idealized role of a guardian of the world's trustworthiness. Subsequently, the ambivalent and vindictive parents can easily discolor their youngster's identity by tarring him with the alleged culpabilities of previous generations.

People who delegate their children with the task of providing unfailing and thus unfulfillable trustworthiness set them up as eventual scapegoats. Such children become living symbols for their parents, proof of the world's continuing lack of trustworthiness, and justification for their own entrenched stagnation. From a purely centripetal, self-delineating perspective, however, these parents have gained a position only at their children's expense.

From his side a child, delegated with the unfair task of compensating his parents for their disappointment in the world, is set up to fail. First of all, he is typically parentified beyond any reasonable call to duty. Secondly, though his parents are trading on their child's concern, the youngster can expect no acknowledgment of his investment from them. In time, the failure of trustworthiness in his own world is bound to permeate the youngster's attitudes and behavior. The young child whose inherent entitlement to parental consideration remains unmet eventually becomes destructively overentitled—paradoxically, a condition he has earned through his one-sided giving. A result of genuine exploitation, destructive overentitlement nonetheless will have grave consequences for this youngster and his future relationships, including those with his own offspring. These may take the form of child abuse, incest and parental abandonment.

Inclusive, fair multilaterality is a context of actualized trustworthiness. In many ways it is an ideal goal which can be only partly realized between relating people. Its inclusiveness refers to a consideration of fairness from the vantage point of every affected person's ledger. A context of responsibly caring continuity is a requirement for the survival of the generations. Moreover, its knowledge is a therapeutic guideline for eliciting relational resources. Some of the questions associated with inclusive and fair multilaterality are: Who else is invisibly involved? How might absent members be affected? What are the consequences for yet unborn offspring? What is the due of an absent member, and what contributions might he still make?

Overriding Fair Multilaterality

It is true that fair and inclusive multilaterality are often overridden as legitimate goals of relationship and therapy. Relationships essentially fulfill internal "object relational" needs. In this context people tend to play defensive games within themselves. They also tend to exploit the target of such projective identification, projection, displacement, scapegoating, and parentification. To be sure, the target of these attempts will rightfully feel victimized; "intrapsychically" based distortion harms the justice of the human order.

Invisible filial loyalty is another instance that can eclipse fair mutuality. It often involves an unfair and inappropriate victimization of another relationship. Invisible loyalty is likely to inflict new injustice even as it serves to protect parents from an offspring's ambivalent or negative attitudes.

In this sense it fulfills the criteria of the "revolving slate" (Boszormenyi-Nagy & Spark, 1973). Other examples of exclusivity, unfairness and unilaterality abound. A marriage can become the victim of one or both mate's overinvestment in parenting. On the other hand, a parent's search for satisfying adult relationships—with an insistence on total freedom of choice—may seriously hurt his or her children.

Overlooking the fairness of the parent-child ledger can lead to bizarre consequences, e.g., expectations of incestuous compliance on the part of a young daughter. It is not unusual for an incestuous father to consider himself loyal for keeping his frustration over his wife's sexual rejection within the family. In these cases the mother often condones the loyalty of such an arrangement covertly or overtly. Contextual therapists generally look out for the balance between the ledgers of self-serving interests among partners, and consequences for innocent others. They are interested in discovering who listens and is not heard by others. They want to know who is beneficiary of the victimization of another, but also how the victim himself is a partial beneficiary.

Ultimately, though, the search for the criteria of inclusive fair multilaterality is the job of family members. The therapist only assists with his interventions based on multidirected partiality.

THERAPEUTIC IMPLICATIONS OF THE THREE ASPECTS OF INTERPERSONAL DIALOGUE

The three aspects of the dialogue discussed above in this chapter represent important, practical therapeutic principles. They guide the therapist in his task of setting goals and expectations for each family member's therapeutic work. Beyond the goals of problem-solving and behavioral control, the applications of the three aspects of the dialogue help the therapist review the course of each client's personal aims and progress. Their understanding helps the therapist in his work as elicitor of his or her client's commitment to responsible action.

Multidirected partiality as a therapeutic method (see Chapter 16) expects each member to develop courage for genuine self-assertion. This is to be done by delineating one's position through proving one's openness toward hearing, and through considering the due claims of each partner's side. In engaging in the never ceasing conflict of the dialogue's claims and counterclaims, the therapist can help family members consider the asymmetrical elements of their respective claims. Regard for asymmetry helps clients avoid the trap of parentification and the ignorance of crucially redeeming acknowledgment. Inclusive, fair multilaterality helps people maintain a viable network of relational resources. It provides a formula for constructive coexistence in extended family and community. It helps recognize and deal with the false security of dyadic closeness at the expense of an ambivalent cutoff from one or both partner's significant relatives. In summary, knowledge of the three aspects of the dialogue helps elicit spontaneous, relational initiative on the part of clients rather than offering prescriptions for technique.

The trustbuilding resources of inclusive fair multilaterality resemble the workings of democracy in societies. Fairness, viewed as democratic, introduces the prospect of a more equitable distribution of burdens and benefits. Previously, authority was ascribed to the privileged minority and their offspring. A great many people were tied to fixed obligations and discriminatory taxation. Fixed inbalances diminished the fairness and trustworthiness of the social order. Democracy represents a claim to a politically fairer and more inclusive multilaterality. Similarly, the therapist has the task of finding options for a more equitable relational balance of burdens and advantages among family members.

In contextual therapy with family members, as in progress toward democratic changes in larger society, work toward inclusive fair multilaterality offers options for increased trustability through creative rebalancing. The therapeutic method of inclusive, multidirected partiality, as defined in Chapter 16 on method, increases every relating member's awareness of the possibility of any other person's persistent exploitation. At the same time, every member is expected to voice and represent his or her own side (of rights and credits) with regard to balances and conflicts. Rather than self-denying altruism, the goal is liberation of both self-enhancing activity and due concern for the plight of the exploited other. At the same time each member gains and gives room for fair, maturely valid self-assertion.

CHAPTER 7

Dialogue Between the Person and the Human Context

The relational bond between human beings includes all four dimensions of reality: Facts, psychology of individuals, systems of transactions, and relational ethics. Relational ethics implies the existence of ledgers and accounts of obligation and responsibility between persons. However, dealing in depth with relationships between specific partners shows that these relationships are permeated by a larger ledger. While ostensibly dealing with a relational partner, one is also in inevitable contact with irreversible consequences for others, especially for posterity and therefore for the chain of transgenerational survival.

It is Martin Buber who comes closest to this concern in his lecture to the 1948 International Congress of Mental Health (Buber, 1948, 1957). "Each man stands in an objective relationship to others; the totality of this relationship constitutes his life as one that factually participates in the being of the world . . . It is his share in the human order of being, the share for which he bears responsibility . . . Injuring a relationship means that at this place the human order of being is injured" (p. 132).

Contextual thinking stresses responsibility for the consequences of actions. The human order of being is seen in terms of transgenerational continuity. The quality of the survival of the species depends on transgenerational solidarity. Each generation benefits from and later conributes to this solidarity. The justice of the human order requires that each person contribute his share to this human order and receive his share of returns from it. Thus, an ethical ledger of rights and obligations exists between a person and the human order. The context of the human order of justice and transgenerational solidarity is a silent partner to intergenerational relationships.

From any individual's vantage point this translates into:

1) Options for and risks in exercising his rights including his creative and destructive entitlements;
2) An obligation to consider the wishes and merits of the preceding generations;
3) An obligation to preserve, enhance and transmit bequests from the past for the benefit of posterity.

Both constructive and destructive entitlement are earned as a result of relating to concrete others. However entitlement is always earned mainly vis-à-vis the justice of the human order as a whole. In other words, the criteria of what constitutes merit and the fact that it has been earned are beyond any one individual's judgment, perception or values. On the other hand, earned entitlement is the property of the individual; he has a right to it in return for taking his share of relational responsibility.

ENTITLEMENT: THE CONSEQUENCE OF EARNED MERIT

Beyond the tit-for-tat, or *quid pro quo* of relational exchanges lies the realm of the justice of the human order. The notion of earned entitlement is only partly requitable in the ledger between the interacting partners. Part of the ledger stands between the person earning entitlement and an indefinable entity that resides in both parties but also between and beyond them. This entity is the justice of the human order which, for us, encompasses transgenerational solidarity for the purpose of human survival.

Here offspring remain accountable to life or destiny as a whole for benefits received from parental and ancestral generations. It is actually the impossibility of establishing equitable, symmetrical repayment to one's ancestors that creates the basis of a generation's unrequitable giving. In addition, grown offspring earn entitlement through unrequitable giving to the next generation. As each generation gives to the next one, it is negotiating with its own destiny. In turn its members accrue personal liberation in addition to what the next generation may be able to repay directly.

Responsible Parenting

Adequate or *responsible parenting* is the chief dynamic principle in the intergenerational order of being. It is the cornerstone of survival, and the matrix out of which interhuman justice grows and flows. *The matrix of justice* between individuals amounts to a transgenerational scheme for survival, one that applies to mammals and birds as well. Higher animals care for their young as they themselves were cared for by their parents. Responsible caring and just balances of give-and-take are thus directly linked. The intrinsic problem in this reality lies in the fact that when a creature has received too little care from his parents, he is hard put to offer adequate care to his own children. Responsible parenting begets responsible parenting from generation to generation. It is difficult to become an adequate parent if one has failed to receive adequate care.

Repaying Parental Care

Adequate parenting is one premise of a transgenerational order of being. Repaying parental care is another. Since it can only be accomplished through giving to the next generation, the direction and criteria of repayment between parent and child can only be grasped through a consideration of at least three generations. Otherwise, the arc of justice is truncated, incomplete, unfulfilled. At one level, of course, the receipt of parenting is a debt that can never be repaid. A parent's insistence that her child return her care in equal measure is a tragically destructive demand. This attitude typically characterizes parents made remorselessly insensitive by injustices suffered in their own childhood. Still, proceeding under the burden of past suffering, a parent is unlikely to note the injustice of his or her own demand.

Parents deserve acknowledgement of their care and contributions. There are also times when they require their children's care and concern. At base, however, the direction of *repayment is forward* rather than backward. Parental investments are most fully repaid through an offspring's due contributions to posterity. Simply put, a person receives from his past and his parents, and gives through his children and his future. Direct, symmetrical reciprocity is only one aspect of justice in the matrix of the human order: Acts of caring between people are inevitably private and personal. They are also motivated by the factual consequences that receiving care implies the obligation to offer care.

Earning Entitlement

Adequate parenting and repaying parental care constitute two premises of the transgenerational order of being. Still another premise has to do with the self-gain or benefits linked to offering care: The person who gives care earns merit or *entitlement* as a reward. Effectively earned entitlement results in personal liberation, i.e., in the individual's security to let life unfold. In other words, caring about the justice of the human order intersects with a person's own satisfactions and functions. These include:

- A capacity for personal enjoyment;
- A creative use of life's endowments;
- A capacity to develop inborn talents and abilities;
- A capacity to enjoy success at work;
- A condition of health that is relatively free of psychosomatic symptoms and problems;
- A continuing and growing capacity to risk investing trust in new relationships;
- An ability to enjoy a partner's emotional satisfactions as well as one's own;
- A growing freedom to claim one's own side in relationships, including a person's independence from parents;
- The motivation to contribute to the welfare of future generations.

The consequence of responsible caring is autonomy in it fullest and richest sense. High levels of earned entitlement allow a person to make freer use of options than are already available to him. In effect, entitlement is a bridge between self-gain and the offer of due care. It is a new synthesis born of a dialectic between thesis and antithesis: between selfishness and altruism.

Developmental Implications of
Fair Consequences

Self-gain and justice in the human order interlock. Preceding and succeeding generations offer continuity of consequences that is partially based on psychology, partially based on transactions, and partially based on relational justice. The child of parents who are well cared for and are caring themselves tends to become a beneficiary of unmerited good fortune. Many of the resources in his or her life were shaped two generations before with no specific thought of him. Still he is in receipt of options indirectly conveyed.

Conversely, the child of disappointed and mistrustful parents tends to become the undeserving victim of bad fortune. Many of the detriments in his life were shaped by his grandparents' (and other ancestors') inability to provide his parents with adequate care. Well cared-for parents and exploitatively deprived parents are both likely to pass their fortunes on to their children. The consequences of persistent relational injustice tend to be uniquely irreversible as well as delayed in time. On the other hand, the consequences of fair consideration tend to be uniquely redeeming: A person who has struggled to improve the lot of the next generation over the lot of the previous one has not only contributed to posterity; he has also earned the freedom to claim his own just due in the world.

The newborn is inherently entitled to care. He does not have to earn merit through his actions in order to earn this entitlement. The helplessness of his condition grants him the right to be nurtured or else he would not survive. It is the violation of an individual's inherent entitlement that constitutes the heaviest component in the development of destructive entitlement, i.e., the intrinsic right to a grudge.

Justice criteria also function as a set of determining factors that can constitute preconditions for *psychological maturity*. The root cause of difficulties in adjusting to life's complex demands are frequently linked to *consequences* of a lack of an ordered capacity for planning and long-term relating. A capacity for ordered reality-based discipline is usually a result of a learning process that emerges from a formative environment that is trustworthy and caring. Good parenting requires both empathic caring and an ordered capacity for consistent relating.

Having missed a caring, early environment, children can lose their option for ever gaining basic trust. This reality in a person's life is akin to the fact that in animal development there are critical periods for imprinting which, once missed, do not return again. In humans a critical loss of early care can result in a lifelong narcissistic, autistic or sociopathic character formation, developments that can render a person incapable of making the commitments required by the demands of ongoing relating, e.g., marriage and friendship. Once again, an ounce of prevention is worth tons of therapy.

Conversely, parents who consider their infant's needs in terms of the baby's own growth and autonomy engender a capacity for trust: A child raised in a caring milieu gains the option of becoming a mature, considerate and appropriately assertive partner and parent. A successive chain of maturely parenting generations, then, is a result of consequences that establish trust: A capacity for adequate parenting is conditioned by learning and imprinting. The degree of *fairness and trustworthiness* born of caring between parent and child is a significant regulatory requirement for healthy functioning and satisfying relating. It is also an investment that is likely to have matching "funds." Born into a world that offers care and engenders trust, offspring are dynamically obliged to rebalance the benefits they received through offering more of the same to subsequent generations. Thus a transgenerational chain of credits and debits is fostered and established, one whose domino effect is a causative phenomenon in its own right.

Children should not carry the chief responsibility for repaying their parents for benefits received. It is also true, however, that offspring owe their parents generous consideration even when parents seem to have failed them.

Exoneration

How then can the distribution of credits and debits be fair? Answers to this question almost always depend on an offspring's readiness and willingness to try to exonerate his parents rather than subject them to endless condemnation. It is still another function of justice criteria that children in quest of entitlement inquire into their parents' sides. *Regardless of outcome*, attempts to *exonerate* a parent earn entitlement—that is, an offspring's efforts to be fair to a resented or even despised parent—can lead to a self-sustaining spiral of motivation that enables positive behavior in other relationships.

By contrast, one alternative may be a repetitive behavior that reflects a stagnant captivity to patterns of chronic blame. For example, "My mother beat me and I hated it. I vowed never to subject my children to that kind of behavior. Yet here I am screaming and hitting my five-year-old and it makes me feel ashamed! Why am I treating her in ways that I despised?"

Exoneration of her parent might be gained through learning that her mother desperately wanted opportunities for her child that she lacked in her own childhood. Her frustration to "make everything right" led to unreasonable demands which, in turn, led to mother's tendencies to lash out at her daughter when she failed to perform. Grabbing hold of her mother's fundamental truth can free the young parent from repeating unintended destructive behavior, and from continuing to suffer from chronic resentment and shame. However, the experienced therapist explores the timing: At what point is a client ready to work on exonerating his parents.

Exoneration of a seemingly "bad" parent should be understood as an attempt to grasp a fundamental *truth of relational reality*. A deeper level of truth is neither a paradox nor a function of insight into the sources of emotions. The family members' commitment to care about fairness for each other—especially in the midst of tendencies to blame—earns entitlement for them. As a matter of fact, a parent's spontaneous attempts to exonerate his own parent often become a turning point in the treatment of a family.

A therapist who helps family members spell out the universal truth of earning merit through giving due consideration is functioning to unburden them. A therapist helps diminish the myth of one-sided accountability by rejecting the notion that one person can ever be the sole source of a given family's ills. In the process he facilitates a reconsideration of fairness, through eliciting each member's just claims to relational merits. Defining the fair balance of their own relational reality offers people the option to earn entitlement, a healing alternative to stagnation and existential guilt or blame. Equally significant, it can result in a fairer distribution of credits and debits, and in a redistribution of burdens and benefits.

Therapeutic Implications

A family's new concern for redistributing burdens and benefits may be comprehended as "change" or as restoration of viable continuity of relationship. From a contextual perspective, self-sustaining continuity of responsibly caring relationship is more valid and specific a goal of therapeutic intervention than is the goal of mere *change*. In the first instance, the process of restoring viable relationships in the midst of injustices and mistrust requires a measure of intergenerational integrity. The ability to define one's own fundamental truths and entitlements is the beginning of such integrity. It is also tantamount to improving the quality of life itself.

Relationally, every mature human faces the necessity of validating his existence through earning merit. The term *merit*, as used here, is an ethical surplus independent of return received from the partner. In asymmetrical relationships, the process of validation is double-faceted and consists of 1) earned consideration in current relationships and 2) due consideration of past legacies and mandates for the future. Why, though, do people have to validate themselves? Isn't it every person's right simply to exist? Isn't a person justified to get what he can from life? Is the nature of all getting characterized by borrowing? Don't people have anything that intrinsically belongs to themselves? From a contextual view, the issue of justification by merit is neither preconceived nor moralistic in intent. It is a conclusion drawn from empirically gained knowledge from our own relationships as well as from families in treatment.

Merit is a self-motivating factor (Boszormenyi-Nagy & Spark, 1973, pp. 169-76) that addresses and transcends inevitably conflicting interests between a self and a significant other. Acts that earn merit benefit both the actor and the partner. Gain attained by the self predisposes the earner to try again. It represents an investment in reality that can rise above the abyss that exists between the polar opposites of self-centeredness and self-sacrifice. It is an overdue recognition of the relational dynamic through which the self is served by its due concern for the terms of another. It is one side of the dialectic in which a person's concern for her partner can produce self-serving benefits *regardless of the partner's response*. It is a chosen direction of a person who can risk drawing on the untapped reservoirs of residual trust that characterize long-term relationships and predispose that person to acquiring further trust. Self-validation by merit is the process through which entitlement is earned, that is, through which a person develops the courage

- to take the risk of investing trust in new relationships;
- to hear people on their own terms (centrifugal concern) without abandoning one's own position (centripetal concern);
- to claim one's own side and, in the process, to gain autonomy.

In summary, a capacity for self-validation entitles a person to become a mature partner in each of his or her relationships. It also enables one to maximize one's capacity for the enjoyment of creativity, sexuality and shared affection. Entitlement enhances the chances of therapeutic progress and even of psychosomatic health.

Brief examples of the life situations of a young, unmarried man may clarify the implications of self-validation. David, age 24, is the middle child of middle-class parents. His father is a pastor, his mother a secretary. From the time of his birth, his mother "didn't know what to do with a boy child who could never be pleased." As he remembers it, his father was always away: "He managed to find time to spend with other people's children but rarely with me." David has had a rocky situation for as long as he can recall. To learn to earn entitlement and to feel entitled was almost out of his reach:

"My mother has always preferred my two sisters," he says. "I don't know who my father likes best. I do know that he needs me to be sick. I can never be with him without being analyzed. Nothing I ever do seems right to him so I try to keep my distance. I've just moved back into the house until I start my new job. I pretty much stay in my room. Sometimes I watch television in the family room but if he comes in, I leave. When I try to do something for my parents, they don't seem to ever want to accept it."

Desperately loyal to his family, David nevertheless feels used. His personal life is characterized by loneliness, even isolation. "It's just safer," he says, "to stay to yourself." "Anyhow I'm always self-conscious when I spend time with the guys. Nothing I ever say sounds right." When it comes to women, David doesn't date. "I'd like to," he says, "but I was almost engaged to a girl who broke things off without any warning. I still don't understand why. I'd still like to call her and find out but I can't do that. Besides, it's hard to meet women."

David has been enraged for a long time. He retains affection for his parents but doesn't know how to please them. As far as he is concerned, they have never acknowledged him for anything he has done. So, for a long time, he stopped trying. He was able neither to earn sufficient entitlement through due contribution nor to gain the security of feeling entitled through earned merit.

David's parents, Mr. and Mrs. Ross, were confused by their son's behavior which they characterized as "rejecting" from the time he was a little child. Over the years, marital difficulties between the couple led the family to several psychologists. One of them diagnosed David as paranoid-schizophrenic, a questionable opinion which, in any case, confirmed his parents' deepest fears and left the youngster more isolated than ever.

Eventually, his father found his way to a contextual therapist. Depleted from unsuccessful efforts to make things right for his family, Mr. Ross was considering divorce. He needed more consideration than he was getting and he didn't know what to do. Angry at his wife's disengagement from him as well as from their son, Mr. Ross began to function as David's advocate—with the result of driving David's mother even further away from both of them.

Depressed and depleted in her own right, Mrs. Ross agreed to reassess her marriage. Whenever David's name came up, she fell silent and her husband became indignant. Mr. Ross decided to initiate more frequent contact with David, who began to visit the family home. Eventually, David and his sisters came to some therapy sessions, after which he asked to begin to see the therapist alone. In the joint sessions, David was able to state his grievances but was unable to tell his parents what he needed from them now. In his private sessions with the therapist, David was able to state his anger at his parents' unfairness and began to explore his own terms for relating to them. He was unable, however, to make claims on them outside of the therapy room.

Mr. and Mrs. Ross were committed to opposing expressions of their religious faith. Caught in the predicament of split loyalties, David had stopped going to church. But he recognized how his mother's fundamentalist commitment had isolated her from the rest of the family. He commented on her isolation and, over time, his mother began to identify with him. He offered to go to church with her one Sunday morning. He didn't like it much but he was thrilled by his mother's gratitude at his presence. Over the ensuing weeks, FOR THE FIRST TIME IN HIS MEMORY, his mother began to thank him for little things like picking her up at work. When he learned how overwhelmed his mother felt over the demands of the oncoming holiday, he offered to help cook the holiday meal. He also offered to help clean up. He had wanted to be helpful to his mother before but had rarely seen the point of trying. Didn't she always have some complaint? Now, though, something had changed. He couldn't put words to it but still he knew that things were different. David had begun to duly earn his mother's approval, and she had begun to earn his.

Near Christmas time, Mrs. Ross' mother died unexpectedly. Her first response to the death was, "Now maybe my father will finally have some time for me." She knew that her father loved her; he had told her so many times. But when her mother was punitive—which she was frequently—she expected her husband to take her side automatically. Mrs. Ross came to expect the same kind of blind, one-sided advocacy from Mr. Ross even where their children were concerned. Over the years, it seems, Mrs. Ross' father would come to her after she and her mother had had a fight. The first time it happened was when she was 16 years old. He had agreed with his daughter on many occasions and apologized for not saying so in front of his wife. "But you know how mother is!" he would always say. Men were a "confusing business" for Mrs. Ross. They seemed to say one thing but act out another. Unable to please her mother and chronically unacknowledged by her father, Mrs. Ross had learned to protect herself by distancing. She had gotten some mothering "back" when their little girls were born. David's difficult and demanding infancy, though, had evoked many of the doubts that she had always had of herself. Even with herself she could never justify her merit.

Gaining strength through being approved by his mother, David no longer had to rely on a power alliance with his father to protect him from his mother. Validating himself with one parent, he found the courage to begin to validate himself with the other. He wanted to relate to his father on adult terms but that wasn't as easy as it might seem. For one thing, his father was always the "good guy." For another, his father never had any time for him—though maybe that was no longer totally true. It had seemed that way when he was growing up. In any case, David wanted to be taken seriously by his father, and to have his claims addressed. He was tired of doing things solely on his father's terms.

Once David had begun to take his first halting steps towards his mother, his father had lost his role of advocate. Mr. Ross felt confused by what his son was asking. He also felt stripped and bereft. He was shaken to discover that he was treating his son like a "patient"—something that he had never intended to do. Now he wasn't quite sure how he was supposed to act. In many ways, Mr. Ross guessed, he had treated his own parents like that. Their marriage had been a lifelong sequence of arguments, as he now saw it. With a lot of practice, he had learned how to keep the peace. An only child, Mr. Ross eventually became the permanent peacemaker for his parents. Any show of conflict between them was cause for his immediate concern. He still reacted that way when people were upset. In fact, as he began to reflect on it, his whole life seemed like a peacekeeping mission. He was always helping people handle their conflicts—to the exclusion of ever directly stating his own needs and wants. Inadvertently, Mr. Ross had frozen into a permanent helping role whose inflexibility was underwritten by his profession as pastor. Now he had to find other ways to act. Upset by his son's challenge, he nevertheless saw the merit in it—for himself as well as for his son.

Mr. and Mrs. Ross were able to acknowledge the impact that their legacies had had on them. Each seemed to have been victimized by their respective backgounds of split loyalty. Harder by far was the ability to see how they had colluded by undercutting his reasons to trust in the adult world, and how that built up David's own destructive entitlement.

Many of David's inherent childhood entitlements had gone unmet out of his parents' subtle efforts to transform him into what he couldn't be, and thus to parentify him. His own identity was tarnished with the culpability of previous generations: To what degree Mrs. Ross expected or needed her son to be her advocate and, instead, wound up with an unruly charge is hard to know. Surely some of that had to be there; it still was. To what degree Mr. Ross longed for a conflict-free camaraderie with his son and, instead, wound up with a set of estrangements between David and Mrs. Ross that were disconcertingly similar to what he had seen in his parents is equally hard to know. Some of that had to be there too; it still was.

What is indisputable here is that David took a long time before he was able to gain approval in his own eyes as well as with his parents. That he was able to come to it at this juncture in his young life in no small measure belonged to his father's initiative, to his mother's religious commitment to reworking relationships, and to his own courage and tenacity. Moreover, his parents' entitlements were heavily wrapped up in making good to David. Their daughters had struggled but never like him. Hard put to validate their own merit in their parenting of him, Mr. and Mrs. Ross found it difficult to credit their son.

What is also to be noted here is that, despite real and felt injustices among these family members, their long-term involvements with each other had established a reservoir of trust. They talked sincerely, if not easily, to each other in even the earliest family sessions. For all of the anger, resentment and regret that each of them carried, the residual resources that still existed among them gave them the courage to surface their sides, to set their terms for future relatedness, and to acknowledge the other person's claims, that is, to offer fairness and to require it.

Under the impact of therapy, each family member could begin to benefit from offering the others their just due. Everyone gained justification and earned the entitlement that comes from bridging the gap between centripetal and centrifugal concerns. Helping the family members gain entitlement was made the major goal of therapy. Entitlement could not be provided by the therapist, of course, nor could it be prescribed. However, she could elicit the family members' interest in self-gain, helping each of them actualize their longings to invest anew. To recast Martin Buber's phrase, she could help them towards "healing through meeting" with offers of care.

Characteristic of people relying on their destructive entitlement, one of the paradoxes in this family was that, for a long time, each of them *felt* that they were entitled to more than they had received. Searching for answers to their felt deprivation, Mr. and Mrs. Ross occasionally blamed their children's unhappiness on neighborhood kids. Like many others, though, they had failed to turn to each other for help in assessing their situation. Even if they had done so but stayed focused on their feelings of entitlement or sense of justification, it is unlikely that the simple expression of these feelings would have propelled them very far. For feelings of entitlement are a psychological state or phenomenon that can differ radically from the process of earning entitlement. Earned merit is, in fact, the opposite of a mere arrogant claim to entitlement to superiority.

Feelings of entitlement may or may not parallel actually earned entitlement. A person's, especially a child's, sense of entitlement may be manipulated regardless of his or her offers of care to others.

Earning entitlement has become one of the key goal notions of contextual therapy. The therapist elicits relational moves whereby each family member can earn entitlement to promote a positive relational climate and also to help gain satisfaction from every member's vantage point. The discovery of ways in which a person can earn entitlement both diminishes the cost of reciprocal due consideration and becomes a forceful motivational factor for maturation (Boszormenyi-Nagy & Spark, 1973). Earned entitlement benefits the donor through self-validation. As he experiences the resulting inner freedom and health, he will not only be capable of living a fuller, more enjoyable and creative life, he will be interested in trying to earn entitlement again. Efforts to accrue entitlement are not only a method but a mechanism of therapeutic change and a therapeutic goal.

As each member moves toward this goal, a climate of ongoing responsibility for consequences develops. As a result, any member's need for pathological, exploitative modes of relating is expected to diminish.

DESTRUCTIVE ENTITLEMENT: WHEN EARNING MERIT FAILS

The more relatively helpless and vulnerable the victim and the more injurious and irreversible the harm suffered, the more the victim is likely to accumulate destructive entitlement. Like its counterpart, constructive entitlement, earned destructive entitlement accrues vis-à-vis destiny, the justice of the human order, as well as in the ledger between victim and victimizer. People are reluctant to own up to accountability for the perpetration of injury. Under the circumstances, the victim is not only inclined but actually entitled to seek reparation. Yet, there may be tragic contradictions. The destructively entitled person characteristically overlooks the fact that he is not entitled to take out his basically justifiable grudge on innocent others. Without considering the ethical contradiction implicit in destructive entitlement, the therapist can hardly hope to penetrate the origins of what psychologically qualify as "character disorders".

Earned merit is the basis of self-validation and the coinage of constructive entitlement. Conversely, a person can accumulate valid justification that results in destructive entitlement. Paradoxically, through being victimized, a person can also earn the "right" to be destructive. This right is not essentially psychological either in attitude or content. Nor is it faulty learning, "basic fault," displacement, or projection. Destructive entitlement is a consequence of reality or the unfortunate vicissitudes of injustice. In other terms, destructive entitlement is a derivative of unacknowledged and unrequited injustice. Not a psychological defect *per se*, destructive entitlement is interwoven with psychological consequences. It is one link in the chain of consequences that are associated with the "hurt" justice of the human order.

Destructive entitlement is one end result of the parental failure to honor the inherent entitlement with which each infant is born. If nurturant care is significantly withheld from the young and dependent child, he or she is unjustly, and often even exploitatively, injured. *Ipso facto*, the baby merits due consideration. Physical and material neglect comprise only one manifestation of parental failure to consider a child's merit. Others include:

- Parental assignments of essentially unreachable goals;
- Parental manipulation of a child's sense of entitlement;
- A chronic imposition of parental mistrust with its inevitable consequence—a depleting drain on the child's generous loyal availability;
- Making a child a singular and overresponsible source of parental trust;
- Forcing a child to betray one parent in order to retain the affection and concern of the other;
- Reversing the direction of parenting through utilizing the child's own devotion and causing him to feel guilty in the midst of his attempt to give his heart and soul.

Parental neglect and exploitation of a child's intrinsic merit constitute the basis of destructive entitlement.

The degree of destructive overentitlement seems to evolve in direct correlation to 1) the child's dependency and helplessness, 2) the scope and intensity of the injuries, 3) the extent to which such injuries are irreversible, and 4) the ongoing failure of parents to offer their children some means of redress. The parent whose child abuse led a protective agency to remove the children from her home finds some vindication in her desperate efforts to be "retrained." At age 40, she is still being humiliated and attacked by her mother and emotionally abused by her siblings. She can acknowledge how a child needs a nonabusive parent; she just doesn't know how to get there.

On the other hand, consider the mother who refuses to acknowledge the long-time exploitation of her youngest son. "We've been close friends from the day he was born," she reports, "and he has no wish to break up that friendship by going away to school." The youngster who is always at his parent's bidding and rarely, if ever, at his own can eventually be driven to revenge. The tragedy here is that the consequences of destructive overentitlement become essentially transgenerational. A discredited and exploited person may become a relational "monster." He may also confer "monsterhood" on children yet unborn.

Credit earned by victimization predisposes people to repetitive, substitutive claims for restitution. In addition, such people are disinclined to feel pangs of remorse or guilt. The destructive entitlement that ensues can sometimes be uniquely incorrigible. With no inner or outer reins that can check their destructive bent, people can justify their own punitive behavioral patterns in marriage and parenting alike. It seems safe to say that the derailment of merit in the family of origin can be viewed as a root cause of marital breakdown and divorce.

It also seems clear that destructive entitlement is composed of a valid factor and an invalid factor, each operating at the same time. The two factors stand in internal contradiction to each other: The valid factor is a person's historically-rooted grudge and self-justifying claim to compensation. The invalid factor is that substitutive revenge, particularly on innocent third parties, cannot be justified in the long run.

In clinical language, destructive entitlement may manifest itself in any of the following terms: incorrigibly paranoid attitudes, hostility to all authority, hostility between the sexes, cutoffs from parents, self-destructive patterns of day-to-day life, and severe addiction, among others. The person who is driven by the intrinsic "logic" of destructive entitlement keeps circling in recurrently stagnant relational patterns. None of these patterns serve to earn him constructive entitlement. The depression which is often present in people caught in this circle is a natural consequence of their inability to make helpful contributions to others—and their feeling some guilt over this disability. Moreover, destructively entitled people are typically burdened by their self-estranging and self-depleting efforts, apparently sucked into the quicksand of their own depression and despair.

This effect is the reverse of the one engendered by efforts to earn constructive entitlement. The self-validation gained by actively considering other people and contributing to their well-being results in a self-reinforcing spiral of motivation. Successful efforts to earn entitlement produce a gratifying and liberating experience which, in turn, leads to new efforts to earn entitlement.

Merited entitlement motivates people to want to earn more of it. Why then do we need to be helped with relationships? Why can't we discover the process on our own? If my self-interest is served by helping my daughter stay close to her father after a bitterly contested divorce, why do I want her to hate him, the way I often do? Some answers to these questions obviously lie within the realm of psychological limitations, e.g., anger, resentment, narcissistic personality development, or regressive dependency. Some answers can also be found in the realm of relational consequences that link a person's past injuries to his or her ongoing retributive tendencies. The unmitigated impulse to wreak revenge is an outgrowth of destructive entitlement.

People actually earn the "right" to be vengeful and destructive. Consider the man who had lived in his adoptive parents' home by "the sufferance of his mother" and by the exploitation of his father. The unrequited suffering of his childhood now seems to justify his wish to extrude his own adolescent son from the family. Father has lost all his motivation to be concerned or considerate of this child. Never a priority for anyone in his own upbringing, this parent no longer feels obliged to consider the valid life interests of his "ill-behaved" youngster. To the contrary. He is now motivated by an opposite force. Here a person's past deprivations function as a demand for advance compensation. From his perspective, no one really understood him when he was his son's age. No one seemed to care about his vulnerabilities or knew the futility of his repeated attempts to help indifferent parents. Why then is he obliged to work harder for his son than his parent worked for him?

Past injuries can serve to cancel out a person's prospective remorse over his or her own unjust acts. The tragic paradox of destructive entitlement lies in the fact that the son, like his father, will probably wreak vengeance on innocent third parties.

The person whose destructive entitlement results in remorseless victimization of innocent third parties becomes more disappointed and indebted rather than gratified or free. His past injuries may provide genuine justification for his present behavior. But now he, too, has injured the justice of the order of existence. He may be unable or unwilling to earn constructive entitlement vis-à-vis his son. Still, his destructive input into his child's life has decisive consequences for both of them. His treatment of the boy incurs additional indebtedness for the father, and his claim to overentitlement from the past obscures the option of accruing merit.

It is not a sense of existentially incurred guilt, then, that compels the primary attention of contextual therapists. Our emphasis does not focus on the tension between self-assertiveness and guilt (or guilt feelings) that comes of choosing the self over the other. Our interest is rooted in the relational ethic that offers a balance between self-concern and concern for the other: Entitlement to personal gratification and gain on the one hand and, on the other hand, due consideration of the people who depend on the consequences of one's relationship with them and who have significantly contributed to one's life.

Therapeutic Implications of Destructive Entitlement

The technical armamentarium of contextual therapists consists of tools that mainly help people validate themselves through constructive options. These options, as we have already said, are fundamentally dialogic. The dialogue itself is composed of a self-delineating aspect and a self-validating aspect that is made reciprocal by offers of care rather than by vindictive demands. Given these goals, contextual work requires:

- That the therapist's knowledge be oriented towards life's intrinsic and spontaneous potential, resources and options. He has little interest in prescribing specific behavioral formulae;
- That in cases struggling with the consequences of childhood deprivation, the therapist be able to distinguish between actually incurred, factual hurts that have genuinely injured the order of justice, and psychological defect, deficiency, anger, or guilt;
- That the therapist have the initial ability to offer due acknowledgment of his past victimization to the person who is currently victimizing the people who are close to him;
- That the therapist have the simultaneous ability to offer due acknowledgment to the family members who are currently being victimized;
- That the therapist develop a therapeutic relationship whose empathic character can help heal psychological defects, rebalance relational benefits and burdens, and help increase each family member's capacity for growth;
- That the therapist learn how to credit each and all family members even when their basic self-interests conflict; he accepts an attitude and methodology that is multidirectionally partial;
- That the therapist elicits in the destructively entitled person a capacity for being responsible for his own victimization of others.

The therapist's capacity to empathize with each family member's justifications and to credit their relational merit is likely to have a catalytic effect. As they experience the impact of due acknowledgment, they may eventually be able to extend their just due to others as well as seek it for themselves. It is important to note, though, that acknowledgment by the therapist is not the essence of therapy. Family members have to find their own ways toward earning contructive entitlement. They have to validate their own existence by choosing options that make sense to them. The therapeutic task is to guide family members towards self-rewarding avenues of autonomy and trustbuilding. It is this self-reinforcing process rather than therapeutic acknowledgment *per se* that ultimately functions as a healing source.

The shift from relying on destructive justification may be a long pull. The therapist may have to offer a moratorium to the injured party who may have to receive a period of unilateral acknowledgment and credit for his claims. Care must be taken to give people adequate time and room. No delay is to be brooked, though, when it comes to damage being done to the very young, even if therapeutic intervention threatens to antagonize attention-seeking parents. When multidirected partiality is at play, ''losing'' the parents' therapeutic involvement is unlikely. Naturally, they will learn that the therapist cares about their own just due, too.

A more complex and demanding task falls to people who want to earn entitlement vis-à-vis their deceased parents. Obviously, such a task is best begun and achieved while aging parents are still around, though many people shirk facing them. Still it is possible to gain entitlement that comes of exonerating our parents' sides. Posthumous exoneration, of course, constitutes an almost totally unidirectional task. However strong our memories, their one-sidedness is a limitation. Who the parents were to themselves, to us, and to others can be reconstructed, but dialogue cannot occur. It is a point at which our parents themselves can receive nothing back despite our good intentions. Even so, their children as well as their children's children can be rightful beneficiaries of the process.

Social and Preventive Implications of Destructive Entitlement

Destructive entitlement invariably destroys an individual's capacity to validate himself through offers of due care. A woman's hapless deprivation by her father may have been horrendously unjust. It may have left her feeling enraged and massively bereft. Nevertheless, there is nothing to justify her chronic manipulation of her husband and sons, or the fact that she feels no remorse in having her way. People may have a well-founded, undeniable basis for their retributive behavior. Still it seems fair to ask how long anyone is entitled to use past injustices to cancel out the necessity to make fair investments in the future.

Destructive entitlement undergirds attempts at self-vindication that are removed from a concern for significant others. It is also manifested in attempts to use indifferent or negative modes of relating to define one's personal identity. Addictive behavior, an obsessive focus on money and the accumulation of material goods, and paranoid preoccupations are all forms of self-mastery that indebt people by omission or by commission. In any case, the chronic use of power schemes and manipulation results in massive exploitation. The destructively entitled person may finally be collecting his ''just'' due—but he is taking what he is owed from the incorrect source. In contrast with the individual-based confines of projection or displacement, the relational pattern of destructive entitlement recreates an actual new context of unfair social interaction.

Self-survival as a primary attitude towards nature and society is a human preoccupation. People can never entirely transcend their own self-serving, one-sided perspective of a given person and relationship. Expediency based on self service is of course, a fact of life. In the main, men and women would rather be included in a power system than be part of an exploited crowd. Overtly or covertly, members of loyalty groups expect their group leaders to secure as much advantage and power as the in-group holds—while simultaneously excluding outsiders. Something in people compels them to a view of justice that is tempered for themselves and sharply honed for others. A common human characteristic, expediency, has, nonetheless, serious shortcomings as a sole criterion by which to raise the young. However effective in the short run, temporarily expedient solutions are often permanently damaging in their consequences for posterity.

If expediency is an insufficient guideline for human behavior, what are the alternatives? What can still be assumed about human integrity as a genuinely guiding force? For many "average" people, "love" and "the family" have been defined as the balancing forces of human intimacy. Like other family therapists, we have discovered how often the adult's wished-for island of human integrity is provided by the trust offerings of the very young. Given their loyalty to the parent generation, young children stand in jeopardy of having their trust exploited. Their naive assumptions about the adult world can lead them to be abandoned. Conversely, they may have their "understanding" of adult difficulties manipulated.

Disintegrated family patterns are forcing adults to draw heavily on the trust resources of the future. Even if inadvertently, contemporary children are exploited and parentified to a degree that should be alerting the helping professions. Desperate parents may cling to their children in inappropriate, if understandable, ways. Exploitatively inverted parenting always has lasting consequences that negate any personal gain for either parent or child.

The issues created by inverted parenting pose a penetrating challenge to psychotherapy in general. They underscore the fact that reciprocally enhancing responsibility has to be linked to the efforts of a family member who is willing to take a lead in building trust. It is illusory to assume that any kind of therapy can help family members attain a measure of multilateral fairness without one of their own taking appropriate, trust-building risks. Without some coinage of good faith among family members themselves, a therapist is unlikely to be able to guide people towards the creative actions that undergird creative responsibility.

Relational responsibility of this kind evolves from therapies for which trustworthy transformation may not be a purposeful goal; but neither can it be secondary nor incidental. Reciprocally enhancing responsibility in relationship does not necessarily emerge even from successful, insight-oriented, transference-based individual therapy, nor from systemic structural therapy with its emphasis on transactions, rules, patterns and boundaries.

Non-dialogic notions obstruct the dynamics of dialogic trust. People are not automatically motivated to assess both sides of a given situation or conflict. Rather, men and women are inclined to be led towards parallel and discrete differentiation and maturation. They may be taught how to establish a collectively well-flowing, feedback pattern of communication and transactions. They may be guided towards formal compliance (direct or paradoxical) with their therapist's prescriptions. All of these methods, however, are essentially non-dialogic even when they are done in pairs. *Ipso facto* they are unlikely to provide people with a self-motivating and enduring search for trustworthy resolutions between the colliding entitlements of parties. The relevant and precise terms of a client's partner are frequently ignored in individually-based therapies.

For their part, transactional-systemic approaches make few allowances for the uniquely private existence and experience of each person, or for the subjective sides of relationships that may span generations. Yet, ultimately, detrimental "enmeshment" can be cured only through each family member's progress toward individuation, i.e., each person's ability to both assert himself or herself and to consider the other side. In contextual terms, that adds up to a dialogue between responsible partners. First of all, healing emerges from the residual trust resources of people who are significant to each other rather than from a therapist's attempt to repair role boundaries or correct rigid transactional patterns.

Therapists are daily burdened with the demands of destructively entitled clients. This tragic example of two teenagers is, certainly, an extreme and explicit case in point.

> Within seven hours of meeting for the first time, Shirley Wolf, 14 years old, and Cindy Collier, 15 years old, collaborated in the brutal murder of Anna Brackett, eighty-five years old (McCall, 1983). In June, 1983, Shirley wrote in her diary, "Today, Cindy and I ran away and killed an old lady. It was lots of fun." Tried as juveniles under state law, both Collier and Wolf were found guilty of first-degree murder and Collier was sentenced to the maximum for minors—incarceration in a California Youth Authority facility until she turns 27.
>
> In Wolf's case, the insanity issue will be heard as a separate phase of the trial. "We've got a judicial system that does not work," says Carl Brackett (the murdered woman's son). "I'm thoroughly dis-

gusted." "Next month, when the proceedings resume, lawyers and psychiatrists will explore the troubling questions which remain: How did two young girls become monstrous killers? What furious impulses drove them to murder an innocent old woman who offered them only kindness?"

"Anna Brackett's killing was a nightmare of Shirley Wolf's life. Sexually abused from infancy by her father—and occasionally by her paternal grandfather and uncle as well—Shirley's disruptive behavior drew the attention of an alert teacher as early as kindergarten. But the teacher's recommendation of psychiatric help was ignored and Shirley ran away for the first time when she was six. But the mean streets of Brooklyn, where she was born, seemed even more terrifying than staying at home, and she returned within the day." From the time Shirley was nine, "her father sexually assaulted her whenever an opportunity arose—sometimes three times a day—and obtained birth control pills for her when she reached puberty.

"In her statement to police the night of her arrest, Cindy revealed that she once had been raped by a family member as well as by another man who then threw her down a flight of concrete stairs . . . 'My childhood has been rotten. I've been beaten since I was born and I've been raped a few times. I have tried to kill myself before and all I did was to bring frustrations. So I take it out on others. I don't like them because they probably think they're better than I am. I don't want them around. I want them to pay.'"

Most instances of destructive entitlement take milder, more everyday forms. Society understandably sees extremely destructively entitled people as trouble-making and unproductive members, and resents the fruitless outlay of time, money and energy on their behalf. Therapists themselves are ambivalent about them, and are often torn by the ethical conflict posed by the tensions that exist between society's normative expectations and their clients' desperate needs.

This tension may be a root cause of the therapist burnout that is so prevalent in public mental health centers. In any case, these clients do test therapists to see what signs of trustworthiness can be delivered out of their professional integrity. Sometimes this testing goes on at real cost to a therapist's personal relationships. Yet people burdened with destructive entitlement have a powerful need for ongoing consideration—from any source. Whereas society deserves protection, these people deserve and need retrospective acknowledgment of their suffering if they are ever to be moved to offer society more trust. The bind for mental health workers, whatever their training and preferred modality, has to do with the fact that in the long run no society can finally afford to become instruments of simple expediency or of subtle exploitation of the weak by the strong. The preventive implications of the concept of destructive entitlement are huge and costly.

INTERGENERATIONAL CONSEQUENCES AND EXPECTATIONS

Another phenomenon to be considered as truly asymmetrical is the fact of *transgenerational consequences*. Clearly, the parent generation is in a better position to affect the offspring than vice versa. Each intergenerational act is asymmetrical in the sense that the filial generation is onesidedly more exposed to influences because it is going through phases of formative development. Also, because of its age, it is less powerful and efficient than the adult generation. The offspring's natural, existential indebtedness to the parents can, therefore, be manipulated into guilt feelings. Moreover, influences affecting the child at an early age tend to become irreversible foundations of personality development. A particular type of such irreversible impact on the child can take the form of binding injunctions, also described by Stierlin (1974) as "delegations." Although the child owes selective consideration to the parents, ultimately, the transgenerational mandate for the good of posterity has to prevail as the uppermost consideration.

As already noted, birth itself creates intergenerational consequences. As parents become responsible for helping their helpless infants thrive, children eventually become accountable to the people who, alone among all others, gave them life and the capacity to survive. The fact of a new life and its intrinsic attachments establishes a unique source of interlocking obligations and these produce an ineradicable basis for claims for due consideration. A parent cannot help but exert a lasting, irreversible influence (positive and negative) on a child and his or her well-being, with all its attendant consequences for posterity. A child cannot help but inherit the consequences of the past's relational endowments. Consider, for example, the following situation.

Estrangement in the Price family seemed to be at an all-time high. It was Charles, though, against whom the charges were made. Now 16, he was born armless and required extensive physical care which his parents and sisters gave him. His current bahavior, they feel, ignores how much they've done and still do for him. Why else would he use marijuana, cut school, violate his curfew, and associate with "unreliable" friends? Charles' behavior was certainly causing his family grief but the intensity with which they were reacting didn't seem to match the level of Charles' "transgressions."

Like his wife, father was unable to state any personal goals that were unrelated to Charles. He was able to state how confused and wounded he was by his children's response to his having been a Marine. "I feel deeply attached to my children including my son. When I went into combat, I wrote him a letter that I tore up when I survived. I wanted him to know who I was. I might not have been a hero but I wasn't an uncaring guy. They all think that I killed innocent people. They don't seem to understand that sometimes you do what you have to do." "He did kill innocent people," Charles retorts, "people who never did him any harm. If he really cared about them, he could have found another way!"

Charles, father feels, is hardly in a position to talk about care; he has gotten so much of it. Not so the father—nobody even wanted him: "I lived in my parents' home at the sufferance of my mother. They had lost their child when she was only three and then they adopted me. The adoption was my father's idea not hers. Maybe it was a way of keeping their marriage together. I also know my mother never wanted me."

Given up by biological parents and an apparent matter of indifference to his adoptive parents, Mr. Price's world was untrustworthy and unjust. For him service in the Marines was a significant source of parenting, given his adoptive mother's early death and the infrequency with which he saw his father after that.

Mrs. Price's family background also had consequences for her son. Charles can count on his mother's love and support—even against his father as long as he meets her need to be needed. Should he try to find his own way, however, he can count on her displeasure. Charles also has to make sense of his mother's preference for and more lenient attitude toward his sisters, "Our daughters had their problems in adolescence too," she said. "They stayed out late and smoked pot but never like this." Here mother's disappointment in who men are began to come into play. She had assumed they would all be like her father. She had hoped that her husband and son could meet her idealized expectations of a man who is long-since dead.

Charles' backgound burdens him with destructive and shameful factors which he obviously did not choose. Still his physical existence and survival skills, conveyed to him through his parents' massive efforts and investments, have *ipso facto* established the baseline for his filial indebtedness.

At the same time and in the same process, birth indebts a youngster to an obligation of filial loyalty and to a mandate to care for posterity. The source of this dual indebtedness is existential in nature, and usually links deeply with most parents' motivations. As a rule, people strive to be at least as giving to their children as their parents were to them. A person characteristically offers the next generation the same quality of unilateral caring that he or she received as a child. Adults are typically motivated to offer special consideration to the people who over time have endowed them with special contributions and benefits.

At the very least, parents deserve a considerate hearing so that the healing aspects of their life's realities may be accurately transmitted to posterity. To be sure, it is the offspring who is finally responsible for the appropriate transformation of parental "messages." Only so can past truths impart meaning in terms that apply to future generations. Take the example of a dying mother's plea that her three adult daughters "stay close to each other after (she's) gone." Her request is likely to be significant to them however they choose to respond to her efforts at binding delegations.

Her daughters may be forced into a loyalty bind by their mother's exhortation. They may try to ignore their personal issues with each other, some of them linked to differences in how their parents treated them. They may try to deny old sources of anger, resentment and guilt among them, sources that are invisibly activated each time they come into each other's company. Or they may decide to go their separate ways once their mother is dead. On the other hand, they may take note of how costly it has been for their mother to be estranged from her own siblings. Ill though she may be, while she is alive their mother can help them comprehend the legitimacy of her request.

The crux of mother's message lies in the fact that she removed herself from relationships with her own brothers and sisters when she was very young. She only did so, she recalls, because her bridegroom felt competitive and said that he disliked them. Over the ensuing years, mother became increasingly isolated from her family of origin by virtue of her marriage, and increasingly isolated from her marriage by virtue of her husband's alcohol use and abuse. Before long she was turning to her daughters to meet her deep-felt needs. Profound piety was her only alternative source of emotional gratification. Today her children and others still picture her as a saint. There seem to have been no trustworthy relationships to which she felt free to turn in her family or in her community.

The lack of options for real dialogue between her and other adults isolated mother and, in essence, abandoned her to the limited resources of her nuclear family. Her isolation was onerous and depleting on a day-to-day basis. It also functioned to obscure the degree to which isolated and self-isolating people contribute to breakdowns in their significant relationships. For example, it is likely that she may never have realized her own part in abandoning her siblings for her husband, and her husband for her children. It is likely that she never intuited how she had helped to turn "her" girls against their father; how she had contributed to their definition of their father as their mother's vitimizer. Even now in their adulthood, these women seem to carry a deep mistrust of men and replay it in part on their husbands and sons. "You can't count on men" is certainly one aspect of their dying mother's message, but so, too, is her counsel that siblings can be helpful, even necessary, resources to each other. Her regret over her own choices makes her want to encourage her adult children towards other options, options that might save them from repeating the same mistakes and suffering the same degree of pain.

How her daughters interpret and apply their mother's message now becomes a major issue for them and for their children. They may choose to focus on mistrust. "Your father was unreliable" can translate into retributive action against all males. Or they may choose to focus on the resource side of their mother's concerns: "I suffered unnecessary loss when I gave up relating to my siblings; please don't repeat my mistake." "Choosing between two loved ones doesn't prove to be the best way." "My siblings might have given me strength to help your father win his battle with alcohol." "You can lend each other courage; explore your relationships." "It's true you've hurt each other but you can do better than that." How these women respond to their mother's message once she has died is obviously up to them. One of them may retreat from facing the meaning of their mother's exhortation. One may move forward to see what can be done. One of them may feel angry and confused about what is required of her.

Intergenerational consequences can be lasting and serious. If a mother is unable to resolve the conflict between her filial and marital loyalties, she becomes the source of her children's split filial loyalty. The delegation issuing from one parent's contempt for the other not only harms and parentifies their children but tends to interfere with the children's legacy of parental accountability. As the children inevitably become destructively entitled, the next intergenerational "revolving slate" endangers their children's inherent entitlement to a trustable, caring nurturance. Ultimately, of course, it is in everybody's interest that the legacy-based expectation of posterity's good will conquer the damaging consequences of split filial loyalty induced by detrimental parental delegation in the first place. The therapist's task is to help people sort out the agenda required by genuine transgenerational legacies from self-serving or destructive parental delegations.

As always in contextual work, the existence of pathology has its own significance. It also has significance as a guideline to future rebalancing. The identification of past injustices and mistrust inevitably points beyond itself towards residual resources, trust-building options, and opportunities for the present generation to build on the wisdom received from parents' lives and contexts. It may be that the wisdom conveyed from one generation to another is one of the fundamental returns to be gained by adult children when they minister to frail, ill or aging parents.

Parents *qua* parents are entitled to a fair hearing from their adult children. They are also entitled to personal consideration in their times of particular vulnerability and stress. These times present offspring with options to earn their own entitlement through offers of availability and care. The son who is there to lend courage to a frightened father facing surgery is winning his own future freedom as well as meeting obligations from the past. It should be noted, then, that the process of earning entitlement means that neither parental nor filial accountability should be essentially an enslaving one. Ministrations that acknowledge the past redeem the validity of what was received. Injunctions that flow from the past help forge the terms of an offspring's future.

Clinical experience discloses the frequency with which an adult child discovers hidden affection for his or her "stricter" parent. The parent who risks making demands for responsibility on her child is characteristically preferred to the one whose leniency borders on indifference. Parents can be chronically overavailable and dependently possessive at one and the same time. Captivity to this kind of parenting may cost a youngster his personal autonomy. It may also undercut the option of fulfilling his mandate to posterity. Parental expectations that are clear, direct and meaningful though strict are in the best interests of the young. Parental guidelines that aim at helping a child cope with life's demands and realities will ultimately prove beneficial—despite a child's temporary or short-term, resentful response. In a fluid society in which "anything goes," parents are increasingly confused over what demands they are entitled, much less obliged, to make of their children. Blame or permissiveness are the characteristic, if contradictory, modes in which increasing numbers of adults parent their children.

In family therapy sessions, tedious discussions over a youngster's at-home use of drugs is a common case in point. Parents often forbid the use of drugs in their home and develop an intricate "spy system" by which to enforce their prescription, a solution which is doomed to failure. They sometimes join their youngster in using drugs and so try to meet their own unfaced needs for a source of permissive parenting. Rarely do they know how to claim their right to a drugfree home on the basis of fairness. The parental capacity to tell children what is required of them presumes that parents know their own terms and can find the courage to convey them fairly. Unfortunately, when it comes to drugs and sex, parental behavior is often passively reactive. The end point of parents' chronically reacting to their children's behavior rather than establishing terms of their own is poignantly documented by Robert Lindsey (1979) in *The Falcon and the Snowman*. Here he reports the life journeys of two youngsters eventually committed to Federal prison. Lindsey cites (p. 351) the comments of one of the young men's lawyers:

There is nothing in (Andrew Daulton Lee's) school records, or in the memories of their friends or teachers to indicate that (he was) anything but a devout Catholic boy growing up in a happy warm family in one of the most affluent suburbs in America (Palos Verdes, California) . . . The kids got in trouble over drugs but shouldn't the parents have to take some of the blame? The only thing those kids had, a lot of them, was what money could buy. Their fathers were into making money as fast as they could, and their mothers were up to their ears pursuing their social interest, and they just blinded themselves to what was happening to their kids. I know a lot of these kids were smoking pot and snorting coke and heroin when their parents were in the house; some of them dealing right out of the houses, the parents were oblivious to it. It was incredible. The parents gave their children all the material things, and that made them think they had discharged their duties; it gave them a clear conscience so the father could go back to making money and the mother could keep up with her tennis and social life. Then, all of a sudden, when their kids are seventeen or eighteen, or on drugs, they ask "What happened to my children?"

The issue here has little to do with imposing rules or setting limits. Our concern is neither with "tough love" nor with "being right." Our concern has to do with long-term, deep-rooted parental investments that eventually instruct children about the two-sided nature of significant relationships. The emphasis here is on meaning, not on enforcement which in any case is a literal impossibility. Obviously, youngsters are creative in developing ways to sidestep parental requests. Less obviously, perhaps, they are in desperate need of parents who, out of their own lives and contexts, stand on ground that is congruent with their offsprings' absolute and nonnegotiable need for life's meaning.

The genuine, long-term interests of offspring are never served by the evasive conflict-avoidance of insistently permissive parenting. A person whose parenting is grounded in noncontroversiality poses a severe existential conflict for her child. Buffered from the experience of learning how to convert conflict into cogency, youngsters are left with the onus of floundering for meaning and repeating patterns of evasion, avoidance and denial that they have learned from their elders. An adult's inflexible standoff from conflict, "Peace at any price," is also a result of her failure to take what is valid from her own past (legacy options) and translate and transmit it to the future (mandate options).

Posterity is profoundly affected by the degree to which parents and parenting figures transmit their cumulative, intergenerational wisdom. This reality mandates the adult world to care about the transgenerational consequences of actions and decision-making. The empirically-rooted "ethic" of responsibility for the consequences of a person's impact on his child's life is linked to the fact of the helplessness of the successor generation. The following shows how a father is called to account by his 16-year-old's behavior:

> I can stay bound to my long-entrenched tendencies to avoid controversy at any cost. I can have ample insight into the fact that I prefer to emulate my father's withholding silence in order to protect myself from the trauma of my mother's smothering, all-enveloping garrulousness. I can overlook all of my own hard-earned learning and wisdom, and delegate the task of my child's guidance and discipline to my mate who is a professional counselor. But when my youngster begins to punch his mother and to escalate his destructive behavior in school as well as at home, I (hopefully) will be forced to reassess my own position and behavior: Am I being faced with the unintended consequences of my long-term if invisible relational choices? Is our son asking me finally to disclose who I am, what I think and feel? What it is I want? Is my legacy strengthening or undermining my intrinsic mandate to be responsible to my helpless and unsuspecting son?

Asked to reflect on the causes of his anger, the youngster is absolutely clear: "How come women always get the upper hand? My mother doesn't talk, she lectures. My girlfriend is just like her, stubborn and a pain in the butt! And my father's mother rolls over him; she always starts yapping away. Why doesn't he ever put it on the line?" Our children's insistence on being taught fair ways to relate poses hard questions: For example, what can adults do about the consequences of their behavior that may take decades to evolve, often through the personality formation of their offspring? How can parents be accountable for actions whose consequences they can't anticipate?

Parentification

An important consequence of any form of misuse of parental authority can be defined as parentification. Essentially the misuse disregards the asymmetrical nature of liabilities in the parent-child relationship. The essence of *destructive* parentification is usually inadvertent use of the child's filial obligation to reinforce his captive availability to the parent's exploitatively dependent aims. The implicit bind of guilt is then a powerful reinforcement of the child's helpless compliance. So is his spontaneous loyalty and his investment in keeping the family together.

Parentification takes many forms, ranging from an overtly obvious role reversal to subtle "infantilization" of the child. Possessive, overprotective parental attitudes can lead to crippled development of the child's personality. The child may remain permanently available to the parents. The child's failure to grow amounts to the most formidable parentification (e.g., in cases of addiction, criminality.) Almost every failure of responsible parental leadership is bound to lead to an automatic, complementary "recruitment" of the child into roles of prematurely heavy, crushing over-responsibility. The more explicit the recruitment, the more manageable it is from the child's vantage point. For instance, periods of actual sickness or disability of the parent or other emergency situations may demand adult-like responsibility from the child. Yet this experience may enhance the child's emotional growth rather than handicap or destructively exploit him. Learning responsible management in emergencies can be a healthy gain for the child.

An important criterion of destructive parentification lies in relational factors rather than in a role shift itself. If the child is acknowledged for his helpful and useful availability, the experience is incorporated into his future self-confidence and sense of competence. An overt request for help is already an implicit acknowledgment. By contrast, withholding acknowledgment, coupled with guilt-bound allegations, is a tremendous combination of destructive, if effective, manipulation. The more subtle the imposition of guilt, the more the child is entrapped in destructive parentification. An important therapeutic guideline is present here. The emergency in the family situation may be unalterable, but the parent can at least learn to acknowledge the child's contribution. Acknowledgment or crediting is the opposite of guilt inducement.

No human services profession is currently in a position to make predictions that are scientifically knowledgeable. On the other hand, the escalation of disintegrative relationships in technological societies warns against inertia. A lack of readily accessible answers can be overwhelming. Worse, the very complexity of contemporary relationships can lead social scientists and psychotherapists towards a position of weary indifference.

Hopefully, other alternatives still exist. There is mounting evidence about just how significantly posterity is affected by the consequences of the past. Family treatment in the last three decades provides ample clues to how even unborn generations are heirs to adult relationship patterns. Research has underlined how deprivation and exploitation in the young can lead to irreversible developmental damage. A child's captive investment in his parent's well-being has a unique, if equal and opposite, reality: On the one hand, children are entitled to parenting by virtue of their relative helplessness in the world. A decisive lack of parenting is likely to result in destructive parentification and the child's own build-up of destructive entitlement. On the other hand, parents earn entitlement for themselves in the process of offering due care. How parent-child balances are attained over the long run has intergenerational consequences which need to be addressed on both preventive and methodological levels.

Delegation

From the standpoint of contextual therapy, legacies that contain valuable aspects of transgenerational heritage are to be distinguished from parental delegation that is actively imposed by adults on their offspring. Stierlin (1974) writes,

> The delegating mode obtains where a child (particularly an adolescent) is allowed and encouraged to move out of the parental orbit . . . to a point! He is then held on a long leash as it were. . . . The delegate, although sent out, remains beholden to the sender. He remains bound . . . in a special and selective manner that implies a strong yet often visible loyalty (p. 249).

Delegation often serves the interests of the young but the process lends itself to many possibilities for derailment and exploitation. From the perspective of the delegating process, obligation is a relatively unilateral phenomenon in which the parent's psyche is determinative. Conversely, the process of addressing legacy issues and options is inherently dialogic. In reviewing his parents' and other predecessors' past action and in reassessing his own, it is the offspring whose position is likely to be determined. It is the offspring who is left to balance the legacies from the past with the mandates for the future. It is the offspring in whose hands decision-making will lie. It is the offspring who, if he or she so chooses, can peel back the years' long layers of intergenerational delegation and imposition. In the process, it is the offspring who can begin to attain—for his and posterity's good—a fairer distribution of burdens and benefits, a more viable balance of freedom and responsibility that is uniquely his or her own.

The Predicament of Split Loyalty

An adult assessment of the consequences of parental behavior patterns can lead to a poignant discovery of parental limitations. As often as not, parents inadvertently entrap their children without ever consciously intending to exploit them. The predicament of split loyalty characterizes the unconscious ways in which exploitation occurs. A child chronically forced to function as a referee between her mutually mistrustful parents eventually suffers a severe loss of trust in both of them.

It is a common phenomenon these days for adults to acknowledge their children's need and right to easy access to both their parents—even while they undercut the possibility. This situation is compounded by the last generation's failure to act on burdens coming from their pasts. The mother who long ago "chose up" mother over father is unlikely to be able to see her own part in laying the same imposition on her children. Here she is not consciously acting against them. Nonetheless, the consequences of her behavior militate against the children's future well-being.

The predicament of split loyalty is singularly destructive in its capacity to demolish intergenerational trust. We do well, however, to differentiate between the negative consequences linked to this sort of impasse and the positive consequences linked to the filial task of integrating parental legacies. It is both common and reasonable for people to expect their children to find ways to resolve legacy conflicts.

The colliding legacies that evolve from the parents' respective families of origin present offspring with legacy conflicts that require integrative resolutions. Otherwise, children inherit legacies that seem intrinsically incompatible. In its most apparent form, what is Johnny supposed to do if his mother is a pious Christian for whom scrupulous ritual observances are a family legacy; but his father takes pride in the fact that his family of origin always was proud of their enlightened, cosmopolitan, humanistic atheism? Mixed religious, racial and national origins represent the clearest examples of potentially incompatible parental legacies. However, the task of integrating diverse legacies exists in every two families whose children have grown up and have children of their own.

A parent's own success or failure in resolving conflicting loyalties significantly affects a child's ability to integrate both sides of a family's legacies. What is a youngster to make of the fact that his father is always caught between his mate and his own parent? Collisions between primary loyalties (family of origin) and marital loyalties can produce unremitting conflict for everyone involved. Youngsters who are caught in their parents' irreconcilable loyalties are faced with an impossible task: They have to choose up sides. In other terms, they lose the opportunity to earn constructive entitlement from both of their parents. Repeatedly trying, they inevitably fail. Eventually children learn to stop trying. They conclude that they simply cannot master the impossible. Loyalty conflict in the parent generation causes the dilemma of split loyalty in the offspring. Consider the boy whose recurrently psychotic mother has delegated him to compensate for her years' long estrangements, first from her parents and then from her mate.

Bruce has finally chosen for his dad over his mom. Even worse, he is in close touch with his maternal grandmother from whom his mother is totally estranged. Over time he has developed patently unrealistic expectations of what he is due. In his view he is entitled to cars, money, stereo sets, vacations abroad, and tuition for Ivy League schools. His expectations are barely affected by a divorce "settlement" that awarded four-fifths of his father's assets to his mother despite the fact that she is able to work. At 21 he still operates on the expectation that to get exactly what he wants, all he has to do is ask. He makes massive demands on his father and his father's new wife.

Bruce typically has to be forced to help out when he is at home. When the therapist enumerated the burdens that his stepmother carries at home and at work, Bruce unselfconsciously remarked, "Isn't that what mothers are supposed to be for?"

Destructive entitlement has effectively blocked Bruce's motivation to earn constructive entitlement. Past deprivation has taught him to get what he can regardless of consequences to himself or someone else. "Why continue to invest in people," is his essential question, "when none of your investments ever pay off?"

Parent-child relating merits special consideration beyond simple reciprocity of a symmetrical nature. This is mainly required because of the *consequences* of the relationship. The heavy consequences are like a third party; they require consideration beyond the simple, ordinary rules of equitable give-and-take. It carries heavy costs in consequences for a parent to say to a child: "What if you are adopted? It is your problem; don't expect extra consideration for it from us." The consequence of such parental attitudes would be the violation of the justice of the human order.

The same can be said of the adult who tells the ailing old parent: "To me you are no different from the millions of other human beings. I have no time to give attention to your needs, anxiety, pain, and worries. I hope you will fend for yourself like other people do." In both cases, the justice of the human order is a third party to the relationship between parent and child. Ultimately, such violations have the consequence of harming innocent others.

It is the therapist's task to find out about the consequences of violated intergenerational fairness—first through eliciting everyone's position (multidirectionality), but also through listening with an invisible ear for curiosity about fairness. Partiality to each affected family member means an injection of factors linked to relational ethics (Dimension IV). If listening with the "third ear" means an injection of each member's unconscious dynamics (Reik, 1948) the question of fair consequences means listening with a fourth ear too.

Unrequited intergenerational fairness is the frequent cause of various forms of injustice: e.g., harming another relationship in invisible loyalty to an ambivalently resented, despised or otherwise avoided parent-child relationship. Invisible loyalties are at the basis of unmanageable loyalty conflicts that lead to marital failure.

TRANSGENERATIONAL MANDATES AND LEGACIES

Transgenerational mandates and legacies represent ethical imperatives that originate from justified claims for consideration on the part of both our predecessors and our successors. As we depended on the inadvertent, generative generosity of our parents and ancestors, posterity depends on our responsible concern. That which benefited us from our heritage can be converted into posterity's benefit. It is the task of the present generation to sort out that which is beneficial and translate it into terms of benefits for future generations. In doing so, each generation earns entitlement vis-à-vis its descendants *and* the justice of the human order.

Issues like self-validation and earned entitlement are obviously linked to the matter of transgenerational legacies and mandates. We have argued that a person can achieve relational integrity—that is, a person can validate his existence by offering family members their due. In the process, he enhances his own personal freedom or entitlement. The forum for doing so is double-tiered: One is through interpersonal relationships that allow for a direct exchange; the other is between a person and the human order through transgenerational legacies and mandates that, in their asymmetry, are indirect and one-sided, although not without reward.

Of universally pervasive significance in human life, these legacies and mandates form a distinctive feature of the contextual approach. People can achieve undreamed of success in the vast arena of private and public enterprise. These achievements, however stunning in and of themselves, fail to mitigate the unrequited injuries that fester between the generations. The essence of the legacy is the mandate for forward-thrusting care and concern for the future, a use of the assets of the present to enhance benefits rather than detriments from the past.

The life of the individual is cast into an undulating balance between freedom and unfreedom. Helplessly cast into life, the newborn is forced to rely on a generous response from the adult world. He can later repay what he received only through offering care to future generations. In our view, at least three generations are involved to complete this repayment: the first that transmits lasting consequences to the second, and the third that is to reap benefits from the concern and redeeming efforts made by the second. No one is ever completely free of transgenerational obligations to care.

For all of that, life can and usually does offer options for discharging reasonable obligations without running over people, or imposing guilt feelings for failing. The delicate balance between discharging debts and finding personal freedom is broken and toppled by unfulfillable expectations whatever their source. Moreover, when unrealistic expectations are disappointed, as they inevitably will be, relationships are burdened with attendant feelings of resentment and guilt. Yet few things are as commonplace as parents who delegate unrealistic and unfulfillable expectations to their children who, perforce, are made to bear the onus of invisible loyalties.

The more subtle or inadvertent the parental expectations, the more difficult they are for the young to address. By contrast, the expectations that are placed on the present generation by virtue of their legacies from the past can be addressed, handled, and translated into benefits for posterity. The issue here transcends the boundaries of individual psychology and interpersonal transactions alike. Transgenerational legacies and mandates incorporate multi-individual and systemic determinants although they have to do with that part of relational programming that goes well beyond here-and-now interpersonal dialogue, and beyond transactional and communicational feedback.

Genetic continuity maintains the identity of species through shape, color, size, and movement patterns, among other determinants. On the other hand, each new combination of two sets of genes in each newly-formed individual represents a bold and innovative experiment. Each new generation depends on the formative input of its entire phylogenetic past. Similarly, subsequent generations depend on the free choices made in the present for mate selection. On the one hand, the individual is an autonomous universe, the source of self-contained development programmed for growth, longevity, obsolescence, style, and even "free will." On the other hand, the individual is an essentially ephemeral epiphenomenon, a link within the chain of genetic continuity that by now spans billions of years from the time of the formation of the first organic matter.

The causal linkages between the generations can be characterized more by the image of telescoping than by the notion of circular feedback. Generational consequences can neither go backward nor affect the defunct past. Moreover, as a causal determinant of reproduction, there is a difference between genitality and generativity. Genitality originates from preexistent, instinctual configurations in the individual. While it represents an individual characteristic, generativity is teleological in nature. It serves to sort out the prospective options vis-à-vis mandates for posterity. The future is unilaterally, thus captively, exposed to the consequences of the present reality. Our responsibility for the future of our offspring, our concern over our mandates for posterity require—no, demand—the highest human priority precisely because the future is the most vulnerable of any of the targets of relational consequences.

Informed by this reality, contextual work proceeds from the premises that 1) the individual is vitally invested in transgenerational benefits, received and conferred, and 2) the individual is vitally invested in the personal gain that issues from offers of care and concern specifically geared towards posterity. In their therapeutic design, contextual therapists place a high degree of importance on helping people sort out which of their options can best prevent inadvertent damage to small children.

Parent-child relationships provide the matrix of intergenerational expectations. These expectations, their fulfillment, and their failure to be fulfilled are characterized by emotional bonds that range from the sublime to the ridiculous. As everyone knows, these include love and contempt, devotion and guilt, gratitude and resentment, the need for comfort and the demand for distance. Our experience with transgenerational and intergenerational consequences underscore just how costly it is to ignore them. The implications of these consequences have commanded the attention of the human heart and mind for centuries. Over 2000 years ago a commentator observed that when a parent eats sour grapes, his child's teeth are set on edge (Ezekial 18:2; Jeremiah 31:29). History, drama and literature are replete with references to linkages, punishments, curses, and other manifestations of the interweaving destinies that lock the generations to each other, whether they will it or not.

When we make reference to legacies, then, we are indicating the relational roots of transgenerational consequences. We are describing a pervasive task spanning generations whereby each person becomes a linkage between past expectations and expectations which actively telescope into the future. Ultimately, legacy as a mandate for the future has to be enabling to posterity. In any case, legacy-bound messages always function as guidelines of action for the future, whether the future means only biological offspring or posterity as a whole.

Used conventionally, the term "legacy" can convey a static quality. To review it from a contextual perspective, legacies are NOT merely a set of customs or conditioned patterns handed down from the past. Nor are they simply unmet debts still to be fulfilled. Obviously the past does not admit of change. Nor are legacies meant to indicate a special obligation to worship or specifically revere unrealistic and godlike images of one's ancestors. Parents can and do delegate certain missions to their children that loom out of the past. For example, in some families, college age children always spend a year in their ancestral homeland, a communal and parental expectation that is often forcibly conveyed. Even this, however, is not the essence of transgenerational legacies which are always far more than the delegations or personal wishes or personalities of parents.

Furthermore, legacies are not to be confused with injunctions originating from the superego. That is, they are not simply guilt-bound over-allegiances to parental norms. The fruits of past legacies are the benefits we have enjoyed in the form of language and culture, material survival, and the skills with which to take pleasure in life. In its own turn, each generation is obliged to benefit the next through specific manifestations of its care. These might include work on ways to prevent air and water pollution, radiation contamination, and other destructive use of science and industry. Making the world safe for survival is the very least that one generation owes to others. Existence may be characterized by resources, creativity, flexibility, and still unexplored human potential and possibilities, but these are not boundless. In this as well as in less cataclysmic concerns, care needs to be taken for the irreversible consequences that characterize transgenerational mandates.

The existence and impact of transgenerational mandates document the fact that the asymmetry of parent-child relationships extends beyond the issues at play between two parties. The infant is not only a justified recipient of parental investments but is also the legatee of the lives and actions of all of the lineage that preceded him. Eventually, he can balance the scale of what he has received from the past by becoming a benefactor to posterity. In this he will be a link between the generations, conveying legacies that are founded on 1) roots from the past that are, for example, ethnic, racial and religious in nature, and include family requirements of loyalty and recognition, and 2) each individual's basic characteristics, e.g., male or female, healthy or genetically impaired, physically gifted or intellectually endowed.

In addition, each generation of offspring is forced to find ways to bind together the legacies of two families. They are also obliged to fulfill mandates of caring even in situations of bitter estrangement like divorce. Obviously, asking fractured families to help small and dependent children retain their relationship with a parent who has caused the other parent such pain can be a massive and difficult demand. Yet, without at least an attempt at lessening the child's predicament of split loyalty, the burden of responsibility would shift from the adult to the child. Transgenerational legacies have consequences whether or not people choose to recognize them.

Beyond consideration of the fairness of parent-child relationships, each generation is invested in the long-range good of posterity. Consequences of injustice can injure trust and trustworthiness for generations to come. Transgenerational consequences may be determined by factual circumstances like belonging to a certain sex, race, ethnic group, or religion. Other factual circumstances may follow from inheritable health conditions, migration, genocidal past, ancestral habits, alcoholism, etc.

The good of posterity has to be supported in the face of the negative odds of burdensome heritage. The term legacy implies both the factual inheritance of detrimental consequences and the fact that posterity's good depends on the present's capacity for counteracting the detrimental nature of consequences for the future. The legacy of alcoholism, for example, cannot be the mandate to make drinkers of the offspring too. On the contrary. The legacy is to help them overcome the consequences of such a heritage. Any act of enhancing the lot of posterity constitutes an opportunity for the present to earn valuable entitlement vis-à-vis the justice of the human order. An honest talk about the circumstances of the past can help offspring gain more trust in the world through understanding the humanity of their ancestors. The religiously liberal father can help his agnostic children to connect with the religiously orthodox grandfather's world of values. Adopting parents can help their adopted child to discover the redeeming factors of his or her biological parents' origins.

III. ASSESSING THE CONTEXT

CHAPTER 8

The Client-Therapist Dialogue

From the first meeting on, the therapist and client(s) enter into a dialogue. The therapist immediately begins a process of collecting useful information. Simultaneously, he begins to encourage family members to develop both phases of dialogic exchange. However skilled and helpful the therapist, though, it is not he who provides the essential context of a person's self-delineation and self-validation. These are anchored in each client's relationships with close relatives and with other significant parties in his or her life. The assessment of a family's relational reality and the disclosure of their therapeutic resources are interlocking processes that can immediately establish a trust-building intent from the beginning moments of therapy.

An assessment of relational reality is more comprehensive and complex a procedure than an assessment of an individual who has essentially been extracted from his context. For each person is anchored in a relational world that incorporates others. Each partner in a relationship interdependently carries some of the family's burdens and some of the family's benefits. Shared burdens may include a family name that is tarnished by shame, or the cost of being heir to parents who have survived genocide or revolution. Assessing the existential context of life is a far more comprehensive task than defining the structures of here-and-now power coalitions, role complementations and other behavior patterns.

Genetic illness, a family business, the sudden and unexpected death of a family member, inherited wealth, and prominent parentage all imply burdensome or beneficial consequences for family members. Consider, for example, the situation of an elderly woman and her two adult children.

Twenty-five years ago when he was 15, Jonathan, the youngest of three siblings, was struck by lightning on a golf course and killed. The consequences of that event had a massive impact on the whole family and on each individual. First of all, the event was never discussed. Mother still carries the details of the moment as if it had occurred last week. Until they gathered for a family assessment initiated by Sarah, age 47, no one had had the courage or the energy to share the implications of Jonny's death for his or her own life. They had not wanted to hurt each other.

Sarah was living abroad at the time of the tragic event. She still feels locked out by the way in which their father handled the funeral arrangements and their aftermath. The funeral was held before she could get back home. When she did arrive, she remembers her father saying, "Jonathan's dead now, Sarah. There's nothing to be gained from crying over something that can't be fixed." No one in the family can recall how the father handled his own grief. What they do remember is how his behavior seemed to allow no room for them to handle theirs.

Will, the family's surviving son and a parentified child, remembers consoling his parents at the time of his brother's death. He, himself, was offered some consolation by a family friend. His parents, though, were unavailable to him. Presumably, they were so bereft that they never found time to help Will with his grief as he had tried to help them with theirs. Or, perhaps, long-term patterns of evading emotions in any domain kept them from reaching out. In any case Will, like Sarah—and perhaps like his parents—was left to mourn alone. During the family assessment, he reported for the first time that he had gone to his brother's graveside for months following the incident in an effort to connect.

Over the years Will, now 44, became heir to the family business. He is president of a small corporation, professionally successful; personally, he is still trying to establish the criteria for sometimes living life on his own terms. One thing remains clear in the midst of his current struggle: If Jonathan had survived, Will might not have to be in corporate life. He might have opted to stay in the navy, flying a plane—the long-standing love of his life.

Obviously, any attempt to help this family evaluate their situation involves sharing their personal aspirations and disappointments. It also involves surfacing hopes and dissatisfactions that are linked to the burdens and benefits of their shared lives. Through no one's intentions but by the act of destiny, a death in the family altered their collective and individual lives. Discussing Jonathan cannot alter the fact of his death but the family's ability to talk openly about him has lifegiving implications. However brief, his existence had consequences for this family and can still function as a resource for his survivors. Through a shared review of their options for doing and caring for one another, the family members discover new avenues for self-delineation and self-validation.

Multidirected Partiality

Multidirected partiality is the methodological cornerstone for eliciting intermember dialogue in a family. It is also the most productive approach to collecting relevant information about relationships. In each case, it is a methodological procedure that helps its members surface questions about the family's balances of fairness and unfairness (Dimension IV). Such questions always lie close to the heart of people's relational needs. In therapy, then, it always makes sense to establish a multidirectional perspective immediately. Within the first half of the first session, a therapist can help people begin the process of delineating and validating their respective terms and positions. To do so, he has to take consummate care *not* to define a family's situation simply by virtue of its pathology. He must also take care to resist an overquick definition of who is the victim and who the victimizer. For example, consider the situation of a man who called to arrange for therapy.

On the phone and in the early moments of the first therapy session, he identified himself as a child-molester. His therapeutic goal, he said, was to uncover the causes of his "child-molestation." Eleven years ago, he and one of his daughters, Jan, now 25, entered into a year-and-a-half period of fondling and lovemaking that apparently stopped short of intercourse. Three years later he was involved in an extramarital affair. Now he is withdrawn, depressed and impotent. He is also guilt-stricken, self-blaming and, to hear him tell it, bereft in any terms of his own. He is the victimizer, he declares, and his child the victim. What else is there to say?

He was contracting for therapy, he said, because his daughter ordered him to do so. Currently ill with ulcerative colitis, she is enraged at her father. She has hinted that her childhood experience with him has led to a revulsion with men and to a homosexual relationship with a woman. Jan made some attempts to discuss her struggle with sexual identity with her father but he couldn't find the courage to pick up on her prompting. She has since moved three thousand miles away. Mr. Santangelo wants her to get well. If it makes her happy for him to see a therapist, he means to comply with her wish. On the other hand, he and his wife have just ended eight months of therapy that "failed." His wife had to do all the talking during those sessions, she complained. When their daughter came to therapy once, she was bitterly disappointed. No one would discuss what had happened between her father and her; the therapist focused on the Santangelos' marriage.

Mr. Santangelo was engaged within minutes of his first contact with a multidirected approach. "No," the therapist couldn't help him if he were attending sessions just for his daughter's sake. Nor could he begin to hope to heal the scars of his family context if he continued to take constant refuge in his job. "Therapy can't proceed along a categorical definition of good and bad, or victim and victimizer, even in cases like this," the therapist explained, but she can help him and the rest of the family assess what is possible between them now. Here the therapist's questions are geared to elicit a dialogue between family members.

Can Mr. and Mrs. Santangelo and, where applicable, their children begin to address questions like these?

- Were 15 hours of work a day preferable to intimate relating?
- What was Mrs. Santangelo's part, if any, in the relationship between her husband and daugher?
- To what degree did the children run their parents' lives (parentification)?
- How had he learned that it was less trouble to be quiet than to speak?
- What did he do with his mother's inability to acknowledge "frailty" in men?
- What were the costs in his family of origin for saying his side?
- Why were their sons more accepting of him than their daughters?
- Why did Mrs. S prefer their sons to their daughters?
- Clearly Mr. S wants Jan to get well. But can he say what he wants for himself and for his marriage?
- Is the couple prepared to reinvest in their marriage, and on what terms?
- Do they want to become marital partners again as well as a parenting team?
- How can Mr. S parent his daughter Jan anew?
- Can he find the courage to speak directly with her, or is he still compelled to leave the task of relating to his wife?

Information-gathering in contextual therapy is tantamount to exploring past and current balances of fairness and unfairness. Both are inseparable from attempts to identify and to shore up interpersonal resources so people can more readily enter into a spontaneous, trust-restoring, dialogic process. A knowledge of past events is intrinsically valuable only if it is useful for the future.

Reliability: Its Aspects and Resources

The chief resource of any relationship is rooted in its long-term, fair reliability. Relational ethics are founded on the fact that, over time, a person has been sensitively attuned to his or her partner's essential needs and interests. Thus, on balance, people are there for each other when it really counts and so manage to sustain the relationship.

A relationship may be characterized by injuries and exploitation. Nevertheless, it is likely to be trustworthy if it is also characterized by reliability in the long run. In the first instance, what is at work here is the earned merit of each partner in offering each other care. Also at work is each partner's responsiveness to the earned merit of the other.

Obviously, no one is capable of sustaining a continuously ideal performance vis-à-vis his partner all of the time. On balance though, reciprocity of commitment (Boszormenyi-Nagy & Spark, 1973, p. 161) can be assessed with relative ease. Consider the situation of the family whose 20-year-old had been brought home drunk by the police.

Thirty minutes into the first therapy session, his mother reported that Paul had always been her "good boy." Now he was drinking a lot and had been in three automobile accidents since high school. "One of my own brothers was killed in a crash only 11 years ago," she said, and Paul just doesn't seem to want to hear. He didn't do well in college and his father made him quit. Now he has one of those little, part-time jobs, and he's so bright." Everyone, including Paul, agrees that he is the family failure. The last of five children to be at home. he feels hopeless and undirected.

In the second of four assessment sessions, Paul reported that his greatest fear lay in hurting his parents. Not hurting them, though, sometimes became a challenge. For one thing, they argue a lot. He was often in the position of begging them to "grow up." "It's always about silly things," he says, "And nothing ever really gets settled. My mom wants to talk a lot and my dad wants to watch TV. She wants me to go to college; he didn't go and doesn't care if I go. When they fight, I try to calm them down. Things got worse a couple of years ago when mom had a falling-out with her parents. We never visit them anymore, at least not as a family. They never did like my father much and, recently, my grandfather yelled at mom."

Paul was relieved after the first session. "I began to realize," he said, "that things were more complex than they originally seemed." The therapist was able to help the family look beyond the presenting problem of Paul's drinking. She managed to point out the youngster's long-term reliability, including the fact that he functioned as his parent's referee. His behavior managed to contain the anger in his parents' marriage. He was his mother's advocate with her parents. But he was enraged by her wheedling and her seeming helplessness. "It's never occurred to me to work on my friendship with my dad. My mom's always so lonely, I figured she needed me more." Paul was also his family's therapist. "Mom needs me," he says, "to make up for her aggravation over grandpop."

Paul's parents had sought family therapy after unsuccessful marital work with their minister, who remained a resource to the family and to the therapist too. Paul and his "failures" had then been the primary focus of the couple's concern. It was up to the therapist to acknowledge their frustration but also to credit Paul's contributions. It was also her task to illustrate how Paul had subtly become his parents' benefactor. Identifying the criteria of family fairness, the therapist could quickly establish its members' reliability which, at the very least, functions to balance manifest pathogenicity. Pointing to the evidence of reciprocal commitment, the therapist is able to avoid a judgmental attitude towards her clients.

A fair consideration of the earned merit and the vital interests of matched partners establishes viability in peer relationships. Mutual commitment and caring about an equitable return over time are the primary criteria for assessing fairness in symmetrical relationships. Reliable marriage, friendship and collegial relationships are typically characterized by direct, external and equitable returns between autonomous adults. Exceptions to this fact exist when, for example, chronic illness or divorce occurs and burdens a relationship with radically new expectations and conditions.

On the other hand, an equitable balance of give-and-take cannot function as the measure of asymmetrical relationships. Here the evaluation of fairness is more likely to depend on internal rewards like earned entitlement and emotional satisfactions over a youngster's growth, achievement and success for himself. In family situations in which one person is dependent on others by virtue of infancy, illness or senility, everyone else is faced with a costly demand. How they opt to handle that demand has massive practical and ethical consequences for the present and future alike.

A family's treatment of its extremely needy and bereft members provides important clues to a therapeutic assessment of the balance of burdens and benefits among its members. For example, a woman dies in a car crash, her husband remarries within a short time, and his new wife resents having to care for his chronically depressed, 10-year-old girl. Over time, Joan is moved from place to place. She becomes increasingly depressed and eventually develops anorexia. Finally, her maternal aunt, Mrs. Curtis, agrees to take Joan and raise her. What does this kind of decision cost Mrs. Curtis, her husband, and her three children? What practical consequences does this kind of decision have for their lives?

On a practical plane, the Curtis family obviously had other options. On an ethical plane, however, Mrs. Curtis saw no other choice. "She owed it" to her parents and her dead sister to raise Joan. She may owe it to her children as well. Is she entitled, she wonders, to go about her life as if nothing of this nature had occurred? She is now her parents' only surviving child. Is she free to ignore the pain they continue to suffer over their daughter's death and their grandchild's plight? Given her own relationship to her sister over the years, can she proceed to mother her own children and be indifferent to what is happening to her sister's child? The Curtis family lives on a sprawling farm. Would it be so much trouble to take care of just one more child?

The high demands imposed on a family through one of its member's extreme neediness, especially a young child's, are framed in limitless ways: For example, an infant is born with a severely cleft palate. From the start of his life, the infant has difficulty nursing and has to undergo multiple operations. How do his nonnegotiable needs affect the quality of his parents' marriage and lives? What do they put at risk by considering having another child? In each of these situations, an adult's decision to offer responsible care is an indisputable signpost of reliability and trustworthiness. It inevitably involves a degree of self-sacrifice and deprivation. It is also a measure of earned entitlement. Equity of return is never a real possibility in situations such as these. The primary return comes instead from the internal freedom that is earned from appropriate giving.

The contextual therapist draws on broad, multifaceted criteria in evaluating a family. Among them are interpersonal conflicts of interest (colliding entitlements), legacies and legacy conflicts, and the context of potential, if unutilized, resources. All of these aspects provide clues that identify the balance of peoples' relational reliability. The resource orientation subsumes rather than contradicts the dynamic, individual and systemic relational orientations to therapy.

Interpersonal Conflicts of Interest

Interpersonal conflicts of interests between two partners are inevitable and unavoidable, and are not to be equated with failure in relationships. The existential interests of parent and child, of man and woman, and of sibling and sibling converge and diverge, blend, collide and find resolution or fester and build. Parents, for example, characteristically want to be able to rely on their children, if not to possess them. Adolescents, on the other hand, increasingly want independence *in their context*; they need the freedom to experience and grow. Sue, for example, is 16 years old and her mother is threatening to disinherit her.

Sue is involved with Tom who is 28 years old. She has her own doubts about him and the fact that he takes drugs. But his family is nice to her, and Tom reminds her of her father who was killed in a plane crash five years ago. One of 12 children, Sue had been her father's favorite, his "blue-eyed, blond-hair girl." She had far surpassed her mother in his affection, she was sure.

With her father gone, Sue felt like a needed resource; yet she had to find something for herself. Educated in parochial schools, she considered herself to be deeply religious but still was entitled to love, she said; and Tom, she was sure, was the only person in her life who could provide that love. Paradoxically, she was constantly worried about her mother who now had no one on whom to depend. What was worse, in her view, Sue plans to leave home as soon as Tom gets back from school; but who, she worried, would take care of her mother then?

External circumstances, vested interests, personal predilections, and transgenerational and individual expectations are all factors in this hurtful, inevitable collision between mother and daughter. In fact, some collisions between them are predictable. It would be a mistake, though, to use their conflicting interests as the sole measure of their relationship or as the primary focus of therapy.

Like parent-child relationships, asymmetry in the reproductive process also exemplifies how inevitably conflicting life interests between two caring partners are not necessarily elicited by a breakdown between them. The intrinsic conflicts for them lie in the differing degree of risk that pregnancy holds for a man and a woman. Pregnancy may, of course, jeopardize the health or even the life of a prospective mother while representing gain for the prospective father. A prospective father may choose to mitigate the demands that the reproductive process puts on his mate but he can never eradicate them. He can balance them, though. For example, he may help his wife as she delivers their baby. He may rearrange his professional commitments in an effort to parent his child in contrast to how his father failed to parent him. Still the asymmetry exists. No amount of male effort or good intentions can obscure the risks of pregnancy and childbirth that are determined by the fact of being female.

The undeniable costs intrinsic to becoming a mother are present even when natural parenting is negligent or absent. In cases of adoption, for instance, the significance of the biological parents is always a factor. The time, place and circumstances of birth are characteristic developmental and relational issues for adopted children. Their biological mother's contribution to their existence can never be gainsaid. In adoptive situations, as in any family situation, the fundamental asymmetries between being male or female deserve a thoughtful assessment in therapy. Sensitive clinicians, however, cannot afford to ignore fundamental, existential elements of relational reality.

The possibility of organ transfer surgery creates another extreme form of asymmetry between two closely related partners. Potentially severe conflicts of interests are linked to the anticipated degree of gain or loss between immunologically compatible relatives. When, for example, does a person's offer of his vital organs to a sibling threaten his availability as a healthy and functioning parent to his children? Or, to what is a person entitled if he faces death without a transplant if his relatives, who are potential donors, are resistant to the idea? A recent case of colliding interests had to do with the legal rights of a man who faced death without a compatible marrow transplant. Adopted at birth, he petitioned the court to gain access to his biological parents in the hope that they would help him. What was the court's obligation, and to whom? If contacted, what did the biological parents owe? Did the court have a right to protect the privacy of the biological parents against the survival of the child to whom they had given life? In a case like this, how do legal rights differ from birthrights?

A fluid society with innovative contributions has a massive impact on family relationships. One of them has to do with the illusion that people are free to live as they please without having to contend with the limits imposed on life by the nature of creation itself. For example, the swing from traditional sex roles to fluid ones tends to obscure the legitimacy of gender-based asymmetries. A fluid society with changing expectations also tends to obscure the immutability of intergenerational demands. The claim that parents and children are dynamically indebted to each other may sometimes be a highly unpopular fact. Nevertheless, parental accountability and filial obligation are dynamic realities that figure into every contextual assessment. Here again, we are addressing asymmetrical balances that stem from reciprocity of commitment rather than from expectations of direct or immediate returns.

Intergenerational Expectations and Legacies

The burden of intergenerational expectations points from the past to the future. Every child is inevitably faced with expectations conveyed from the past. The filial question is never "Shall I be loyal or disloyal?" for loyalty is the glue of parent-child relationships. It may be positive or negative in form, but it is always the basis for asymmetrical relationships. Rather, the question before each maturing adult has to do with whether or not to embrace or discard certain, specific parental expectations. The legacy of filial indebtedness may indeed convey the imperative to consider one's father and mother. It also presents adults with the life task of sorting out the best of the past's input—for posterity's sake as well as for the sake of the present generation. Honoring parents never implies an unquestioning subservience to all intergenerational "delegations" (Stierlin, 1974). The ultimate measure of an offspring's honor for his or her parents has to do neither with having to submit to parental values nor having to rebel against them. Filial respect for the past is most creatively embodied in a person's entitlement to take what has been given in the past, assess its merit, and, finally, recast it into more effective modes of offering future care.

Intergenerational expectations set up a potential clash between what is conveyed and what is embraced. Consider the situation of a brother and sister who, as teenagers, emigrated from Cuba to the United States.

Each brings a set of dual expectations, one from lifetimes spent in a Spanish, Catholic milieu, the other from their parents who are Polish Jews by birth. These expectations are partially cultural, but they are clear about their family's expectations had they remained in their native land: In her view, the girl would have been expected to marry early, have children, and, perhaps, work in their father's store. The boy would have been expected to graduate from high school, have a family, and succeed his father as an entrepreneur. It also would have been expected that each of them live in close proximity to their city's Jewish enclave.

In their new environment in the United States, they were subjected to still another, diverse set of demands. Placed in foster care until the adults in their family could emigrate, they were forced to rework many family loyalties that were, of course, deeply ingrained. For one thing, there was no longer a shop, owned by a parent, in which each had a place. For their father, an immigrant to Cuba from Eastern Europe, owning his own business was a buffer against prejudicial behavior from unfriendly governments. In their homeland, an individual's private enterprise could be a hedge against intrusion by authorities whose predisposition towards Jews could be a destructive one. In Cuba, however, his store had become a "capitalistic offense." In their twenties, his children opted for professions with an entrepreneurial bent in which they could retain a high degree of personal independence.

The cost of forced migration altered their family's vocational expectations of this young woman and man. It also took a high toll on their personal lives. Father was initially very disappointed that his daughter had chosen a profession instead of early marriage. His daughter waged a furious battle against her father's disapproval. A delegated conflict set parent against child and child against parent. Eventually, though, it was for the adult child to choose for posterity's sake. Whether the world was safe enough to justify having children was one of the reasonable questions that faced these young people. Obviously, what served their father in his lifetime might not necessarily serve them. Theirs was a reasonable inquiry for offspring whose family was forced to flee its homeland twice in two generations. The legacy requirement of the daughter's accountability to her father outweighed issues that can be viewed as delegated interpersonal expectations.

Their father's expectation may have been valid in his own life and place. Like all parents of adult children, he is entitled, even obliged, to convey his expectation to the next generation; for parental expectations that emerge from his own family of origin and from his own life experience comprise the cornerstone of his children's ability to build lives of their own. On the other hand, there is nothing that entitles him to *impose* his own expectations on them. They owe and deserve to be able to choose the options that best serve them and help them responsibly care for posterity.

It is for his children to hear and acknowledge their father's expectations, but to resist submitting to them simply because he is their parent. For all adult children are entitled, even obliged, to sort out from the past what they deem best for the future. Filial obligation is always tempered by the parental accountability that offspring assume as adults. No parent can autocratically impose his or her own life expectations on children without taking the risk of imposing destructive costs. Conversely, parents who can honor their past, without freezing it into a bludgeon or ideology, can help their offspring make constructive choices. How else can the tragic loss or shame that may have burdened the past be transformed into learning that can create a healing and positive stance towards future generations?

Unutilized Potential Resources

Unutilized human resources provide the currency through which people's past losses and shame can be transformed and redeemed. Evaluating resources is always a primary task in contextual therapy, one that must be undertaken very early in the therapeutic process. Consider the example of youngsters placed in the hands of child care agencies. At a visible level, attempts to put an abused or neglected youngster into foster care appear to transfer the responsibility for care from biological parents to people who can function in their stead. Here common wisdom suggests that adequate and responsible parenting figures in an average group or foster home will compensate for inadequate and destructive family members.

In point of fact, surrogate parenting is a necessity in many situations and must be regarded as a resource. Still, no surrogate can finally function as a permanent substitute for the people in our family of origin. So it behooves child care workers, as well as other helping professionals, to assess natural family resources at the same time that they are providing children with alternative sources of nurturance and support. One need be neither naive nor blindly optimistic about human nature to assume that, characteristically, most children have at least one relative who is concerned about him.

Typically, someone in a child's family of origin is willing to accept the validity of the youngster's deprivation, and offer some responsible input—if and when that person is asked! Consider the situation of two girls whose father is thought to have molested them. Given this possibility and a long history of physical violence in the family's midst, the court removed the children from their home *and* mandated the family to seek therapy.

Mother and the children complied and went to therapy sessions even after the youngsters were removed from their home. Father stayed away, both ashamed of his situation and doubtful that anyone could ever understand his plight. His constant failure to cooperate or comply was a factor in leading the court to consider adopting these children out to their foster parents. This option was put in abeyance as long as mother protected the children from ever being in the company of their father.

In fact, if not in intent, the court placed mother in the untenable position of having to choose between her children and her mate. She immediately chose for the children for fear of losing them permanently. Over time, though, she maintained her attachment to her husband and became pregnant by him again. Inevitably, the two girls went home for a weekend and found their father at home. The child care agency was now faced with the dilemma of whether or not to fight for the girls' adoption and, with it, to press for immediate termination of their mother's and father's parental rights.

We posed the question of what anyone in the family could gain from this kind of legal action. At best, the termination of parental rights is a legal fiction that attempts to alter the reality of the parent-child linkage. It does so in the name of shaping a better future for children, of course, and in instances of infant adoption establishes boundaries for the safety and security of all the parties that are involved. But its usefulness remains undocumented at other levels. Obviously, children are entitled to protection from abuse; but what kind of abuse is involved when society imposes a lasting exile on two people who are bound by close biological ties? In any case, a judgment ordering the termination of parental rights is far removed from the family dynamics let loose by its implementation, so we suggested an alternative.

Four family evaluation sessions were set up and all of the family's workers, advocates and therapists were asked to attend. We then began to identify what additional family resources might exist to help actualize a new balance of fairness for the adults as well as for the children. One of the gains here was the discovery that mother's brother lived in her home, and often functioned as a go-between and advocate for his brother-in-law, his sister and his nieces. He attended one of the sessions in which his significance to the family soon became very clear. His sister's dependence on him and his nieces' affection for him were evident. He also functioned as a resource for the therapist:

Therapist: Can you encourage your brother-in-law to take part in the family evaluation sessions?
Brother: Probably not.
Therapist: Do you think you can nudge him toward getting help for himself?
Brother: Maybe so.
Therapist: What do you think you can do for your sister?
Brother: Well, I'm not really sure, but I wish I could think of something. Our mother still beats her and my sister's past forty years old. It really isn't fair for her to take so much blame. But my sister keeps having children; my mother doesn't like that much and neither do I.
Therapist: Is there a way in which your sister and you can help each other?
Brother: Well, I'm not really sure. I like her husband and I don't want to take sides. On the other hand, I love my nieces. They're good little girls and I don't want them hurt. Maybe I can think of something that will leave us all better off.

However minor the gain, the fact is that this man is a resource to his sister and her family. He is seen as a parenting figure by everyone in that context, and consequently carries leverage to help motivate them—leverage that nobody else may have. What's more, living in their house is a contribution to him. So asking him to help them, if he can, may be a way for him to give back to his sister and brother-in-law.

Still another gain from the joint evaluation came from the children's mother and their foster parents coming face to face. Embattled over long periods of time, mother and foster-mother and foster-father were giving the girls conflicting messages. Caught in still another loyalty split, the children were demanding to be adopted. In the sessions, though, they were free to state just how worried they were about what would happen to their biological mother if indeed they were adopted.

The final outcome of this case is still under negotiation. But mother's evident investment in her girls moved the foster parents from their previously held position. Maybe their subtle forms of blame were intrinsically unjust. Maybe this woman was not just plain rotten. Maybe they could find ways to deal with her that were fairer if she could be helped to change. Could these foster parents be assured of "keeping" the foster children without adopting them? Could these children be kept in the more or less secure environment of their foster home without having to betray their biological mother? The obvious neediness and helplessness of these young children demand adult consideration. Whether that consideration has to be unilateral advocacy for the children—with all its harmful implications for future trustworthiness—is what is under discussion here. Is it possible for society's caretakers to be multidirectional caretakers? Can family members like the children's uncle be viewed as potential resources rather than as nonexistent and nonessential to the family context? Can asking him to contribute to his nieces' well-being be seen as providing options for him to earn constructive entitlement for himself rather than as undue exploitation of still another hapless or limited family member? In our view, a contextual evaluation helps people shift the burdens and benefits of all family members, especially those of the children. It helps them discover resources in and among themselves to relieve the undue conflicts in which these girls are caught. And perhaps, most significant of all is the fact that family members can be helped to offer more effective care and gain something for themselves in the process.

Even in cases of lesser urgency, relatives *always* represent a potential resource for each other. The siblings who have been estranged for many years, for example, can gain a new measure of freedom and meaning from reestablishing their contacts with each other as well as from reconnecting with their parents. Interrupted family dialogue is a sign of broken trust, one that usually embodies stagnant injustice with no hope for redress. Therapists who have failed to address their own stagnant and estranged relationships can easily accept their clients' family "cutoffs" as normal. They can turn away from the potential for fairness and trustworthiness that resides in close relationships—however stagnant. On the other hand, the indications of broken family exchange can provide clues and stimuli for alert therapists in search of residual sources of family trust.

In the long run, family "cutoffs" are destructive, trust-diminishing resolutions for wounded relationships; therapists who ignore them do so at their clients' risk. Consider the situation of three adult siblings who have essentially managed to go in separate directions over the past 14 years.

Two of them have been in intense individual psychotherapy, one for six years and one for 15 years. The third has been institutionalized several times and seems to be able to function well only in a sheltered environment. Their mother, a widow of many years, tends to see herself as a person who gave her all to her children. Their father died several years ago and is rarely a subject of discussion in the family. He remains an invisible force among his sons, but one that is mystified by their mother's unceasing attempts to glorify his memory. All of these young men are desperate to diminish the guilt they feel as they try to individuate. In their own ways, however, none of them feels entitled to live his own life. Underneath massive anger and resentment, all of them are loyalty-bound to their family of origin—including an aunt and uncle who helped raise them, and a grandmother who had a decisive impact on everyone's life.

Their mother's own difficult legacy, her vulnerability, her defensive posture, and her expressions of unmitigated devotion and love overpower her sons who have remained silent rather than risk "hurting" her. This year, Malcolm, a social worker, terminated his long-term work in individually-oriented therapy. "Our philosophies simply collided," he says. "He expects me to get on with my life as if everything else were okay. But it's not okay. I can't commit myself to relationships or even really have a good time. This year my brother was hospitalized again. I've carried an incredible amount of sadness and regret for my indifferent behavior towards him over the years. He had his first breakdown at college. I was too young to know what was happening. I did know that he lived in the shadow of our older brother and that all three of us live in the shadow of an even older brother who died in infancy. Our mother seems to measure us all by her fantasies of who Clifford might have been.

When Howie was ready to come home this time, I asked him to live with me. I thought it would just be for a short time. I hoped that I could give him something, but I needed something too. I needed to reconnect with the whole family instead of talking about how sick Howard is. I needed and still need to find out what's happening to him. I need to be able to tell him what's happening to me. I need to be able to sit in the same room with my mother and brothers to see if something better is possible now from what's been possible in the past. Even if Howie finally can't make it on the outside, I need to know that I tried. At the very least, I need to know that the people who caused him so much pain—either by commission or omission—made an effort to own up to their pieces of the puzzle. Even at this late date I wonder if something different can happen if we take a look at what we do.

Malcolm can no longer tolerate the cost of his family members' "cutoff" from each other. In his own view, he has reached the limits of what individually-oriented therapy can offer him. He is looking for ways to act on behalf of his family—and so on his own behalf.

By a process of testing different options over time, he has begun to grasp the degree of destructiveness and stagnation that seem to characterize his family's modes of relating and nonrelating. Now he hopes that they are willing to explore more constructive options. The least of these may simply be the ability to sit in the same room together. Contextual therapy supports his pursuit. Whether or not any therapy modality can help Howard heal at this late date remains unclear. What is clear here is that everyone will continue to be hobbled in their entitlement to go on with their lives if they fail to reassess what they can do. Long-term family stagnation, even at its worse, can be seen as a significant clue for discovering unutilized resources and strengths in a family and its members— rather than as data to document pathology.

Therapeutic Commitment

Nothing, then, is to be gained from permanent cutoffs between a parent and a child who—despite protestations to the contrary—in truth long for a chance at fair give-and-take. For significant relationships are characteristically imbued with the prospect for just consideration, no matter how much they seem to have failed. Neither sadistic beatings nor sexual exploitation nor any other pathological manifestations of relational behavior is likely to eradicate the implications of fairness that persist even after a parent's death. The persistence of this residual resource is one of the foundations of contextual work and the basis of its therapeutic interventions. It is also the basis for connecting with each family member's most crucial criterion for relationship, i.e., trustworthiness.

The very act of addressing balances of fairness in a family (Dimension IV) from a multidirected perspective provides the leverage to transcend the dead-end traps of relational stagnation and ethical disengagement. A multidirected assessment *ipso facto* challenges the fragmentation and skew of a purely individual approach. For example, consider the situation of a teenager whose "pathological" behavior psychologically seems anchored in lowered self-esteem. The youngster may show signs of depression or anxiety and insecurity. To be sure, these psychological symptoms have their own implications and consequences, but the primary significance of these affects may have to do with an actual loss of worth that occurred in a relational cutoff. What if the teenager is factually unable to refill the reservoir of his actual self-worth (entitlement) because his father succeeds in discouraging his attempts? What if the resources for building the youngster's ego strength are anchored in the events of his childhood's life cycle, e.g., a parent's death, or placement in a foster home. What if his capacities for actually earning entitlement have been determined by real losses and hurts that have also been internalized and "psychologized?" The internal and external realities of people's lives converge and interlock. Their options are almost never confined to one partner's terms, demands or side. Their resources are never totally confined to their psychologies or simply to the external events that have impinged on their relationships.

CHAPTER 9
Assessing Relational Reality

Contextual assessments operate from the premises that people are best helped when they can make use of whatever residual resources lie between them and that an increased sense of trust accrues from proven trustworthiness in relationship. Concrete "handles" are needed to evaluate these intangible but crucial universals of relational reality, however. Fundamental though they may be, these universals often lack an adequate and readily identifiable language. They also may be personally and culturally suppressed. In practice, the complexities of relational reality can be most fully assessed through the four dimensions or categories to which we have already referred: 1) Facts, 2) Psychology, 3) Transactions, and 4) Relational Ethics. These dimensions seem to include all of the known possible determinants of relational behavior, including the variant of therapist-client relationship.

DIMENSION I: FACTUAL PREDETERMINANTS

The facts of a person's life and context can function as determinative forces that often precede or intermingle with psychological events and transactional behavior. Factual circumstances and their consequences may or may not be partly reversible. For example, a parent's acute illness may go into remission or a child's fantasy about his long-separated parents living together again may become reality. These facts and others, like being born out of wedlock, require therapeutic attention and consideration *independently of the reactions of family members to them*. A comprehensive evaluation always needs to identify the wide range of facts in a given situation, facts and their consequences that help determine people's lives.

The early loss of parents, extreme poverty, malnutrition, child abuse, poor school attendance or performance, the consequences of adoption, and psychosomatic illness in oneself or in one's parents each deserves careful assessment of its influence on a person's development and balances of justice. Combined with the knowledge gleaned from assessing the implications of the additional three dimensions, the therapist can help people develop remedial and reparative options. In addition, there are some facts about a person's life and context that require urgent and instant interventions. A suicidal risk to self and children, a protracted avoidance of school, the dangers of anorexia or of repetitious, secret venous blood drainage (self-vampirism), to name a few, require the immediate structuring of protective measures. A parent's advanced illness or imminent death also demands priority in the therapeutic process.

Factual predeterminants have to do with the events of each family member's life cycle: Birth, school attendance, puberty, parenthood (in or out of marriage), aging, senility, and death are all distinct steps that can be regarded as factual. These stages each have important determinative roles and adjustment requirements for the psychosocial development of the individual involved (Erikson, 1959). A combination of individual life cycle stages also accounts for a family's progress and adjustment requirements. People marry, children are born and then grow up and become independent. Do these facts give a helpful shape to the future, or are they data used to stigmatize the past? For example, a baby is born to his mother when she is 45 years old. For religious reasons, abortion was an unacceptable solution. Over the years she tells and retells how she cried for the eight months after she found she was pregnant. The boy's mother rejected his very right to come into the world. The fact of his birth became a source of mourning for him, one that he replayed in each of his relations with a woman.

A person's successful mastery of each life cycle stage is thus partially built on factual predeterminants. Requirements for mastering these stages also engage the psychological, transactional and ethical resources of various family members. The dynamic linkages of these four dimensions may each be pulled out of their context for the purposes of assessment but, in reality, are always interactive and interwoven.

The assessment of this dimension may yield important therapeutic options even though certain factual circumstances are irreversible by nature. Moreover, their consequences may be mitigated by an affected person's options for action. Tragic and undesirable circumstances can sometimes be transformed into resources for building trust and earning entitlement. The liberating effect of seizing options for action in the midst of tragic circumstances can seep down to future generations, even to the offspring of the still unborn, and affect even their prospects. This kind of option may be presented through the birth of a brain-damaged child, through genetic illness, or through the terminal illness of an aged parent.

Mental retardation or brain damage in a child is a case in point. Irreversible conditions *per se* represent a discouraging psychotherapeutic prospect for the person who is afflicted. On the other hand, family members can help manage their situation-in-common in ways that offer real opportunities for constructive therapeutic progress for each of them. Family attitudes towards an impaired member often make the difference between balanced fairness in context and pathogenicity in a family system.

Faced with severe and irreversible mental or physical illness in one of its members, a family stands to gain when it can be helped to assess which of them is carrying disproportionate burdens. What are these burdens, and how can they be fairly distributed? Who among them can offer additional concern or new kinds of consideration, and earn additional entitlement in the process? Does someone's contributions go unacknowledged? Why? Are the family member's frustrations over their unsought chores and demands converted into blame? Do the family members every acknowledge the impaired member for his or her contributions to them? Or do they limit their view of him to a person whose condition creates an endless source of irritating consequences for the entire family?

Long-term demands for consideration are obviously onerous and typically evoke guilt or resentment or both from everyone involved. Nevertheless, the reality behind such demands can also provide the fulcrum for a constructive relational reorientation in a family. In the case of a parent's terminal illness, for example, mother and her adult daughter can begin to rework a long time cutoff between them. When Mrs. P. learned of her mother's illness, she opted to offer care to this person whom she had long regarded as distancing and rejecting. The whole family eventually stood to gain from the improved intergenerational trustworthiness that Mrs. P. had set in motion by her choice for active care (Boszormenyi-Nagy & Spark, 1973, chapter 12). In this situation, as in so many others, the broken dialogue among people of significance to each other could be reestablished in a time of crisis.

In point of fact, entitlement earned through creative giving is typically a resource even in the midst of deep and entrenched mistrust. Real and threatened loss characteristically offers options for new risks and initiatives for trustworthy action and behavior. Only so can people begin to convert linear, self-serving avoidance into a stance that may evoke an unexpected (if deeply hoped for) multipersonal return. Even terminal illness in a young child offers options and represents resources. In instances like these, clinical work typically focuses on the youngster's condition, on the family's anticipated loss, on the parents' depletion, and on the child's options to participate in life through the ever remaining alternative of earning entitlement.

Characteristically, everyone in the family functions under the obligation to give and to care in direct proportion to the neediness of the sick child. The parents' neediness is usually ignored; yet parents in this situation can be more emotionally depleted than the dying youngster himself. Given this likelihood, it is often possible to generate resources for the grieving parents through enabling their child to give to them. In the process, the youngster's life is enhanced by his ability to tender care. "Help me tell my parents I'm going to die," a youngster in a pediatric oncology unit asked of a worker. The request cut across the worker's protective tendencies and professional training alike. The sick child can benefit from aiding the depleted grown-ups. There was loyalty, meaning and dignity in the request. The child's active offer of care to her parents also contributed to the parents' capacity to struggle with their grief and their need to continue to offer care.

The same kind of consideration applies to less dramatic situations, e.g., to families with a blind or deaf member who is constantly being protected. A family's chronic overprotectiveness of its handicapped member underrates and undercuts that person's potential to contribute to himself as well as to others. It reduces that person's life to an extension of his handicap. It makes one person's physical pathology the chief measure of everyone else's indebtedness. It induces withdrawal and a self-serving caution in family members whose protectiveness robs its handicapped member of the option to earn constructive entitlement. Consider the situation of two adolescents, both of whose parents are deaf, for example.

George, 16, has developed a violent temper. His father works at night, his older sister leaves to baby-sit, and he is left alone with his mother every night. If he leaves to do anything that he might enjoy, she drinks—heavily. The youngsters have grown to hate their mother's deafness. It isolates her and overburdens them, and has left everyone with feelings of helplessness and hopelessness. No one expects mother to be accountable for her demands, let alone help them with theirs.

When George's fury at his situation was played out in school, however, family work began. The therapist's multidirected intervention started with her use of an outside expert in sign language, thus releasing the children from being an addendum to their parents' handicap. *Ipso facto* each family member's needs were acknowledged as equally important. At least for the therapeutic hour, everyone could be addressed as a separate entity with separate goals as well as common obligations. Up to this point, no one had ever given words to their entitlement to live individuated lives.

In sum, overprotectiveness of one, heavily encumbered family member amounts to a loss for everyone but, worst of all, is an additional handicap to the person who least needs more burdens. Even more significantly, perhaps, it prevents one family member from gaining the liberating consequences of contributing to the welfare of others. Factual predeterminants and options are obviously limitless in form: Available social agencies, the usefulness of appropriate medications, large-scale social trends all hold factual significance for families and individuals. The sexual revolution, legalized abortion, single parenthood, the widespread phenomenon of legal divorce, the implications of remarriage, and the diminished functions of the extended family are all important factual determinants of relational dynamics. So, still, is the conception and birth of a child—events that continue to be factual consequences of the highest human order.

DIMENSION II: INDIVIDUAL PSYCHOLOGY

Contextual evaluations include the perspective of psychology which is always an individually-focused one. There is simply no psychological theory that simultaneously encompasses mental events of more than one person. Yet external events are activated through the perceiving, acting and reacting psyches of relating individuals. Individual motivations, then, have to be part of any comprehensive, relational assessment process. The psychological dimension involves a number of schools and orientations, of course. These include learning, conditioning, developmental and behavioral, hypnotic modalities as well as Adlerian, Freudian, Jungian, Rogerian, Gestalt and Sullivanian ones, among others. It is neither our task nor our goal here to diminish the wisdom or methodologies of these psychological approaches. We do mean to convey, however, that the factual, transactional and ethical aspects of relational reality are only partly translatable into the terms of the psychological dimension.

Psychological dynamics are essentially rooted in the dynamics of human striving for satisfaction or pleasure as noted by Freud. Contextual therapy acknowledges the pleasure-based foundations of existence but argues that capacity to sustain life and the freedom to enjoy life also come from offering responsible care and so from earning entitlement. Put in other terms, satisfying the multilateral criteria of relational ethics frees a person for optimum use of his or her psychological endowment. The signs of this liberation are partly psychological and partly physiological. On the one hand, entitlement results in improved self-esteem and a heightened sense of worth. On the other hand, it results in improved psychosomatic health, better sexual and reproductive functions, and sounder sleep.

Conversely, people often pay a high personal price when they are unable to transform their filial loyalties into some form of just due for long-rejected parents. The resultant failure to earn entitlement often cripples a person's capacity for enjoyment of any kind, and can result in chronic displeasure and dissatisfaction with life.

Diagnostic Aspects of the Psychological Dimension

The psychological dimension of relational reality is always associated with a descriptively diagnostic assessment of people in treatment. Psychobehavioral diagnostic categories fall short of full scientific validity almost by necessity. Besides, too often they are only loosely connected to the dynamics and planning of individual therapy. Diagnostic categories, however, also carry an administrative and legal significance. At best, they have a somewhat predictive value in terms of a person's behavioral tendencies. At worst, diagnostic categories can be misleading. They can emphasize and overstretch the significance of some general or partial truths and they often discourage a comprehensive grasp of relational motivations. In our view, it is insufficient to base therapeutic planning on a diagnostic scheme. For such schemes are not analogous to medicine. Diagnostic categories cannot transform psychotherapy into a method based on scientific evidence of causation.

Any analogy between medicine and psychotherapy is even further stretched if a "family diagnosis" is used as an indicator of relational therapy. First of all, a unitary scheme for relational diagnoses will be a long time in the making by family therapists and allied workers. Even if such a diagnostic category were attainable, it might easily lead to a false conclusion. If a "family diagnosis" were used as an alternate scheme to individual diagnosis, it might lead to the mistaken notion that family therapy is indicated only when a family diagnosis accompanies the identified patient's individual diagnosis.

In point of fact, indications for contextual therapy naturally evolve from individual diagnoses or from "symptomatic" designations. Families typically seek help for the alleged malfunctioning of one of the members, e.g., a school phobic child, an addictive adolescent, or a depressed mate. The symptom as the definition of underlying pathology, however, has already been transcended by dynamic, individually-oriented Freudian theory as well as by family therapy. At this time, attempts to create a scientific psychopathology to explain behavior, mental function, or even psychosomatic illness lack the rigor and data to prove scientific causality. Diagnostic categories like narcissism, depression, paranoia, or schizophrenia cannot be treated like objective data of physical medicine though they do have a practical value. Like psychotherapy itself, they represent a resource for help. Psychotherapy's scientific claim and rationale are rooted in the definability and consistency of its helping methods rather than in the comprehensive sweep of its diagnostic categories.

Individuation and Differentiation

Therapeutic assessments of any kind are always concerned with issues of individuation and differentiation to some degree. How they are addressed has to do with core notions that run through individual and family therapy alike. Issues of identity, for example, are viewed in a cognitive sense at times—knowing one's boundaries. At other times, identity is described in a dynamic, structural sense—referring to a person's cohesive or fragmented self. Differentiation also has to do with identity. As Freud saw it, identity formation indicated a person's emergence from a primary fusion or merger. In the language of classical family therapy, it can also be seen as an ongoing interpersonal struggle among relationships characterized by symbiosis, enmeshment, pseudomutuality, or an undifferentiated ego mass.

The contextual approach views self-validation via personal responsibility in relationships as the most significant criterion of individuation and differentiation. That is, the best way to consolidate a basis for secure, relational functioning is to offer fair consideration to significant others, including oneself. Contextual therapists help people explore each family member's options for earning entitlement or gaining self worth. Here the therapist is forcefully allied with everyone's individuation and differentiation. A full assessment of the existence of individual and family options within an organic context of indebtedness and entitlement is always indicated. The capacity to enable such assessments depends on a firm if flexible therapeutic expectation that clients take the risk of trying.

Consider the psychologist whose depletion was so complete that suicide seemed a reasonable and consistent option. Self-medicated and very astute, he presented himself as a "finished product," i.e., as someone who had forged his own personal and professional identity by massive and dedicated effort. His presenting problem, he insisted, was a marital one. His wife was coming into her own right and he felt threatened and abandoned by her successful attempts at autonomy.

His wife, as he saw it, had been his salvation, even his savior, for she had effectively "rescued" him from his family of origin. She had been everything that his parents were not: kind, understanding, enduring, acknowledging, compassionate, loving. Even they regard her as a saint. Life for him would have no meaning if his wife's personal and professional growth left him alone in the world, again isolated as he had been when they first met.

In assessing the situation, the therapist needed to differentiate marital issues from family of origin issues. Clear consideration had to be given to the client's despair, its sources and its consequences. His disappointment in his wife's need to shift the terms of their marriage contract *per se* is a legitimate life concern and a proper focus of therapy. From a contextual perspective, however, this man's primary therapeutic task had to do with long unsettled accounts with his family of origin.

Later sessions would disclose how his wife's unfinished business in her own family of origin was also skewing their marriage. Her husband and in-laws valued her peacemaking characteristics, a trait that so "differentiated" her from them. In her own context, though, her obligation to be the family peacemaker robbed her of the chance to act on her own entitlement to needs and claims. Peacemaking was a function assigned to her in early childhood; and it was one that she continued to perform in most relationships—to her own detriment. She was still invisibly loyal to her own family of origin, an indication of relational stagnation and ethical disengagement that obstructed her road to individuation.

In summary, the contextual therapist is certainly open and flexible to the legitimate needs of this couple to rebalance the entitlements and indebtedness that have accrued over an 18-year-old marriage. On the other hand, she is also obliged to identify 1) the roots of the couple's dilemma, 2) the fact that they are victims of each other's revolving slate, 3) the fact that they are most likely to rework their marital stagnation by addressing the imbalances that remain between them and their roots, and in the process, 4) the fact that they have options through which to earn increasing entitlement to individuate. The psychologically anchored goals of self-delineation (Dimension II), have to be complemented by effective efforts at each person's self-validation (Dimension IV).

One aspect of individuation falls under the rubric of *psychic development*, a process concept. In this view there is a phasic, sequential emergence of personality formation that extends from a human being's late embryonic stages to his or her death. Theoretical concepts as well as the observation of the young (people and animals alike) support the probable existence of an inner timetable of psychic propensities that is called critical phases in animal ethology. "Graduation" from one state to the next is predicated on the convergence of these critical phases with suitable environmental input, e.g., early imprinting.

Erik Erikson's theory of psychosocial development (1959) is prominent among the psychodynamic theories of development. For Erikson, the foundation of personality formation is essentially linked to the emergence of basic trust. The potential life dilemma here has to do with the infant's readiness to receive trustworthy parenting, as well as the question of whether the adult environment can live up to the infant's needs. Furthermore, all later stages of development presuppose a prior establishment of basic trust. Still further, new tests of a person's capacity to trust or mistrust are constantly occurring in adult relationships. The courage to risk trust in relationships is a primary requirement for commitment and devotion. Conversely, a blatant lack of courage to risk trust characterizes paranoid, suspicious people and an empty, disengaged and lonely life.

Subtle forms of mistrust permeate peer relationships, including marriage. Lasting marital mistrust often carries ominous consequences for the next generation, consequences most frequently associated with the predicament of split loyalties. An insufficient foundation for dealing with basic trust and mistrust leads to countless intergenerational and interpersonal injuries and injustices. It leads to clear manifestations of relational stagnation. It also leads to an unknown variety of developmental deficiencies for, according to Erikson, the mastery of the phase of basic trust and mistrust in a child affects the sequence of all of the later phases of his psychosocial development.

The consequences of an insufficient trust base in a person are readily identified in a variety of later function disorders. A case in point is the matter of regression, a "pathological" and age-inappropriate return to an earlier developmental level of functioning. For example, a psychotic adult can demand that his parents treat him like a baby, i.e., literally feed and dress him. Here, as in any severely regressed condition, the person may require institutionalization for the well-being of everyone involved. Usually, however, people are likely to make more progress in a prolonged struggle to grow if they continue to relate to their family members.

The degree of psychotic regression is not necessarily proportionate to an ultimately poor prognosis. In our experience, regressed people tend to stay inwardly receptive to honest and trustworthy input from significant relatives and caretakers. Indeed, if a language exists that can penetrate the psychotic's "crazy talk," it is the trustworthy language of relational fairness and devotion—whether or not it evokes an immediately appreciative response. The psychotic person's mistrust is entrenched and enduring and puts a special burden on his caretakers. Therapists are obliged to avoid exploiting that mistrust, either through silencing a manifest symptom or through manipulating a superficially "well-adjusted" transactional pattern.

A capacity to relinquish relationships and to draw strength from the process is an additional facet of the developmental point of view. Growth *per se* requires the acceptance of a continuous loss of old relational modes. It also requires people to risk the acquisition of new relational modes with the same partner or with others. People struggle with a lifelong need to tolerate radically shifting relational modes, starting with the child who absorbs the traumatic loss of breastfeeding and has to adopt a new pattern of relating to her mother. The concept of mourning work emphasizes each person's need to face up to losses and to develop the ability to remodel old patterns of relating into new ones. An inability to do mourning work or to divest oneself from lost relationships typically characterizes relational stagnation. The concept of mourning work connects the internal relational world of a human being with the interpersonal world. Therapeutic progress is heavily dependent on each person's capacity to "work through" his losses. In this regard, it resembles the work of mourning.

An Object Relations View

The object relations view of personality, especially with Ronald Fairbairn's formulations (1952), has been a major contribution to the field of psychotherapy from the psychoanalytic school. According to Fairbairn, the mind's relational structure does not begin at the time that it internalizes parental structure in the form of the ego ideal and superego. Rather the mind is inherently relational from its beginnings. Therefore, to paraphrase, an internal self or "ego" is intrinsically matched with an internal partner or "object." In this construct, it is painful for a person to invest in the bad aspects of his or her internal partner. So the self turns to an idealized, good internal other and thus creates a balance. In addition, the self usually projects the internal partner's bad attributes onto an unsuspecting, external partner.

Unfortunately, a person who represents a significant love relationship is the likely target for "projective identification" which is obviously one use of a relating partner. However, projective identification is unilaterally exploitative unless reciprocally practiced by both partners. It is exploitative to relate to a person as if he or she were simply an externalization of one's internal partner. For, in so doing, we fail to engage with a whole human being in a genuine dialogue. In Buber's (1923/1958) terms, our use of people in such ways reduces the quality of human connectedness, puts relationship on an I-it basis, and eliminates the option of an I-Thou exchange.

Projective identification can be associated in part with the contextual concept of parentification. Many parents discover that even their two- or three-year-old child can turn into a responsible caretaker. Very often, the young's capacity to function in such a role may exist in direct proportion to a parent's lack of responsibility. In any case, parentification can be an exploitative, dependence-seeking behavior. It can be a selfish use of relationship in which I create a "parent" who will relieve me of the hard demands of completing the work of mourning over past, lost relationships. Under the circumstances, I can continue to project attitudes of chronic dependence or to vent vengeful feelings on a parentlike figure. At the same time I can evade the fact that the burden of these feelings and attitudes were originally patterned for my deceased or otherwise "lost" mother and father.

Parentification is not always a destructive process. At one time or another, most parents cling to a child or lean on him or her emotionally and even physically. Children can benefit from these moments in terms of establishing trustworthiness, and in terms of self-esteem. Still, there is a realm of undue gain, psychological and transactional, that comes from 1) possessively holding onto a child, and 2) deriving unilateral benefits from him. When a parent's support and respect for a child's personality growth is obscured by goals that are essentially possessive and self-serving, then destructive parentification sets in. This kind of parentification does not necessarily have to take a form that is transactionally adultlike, efficient, "parental" child behavior (Minuchin, 1974). To the contrary. The worst manifestations of destructive parentification may be embodied in a child who is immobilized by failure, e.g., psychosis, delinquency or addiction. A child's immobilization may shield her parents from ever having to mourn the loss of their possession.

A full assessment of the degree of destructiveness in parentification includes an evaluation of the parentifying parent's capacity to eventually acknowledge the child's actual availability. A subtle but pervasive form of parentification consists of the destructive idealization of a child or adult. The idealized person is ascribed a superhuman degree of perfection and trustworthiness. This "use" of a person lets people externalize an internal need for a good parent. It also serves as a wishful allocation of trustable behavior, one that is free from deceiving an actual partner. Usually, destructive idealization is the first phase of destructive parentification. Inevitably the idealized person falls short of perfectionistic expectations, then becoming an alleged traitor and a target for "well-deserved" blame.

It is to be noted here that a combination of elements go into the kinds of displacement under discussion. The blind projection of internal partners onto other partners is rooted in psychological, transactional and ethical dimensions alike. For example, a person who has been exploited in childhood is likely to have earned destructive entitlement, too. For its part, destructive entitlement can add to the pleasure-based motivations of psychological regression. It can function to avoid the pain of the work of mourning that is required to relinquish inappropriate relational patterns. In a parallel vein, family members can consciously or inadvertently collude in avoidance and so transactionally reinforce regressive psychological patterns. A relationship may delay individuation and growth on everyone's part, and still be maintained because the need configurations of colluding partners fit into a pattern of mutual complementation.

Affect as a Contextual Indicator

In psychological theory, psychic events like affects are seen as being among the primary determinants of a person's behavior. In contextual theory, feelings, moods, emotional states, satisfactions, frustrations, sorrow, happiness, and exaltation among other affects are chiefly viewed as indicators of fundamental relational imbalances. Simply put, sustained affect is likely to be a legitimate indicator of the fairness or unfairness with which merits and debts, burdens and benefits are distributed in a given relational context over a given period of time. An entitled, if exploited, person is likely to be angry; an indebted, if ethically disengaged person, is likely to feel guilt. Affect then can be psychologically derived from personality development and from the relative fluctuations of satisfaction within a person. On the other hand, it can roughly indicate the balances of merit between people in the ethical dimension.

Subtle distinctions differentiate psychological reality from existential reality. A depressed person, for example, may experience a low sense of entitlement and a low sense of self-esteem. These feelings may exist whether or not that person is actually in the relational debt of other people. In different terms, a person who is actually in a high state of earned merit can nevertheless be manipulated into feeling guilty. Many people, for example, are conditioned to experience guilt on the occasion of any form of sexual satisfaction—whatever their degree of entitlement. Psychological guilt seems to abound for reasons that are both frivolous and profound. Nevertheless, in contextual work it is not to be confused with the existential guilt that occurs when the justice of the human order has been ruptured and injured (Buber, 1948). Paradoxically, perhaps, existential guilt can exist without concomitant psychological guilt. Whatever the juxtaposition between affect and entitlement, contextual therapists will take the opportunity to determine the ways in which a depressed person has cut himself off from options for earning merit.

A person exhibiting an uninhibited manic (or hypomanic) affect may have earned a high degree of merited entitlement. Or based on his childhood victimization, he may psychologically experience an ethically invalid sense of entitlement which diminishes his need to consider other people's terms. A person's warped feelings of entitlement may desensitize him to doing harm to innocent parties in current relationships. His insensitivity itself may be a consequence of the destructive entitlement of past injustices and victimizations. A close look at the revolving slate (Boszormenyi-Nagy & Spark, 1973) with its internal ethical contradictions is always indicated in the face of heightened affect.

In summary, a person's affect can indicate the approximate balance and imbalance of fairness in a given set of relationships. *Ipso facto*, though, affect cannot function as the sole measure of earned entitlement. To complete any assessment of a relationship's balances of entitlement and indebtedness, partners' terms and entitlements have to be considered. For the difficult truth of relationship is that one person's self-satisfied attitudes of altruism or generosity are not necessarily consonant with another person's rights and needs, however close or beloved that person may be. What is more, one person's criteria for due consideration have to be tested even if they prove to be remarkably similar to the partner's expectations and terms. Earned merit simply cannot be separated from its context of multilateral reality, nor can it be earned outside of dialogic claims and counterclaims.

Relational merit is not a possession, it is a teleological entity. It is a goal or direction at which we can aim through offering due consideration to a significant partner. Merit can be earned regardless of how momentarily entitled or indebted a person is to another person. A contextual assessment helps people explore *all* of their future options for earning entitlement in a heretofore stagnant relational context. A therapist hinders this process if he is sidetracked into passing judgment on who among the family members is the most or least meritorious.

Mature Strength

Maturity, from an individual perspective, is equated with a person's capacity to function with a minimum of intrapsychic conflict. The limitation of this definition is that it stops short of assessing the relative strength of relating partners. For example, if a mature person becomes more open-minded and accessible, is his maturity bound to be undercut by his partner's narcissism or effective manipulations? How do maturity and power gains converge and correlate?

In close relationships, one person's short-term power gains over another have to be balanced by a consideration of long-term merit. Unilateral expediency is always struggling for balance with the long-term ethical (merit) and psychological consequences for the actor. Self-serving manipulations are also in a struggle for balance with the generative responsibility of being a trustworthy parent. For example,

Larry, a married man, had a lover and decided to leave his wife. Over several years he lived away from home and entered into his children's lives primarily at his own convenience. Financially well off, he lived pretty much on his own terms, in part as a result of his own destructive entitlement. Eventually, he returned "home" when his love affair seemed threatened. He found that the former incompatibility between him and his wife had grown and decided to seek a divorce. His plans to leave for good were interrupted, however, when his 12-year-old began to "act out" at school. Teachers reported a sudden rowdiness and demand quality to the boy's behavior. At about the same time, the youngster drew a picture of a sad and frightened boy who was saying, "Mother, Dad, help!" "This changes everything," Larry reflected. "I've handed my own miserable legacy down to my son, and that was the last thing I wanted to do."

Larry's power manipulations and unilateral expediency worked for him for a long time. Eventually, though, they had consequences for his own life and context: They furthered his indebtedness and wounded his deep-felt, legacy-based commitment to offer his children a "better life" than he himself had had.

The loss of entitlement, that is, the consequence of relying on unfettered power aspirations can show itself in a variety of ways. These include a diminished freedom to enjoy the aspects of life that are creative and pleasurable. They also include loss of sleep and appetite, and psychosomatic illnesses. In Larry's case as in any other therapeutic situation, a contextual worker will be helping each related member develop options for earning entitlement. Larry's effective manipulations and self-serving expediency had a life of their own, but one whose consequences eventually provided impetus for him to reconsider their effect on the next generation. Here, as in all other efforts, contextual therapists will have little interest in helping partners equalize power-based transactional gains. Their primary interests in helping Larry and his family will be in building the foundations for the equity of genuine dialogue.

Individuals in Dialogue

In our use of the word, dialogue is meant to convey a mutuality of commitment rather than a verbal exchange. Moreover, in our view, mature dialogue is the greatest of all the resources of relationship. A mutuality of commitment to responsible care embodies both communication and action, and characterizes intergenerational exchange among people who significantly contribute to each other. It is a simple fact that the members of each new generation *have* to receive responsible care from members of preceding generations. The commitment to provide care to the next generation is forward-thrusting rather than feedback-like. Like other animals who are responsible for feeding and sheltering their young, human beings engage in a protective dialogue with the future of their progeny. For example, our present concern (or lack of it) about the clean air and water requirements of posterity is essentially a dialogue with our children's right to life.

A contextual assessment of family resources incorporates both the self-delineating and the self-validating phases of the dialogic process. The self-delineating phase is chiefly psychological in nature: One person relies on others. In so doing, he gains a chance to test himself against them as his ground. A lonely father decides to telephone his son, for example. His son's reactions to the call may be impatient or rejecting. Still the father retains the chance to relate to someone who is a source of meaning to him. On the other hand, his call to his son may be self-validating. Perhaps the son, too, is lonely and benefits from the sound of his father's voice. The prospect of diversified and mutual benefits is a built-in feature of relationships, and makes them natural arenas for personal (centripetal) gain for each partner. Assertive mastery, e.g., the capacity to speak up or to overcome sexual fears, are among the self-serving benefits to be gained from relationship.

A person's lessened reliance on internal relational patterns is also a caring offer (centrifugal) to his or her partner. The withdrawn psychotic who depends on the "presence" of hallucinatory or imagined partners is an extreme example of self-confined, internal reliance. In these situations, people sometimes refer to the "voices" in their lives in warm, complimentary tones (Hollender and Boszormenyi-Nagy, 1958). They act as if they were speaking of trustworthy companions who have altered a felt condition of profound loneliness. Intermediate, internal and external relatedness all shows in projective identification (Klein, 1948; Fairbairn, 1952). In the doing, the "other" is forcibly cast into an image of the internalized relational partner, typically one of a suspect, negative character. From his side, the captive target of projective identification usually finds it difficult to realize what benefits accrue to the desperate projector from this process of maligning.

The fact remains that two "live" parties who test their perceptions of relationship against each other can reduce the consequences of one-sided exploitation. Exploitativeness characteristically gives way to fairness if partners can take the risk of surfacing their own needs and claims. People also increase their own self-gain if they can make room for the genuine needs, interests and entitlement of their partners. Making room for the needs of others while honoring one's own needs are the rudiments of constructive entitlement and interpersonal maturity. Conversely, a permanent inability to be responsive to the needs of others is characteristic of psychological immaturity as well as of destructive entitlement.

DIMENSION III: SYSTEMIC PATTERNS OF TRANSACTIONS AND POWER

Like the psychological dimension of reality, the transactional and communicational dimension of reality is a significant component in contextual assessments. Here it is useful to draw on the traditional descriptions of classical (systemic) family therapy. Terms like patterns or structures of manifest behavior, role distributions, subsystems, power alignments, generational boundaries, triangulation, enmeshment, marital schism and skew, pseudomutuality, cutoffs, and double-binding communications all apply to

Dimension III. This dimension of relatedness is typically observable in the form of feedback.

Behaviors that are linked to the family of origin connect one person's patterns with those of another person. The motivations and purposes of close relatives eventually collide or converge with each other. In the process people are competitive and enter into alliances with one another to strengthen or consolidate their own directions or goals. The patterns of hierarchy, competition and alliance can be interpreted in power terms. In these instances, power can be defined as survival efforts, or purposive, competitive striving. To be sure, power dynamics are part of human survival. Yet a view of therapy that excludes psychological and ethical determinants of human behavior is reductionistic, shortsighted and dangerous.

Power is diffuse in all systems of life, of course; and its fluctuations are always creating a new victor and victim. The process of victimizing or being victimized is of significance to the people who are involved. Even more significance, perhaps, may be attached to the consequences of the victimizing process for posterity. A case in point ostensibly has to do with the consequences of a woman's choice to enter into a second marriage shortly after her first husband's sudden and untimely death.

A woman loses her husband when he is 39 years old, and marries a family friend. She is soon disappointed, even ashamed, of the ways in which he responds to her children. He is stern, distant and possessive of her whenever the youngsters are present. She accommodates to the marriage for she sees no other choice. She had been severely traumatized by the circumstances and consequences of her first husband's death, a series of events that convinced her of life's unreliability. She has also been frightened of long-term loneliness.

Her second husband's destructive demands and her compliance with them certainly victimized her but had massive consequences for her children. Anger, depression and resentment have characterized their lives together, and fundamental questions remained unaddressed: Was their mother a saint? If so, how could they ever measure up to her? Or was she simply a composite of everyone else's expectations, without even a core of self? If so, could her own children ever be entitled to selves of their own?

Here patterns of power as a dynamic force were of extreme significance to each of the people involved. But the relationship as a whole can hardly be explained away as a power struggle or as forces of a self-maintaining feedback system. To reduce human struggle like that and to ignore the existential perspectives of each striving and feeling individual is to trivialize life. This kind of reductionism is akin to explaining a city's traffic pattern as a self-sustaining dynamic rather than as a composite of cars, buses and trucks driven by people motivated to earn a living by getting to work.

In our view, then, power-based transactional patterns are usually only determinants of short-term behavior—even when they appear to be regulators. The complementary aspects of overdependent and overindependent behavior, for example, often reinforce each other in molding a pattern of dependent relating. Even so, a transactional pattern alone cannot account for the fundamental determinants of two people's behavior. The basic determinants of human behavior originate from a mix of personal goals, motives and capacities. However, some of these factors are anchored in complex balances of fairness in relationships.

Close relationships cannot survive or thrive simply on power dynamics. Nor can close relationships be assessed solely on the basis of competition. Family life is not analogous to the power-based aspirations of the marketplace nor of national and international politics and exchange. Where is the room for emotional reliance, generosity, nurturance, love, and gratitude if the rules of businesslike behavior invade and dominate the home? Power and competition exist in families but there is no future for parent and small child if they alone are the bases for care. Nurturance of the young always requires a responsible and caring investment on the part of the parenting adult.

The essence of parent-child relationships can never be explained away by neat-sounding, power-based formulations if they are to survive. Even male-female relationships require a generous allotment of room for care, despite the degree to which they are shaped by emotional needs and power-based transactions. Beyond the life of the couple's relationship is the intrinsic responsibility for real or prospective children as well.

Contextual therapists, then, learn to search beyond the power dynamics in a family. They also learn to contain the tendency to battle for the control of power with their clients. A family's resistance to therapy is typically collusive and indicates the limits of the therapist, of the family members, or of both. This collusion may effectively block the therapist's moves for a while. Realistically, though, the therapist cannot be "defeated" unless he clothes himself in the role of a magician who is supposed to perform miracles. Secretiveness, like magic, is not a source of strength for therapists, either. It is surely regrettable if a client has read his therapist's books and the therapist has to discover that her strategies no longer work (Dell, 1981). But, in fact, there is no one technique, method or strategy which characterizes contextual therapy—short of the therapist's ability to rely on each member's willingness to define his or her own side of the relational dialogue. The realities uncovered by multidirected caring provide a source of therapeutic leverage that far exceeds anything produced by the power-based manipulations of family members and therapist, working together or alone.

Our intention here is not to deny the realm of power that exists in families and in other close relationships. It is meant to argue for the possibility that even power can be tempered by ethical concern. For instance, issues relating to wealth and money in families are unquestionably anchored in the dimension of power. Money can buy both things and persons; it functions as one real measure of survival strength. Furthermore, a person's manipulation of relatives through the means of money is an important, if avoided, part of relationships. The following questions exemplify the convergence of power and a relational ethic around money matters: What are the relational criteria by which aging parents leave their material wealth to their children? Is a parent's will a matter of open record to his or her children and if not, why not? Can adult children take the chance of talking about their parents' will or offer advice that may alter its terms?

An overriding focus on money matters in a family always accompanies its members' basic impoverishment of fair give-and-take. Consider the example of a couple and their two sons, age 14 and 11, who for three sessions talked about the stress and tension in their home.

Father's temper stood at the center of the family's myth about why nobody in the family can get along. Finally, after three sessions, Mrs. E began to talk about her in-laws with contempt. Mr. E visibly "shrunk" at her statements, but agreed that his parents and three siblings were "losers" and "takers" who "had never offered a kind gesture or word to anyone," especially to him. He said that he'd given time, effort and financial aid to each member of his family, but that nothing he gave was ever enough. He'd just rather have no contact with any of them anymore.

Mr. E works with his elder brother at the "family store." Their father died two years ago. Since then, his younger brother has taken money to support a drug addiction, and the two older brothers recently fired him. "We would have kept him if he had been willing to seek medical help," Mr. E said. "Instead he moved back home with our mother." Both of his brothers have recently been divorced and their wives' claims on the business have created additional burdens for Mr. E. Furthermore, Mrs. E has made life "next to impossible" for him by insisting that he invite his whole family over at every holiday. "It's good for the children," she insists, and "Besides, *my* own parents live so far away." "She just won't butt out," he bitterly complains. "No matter what happens, it's always the same."

Unaddressed by Mr. E is his anger at paying more for the business than it was worth. "What do you do," he asks, "when your grey-haired mother who lives in a nearby suburb thinks that things are coming to her? "What do you do when your brother embezzles the last of her nest egg?'' Not surprisingly, Mr. E's 14-year-old is the identified patient. Echoing his father's untenable situation, Charles complains that he is always on the ''losing team.''

Like his son, Mr. E is the parentified child in his family of origin. Like Charles, he is reduced to helplessness by the absolute quality of everybody's dissatisfaction with their own lives, and hence with his. But worst of all, is Mr. E's rage at his father who rewrote his will shortly before he died. ''My father tried to rule all of us from the grave,'' Mr. E observes, ''but I didn't learn about it until 11 months after his death.

''My one brother and I technically got everything. The other three got left out entirely. Of course, I've paid for that; they're all resentful even though each of them has gotten a lot of money over the years. Eventually, I came up with a compromise: I estimated the cost of the business and divided it six ways. No one was satisfied though. What's worse, the compromise conceals the real issue. My father robbed the till before he died.''

Inheritances always have consequences for the legatees. In this vivid instance, the relationships of at least three generations were harmed by a husband's and father's close to total lack of fair consideration for their specific interests and needs. Here the family business (and the father's destructive entitlement) overrode any real concern for marital or parent-child relationships. What is more, the marriages of the offspring were also altered by monetary considerations. In this as in other families, all in-laws were treated as if they were inferior; their status was reduced to that of employees in the ''family store.'' The collaborative efforts that still exist in the E family obviously rely on power as their main determinant. The dilemma here is the kind of transactional configurations that are being conveyed to the next generation.

How can therapists help couples establish fairer and, therefore, more effective patterns of cooperation for themselves and for their children? Can therapy influence the kind of teamwork on which the young learn to depend? Despite their good intentions, Mr. and Mrs. E are not only mistrustful mates but also mistrustful parents who play their children like pawns in a chess game. The youngsters' own needs to thrive and gain are secondary to each parent's push to dominate the board. Their mistrustful patterns of relating have already placed their 11- and 14-year-old sons into a tragic predicament of split loyalty. The children inherit the impossible task of having to undo the consequences of parental mistrust.

Relationships obviously have to rely on communications and transactions. However, their costs in power terms can be mitigated or intensified. Mrs. E, for example, appeals to her older son to substantiate her contempt for her husband and his father. ''Ask Charles if you don't believe me,'' she instructs the therapist. In a sentence she manages to split Charles from his father, to parentify him in a massively destructive way, and to demonstrate how useless it is to hope for a cooperative stance from Mr. E. The depth of their parents' mistrust is grossly evident to both sons.

Destructive parentification is rooted in a chronically deep level of mistrust between father and mother, and it comes in many forms. Paradoxically, perhaps, overt expressions of destructive parentification are typically preferable to covert expressions. Underlying parental mistrust manifested in open, even vicious, fighting between father and mother tends to be more easily handled by the young than a set of superficially smooth, well-rehearsed and deceptive interactions. Parentification is not always linked to negative consequences, of course. There are times of necessity in every family when children are expected to act with adult-like responsibility with both helpful and unhelpful results. On the other hand, a parent's failure to acknowledge a young child, instead heaping guilt feelings on him, is destructive *ipso facto*.

The concept of parentification has evolved from an intrinsically descriptive and transactional notion to an increasingly trust-based and ethical one (Boszormenyi-Nagy & Spark, 1973). Minuchin (1974) has aptly used the phrase "parental child" to describe the phenomenon of a youngster burdened with age-inappropriate expectations by the adults in his or her family. This usage continues in the transactional formulations of classical family therapy. From a contextual view, occasional inverted parenting can sometimes be partially beneficial. On the other hand, dependent, parental possessiveness can be most devastating when it is reinforced with unfair blaming and a lack of due acknowledgment. This kind of burden retards a child from growing up and from ever gaining independence. It follows, then, that infantilization is the worst and costliest manifestation of parentifying behavior. Ultimately, the "failing" offspring, that is, the psychotic, the addict or the serious criminal, will never become a maturely responsible adult.

DIMENSION IV: RELATIONAL ETHICS

Relational ethics, that is, the response and outcome of genuine dialogue, is the fourth dimension of relating and the most difficult to assess. The dynamics of fairness, reliability and trustworthiness are omnipresent in relationships. Yet they often seem to defy definition. Psychologically, the word "ethics" is subject to confusion, fraught as it is with connotations of authoritarianism, moralizing and utopian ideals. Transactionally, public life and the marketplace are so characterized by power manipulations and expedient schemes that it is difficult to identify the pervasive relevance of relational ethics. This fourth dimension of relational reality cuts across the psychic experience of individuals and across the competitive power lines that exist between individuals and groups. Therapeutic interest and interventions have traditionally focused on the clues characteristic of Dimensions II and III.

Common usage of the term "ethics" typically connotes an individual's selfless, even self-sacrificing, consideration of persons or principles. "Relational ethics are distinguished by the proposition that no one individual or group can ever function as the sole measure of the whole of *any* relational situation" (Cotroneo & Krasner, 1981). Hence, terms like altruism and self-interest can be understood only in a context that considers all sides. Relational ethics are concerned with the equitable distribution of the benefits and burdens of all partners to a given situation. They simultaneously consider the terms and claims of each active and passive participant who is affected by the consequences of a relating party's actions. Given this measure of human behavior, a therapist can help clients address themselves to the matter of equity among all members of the relational context that he is treating. In the process, he is relieved of the task of trying to decide who or what is right or wrong.

A family's joint assessment of the equity among them is the initial step in the process of implementing relational ethics. This includes an assessment of even unchangeable injustices in each person's destiny. A redistribution of credits, benefits and burdens comes next. The question of distributing credits and benefits is crucial for the family evaluation. On the other hand, people can turn to the sphere of power with its reliance on simple, competitive struggles to accrue additional benefits. From this vantage point, scapegoating is a common phenomenon. Here a family can blame one of its members without ever having to face or to hear the merit on his or her side. In Dimension III, the stronger person or alliance easily "wins" by virtue of greater power and by outright dismissal of the "losing" partner's terms. The spurious dismissal or rejection of one partner's terms is intrinsically exploitative and cannot occur without the leverage of power.

Take the situation of the father who "robbed the till" of the company store before he died, for example. He probably felt that what he took was only his rightful due. He earned it in the first place, he might have reasoned, and so he owed no explanations. On the other hand, Mr. E and his siblings see it in other ways. Their father's actions have had unconsidered consequences for them. Yes, what he did probably fell within his legal rights. Yes, it was his money in the first place, and in part, a yield on his early investments. Why, then, shouldn't he have spent it exactly as he liked? At these levels their father might be considered a winner.

In the family's view, though, their father clearly seems to have "ripped the family off" and left them holding the bag. What are they supposed to do about their mother who now expects financial support from *them*? And what about their younger brother who now needs caretaking too? Where, in the outcome of father's manipulative stance, is there room for anyone else's claims but his own? Where is the acknowledgment or record of the merits and contributions of family members other than father? What about the grandchildren and how they have been pitted against each other by their parents' competing claims? What kind of hope is there for quality relationships between Mr. E. and his siblings who are already mired in blame?

The unalloyed use of power in families has other consequences, too. Consider the 70-year-old man who recently retired from a successful real estate business. He lived luxuriously and wanted for nothing, but was afflicted with intractable insomnia. No medical reason could be discovered nor did the insomnia yield to medication. Eventually, though, Mr. F could identify some doubts he was experiencing over the shrewd ways in which he had wound up his business affairs. Long-trusted associates had been affected and Mr. F was having second thoughts. Sound as it may like a morality play, he could not live with his actions. His insomnia eventually started to give way to some restful sleep when he began to explore options for redressing the injuries he had done to the balance of fairness between him and his associates and their investments.

A person's ability or willingness to face his own attitude vis-à-vis his relating partners' sides *ipso facto* is a positive and promising sign. Conversely, a person's consistent resistance to a reckoning that may involve his own culpability is generally a telling indication of 1) a narcissistic personality structure, 2) a communications and transactional impasse, and 3) a person's destructive entitlement. A client's cold-blooded, remorseless exploitation of another family member provides a therapist with reliable clues about the failure of fairness. It can also evoke a sense of disgust in the therapist and a visceral reaction from her.

Like other people, therapists can be hard hit by the blatancy of chronically unfair relating. A man's sexual abuse of his three-year-old is a difficult fact to take. How therapists use family clues is a matter of real import. Like family members, therapists can block their awareness, and retreat to a "technical" plane. They can follow the clues and draw out implications within a strictly psychological or transactional framework. Or they can choose to incorporate the ethical plane as well. The evaluation of relational ethics can seldom be done solely from direct signs. The evidence of trustworthiness is linked to the continuing, live investments that people make in their relationships with each other. The balance of fairness among them determines the quality of their trust-base. Still, the balance oscillates as relationships go on. No fixed balance can ever finally be established that can permanently stay fair or unfair. What matters over time is the degree to which people care about the consequences of their input and everyone's prospects of a fair share.

Contextual therapists offer their clients a singular kind of commitment by their attention to the ethical dimension. In fact, a therapist's work on an ethical level requires a high degree of commitment on the parts of both the therapist and the client. For here the emphasis falls neither on empathy nor on affect. Here psychological and transactional expertise is secondary to a capacity to risk questions that pertain to inclusive, fair multilaterality.

> Have you failed your family or have they failed you? How? What can be done to transform these real and felt failures? To whom can you turn to help you assess and rework them? Are your expectations of each other realistic? Do you test your assumptions or keep them locked up inside? What will the costs of testing them be? If you're unsure of what you want, can you say so? If not, why not? Do family members retreat to moralisms and ideologies when they lack firm individual and relational ground? When there is violence among you, can you still hear each other's sides? When one of you is judgmental, can the other still state his or her side? What kinds of criticism are shame-producing? Who in the family can affirm people for who they really are? (Krasner, 1986). What do you think you give your partner in return? Can you acknowledge him for what he gives? Who is giving more? How can you tell?

Questions directed to all parties to a situation and to both sides of a conflict are indicative of a high level of therapeutic commitment. Here the therapist is choosing to invite an open exchange between people who are already significant to each other. He is choosing to take the face-to-face risks intrinsic to a dialogic stance. Neither judge nor arbiter, he is choosing to extricate his own terms from the middle of other people's relationships. In sum, he is choosing to help people weave the fiber of close and lasting relationships.

Consider the circumstance of a welfare recipient, the single head of a household with six children. Five of them were present in the session. The sixth child, a mentally retarded daughter in need of massive amounts of care, was absent.

> The interviewer addressed mother. "Who is there to help you," he asked. "No one," she replied. Her answer evoked an immediate response from her eldest daughter, who seemed hurt and distraught. "That's just not true," she cried, "and it's also unfair. I'm there and working all of the time! Doesn't what I do count for something?" Tension and conflict were in the room but so were the beginnings

of a longed-for exchange. The stage was now set for a vital interview in which the life interests of all family members were involved and might finally be joined. Once issues of each member's essential investments could come to the surface, the therapist could step back into an essentially catalytic role.

To facilitate a potentially healing exchange, a therapist has to master the method of multidirected partiality. A capacity to be open to questions of fairness between parent and child, or between husband and wife offers family workers the chance to help their clients in extremely sensitive, even delicate, ways.

The areas of trustworthiness and mutuality of commitment offer people the most effective resources for hope, care and fresh investments of good will. They are also the areas in which a person can suddenly and forcefully feel assaulted, insulted, exploited, betrayed, and desperately alone. Therapists can help to stabilize the emotional volatility attached to this relational dimension simply through their willingness to address justice issues, to acknowledge them as valid, and to structure room for them in the therapeutic domain. A therapist's ability to address the ethical dimension of conflict between closely-related people offers his clients a reasonably safe forum for spontaneously examining justice issues.

People typically confine their concern for justice issues to an internal monologue within themselves, or rely on a forum that is built into their relationships, even if that forum is tentative or peripheral. Now, in the therapy room, a new and intentional hearing place is being offered, a court of last resort, if you will. This hearing place is not to be confused with judging, though. For judging is neither the rightful goal nor the rightful method of therapy, though the use of judgment does, of course, occur. Here, however, a distinction is in order. A difference exists between assuming authority to point to the relative merit of people's integrity and hence the degree of trustworthiness that exists between them, and the availability of therapeutic expertise. Seen from another side, there simply is no way for a therapist to ignore the intrinsic "tribunal" function (Boszormenyi-Nagy, 1983) that is inherent in all mutual efforts, past and present, to build a life in common. Consider the situation between Pam, 37, and her 67-year-old mother, Marian.

Pam came into therapy because she was deeply depressed. "I feel like nobody ever listens," she complained. "My husband acts like my four-year-old and my mother acts that way too. I've been divorced before and maybe it's what I need to do again. I need electricity in my life, romance; or else I want a baby. We've been trying for over a year but nothing's happening."

Over the course of 16 weeks Pam did some individual work and then brought in her husband. It was abundantly clear that they had issues of their own which Bob was ready, though frightened, to face. Pam seemed disappointed in Bob's openness; she wasn't sure if it was even worth trying. It would have been easier for her if Bob had just quit. The marriage was clearly suffering from her past hurts and injuries. Long-unfaced issues between Pam and her parents were constricting her life and undercutting all her relationships. Then her mother came East from Texas and began to come to therapy.

Pam wanted to hear her mother say something good about her father who has been dead for over nine years. Her own memory of her father was of a man who didn't have much time for her and who regarded all women as sluts. She also remembers that just before he died she went to see him and they talked as never before. He told her he cared for her and really always had. He knew that he had been seductive towards her and wished that he could have done better. She experienced some consolation from that exchange but was never able to share it with her mother without getting a negative reply.

Marian saw things differently. Her husband was no good, had given her nothing, treated her mother badly, and was indifferent to Pamela's needs. Worst of all, he had always been involved with other women, never really left his first wife, and lied all of the time. She had lived with him for over five years before he consented to marriage and then only after she got pregnant. Marian wanted to better her relationship with Pam but didn't know how. She was willing to talk about Pam's father but could only say negative things. And her anger at Pam was unremitting though she didn't know it. First of all, she simply couldn't understand why Pam remained attached to her father, given who he was. Secondly, she couldn't understand how Pam could regard her maternal grandmother as her "real mother and pal" when Marian had spent so much of her life energy working to keep the family in food and Pam at the orthodontist's. "You sure couldn't count on him for that!," she exclaimed. "Why can't Pam see the difference?"

The weight of a ledger between mother and daughter had frozen them into hard judgments of each other, but also helped them surface the injuries that each believed they had suffered at the other one's hands.

People tend to think of each other in terms of good and bad, right and wrong. Whatever the temptation to join them, therapists do well to seek another way. If the tribunal function between closely-relating people can neither be eradicated nor overruled, how can its energy be harnessed? How can its forcefulness be tamed? From the perspective of a dialogic stance, therapists do well to help activate a client's capacity to hear out his partner's side and to learn how to become an adequate advocate for himself. A therapist's most effective option is a multidirected one, i.e., the option of eliciting a mutually responsible exploration of the merit of people's claims in the midst of colliding vested interests.

Contextual therapists operate on the premise that they can do no more on behalf of their clients than clients will do for themselves. The dialogic process requires a proportionate effort between client and therapist, including a proportionate response. The therapist commits his or her availability as a curious, considerate and empathetic fellow human being in *direct proportion* to the client's investment of integrity and trust in a dialogic exploration. She is willing to help people explore the balances of the credits and debits that exist between them and to help them identify fresh options for relating. She is unwilling, however, to play the role of judge. His or her ability to accompany people into the dialogic exploration is supported by the reliability of a multidirectional methodology.

Multidirected partiality represents a pragmatic effort to gain access to the prevailing order of justice in a family's relationships. It is a way to harness the energy of the tribunal function that exists between people of significance to each other. The more experienced and skillful the therapist, the more he or she is able to explore the balances of give-and-take between family members—and do so via an assessment that offers fair consideration to the symmetry of expectations. Clients always benefit from a fresh opportunity to activate the built-in forum of the relationship. This forum becomes available when one or more family members can

- Find the courage to open up and disclose themselves and their claims;
- Consider the untoward consequences of taking people's integrity for granted;
- Review the dilemma of taking without giving in return, and of giving and not taking in return;
- Grasp the implications of exploiting a person's goodwill as if it were a weakness.

Multidirected partiality offers an intervention that can penetrate the stagnation that comes of despair, for example, when people have given up their quest for fairness; when they have abandoned all efforts to surface their own claims; or when they have become cynical over ever trying to validate themselves through offering fair consideration and care. A multidirected methodology is the most direct route to reworking damaging, if unwitting, forms of family exploitation.

The Exploitative Aspect of Delegation

Inducing a child to carry out implicit missions for the benefit of his or her parents or other predecessors ranks among the most binding forms of relational exploitation. In this process of "delegation" (Stierlin, 1974), filial motives eventually coalesce with destructive parental expectations. The more subtle the delegation or inducement, the more difficult it will be for the child to extricate himself from it. In our view the concept of delegation is usually meant to describe the consequence of a transaction between parent and child that is solely determined by the parents' self-serving needs. For example, consider the mother and her firstborn, a 13-year-old boy.

The boy's father died when John was four and after a while mother remarried. Neither his father's death, a long and painful one, nor his mother's remarriage was ever discussed so John was left to handle his emotions by himself. Eventually mother and her second husband had children of their own, and the strain between John and his mother became increasingly pronounced.

Mother became more and more discouraged. She knew little or nothing about her adolescent son except that he failed her and drove her to despair. "If only John would obey the rules, offer help instead of waiting to be told, babysit without a fuss, and end his requests for more time and space and privileges of his own, everyone's life could improve." Riveted to his disappointing qualities, she was unable to acknowledge the resources between her and John, the humor, or the momentary bond of their eye-to-eye exchange.

From John's perspective, mother always had her way and he could never win. Look what had happened about the therapy session today. He didn't want to attend but he was here, wasn't he? It was true that he didn't want to babysit but he did, didn't he? And what was wrong with biking to the mall? The other guys did it. Why couldn't he?

Like other teen-age boys, John's size and appearance belied his immaturity. Tall and sturdily built, he towered over his mother and stepfather. Half child and half man, he acted like a colt. In the session he fought back timidly but with strong intent. Whenever his mother spoke, he sneaked glances at her. Whenever he spoke, he turned to her for clarification, validation and support and he tried to protect her when hard questions came her way. It was clear, though, that he felt powerless in the face of her authority. It was equally clear that mother knew nothing of her leverage with her son, and so could only complain of his shortfalls.

Commenting at the end of the session, the therapist acknowledged the tensions between them as well as the nonverbal expressions of caring that seemed to flow between mother and son. "I don't think he really cares at all," mother rebutted. "If he did, why would he always be off on his own? Why doesn't he help when he sees that I'm busy? If he cared, I wouldn't be working so hard."

Mother's own history with men had been generally disappointing. She seems to see her father as a shadow figure. Her first husband's death, just when he was on the verge of success after many lean and sacrificial years, had traumatized and depleted her. Her second marriage is a difficult if caring one, but the professional demands on her husband make him more unavailable than not. As for the younger children, they simply create too many demands on mother that are too burdensome much of the time. And for the most part she is forced to care for them alone.

The issue before us has little to do with whether John owes his mother age-appropriate help. Obviously, he does. It has little to do with whether a 13-year-old has to live by family guidelines. Certainly he cannot function as a free-floating entity answerable only to himself.

The question before us is "Whom can John afford to trust?" If his side is wholly and consistently deemed invalid, what are his chances of ever developing adequate trust in the world around him? Mother may not know it but she has inadvertently colluded in a process in which she has become the beneficiary of her child's parentification. Her actions and expectations of John reach far beyond delegation by transaction. The damaging circumstances that affect one generation can and do impose binding delegations on subsequent generations.

Legacies as Transgenerational Mandates

Inadvertently or intentionally, delegations are externally imposed expectations or missions that one generation places upon another. To compound the problem, life itself poses expectations of the young that are often transgenerational in nature. The very fact of receiving life, nurturance and tools of survival behooves offspring to care about their own contributions to posterity. Thus, in one or another way each of us ponders the question of how our available endowments, conveyed to us from the past, can benefit the future. A cost is associated with transgressing this "law of parenting" that characterizes the entire animal kingdom: A developmental handicap affects the offspring and a state of disentitlement affects the parent.

A parent-like accountability to posterity is each generation's primary mandate. The quality of accountability is an act of loyalty evoked by the beneficence of each generation's inherited endowment and its capacity to bequeath endowment. Obviously, rigid loyalty to the past through an offspring's blind or ritualistic obeisance to all of his or her parents' preferences, customs or traditions is no guarantee of a beneficial heritage for posterity. It can and does behoove members of each generation to consider what in their inheritance is intrinsically valuable and so deserves to be reshaped and transmitted to posterity.

Shame, survivorship, split loyalty, emigration, and the ability to merge and synthesize both parents' legacies into one's own are all aspects of transgenerational mandates that a contextual assessment addresses. For example, a parent's longing that children be loyal to his or her past may require the undoing of ancestral shame. Exonerating predecessors, especially if they are viewed as reprehensible or vicious, may represent a special burden. It may also represent a special resource. For if due exoneration can take place and human error understood, residual trust can be identified, developed and activated. On the other hand, if offspring are convinced that a parent is beyond exoneration, residual trust is automatically eclipsed and mistrust becomes their prevailing milieu.

Nowhere is the "failure of exoneration" between the generations more of an evident dilemma than in the offspring of parents who lived in Germany under Hitler's Third Reich. Examples abound of offspring whose parents' affiliations with the Nazi regime keep them bound in shame, contempt, resentment, and guilt. Consider the person whose deep loyalty to his father keeps him double-bound. In a letter he wrote,

I hope you can be forgiving to the second generation of holocaust perpetrators. I have had to work very hard to face my identity as a member of this generation. I had to pull myself out of a debilitating melancholy and then establish boundaries between this legacy and me. I had to learn that I needed boundaries for my own protection, to help me handle my grief over lost time and a corrupt history. I had to divert the energy I was spending on injured self-love, self-pity and accusations against people like you. Next I had to understand the depth of my fear and resistance to my father. It hurt to admit that, of all my siblings, I am the child most like him. It also hurt to realize how well denial, suppression and evasion have worked for me. I just don't want to come closer to my father. My ability to reject him seems to protect me from rejecting myself.

Recently, I told him that I visited the concentration camp at Dachau with a Jew. He seemed to turn pale. "Why did you do that?" he asked. "There wasn't any reason for it." I finally had my opening. I forced him to talk about the Third Reich, to tell about his part in it. The encounter terrified me so that I couldn't ask any more questions. Since then my emotions are jumbled. I mostly feel pain, sorrow, grief, distance, a lack of comprehension. I'm ashamed that I couldn't respond at the time and that I'm not yet in an (emotional) position to speak to my father again.

I think I well know what patterns run in my family, and what role I play. I also see more clearly how I misuse my son, how I repeat on him the same games that my family played with me. I also know that I can break through all of this only if I can take a step out of isolation and pursue a more reconciling stance. Only then can I break through this negative context and give positively to my son. I *know* all that, but, at the moment, I don't have the energy to do much about it.

You have worked with victims of the holocaust as well as with their children. Would it be presumptuous to say that the perpetrators and their children also need help. Can you help us?

One human being cries out for exoneration for his father, for himself, for his son. At base the courage to rework his shame will not come from the therapy room but from his parents, his siblings, his roots. The legacy of ancestral shame and guilt requires redress *and* exoneration insofar as they are possible.

Another painful, if less dramatic, demand for exoneration can be identified in the situation of the couple who comes into therapy because their eldest daughter Mia, 15, keeps running away. The two younger children are burdened and struggling too. The legacy of a child's adoption carries a built-in predicament of split loyalty with it.

Mother is hardworking, a school nurse who has been in individual therapy for nine years now. She is psychologically sophisticated but ethically disengaged in varying severe degrees. To begin, she hates her adoptive parents with what seems like unmovable intensity. Ellen claims that she gets nauseous if she is in the same city with them, let alone the same room. She says that they are cold, unfeeling, indifferent, hateful, insensitive, destructive, exploitative—in a word, unforgivable. She never wants to see them again. Besides, they are not her parents even though they adopted her at birth.

Ellen was responsive to her own therapist's suggestion that she search out her natural parents. She wrote letters, got several leads, learned in what state, city and neighborhood her biological mother lived, called the phone company and was told that her mother's was an unlisted telephone. And then she got stuck. She either could not or would not push further. She still says that she means to make a project of finding her mother but she simply cannot find a way to go on. She is stuck in other places too.

Ellen argues that she had made peace with her background until her husband Ed and the family therapist insisted on bringing it up. Ed argued back. "It's probably exaggerated," he said, "but sometimes I'm afraid that Ellen will cut me and the children off the way she cut off her parents. On second thought, maybe she won't abandon us permanently but she never seeks us out either." Ed could go on waiting indefinitely for Ellen to take initiative in reaching out to him, he says, but it would never happen. She never seems to want to be with him either for companionship or for intimacy and sex. Ed also recalled a recent occasion when Mia frowned at her mother and Ellen responded with agitation: "That's the kind of look I used to get from my mother. I couldn't stand it then and I can't stand it now."

Ellen can be eloquent in her own defense and sometimes very

open. "I simply don't want to risk an investment in people because I know that eventually I'll lose them. In any case, what's the point in enjoying anybody? The pleasure always has to stop. Sex is fine until I'm aware that I'm enjoying it. Then I freeze up and pull back. I like my job because I know the limits and am beholden to no one. At home it's different. I don't like making plans for social visits and I don't like people dropping in. I don't want to have to give people energy I never have. I'm not as depressed and cut off as I used to be, but I don't like to be obliged to be with people. You never know when you're going to lose what you once thought was yours. Even at church I cover my ears when the music begins. It's too beautiful and I can't stand the pain of knowing that it's going to stop."

Loss is clearly the overriding theme in Ellen's life, loss that is steeped in shame and rage.

"My parents are animals," she cried. "I watched my mother feed Mia when she was just a baby. She took no pride in caring for this pretty little girl. She just shoved the food down her throat until the baby gagged. It made me realize that that's what she did to me, too, just shoved things down my throat. By the time I was 12 I was taking care of them. No matter what I did though, nothing was ever enough. I played the organ, gave recitals, was valedictorian of my high school class. They never showed up for anything. It was my aunt who raised me. I don't owe those people a thing. Even a few years ago when they visited, all they could do was criticize my home, my looks, my housekeeping."

"They come from a rural area so at Christmastime, one year, I took my father to see the sights at a big city department store. Did he enjoy it? No, he panicked at the crowds. I tried to calm him; I took him to a restaurant and sat him in a corner. I soothed him and eventually we got home. He told my mother what had happened and then she got upset. She accused me of abusing him but did not say one word about me. How can they act that way to someone who once tried so hard to make them proud?"

Ellen was clearly grieving her lost childhood and her real and imagined injuries, with good reason. But her unresolved issues of shame over them threatened to engulf and drown her.

Her adoptive parents may indeed be animals in Ellen's perception, but what did that make her? Was she so without worth that two sets of parents wanted to abandon her, and now her eldest child? She had managed to keep people at a distance for a long time now. Why were things suddenly breaking apart? Bring her parents into therapy? The very idea made her ill but her behavior's implicit message to her children also upset her:

"Mothers are dispensable. If you don't like what they do, run away! Avoid them! Put them behind you. Act as though they don't exist! Doesn't Mia know that I love her? If she really knew, why would she run away?"

Ellen communicated little about her adoptive parents' side. Her father was one of 13 children whose own parents had died at an early age. Her mother was raised in an orphanage by German Catholic nuns. After they married, they lived in a rural town surrounded by extended family. How did they treat each other? Ellen didn't know. She did know that, unlike her lonely role as an only child, at least they had each other. She did not know and claimed she did not care how their upbringing had injured them or limited their own psyches, communications and transactions.

Unexplored here are whatever mitigating circumstances existed in her parents' lives. For example, did they ever offer her care which might have escaped her notice? Who was there to care for them? On whom could they rely? Ellen was furious because they took in strangers and cared for them even to this day. Did that earn them any merit? Were they trying to find a substitute for her? To what degree did they originally parentify Ellen because they held her in awe? To what degree did their chronic criticism of her represent how they had been raised? To what degree did they feel rejected by her attachment to a beloved aunt? Little is known about Ellen's relationship with this aunt. It is easy to imagine, though, that in addition to everything else, Ellen suffers from a predicament of multiple split loyalty. She is constantly pulled between her biological and adoptive parents, between her adoptive parents and her aunt, and, perhaps, between her adoptive mother and father.

As indicated earlier, a split loyalty predicament is an especially damaging one. Superhuman expectations issue from the failing adult couple, create an insolvable task for a child, and present a unique impasse. The youngster carries a growing concern and hopelessness over his parents' helplessness in the face of their mounting mistrust, and suffers increasing confusion over what options are available to solve his problem on an adult level. Unfortunately his parents are usually motivated to entrap him further in their conflict out of the benefits they draw from parentifying him. Under these circumstances a child is filled with destructive entitlement. He is also saddled with a lifelong mandate to "repay" his parents through actions that are invisibly loyal.

A predicament of split loyalty flies in the face of each generation's mandate to merge the two discrete legacies that stem from each parent's respective family of origin. Spouses may escape the task of maintaining loyalty to each other's families if only because their mistrust and prejudice towards each other makes loyalty of any sort impossible. However, a merged loyalty to both parents' families is a necessity for the grandchild generation. By definition, both my father's and my mother's families are my family. Adopted children also benefit in the long run if their adoptive parents can actively let them prove their concern for their biological parents. Any semblance of permission for an adopted child to establish trustworthiness with his or her biological roots is a welcome blessing. It is also a token of the adoptive parents' trustability and a gift that diminishes the child's split loyalty predicament.

Legacies of emigration and survivorship are also binding on the young. In both instances people characteristically have survived a member of their family, or surpassed the conditions in which loved ones continue to exist. People who have migrated from lands in which poverty and oppression prevail clearly need to find ways to make good on the endowments that they can put into use in their new situation in contrast to others like themselves. Consider the Chinese youngster who, with other boat people from Vietnam, came to New York city with his family.

He, his parents and two brothers shared one room for several years. The entire family struggled to sustain themselves and to help him go to college. Father had been an educator back home. Dishwashing was the only job available to him in his adopted land. His family saw the job as too demeaning for a person of his stature and refused to let him take it. But his eldest son made good on his father's and mother's losses and presumably on the losses of his countrymen who had been left behind. He became valedictorian of his graduating class and won a scholarship to a prestigious professional school. And he promised that as soon as he was able, he would earn the money to buy a home for his family. He is determined to prove his and his people's worth.

If anything, a legacy of survivorship is even more binding on the young than a legacy of emigration. Here persecution, genocide, disease or economic disaster may function as the destructive delegating factor. Thus, a survivor is indebted to the victims who weren't able to escape. Somehow he has to justify their losses and redeem their suffering. The question that drives survivors is how to make good on the very existence of those who are deceased, how to witness to people who were deprived and persecuted through no intrinsic culpability of their own. Can they find an active outlet? The survivor is burdened with a mandate for posterity or for all of humanity: How can they undo the effects of the crime or at least mitigate its consequences? And how can they prevent it from happening again? The key to ameliorating "survivor guilt" lies in the survivor's options for appropriate action that will ultimately benefit posterity.

Interpersonal Relating Vs. Internal Relating: Balances and Options

In relationships partners discover options through which to validate their own merit. Through them they try to broaden the base of the residual trustworthiness that they hold in common. As each partner takes opportunities to be multilaterally fair, he or she earns constructive entitlement and helps to reinvest in the quality of interpersonal relating (as against internal relating). The immediacy and directness of the dialogic exchange help diminish the exploitation that is intrinsic to projective identification. It lessens a person's tendency to see the other as someone who carries the role of one's needed internal "partner."

Here the client can only offer clues which a therapist will presumably pick up. The therapist himself cannot provide the specific input for a trust-building dialogue, so the client's clues are of central importance. The therapist can use his own struggle with intimacy and trust as a major guideline in this area, along with his expertise on the complexities of the self-validating phase (II) of the dialogue. Moreover, his insight into a client's projective tendencies may lead a therapist towards identifying his own projective distortions. In any case, there are no concrete, objective descriptions of the trust-building resources that exist among people, and certainly no prescriptions.

As a general guideline, therapists can direct their attention to signs of vulnerability, rejection and evasion between a client and his significant relatives. These are signs of relational failure that become especially significant when they are presented unilaterally, that is, when they come from one partner whose power over the other partner seems decisive and immense. For example, consider the parent who expects her child to tell her "everything." Then she uses the information to manipulate the child and hold on to him. Or conversely, consider the parent who makes his child his confidante or captive audience without listening to the youngster's problems in return. This parent may feel that he is giving. In fact, his failure to reciprocate a function which is questionable at best fails to fulfill his obligation to be an accountable parent. It also fails to earn him constructive entitlement.

A person's failure to earn constructive entitlement because of exploitative acts is also reflected in other dimensions of relational reality. An absence of dialogic engagement can be identified as transactional dysfunction and breakdowns in communication. Individually, a person's motivations may be linked with psychological traits, e.g., narcissism, defensiveness, ambivalence, and fear of intimacy, among other factors. In the ethical dimension, these omissions or failures usually indicate destructive entitlement, an outcome of broken dialogue. Furthermore, the exploitative person will continually deplete his actual entitlement, often without sensing it.

In her search for practical solutions, a therapist is always in the position of assessing what resources are available that will help all partners earn constructive entitlement for each other. A person's capacity to earn constructive entitlement is the only real antidote to his destructive acts and claims. In some families, a therapist discovers clues from observing highly honed techniques of deceptive manipulation. A case in point may be the parent whose overgiving patterns initially seem sacrificial. Later it becomes apparent that the recipient of his care is being bound by guilt-laden strings. This manipulative successful pattern is, of course, a crude caricature of self-validation through earned entitlement.

Signs of Broken Dialogue

Diminution of dialogue results in a constriction of resources in both the self-delineating and the self-validating phases. The ethical dimension, though, is most fully concerned with phase II. When people cut off or close off close relationships, they lose a source of self-validation. The built-in tribunal function of relationship then limits its expressions to silence or condemnation, usually indirectly conveyed. And options for dialogue itself deteriorate into exchanges of power measures that are aimed at gaining control and at crushing each other through induced confusion, intimidation, resentment or guilt.

The signs of constricted dialogue are numerous and diverse. Among them are,

- Distance;
- Tension and irritation;
- One partner's inability to listen to the other;
- An inability to respond to each other's positive offerings;
- An inability to initiate trustworthy care;
- A lack of appreciation for the partner's efforts to exonerate her parents, or preserve her loyalty to her family;
- Absence of any intentions of earning constructive entitlement; and
- Insensitivity to how a partner is being exploited.

The constriction of the self-validating aspects of dialogue incurs a state of relative disentitlement for everyone concerned. At best, there is an underutilization of prospective relational resources. At worst, there is a total loss. In addition, the personal freedom of each partner simply fails to evolve.

The failure to earn self-validation from a genuine dialogue with one's relational partner has many consequences. Among them are,

- Depressed affect;
- Unwillingness to risk new investments in relationship;

- An inability to sleep or relax;
- An incapacity for creativity or work;
- The failure to enjoy intimacy and sex;
- A need for psychosomatic manifestations;
- Loss of a will to live.

Depression is a particularly important consequence of the failure to earn entitlement. The depressed person who is dependent, demanding, complaining, and attention-getting cannot manage to earn entitlement. Here the dilemma has to do with the circular motion between a person's failure to earn entitlement and his sense of worthlessness, self-blame and self-destructive motives. The classic symptoms of depression are consistent with a lack of inner freedom that occurs whether a person's family members live nearby or far away.

Assessing Destructive Entitlement

A person who accumulates lasting destructive entitlement often displays psychological defenses of displacement and projection. These defenses are appropriate to a paranoid, narcissistic or antisocial character type. The paradox here lies with the fact that destructive entitlement in a person was initially earned through unfair victimization of the person who is now functioning as victimizer. From his perspective of justice in the human order, his behavior can be vindicated. The adult world that he knew as a child *was* both negligent and exploitative. It offered no listening forum for his rightful claims, no redress in his own youthful search for justice in relationship. He was rendered helpless by an irresponsible, adult environment which should have known better than to do a child in. Why should the "child," now grown, give someone better than what he got? Here lasting damage to the justice of the human order has occurred. The relational unfairness of the last generation has spilled over and become consequential for the present generation.

The person who relies on earned, destructive entitlement acts as if he is free of guilt or remorse. His self-destructive behavior and his damaging acts towards other people seem to evoke no reflection or compassion. They do produce a variety of descriptive characteristics. Among them are,

- Self-endangering behavior patterns, including suicide attempts;
- Paranoid accusations of others;
- Unfair attitudes displaced on children or mate;
- Rerouting vindictiveness from one's parents to one's children, e.g., an invisible loyalty that expresses itself in child-battering, aspects of teen-age pregnancy, overprotective possessiveness, and incestuous behavior;

- Relational cut-offs from parents and siblings;
- Non-receptive attitudes towards a young child's contributions, i.e., availability, concern, gratitude;
- A generalized refusal of anyone's offer of care;
- Chronic exploitation of a youngster's loving devotion;
- Scapegoating the young for adult controversies;
- Setting up a child as a perfect ideal to compensate for a treacherous world;
- Parentification, including sexual use of small children;
- Indifference to the consequences of destructive adult behavior, including actions towards children that lead to the predicament of split loyalty.

Parentification

One of the major concerns of contextual therapy has to do with preventing the destructive use of others. The central aspect of this concern is the relational misuse of small children to satisfy the possessive, dependent, destructive, or sexual needs of one or several adults. The concept of parentification was first mentioned in connection with the families of psychotic individuals (Boszormenyi-Nagy, 1965a), and later in connection with family life in general (Boszormenyi-Nagy & Spark, 1973). The contextual view of parentification is somewhat different from the transactional notion of parent-child role reversals emphasized in the concept of the "parental child" (Minuchin, 1974). In themselves, the phenomena of the reversal of roles across generational boundaries may be harmless or even useful experiences for a child. In contrast, a contextual evaluation focuses on the destructive parentification that brings lasting damage to the young.

Lasting damage takes place when the young experience a massive loss of trust and conclude that theirs is an intrinsically exploitative and manipulative world. It is at this point that children earn destructive entitlement and lose their capacity to develop future trust. Being cast into a mediator role between manipulative parents represents a case in point. The young child who is ethically abandoned may operate with the tact of a diplomat over long periods of time, reluctant to displease the members of her adult world. She consistently tries to honor the terms of the parent who is establishing a confidential relationship with her kept secret from the second parent. Under these circumstances, a youngster is automatically caught in split loyalties and forced to protect the absent parent at the same time that she is pleasing the parent at hand. She is then cast into the identical if opposite scenario with her other parent. Any significant predicament of split loyalty places the child into destructive parentification. Consider the situation of Mollie, a 12-year-old who is torn by warring parents.

"Your father must be brain-damaged from that fall he took several years ago," says mother. "I talked to the doctor about his violent temper and she agrees that his anger could stem from a physical injury." "It's true," Mollie tells the therapist. "A healthy person could keep himself from pounding his head against the wall. There has to be a reason for that kind of crazy behavior."

Mrs. H has suffered from aspergillosis for 12 years. It is a debilitating disease that attacks the immune system and undermines ordinary efforts to live a normal life. She has been hospitalized for pneumonia two or three times a year during those 12 years and sinks into a deep depression each time she has to leave home.

A psychiatrist encouraged Mr. and Mrs. H to consider family therapy. Mrs. H said the presenting problem was her husband's impotence. "I'm hardly impotent," Mr. H replied. "Our marriage was on the rocks even before she got sick. Her mother and brother were always more important than me. She tries to protect her mother when she finds out she has to be hospitalized again. But she acts as though I'm responsible." Mollie listened to her father and reflected that he really had a point. "Mom," she says, "You don't really have to talk about his family the way you always do. It only makes him madder and madder."

Whenever Mr. H spoke in a session or offered a suggestion, Mrs. H not only rebuffed and attacked him, but turned to her daughter for justification. "Go ahead, Mollie, and tell the doctor how sick your father is. Tell her how Daddy beats his head against the wall and walks out every time I try to talk to him. Tell her how he carries on whenever I go to the hospital. Tell her how I have to take care of him when he gets mad, even when I'm in a hospital bed. Tell her how nice Grandma is to him and how he always ignores her. Tell her, the doctor wants to know."

For most of her life Mollie has been forced to advance trust to a mistrustful and untrustworthy adult world. For most of her life she has been unable to restore her diminishing funds of trust from these essentially "bad" investments. To compound the problem, Mollie's contributions to her parents are poorly acknowledged, if at all. That is to say nothing of the situation in which parents dump *blame* on their mediating child. In this kind of situation, the fundamental question facing the therapist has to do with how much Mollie's parents can be helped to acknowledge her contributions, or at least her availability to them. The therapist who can lead the family in the direction of mutual acknowledgment even in the midst of Job-like deprivation has identified a relational resource and can make it work for everyone, preventively and therapeutically.

Patterns of Loyalty Configurations

Mollie's situation is indicative of how profoundly families can bind their members through loyalty configurations. Chapter 1 has already referred to the fundamental concepts of loyalty. In contextual theory, the term loyalty is meant to describe one member's dynamically obligated concern for family members. This concern or investment, for example, can be a response to early care, a return for benefits received. Contextual evaluations are attuned to how loyalties can be denied, ignored, misused, and manipulated. Split loyalties, loyalty conflicts and invisible loyalties are all configurations that require a thorough assessment and review. In each of these instances, what is at stake is an individual's capacity to form, develop and maintain trustworthy relationships in the face of triadic, i.e., third-person, relational claims, rights and needs.

As previously indicated, destructive parentification is characterized by an inadvertently collusive pattern or set of patterns between closely relating family members that reinforces mutual mistrust. The collusion may occur between parents, between grandparent and parent, between parent and sibling, and between a parent and his or her offspring. As individuals, none of these people may treat a child destructively. Rather it is their *combined impact* that can present a devastating, unsolvable dilemma to the young, precisely at their most vulnerable spot—the entitled accrual of trust.

The transactional pattern of "triangulation" is part of the context of the problems of every *split loyalty* configuration. In point of fact, the consummate triangle consists of father, mother and child, plus, perhaps, grandmother. Factually and dynamically, it is literally impossible to address a youngster and one parent as if the other parent were of no import. People try and fail. At one or another time in subtle or blatant forms, father, mother and offspring get involved in allying themselves against each other. After a while, each member of the parent-child triad is likely to have a part in victimizing one another instead of joining mutual efforts at building trust. Over time, all members of the triangle are well-served to assess their own discrete parts in unjust relating and in creating a deteriorating situation among them. Not every triangulation, though, is inherently trust-demolishing or lasting in its destructive consequences.

In essence, loyalty always means making a preferential choice. Loyalty implies that a person has a choice between two alternatives. Otherwise, loyalty would be a superfluous word and could be replaced by dyadic terms like adhering, liking or agreeing. In sum, loyalty presumes an implicitly triadic framework at the very least. It also presumes an actor who chooses between alternatives.

In a contextual assessment, loyalty further assumes adherence to a meaning of relationship that has evolved from earned merit. A contextual therapist operates out of the premise that sooner or later a person's loyalty has to extend to people who have made significant investments in his or her existence. For example, as described earlier, an adopted child is bound to be irrevocably loyal to the woman who was pregnant with her for nine months, who went through the costs of unwanted pregnancy and the risks of childbirth and who gave her life. By contrast, her natural father may or may not be aware of his daughter's existence and so tends to elicit less initial loyalty. In any case, the very fact of adoption places a child in an implicit split loyalty configuration between natural mother and adoptive parents.

Another, less devastating loyalty configuration is the collision between two loyalties, a vertical one and a horizontal one. *Loyalty conflict* is always involved with a choice of priorities of commitment, characteristically between a person's family of origin *and* his or her mate, friends, job, or peers. Loyalty is so basic a cause of marital problems that it sometimes shows up on or before the day of the wedding. Consider the professor approaching 40, who has been inordinately devoted to his mother since his father's death 10 years ago.

Two days before his wedding, Hank's mother came in from out of state. He put her up in his apartment but then found he felt "torn" in two. He wanted to spend the night at his fiancée's home rather than at his place and asked *her* to tell his mother what he preferred to do. Several weeks ago, the couple came into therapy because Hank was never able to tell Joan what he wanted. No matter what the situation, Hank always denied having a preference. He also denied having any anxiety over their forthcoming marriage.

But Hank seemed increasingly angry over his mother's and brother's apparent indifference to his fiancée, and increasingly mindful of how he had "cheated" his dead father of the opportunity to be present at his wedding. He felt deeply wounded by his brother's chronic hostility to Joan whenever they were in each other's company. "Why can't he treat her as a member of our family," he wondered, "the way Joan's family treats me? He challenges every word she says or doesn't talk to her at all. We've been so close all these years, always there for each other. I just don't understand."

Hank traveled several hundred miles to see his brother the month before the wedding in an effort to "explain," but returned disappointed each time he tried. "Tom is fine when we talk about things we used to do but he just won't talk about Joan. My mother's the same way. They act as if she doesn't exist. I know that things would be different if my father were alive."

In other circumstances, a person's attitude towards intimacy may shift immediately after marriage, and he or she may become sexually inhibited even on a honeymoon. At times, loyalty conflict surfaces gradually and expresses itself in a variety of ways, including friction, lack of confidence, sexual problems, and separation. Contextual evaluation of sexual problems requires careful inquiry into a person's loyalty binds. Evidence for the presence of loyalty conflict is often indirect and sometimes difficult to elicit or identify. For example, parents will often give no overt signs of disapproving of an offspring's marriage and only begin to signal negative messages at birthdays or holiday times.

Indirect loyalty conflicts may be channeled through *invisible loyalty* to parents whom an offspring resents or disdains but nevertheless protects. Consider Burt, for example:

> He rarely sees his family and, when he does, the relationship is typically cool and distant. Yet he is depressed a lot over them and often feels deeply hurt over their inattention. "It's always been like that," he says, "even when I was young." His disengagement from his parents is personally wounding to Burt but it is also a relational injury that disentitles him with his wife and elder son, Doug.
>
> Despite his hurt and apparent disengagement from his parents, Burt still makes indirect efforts to prove that they are worthwhile. His retributive withholding from his wife's demands may be one clue to how he indirectly protects his parents. His sometimes punitive parenting of his elder son may be another clue. His parents' seeming withholding from Burt even when he was little has inclined him to be withholding with his own son. For one thing, Burt isn't clear about how to parent him. And when he does reach out, Doug seems indifferent to his father's efforts. No appreciation for Burt there either. One of the dilemmas here is that Burt beat his son when Doug was very young, a fact that intermittently overwhelms him with guilt feelings.

Burt can find ways to earn entitlement through both his wife and son but he can't seem to mount the effort yet. He knows his behavior is unfair and doesn't mean it to be. He also knows that he feels depleted and mistreated. His blindness to how he is mistreating some people he loves can be considered a loyal act that spares Burt's parents from his wrath.

The therapist's task here is to help Burt identify the sources of residual trustworthiness that still exist between him and his parents. The task of identifying these resources is primarily a search for new modes of action. For example, what options exist for him to be more directly loyal to them? Can he find fresh ways to engage his parents, limit his giving solely on their terms, and surface his own options and claims? Secondarily, can he learn to appreciate the linkage between how his real and felt injuries from his parents adversely affect his treatment of his wife and son? His parents' past record may demonstrate that they are unlikely to accept their son's offerings even if he turns to them. Even so, can he grasp the possibility that their own realistic needs may have opened up new possibilities?

Later life can bring loneliness, sickness, anxiety. A child's or grandchild's presence in a person's life may look different than it did 10 or 15 years ago. Aging parents are often ready to talk about their own childhood and their success while acknowledging their regrets before it is too late. Injuries and estrangements notwithstanding, they are likely to welcome their son's or daughter's fresh offer to listen or inquire. They may even find relief from a chance to address hard or unfaced issues. But even if his parents cannot change their attitudes at all, the very fact of Burt's efforts to offer more direct payments of filial loyalty will reduce his inclinations to act on the basis of invisible loyalty.

Split loyalties, loyalty conflict and invisible loyalties produce patterns of relational phenomena that manifest themselves in numerous ways. Among them are:

- Restricted emotional and/or intellectual development;
- Self-disturbances, depression, learning problems, narcissism, psychosis;
- Self-destructive patterns of behavior;
- Suicide, a proclivity towards accidents, social self-damage;
- Delinquency, school phobia, anorexia, addictions, criminal behavior;
- Sexual inadequacy, loss of full range of options for generative heterosexuality;
- Physiological damage as a consequence of psychosomatic behaviors; and
- An inability to accept success.

These manifestations are all indications of the personal failure of individuals who are unwilling or unable to draw entitlement from the self-validating phase of dialogue.

A relational atmosphere that is ethically barren and stagnant produces systemic and structural signals as well as individual ones. Among them are:

- Denial of conflict;
- Martyrlike failure of a person ever to claim his or her side in a relationship;
- A retreat from personal responsibility and responsiveness into relational patterns dependent on manipulation;

- A person's perpetual overloyalty to his or her parents at the cost of losing the chance to individuate;
- An overwhelming emphasis on monetary matters and obligations;
- Attempts to master relational complexity by insisting on extremes, for example, cutoffs or an excessive concern with affective expressiveness;
- Rigid beliefs or ideologies based on prejudices and moralism;
- Paranoid or psychotic withdrawal.

The symptomatic manifestations of loyalty configurations express themselves in individual dysfunction and in systemic malfunction. They are therefore treated via traditional interventions of "pure" individual, systemic or marital therapy.

A therapeutic intervention that consistently ignores or obscures the ethical dimension of relationship simply fails to deliver a comprehensive assessment of a person's context and realities. What is more, therapy itself may contribute to sustained avoidance of the ethical dimension of relating.

IV. THE PROCESS OF THERAPY

CHAPTER 10

Health, Autonomy, and Relational Resources

The essence of contextual therapy lies in the enhancement of the quality of its clients' lives. An improved quality of life remains a constant goal regardless of the nature of individual complaints or systemic malfunction. Obviously, there is a need for symptoms to diminish and malfunction to reverse. At base though, the essential process is linked to eliciting and developing resources for self-improvement and mutual enrichment through a better use of relationships. Each relating individual can thus expect benefits at the same time that he or she is enabling others to benefit as well.

In contrast to isolated individual gains, multilateral benefits liberate each person in a family and help him or her towards greater creative freedom and higher degrees of personal enjoyment. A person's quality of living has a two-fold foundation: 1) the manifest patterns of satisfaction and enjoyment vis-à-vis his suffering from symptoms and chronic discontent, and 2) the understructure of relational balances.

People are not always clear about just how decisively their personal satisfactions and dissatisfactions are anchored in the integrity of relationships. But the more they face into the sources of their suffering and discontent, the more aware they become of how much their relationships function as the crucial criterion of reality. To survive, human beings require basic necessities. To exist, people require relationships. Modern notions of the essentially relational quality of human existence were postulated by one of Freud's early mentors, Franz Brentano, in his theory of intentionality (Spiegelberg, 1960); and again by Freud's picture of instinctual needs, which he believed were anchored in another person (object). In a more active fashion, contextual therapy aims at freeing the processes of every person's creative spontaneity, anchored as it is in a commitment to reciprocal care.

This chapter focuses on process aspects of health, malfunction and healing. A comprehensive concern for the quality of life and health always has to deal with all relating persons' endopsychic processes *and* with their capacity to involve themselves in responsible relating. This reality challenges the usefulness of the debate over whether individual or family therapy is indicated. Ideally, every modality would address both the person and his or her context. A healthy psyche and the freedom for reciprocity of commitment coexist in dialectic relationship to each other. The criteria for healing are confined to neither one nor several individuals' psychology of "feeling good," nor to patterns of behavior systems or structures. Whether or not a patient is treated by himself, relatives will be affected. Conversely any lasting intervention in a person's relational patterns inevitably affects the private motives of every individual.

The process of contextual therapy is geared towards encouraging individuals to use every natural inclination to reach personal goals, among them a basic striving for self-validation through fair give-and-take. The basic therapeutic task, then, is to guide each relating person towards coming to terms with his own and his partner's basic nature, and with their conflicting aspirations. In this process, people are typically able to rework their tendencies towards dependent demands and projective identification. They become more capable of autonomous relating characterized by assertiveness, responsibility and care.

THERAPEUTIC AIMS: CHANGE VS. SOWING SEEDS OF AUTONOMY

Therapy is a complex process that involves motives and interactions, as well as their covert and overt consequences. Change in any one individual is only a part of this process. In any case, the effects of individual therapy have been regarded as mixed; it is often difficult to locate the effects of change given their overt and covert nuances at any given time. Family therapy has demonstrated that overt change in one member typically coincides with visible or invisible changes in other members. It is common for one person's "pathology" to surface and to require attention just as the identified patient's symptoms begin to improve. The phrase "identified patient" originates from classical family therapy. The concept is indicative of a more flexible definition of symptom and change than that found in individual psychology and psychopathology.

Newton's physics identified change as absolute. Modern science has relativized the concept of change even in the inorganic world. Applied to living entities, change is a nonspecific concept of varied and limited value. There is no arguing the fact that life is an unceasing sequence of changes. Continuous dynamic changes help life be a self-sustaining process, capable of defying the law of entropy. Starting from a self-sustaining basis, life's genetic ingenuity can give rise to ever-new forms that themselves can flow into self-perfecting evolutionary trends.

Individual organisms sustain and adjust themselves in basically healthy and positive ways, in basically sick and detrimental ways, and in ways that cover the spectrum between these two extremes. Most of the time, healthy and sick processes coexist in shifting mixtures of composition. For example, malignant tissue is surrounded by healthy tissue. The same condition exists in relationships, too, where people always have to deal with a coalescence of the enabling or detrimental, self-sustaining effects of two or more separate individuals. This coalescence is composed of the simultaneous differentiation of relating partners. If this is so, it may be concluded that in relationships, merging and autonomous differentiation coexist in two simultaneous processes.

Like existence itself, therapy can be understood as part of an ongoing life process that is a mixture of burdens and resources. Into this mixture therapists can plant a seed that functions as a catalytic input. The word catalytic is used here to acknowledge the therapist's creative options *and* to recognize that his or her active self-assertion is limited in its potential consequences without the multilateral efforts of the family. Simply and directly put, a seed can be fruitful only when it is planted in fertile soil.

The catalytic action of therapy is further targeted on the catalytic process of the dialogue between relating partners. A useful analogy can be found in the fact that some enzymatic catalysts regulate the catalytic function of other enzymes in a cell. The catalytic function of contextual work can be demonstrated in an ordinary story in which a therapist elicits the hidden trust resources among sisters.

> Four sisters ranging in age from their early thirties to late forties managed to maintain their connections with each other over time and space. They had two brothers with whom connections were more tenuous. Each of the women wrote or spoke to each other on a one-to-one basis from time to time. But each of them seemed too involved in the demands and investments of daily life to make more than polite inquiries into each other's lives. Of course there were old injuries and hurts among them, though these seemed more related to their parents and brothers than to each other.
>
> First of all there was their parents' deaths within a few short weeks of each other almost 10 years ago. No one had ever really talked about that. Judy, the only single sister, had a lot of leftover

issues and feelings, though. Why, for example, when three older siblings were available, had so much responsibility fallen on her? Why had she been the one to tend their parents as they were dying? Why had she been expected to make all the arrangements afterwards? Why hadn't anyone realized the trauma in doing that? Why had the care and consolation of their younger brother been left to her? Why hadn't anyone concerned themselves with her need for consolation?

Then there was the matter of their brothers, though that seemed related to their parents too. Women in this family were typically defined as "strong." Mother had suffered a lot with many pregnancies and with chronic disease as well. By and large the family had been poor but she had always found a way to make do. Father, on the other hand, was often absent from the house. When he was home, he seemed to capitulate to his wife anyway. He rarely disclosed his feelings and struggled a lot with drink.

In sum, family myth had it that father was "weak" and so were his sons. One of the sisters disagreed with the prevailing family myth. She interpreted most things having to do with her father and older brother differently from her sisters. It seemed fairly clear to the therapist whose primary client was Judy that the siblings were all burdened by a predicament of split loyalty. Chronic mistrust not only existed between mother and father but among the siblings too. Weak father, weak sons? Strong mother, strong daughters? Or heroic, if submissive, father, loyal sons? Overbearing, if caring, mother, protective daughters?

Over the years Judy had suffered a lot from what she called depression. She had had overly high expectations of her colleagues and profession. And though she was more often disappointed in them than not, no one seemed to know about her neediness, a burdensome omission indeed. Judy, like her mother, was supposed to be very strong. Here "strong" meant never acknowledging your own limits and never saying that you had wants. "Strong" meant giving of yourself and doing for others to an extreme. It also meant being angry when people didn't give back in kind. "Strong" meant not even doing for yourself and isolating yourself against anyone's acknowledgment or appreciation of you or your gifts.

Eventually, Judy had had enough. Her compulsion to give to others brought ever-diminishing returns and her emotions became subject to massive swings. In early therapy sessions, Judy was rigorously protective of her family, essentially only able to discuss the unfairness of her parents' deaths. But she was also clear that she couldn't continue to live as she had lived in the past few years. Ever so slowly, Judy began to turn towards her sisters, geographically scattered though they were. She started with her youngest sister and finally incorporated them all. It is difficult to describe the degree of her outright fear and trepidation at approaching them. It is equally difficult to describe her astonishment and awe at their active willingness to respond to her claims.

At first Judy simply tried to tell them who she was on adult terms and to learn more about them. In the beginning, until they understood her priorities, all of the initiative seemed to fall on her. Later, many months later, she began to raise some pressing matters: For example, how did they see their parents? How had they experienced their parents' deaths? What happened to them in its aftermath? Did they ever wonder what happened to her? How did they relate to their brothers? Were the sisters ever ashamed of them?

Still later, Judy brought her youngest sister into therapy and Elizabeth willingly came. The early minutes of the session were awkward; Judy was aggressively protective and reluctant to trust the consequences of having an open exchange. On the other hand, Liz was awed at the option. What could this older sibling, so much brighter, so much more educated, so much more highly accomplished, hope to get from her? "Don't you remember, Liz, how mom used to hold you? I was jealous of that. I felt envious of how close you two seemed to be." "But everyone stood in awe of you," Liz replied, "and that probably included Mom. You were so smart even then. We still talk about how precocious you were; I think you scared us away."

Judy and Liz met for four or five therapy sessions over a period of a year. The phone calls to each other became more frequent, but Liz's husband seemed to be a stumbling block for Judy. He was possessive of Liz and expected her to do things his way. Would Judy's claims for closeness pull Liz in two directions? When Judy was hospitalized for surgery, old feelings of abandonment reappeared. How could she ask for Liz's help when she was busy with her own family and had her hands full with them. "Liz can always refuse," the therapist suggested. "My question is, 'Can you ask?'" Judy asked, and Liz made herself available, glad that her sister might want her comfort and help.

The following summer Judy decided to visit her sisters out West and carefully laid her plans. Yes, she'd like to know their families better. But could they also make time to be alone with her? She returned from her vacation less burdened and more rooted than she could remember being before. Later in the year they returned her visit by coming East and all of them met for four therapy sessions. Here harder questions surfaced with the help of what the therapist already knew. The therapist was carefully multidirected, a process helped along by the trust base that had been established between Judy and her, and by what Judy had previously chosen to share with her sisters.

Special emphasis was placed on the family myth. What did it mean to be a woman in this family? What did it mean to be a man? What did it mean that their older brother was not there? He had agreed to come. What did it mean that their younger brother was not there? Had anyone asked him? What might their mother say if she could be present? And what about their father? Did they all really think that the family members were polarized and split in their loyalty to their parents? How? Why? What happened to each of them when their mother was ill, as frequently happened? Who was there for their father? Why did Judy not tell anyone when she was in trouble? Were they really critical of her choice of a religious vocation? Why had they not told her early on? Could Judy believe that they could change, they wondered. They were not judgmental now.

In a sense, the sisters in this family had begun a fresh and creative way of relating. Their questions of each other were rich and full. So was their capacity to open themselves, be less defensive and more responsive—to people beyond themselves as well as to each other. The therapist had been a catalytic agent. A seed had been planted, watered, fed, and a seedling had taken root. It, too, was nurtured, weeded and staked; and the seedling matured and began to bear fruit. The therapist had merely introduced prospective options that could evoke the trust-building moves which lay contained and unutilized in the sisters' repertory of spontaneous motivations.

In the near future, this family was to suffer a traumatic loss of one of its members. They were also to be available to each other in attentive and previously unexperienced ways. But that is not the point. Therapy can never make anyone's life right, nor protect family members from life's exigencies. It can plow ground though and sow seeds and, in the doing, raise the hidden trust resources that lie dormant among family members. As one member risks initiating a reciprocally responsible dialogue, other members are induced to try to do the same. It can take a while for the planted seed to grow, but how long is objectively hard to tell for its first growth is underground. Long before the seedling's leaves can be seen by the naked eye, its roots have entered into an invisible encounter with the soil. The plant's existence, let alone its capacity for maturation, becomes evident only after it breaks through the ground's hard crust. Therapy like horticulture is a tender and complex art. The seedling's first tendrils are susceptible to pests and rot, as well as dependent on compatible climate and growth. Sometimes it is difficult to differentiate at what stage growth actually takes place.

In point of fact any therapy works when it can enhance life's self-sustaining potential. First, its possibilities are covert: New courage may help a client think and feel differently and enable her to face new aspects of how she behaves and what she expects of herself and her relationships. Later, her early steps can mature into more visible growth and a strengthened capacity to relate. The nuances and complexities of individual growth and viable relationships raise questions about the legitimate target of therapeutic intervention. What is to be strengthened in the life patterns of people seeking help? And what is to be weakened? What needs to improve, and in and between whom? What are the consequences of a given change? Will overburdening others become a consequence? How are the carriers of secondary symptoms to be helped, for example, when a child, once the identified patient, has lost his symptoms and his mother begins to break down?

SYMPTOMS VS. HEALTH

Symptoms are the beginning point of the therapeutic process whose initial definition is based on the disturbances that focus on a "sick" family member or on relational problems. Unlike the etiology of a disease like cancer, for example, the underlying substrate of this pathology is not a scientifically known cause. It is a breakdown of relational resources. This conclusion is not meant to deny the pertinence of damaged personality development in people. Nor is it meant to ignore that fact that conflicts among people are a given that inevitably arise in a family or in a group. It is meant to argue that a person remains an important, irreducible source, a unique receptor and integration of a living gestalt—with his or her own process of self-identity and life cycle stage. No therapeutic change is viable without a coalescence between all of the relating partners' spontaneity and personal needs.

Healthy function, then, is an achievement in human life rather than an automatically given privilege to be taken for granted. In his later work, Freud began to realize the need for individual mental structure, that is, an ego capable of reality testing, one that could absorb the onslaught of changing the instinctual and emotional demands of day-to-day life. People need some degree of structured personality simply to survive the impact of stimulation without "freaking out." The same argument can be made about family systems. No one person can afford to carry all of the other family members' burdens and vicissitudes. Relational (family) therapy first came into existence (in the 1950s) out of a desire to support relational structures that help to temper and buffer individual shortcomings and, intrinsically, to equalize individual burdens. Out of that effort came a discovery of how transactions formed themselves into systemic patterning. Later, contextual therapy offered an ethically integrated perspective of individual and systemic processes.

Earlier family therapists aimed towards a goal of "changing a family's rigid rules." Many still move towards that same goal. It is increasingly clear, though, that rigidity is characteristically secondary to the failure of a well-functioning reciprocity of commitment. This failure is at its most destructive in the failure of parental commitment. Chaotic parenting is a root cause of disintegration in nuclear and extended families. It is the principal source of the "pathogenicity" under attack by therapy and preventive therapeutic efforts alike.

Social Disintegration as Process

Society may now stand at the tail end of a huge, centuries-old process that began with legitimate longings for liberation from oppression. That societal process has had massive consequences, good and bad, for much of the world's population. It has also led people into a dreamland, a world that anticipates freedom from responsibility, a world that essentially offers free options for choosing one's family ties but also one that renounces social solidarity. The post-divorce and post-welfare panorama of our era presents a kaleidoscope of single parent and remarried families with their congeries of stepparents, half-siblings, stepsiblings and stepgrandparents. The complex, interlocking lines of blood and steprelations often seem like a gigantic effort at substitution—an inadvertent attempt to form quasi-extended families, a second chance to try to establish pseudo-genetic resources that can fulfill people's shattered hopes for support and companionship. Divorced parents, their spouses and even their stepchildren and in-laws somehow remain connected through their children's need for parenting. On occasion they may all show up at a family event, a wedding or a funeral in search of something, perhaps for the first and last time.

In the West at least, people tend to believe that their new "freedom" and new relational options enrich the lives of adults and surpass old ways. Not for them the entrenchment of long and enduring marriage. Yet, by now it surely must be clear that the satisfaction of parents is inseparable from their children's welfare. If children are increasingly to suffer as a direct result of unexamined parental choices, then a challenge to "new" ways and options is surely overdue. Whether or not today's varieties of life-styles are satisfying to adults is for each adult to decide. As for the children, it may be that more enriching options for their lives and for their futures came out of extended kinship groups of the past and from their encouragement to couples to stay in and work on shaky marriages.

Symptomatic Change Vs. Intergenerational Consequences

Change by itself is a questionable commodity. By itself, change is a static notion that implies the transformation of one presumably stable state into another stable state, from an old static condition into a new static condition. Change is also the major emphasis of a short-term view of life. A restrictive "here-and-now" therapeutic stance restricts its concerns to observable behavior and patterns, and identifies their changes as its goals. It lacks a perspective of life as a whole. "Here-and-now" therapies notwithstanding, life is a whole, a gestalt with realities and consequences that stems from past causes, spans generations and reaches into the future through its causal input. No one can argue against the fact that life is a series of unceasing changes from moment to moment. But the more significant question remains; change towards what direction?

In the long run, psychotherapy's attitude towards change has been open-ended and evolutionary. In individual psychotherapy, the concept of personality or character formation transcended an ephemeral, symptom-oriented view. In classical family therapy, the concept of systemic homeostasis (Jackson, 1957) expanded the scope of therapeutic understanding even further. Contextual therapy with its integenerational emphasis presses for an even larger gestalt—dialogue between the generations, that is, the reciprocity of commitment that offers posterity a chance.

Parent-child dialogue is a link in the chain of generations which, in itself, is a gestalt that predates the human world. The mother bird or mammal who cares for her young is involved in more than an instinctual discharge. She is investing in what might be termed a "feed-forward" rather than "feed-back" dialogue. She is living out a pattern of relating which will convey from generation to generation. This pattern of relating will extend the benefits of caring to a distant posterity with whom a mutuality of experience is no longer possible. Offspring receive care and, as parents, initiate similar caring with the subsequent generation. Harlow (1962), in his experiments with monkeys, has substantiated the significance of a forward-moving dialogue. He has documented the consequences of early maternal deprivation in the formation of a monkey mother incapable of offering care to her young.

The inability to contribute to the next generation's survival and well-being marks a breakdown of the most fundamental kind. The failure to earn entitlement through offering responsible care to the young (including one-sided exploitation and the imposition of harm) indebts and isolates people in ways that too often bear no redress. A chronically unpaid and cumulative existential debt is itself damaging to the perpetrator as well as to the object toward whom he has chosen to avoid his debts. Its effects are open-ended, unpredictable and never mutual, but they tend to visit implications on several generations. The consequences of scapegoating, for example, are destructive at many levels. Scapegoating lends itself to creating "pathological" transactional patterns. It also functions as a source of hurt feelings. But its most destructive consequences are of an intergenerational nature. Thus, a young person's entitlement to be destructive begins to form in direct relation to the degree to which adults critically undermine his trust.

Over the long run, scapegoating is likely to constrict and to undermine the perpetrator's future freedom. If the scapegoat is a defenseless child, the youngster herself is likely to earn destructive entitlement and, if sufficient, she herself is likely to learn to be indifferent towards her existential indebtedness towards others. To recapitulate, an overwhelming degree of injustice exacted from a child undermines the process of developing basic trust. It also weakens her ability to become a constructive, dialogic partner.

Here the issue of basic trust vs. mistrust underlies individual and relational orientations alike. The psychodevelopmental consequence of character deformation, linked to a failure of trust, eventually parallels the ethical consequence of the injured justice of the human world. The consequences of both span several generations.

THREE MAJOR OBSTACLES TO DIALOGUE

Intergenerational impediments to dialogue are often lasting, self-perpetuating and self-sustaining. The enduring nature of these obstacles tends to block people's awareness of their trust-building options and resources in relationships. As a result, too many of their behaviors and interactions become defensive, provocative, withholding, suspicious, and cunning, that is, essentially wasteful. These reactions can be defined as obstacles to dialogue in the psychological, transactional and ethical dimensions of reality. The factual dimension produces important, determinative input but, by itself, seldom leads to relational impediments that sustain themselves over time.

In the psychological realm, perhaps the most significant obstacle to dialogue is linked to the collision between internal needs and external realities. A faulty alignment occurs when a person's inner, endopsychic relational needs consistently conflict with his or her partner's real identity and needs, and consequently with the requirements for successful interpersonal relating. Projective identification, displacement, narcissistic relating and an incapacity for mourning are among the consequences of this faulty alignment (Boszormenyi-Nagy, 1965a). In practical terms it is a limitation that creates and maintains unrealistic expectations of relationships. So, for example, a person can swing from an initially intense infatuation to a retributive if unintentional disappointment later on without any stages in between. In addition a person can expend herself in frantic efforts to transform her partner into a mold or reflection of her own inner templates of needs.

Rigidly repetitive action sequences and feedback cycles are also obstacles to dialogue and belong to the transactional and communicational dimension of reality. They consist of binding patterns of the detrimental feedback of signals and actions that are mutually reinforced. Some family therapy regards these patterns and their feedback as primary human behavior. Traditional family therapists often picture people as held in the grip of repetition and feedback. They gear their therapeutic task towards interrupting and changing these sequences in treatment sessions. At times, their hope for effectively eliminating these binding patterns on a permanent basis is too strongly tied to performance in the therapy room. Another questionable premise here is the assumption that new replacements for old sequences will have more favorable results for everyone. An additional question mark in classical family therapy has to do with its prescriptive mentality. The direction of change is often prescribed or dictated by the therapist's convictions about subcultural or generational norms.

We have already reiterated the obstacles to dialogue in the ethical dimension in numerous ways. A person who is entitled to retribution and displays no remorse in taking it is clearly rebuffing a dialogic option. The permission to retaliate is partly an earned credit, but also a self-contradictory one. It either stems from an invisible loyalty to parents or is the destructive outcome of unredressed injury or misfortune. This condition can persist because of a built-in mechanism that cancels out a person's guilt over his own destructive behavior or supersedes remorse. Tragically, the destructively entitled person actually has a "right" to his vindictiveness. On the other hand, no one is ever entitled to pass his injuries on through victimizing innocent third persons.

Collusive Postponement of Mourning: A Cause of Stagnation

Relational difficulties in families disclose themselves through a form of transactional structuring, that is, through an apparently multipersonal script. For example, a scapegoating pattern can be viewed as destructive, overt behavior composed of a series of communications and interactions. Yet the overall process of relationship is much more complex. The collusion between mutually scapegoating partners or between a scapegoat and a family healer can fall into contextual Dimension III. Its characteristic triangulation marks the exchange as a transactional pattern or structure. Simultaneously, however, family members can benefit from casting each other into roles that represent internally needed and programmed partners.

These rigidly held relational patterns constitute defensive bastions, that is, reliable ground that functions as a unique reference point for each family member's self. For example,

Therapist: Your son is devoted to both of you. Can you find less critical ways of treating him as well as some ways to enjoy each other?
Mother: He never seemed to enjoy me so I learned to enjoy his sister instead. I don't see that he wants to be with me even now.
Father: I just want to be done with him, send him to his own psychologist, let him work it out that way. Treating William right has no reasonable payoff for me. He needs to get a job and stop all this loafing and taking things out of our skin. I never enjoyed him before either. How could I imagine enjoying him now?

Forcing William, the elder child, to comply with his parents' own internally prescribed role expectations has led to power confrontations: "William has to get out of the house at any cost. What's happening belongs solely to him, and no one else is at fault." Conversely, it can also lead to generous compliance on the part of each partner: William's parents will spend large amounts of time and money to put him in the "hands of a therapist who can help him find a job." On the other hand, the situation in William's family has been going on for years. Everyone has taken care to retrench rather than rock the boat. William has complied with the pattern through his predictably objectionable behavior. The reluctance to join hard issues and rework destructive behavior amounts to a "collusive postponement of mourning" (Boszormenyi-Nagy, 1965b). Their collective "decision" to defer mourning spares all of them from facing the losses involved in relinquishing their rigid patterns.

Ethically (Dimension IV), the question of exploitation can surface simultaneously with the psychology of projective identification and triangulation. William is operating out of a deep-seated loyalty to his father who feels that his own mother has abandoned him. Moreover, father has a history of losing job after job. William's inadequacy may well function as a mitigating factor in his parents' rocky marriage. It may also serve to protect father against the trauma of William's potential success. William's loyalty to his family may be misguided but it is real. Unfortunately it also functions to strengthen the bind that his struggling parents have imposed on him. On the other hand, father is unknowingly victimizing William out of invisible loyalty to his own distanced and resented parents.

Finally, the factual circumstances (Dimension I) of the family's disturbed functions deserve serious consideration. For example, if William's isolation and depression continue to escalate, his life and future may be at risk. Can this family do something new to intervene in these circumstances without irreversibly damaging consequences of their own?

It is obviously easiest to design changes for visible behavior patterns. But knowledge of a person's subjective world can make the therapist's work much more effective and relevant. Even more, in the face of future consequences, interventions on behalf of posterity may provide the firmest ground of all. There is ample reason to argue for the efficacy of Dimension IV as a therapist's major guideline. William's parents never meant to exploit him. At age 20, however, he is trapped in a corner with nowhere to go short of telescoping destructive facts into the future. Still, like his sister and parents, he too deserves consideration in the family.

Here the therapist can be overwhelmed by every member's palpable deprivation, but not if she holds onto the ethical dimension. Her greatest therapeutic leverage lies in her clear conviction that the present is dynamically invested in the welfare and well-being of the future generation. For his parents to hold on to William in a stagnant, scapegoating manner is already causing them profound remorse and existential guilt. A fundamental grasp of this ethical aspect of reality is one of the most important process rules of contextual therapy.

Dimensions of Impaired Mutuality

If reciprocity of commitment and earned entitlement are so fundamental to a viable and balanced life context, why has the ethical dimension in family life basically remained unaddressed? Why has psychotherapy so consistently ignored the existence and implications of this dimension? What are the factors that undermine the realities of Dimension IV and serve to corrupt it? Why is the process so subject to corruption? Consider Danny's situation.

Danny, 11, is described as rebellious. Suddenly, it seems, he has changed from being "mother's closest child" to being a troublemaker. He knows that he does things to which his parents object. He also knows that he will be punished for what he does. "But I do them anyhow," he says. Danny is the middle child of a "remarried family." He and his sister Julie, 13, live with their mother and her second husband who have had a child together, Chet who is seven years old. Danny's and Julie's stepfather has no children from his previous marriage. Their mother and stepfather have been married for 10 years and raised the older children almost entirely by themselves. Danny's and Julie's father lives alone.

Factually, Danny is burdened by a predicament of split loyalty. His natural parents resent and avoid each other. His father still sends child support payments to Danny's mother, but they are typically one or two weeks late. Danny sees his father on Saturday and mother expects Danny to ask whether or not the payments have been sent. His mother's remarriage has placed the boy into a difficult split-loyalty conflict between his biological father and his stepfather. He also carries the weight of the triangle created by the presence of two men in his mother's life. Remarriage *per se* has inevitably produced a male-female triangle and a legacy of split loyalty for him. Danny is somehow indebted to all of the adults. He owes something to each of them and tries to find ways to be loyal to his mother, father and stepfather alike. But that is hard to do since their relationship with each other is intrinsically conflicted and full of mutual mistrust.

Psychologically, Danny is in the throes of a dilemma. His identity and trust needs require a reliance on parents whom he can regard as essentially good and trustworthy, that is, the good internal ego requires a matching good internal (parent) object (Fairbairn, 1952). Throughout his young life, though, Danny has consistently experienced mistrust between his divorced parents. As he sees it, they have always acted like hostile, destructive adversaries. The direction of parenting has been inverted as a result of their behavior. At age 11, Danny has long since become their parent and forfeited his need to be their child. In the process, he has begun to retreat into increasing reliance on his internal relational world. Only thus can he hope to avoid the contradiction that exists between the parent(s) he needs and the parent(s) he actually has.

His mother's repeated warnings to Danny against trusting his father's promises are a revealing case in point. Danny wants to trust his father and, overtly or covertly, has continued to defend his father's integrity. Neither his mother's warning and accusations nor his father's unreliable behavior can successfully cancel out the boy's internal image of a reliable father. At the very least, Danny is able to protect and possess his own internal relational world. He cannot grasp the reality of who his parents were. He consistently projects or displaces an image on them that is inappropriately good or bad. The more desperately he clings to the internal other, the less invested he becomes in choosing realistic options offered in his actual interpersonal relationships.

Danny's struggle to align his internal images with interpersonal reality was paralleled by his parents' analogous struggles. In parentifying their son, they too relied heavily on their internal object relations. Neither mother nor father gave themselves a chance to relate on a constructive plane. Each of them carried profound despair over repeated failures in close relationships and learned that their best defense was to assign blame. But neither wanted to fail with Danny whom they placed into a destructively idealized role. At some level of their existence, each parent imagined their son as a healing judge, a referee, a redeemer of everything that had been evil or bad in their lives. Danny was bound to fail as a consequence of his parents' idealized parentification. And in the wake of his failure, he was bound to be cast into a negative, scapegoat-like role.

Transactionally, Danny is caught in behavior patterns that 1) cost him the satisfactions that come from childhood dependency, 2) force him to function as a precocious parent to his mother, father and stepfather, and 3) brings him into painful conflict with all of his parenting figures. There were times when he refused to visit his father who constantly disparaged his mother. Other times, Danny became his biological father's unwitting agent in his mother's home. Then he would do things that he knew had his father's approval but which were disagreeable to his mother: Staying up late, playing the stereo at full volume, spending his money however he chose, a million little acts that built into a major offense. But as Danny had already said, "I'd still do it even knowing I'll get punished for it." Continuing loyalty to his father's ways forced Danny's behavior to become controversial in his mother's home.

Ethically, Danny's parents are protected from facing their share of responsibility for destructively scapegoating their child. Operating out of the suffering of their own childhood injustices, each of them functions with little remorse. They may even feel entitled to scapegoat Danny in order to spare their respective parents from any blame. Danny's own victimization will pose the same long-term consequences. In time to come, he too is likely to function with little remorse over victimizing his children or other innocent third parties.

Danny's situation is paradigmatic of the coincidence between internal, psychological programming with its displaced hostility and the ethical dimension of reality in which the failure to earn constructive entitlement yields to substitutive vindictiveness.

It is clear that there is no ethical validity to substitutive victimization, whatever its secondary gains. Rather, it is a self-contradictory predicament for everyone involved. The relational impasses in Danny's family are linked to interrupted dialogue. Failing fairness and the incremental buildup of trustworthiness that comes from ongoing investments in considering each other's sides, they settled for exploitation. Unilateral use of each other may not qualify as dialogue but they simply did not know how to get to another point. People can and often do live out their lives taking whatever advantage comes their way. It augurs well for a retreat into power games and into the thrill of stimulations. Yet an essentially exploitative relationship is a wasteful use of the psychological endowments of all relating parties.

In Search of Stimulation: An Avenue of Escape

Everyone has moments when alienation and a lack of meaning in relationships drives them into anxiety and despair. At these times, people seek out diversion through travel, television and entertainment that comes in ever more exotic forms. Our era is full of possibilities for distraction through the increased stimulation of human senses and fantasies. Options always exist that can help people evade a confrontation with their lack of viable, responsible relating. Substitutive stimulation can even give the illusion of meaning in people's lives. At the same time a flight into stimulation also has its costs. Psychosomatic illness, destructive behavior and sexual difficulties are among the frequent consequences of chronic evasion.

Obviously, the quest for stimulation cannot be reduced to motives of evasion. New experiences and fresh stimulation can be enjoyable and creative and are part of life's legitimate driving force. Yet the search for stimulation requires perspective. People need to balance their right to stimulation with the requirements of relational reality. The necessary balance is violated by a misuse of entertainment, nonstop exposure to television, and chemical abuse. The imbalance between due responsibility and the quest for stimulation is also disclosed in the failure of dialogue, that is, when closely related people live in tiny, isolated boxes and confuse monologic attempts to "communicate" with the demands of trustworthy exchange. All too often, people use excitement and thrills as a substitute for trusting relationships.

CHAPTER 11

Rejunction: Reworking the Impasse

WHEN SYMPTOMS ARE REMOVED

Historically, psychotherapy is a record book of professional investments in discovering healing interventions for personal and interpersonal suffering. Whatever their preferred modality, experienced therapists know that a client's initial symptoms can quickly yield to many non-specific therapeutic effects. Among these are:

- The generally supportive effect of therapeutic intervention of any kind;
- The power of the therapist's suggestive influence over the client;
- The persuasive power of the therapist;
- A client's dependent reliance on the therapist;
- The beneficent effect of transference, that is, a client gives up her symptoms in exchange for the therapist's care ("transference cure");
- A shift from one to another symptom, e.g., phobic behavior can give way to delusional thinking; and
- A homeostatic rearrangement within the family, e.g., one person's loss of symptoms can result in the emergence of another family member's newly manifest disturbance.

Therapeutic Interventions After Symptomatic Improvement

Once a therapist has helped a person towards symptomatic improvement, the client has choices to make about what constitutes the next direction for therapeutic gain. Has the causative substrate underlying a client's recent symptoms changed along with his visible behavior? Or do burdensome conditions still remain in the person, and between him and his relational partners? Individual and family therapies have all developed their own emphases and directions for addressing these kinds of questions.

Psychodynamic approaches characteristically try to help clients heal in the following ways.

- Gaining greater awareness of one's real sources of feelings and neurotic mechanisms;
- Gaining insight into the neurotic games one plays with oneself and so achieve stronger leverage for change;
- Facing and renouncing unhealthy patterns of behavior that follow the loss of familiar relational patterns;
- Replacing lost relationships and patterns with new ones;
- Completing the steps of mourning that are required for the process of "working through" (Rado, 1925).

In general psychodynamic terms, the person undergoing these changes will be involved in performing the following tasks.

- Correcting his reality testing;
- Subordinating an undisciplined pleasure principle to a reality principle that considers the consequences of a person's actions and behaviors;
- Undergoing possible changes of character or basic personality; and
- Diminishing the use of narcissistic relational patterns.

In other words, a person who undergoes successful individual therapy will probably succeed in reorganizing his energies in order to master his or her reality more successfully. He will expend less time on previously held neurotic preoccupations, establish a new basis for relationships, and make himself available to them. If the person accomplishes his goals, his relational partners will also gain from how he has changed.

The evolution of object relations theory provided additional nuances to the psychodynamic approach. The concept of internal relating adds the following demands to a client's tasks.

- Diminishing one's reliance on the supremacy of internal sets;
- Developing a capacity to perceive the actual actors in interpersonal relationships; and
- Forming a new and more realistic alignment between the processes of internal and interpersonal relating.

However theoretical in concept, these tasks are all based on the deeply practical issue of each person's primary need for a realistic relational framework. By themselves, however, psychological explanations never capture all aspects of relational reality.

Transactional or systemic (classical) family therapy approaches characteristically define transactional behavior and "feedback" in both symptomatic and causal terms. They work on the implicit assumption that therapeutic interventions can alter the chain of recurrent, circular feedback. Frequently, they assume a therapist's capacity to transform people's actions and interactions into what he or she considers more appropriate patterns. The word "appropriate," of course, ignores the issue of content. At times, behaviorally "structuring" intervention is indirect and paradoxical from the vantage point of clients. Often, there is a lack of candor that would help them define their options or let them know they have a choice.

We have already mentioned our concerns over the assumptions of behaviorally defined therapy, assumptions usually made with little regard for the motivational processes that are at work within a family's individual members. Another questionable assumption has to do with the relevance of the therapist's capacity to judge whether or not a family's interactions and patterns are significant or useful. "Significant or useful to whom?" is our question. Abstract observations about what patterns "fit" into a particular life cycle, age group, generation, or subculture may be used as a mean. But such conclusions are categorical rather than contextual, and ignore the uniqueness and specificity of persons and families alike. In a similar vein, a label like "rigid" may be applied to a family's customary interactions as a justification for change. Again, the questionable assumption has to do with the goal definition of a form of therapy that often uses criteria for "good" and "bad" transactional patterns that mainly reflect the therapist's own values (Selvini-Palazzoli, 1978).

In effect, some families conform to their therapist's behavioral value preferences and other families resist these prescriptions of patterns. Many people are bound to find comfort from pleasing authority figures whose approval they eagerly seek. On the other hand, even when families initially comply with a notion of what will "do them good," it is usually only a matter of time until they find it more rewarding to swing back to their old behavior and so reject the therapist's preferences. The inclination to give up an imposed intervention may occur before or after the termination of therapy. In our view, without a meaningful coalescence with people's genuine spontaneity, behavioral changes do not lead to significant therapeutic gain.

CONSTRUCTIVE AND DESTRUCTIVE COALESCENCE

In our view health is a coalescence of constructive vital forces that originate from the genes and give rise to numberless options. Conversely, illness can be defined either as interference with these constructive forces or as faulty, destructive coalescence. In physical illness, infections and injury exemplify interferences with constructive, vital forces. Here pathology is incidental to life, interfering as it does with basic design and spontaneous construction. On the other hand, genetic and hereditary diseases or malignant growth exemplify faulty, destructive coalescence. Here pathology is a self-perpetuating life process that actively antagonizes the body's capacity to maintain healthy tissues.

A coalescence of constructive vital forces in physical health has an analogy in personality development. Here, a coalescence of constructive vital forces occurs between a child's inner need and readiness for trust development on the one hand and a trustworthy environment on the other. This coalescence forms the epigenetic core of further personality growth (Erikson, 1959). It leads to a baby's capacity to risk trusting the adults around him and, potentially, to the lifelong development of trust. A coalescence of constructive, vital forces is postulated in contextual theory, too. Here the criteria for fairness in a child's life and context are presumed to evolve out of a converging flow of fortunate circumstances, the fairness of fate, so to speak. Fundamentally, a child's inner needs for trust coalesce with his good fortune, including his parents' capacity to offer the care on which he can survive and thrive. Given an adequate parenting environment, with nurturing and reason to trust, the young are likely to grow into people capable of healthy relating. That is, they can risk and are beholden to offering their love and trust to others, they can discover the liberating aspects and effects of giving, and they can induce others to give in return. Or, if others fail to give in return, a healthy youngster can learn to recognize the loss and turn his relational needs in another direction.

Put in negative terms, it follows that certain children are more fortunate than others. A child can be born a victim of crippling and unjust destiny and life circumstances that are bound to lead to developmental consequences. Yet people are not inherently programmed to be encumbered by destructive entitlement which, as a process, is close in nature to the self-perpetuating, faulty destructive coalescence of malignant, psychological growth. It tends to dominate and to prevent healthy development: Unjustly hurt, injured children soon lose their inherent store of trust. Under the burden of further exploitation, their ethical entitlement to vindictiveness coalesces with their psychological potential for mistrust, as well as with their subsequently disturbed psychosocial development. Here, as a result or as a retreat from relating, the internal good and bad image of another in a child's psyche takes precedence over his tendency to risk trust in real people. Consequently, the child pays a price. His retreat into the confining, if safe, world of inner relationships is likely to result in a monologic existence characterized by paranoia, depression or narcissism.

The destructively entitled person may be inconspicuous or superficially pleasant. But his or her thin veneer is likely to crumble under the real tests of relational health. Patterns that reflect fundamental mistrust tend to surface under the stresses of facing serious commitments to peers. These include engagement, marriage, sexuality as an expression of trustworthy exchange, childbirth, and serious loss. Childhood trust is irreplaceable. Once missed, it cannot be recovered. Moreover, there is simply no time limit on the consequences of destructive entitlement. Psychologically, the loss is lasting and irreversible. Even so, the careful therapist is not working in an entirely barren sphere. In this kind of situation, a therapist needs patience and the insight and skill to make ample allowances for therapeutic moratoria except in life-threatening circumstances.

Ethically, then, the therapeutic effort to change patterns rooted in profound, justifiable mistrust may eventually prove successful to some degree but is never an easy task. A therapist may lead her client to a renewed risk of trust. Obviously, though, how relatives respond can never be guaranteed. What can be promised is the return intrinsic to a dialogic stance regardless of the interpersonal outcome of a person's actual attempts. The very process of risking trust anew results in a buildup of self-esteem that comes from relying on one's own entitlement. Furthermore, the attempt itself helps a person gain freedom and relief. All in all, renewed efforts at risking trust invariably constitute a fresh motivational basis for adopting new and constructive relational patterns, particularly those having to do with the dialogic phase of self-validation.

The process behind these significant changes lies in the hands of clients of course. Still, the therapist's conviction and perseverance are of paramount, "catalytic" importance. Here, however, a differentiation is to be made between a coerced intensity or technical intimacy that often occurs on weekend marathons, for example, and a therapist's capacity to be in touch with his or her own relational processes. It is the therapist's relevant concern for the consequences of his clients' situation that provides the basis for active involvement, not a talent for stimulating interest in his values or methods.

The therapist's concern about these consequences is conveyed to clients through a careful assessment of the processes in which they are caught. The assessment is furthered and transformed into a process of its own through the mechanism of crediting. A capacity to credit others in the midst of a hurtful and volatile situation is not only an invaluable part of the dialogic process, but also a preface to "facing." Facing, in a contextual framework, has more to do with taking a stand about credits than with a cognitive confrontation. Facing people's contributions as well as their deficits is also the opposite of retreating into an internal relational world.

The Constructive Coalescence of Spontaneous Motivations

Contextual therapy aids the process of constructively coalescencing people's spontaneous motivations. This process is constructive insofar as it guides the emergence of a coalition that can mobilize the unutilized resources that exist among them. In this sense the coalescence of individual forces has to be consonant with the intrinsic tribunal function of close relationships. Everybody's interests, especially those of posterity, have to receive due consideration. The formation of a coalition is then subordinated to the principle of multilateral fairness. Yet no matter how constructive the attempt, it does not work without harnessing everyone's spontaneous motivations.

In the case of an incestuous father, for example, the therapist aims at a workable formula that will protect everyone from both the reemergence of destructive acts and the consequences of past actions. The father has to be protected from moments that would tempt him to repeat his actions, and also from his own tendency not to face his responsibility for the welfare of his children. The child has to be helped to work on her problems with her family of origin. And the mother has to find her place amidst implications of conscious collusion or callousness. The ultimate goal is a coalition for fair consideration of everyone's interests instead of a coalition of one segment of a family against another.

Picturing a Retreat into an Inner Relational World

How can we picture a retreat into an inner relational world? Persistently painful, failing attempts to relate with actual people can eventually force a child or an adult to turn to the safer, less risky internal formula of self-other relating. It follows that destructive entitlement may result in abandoning people as well as driving them away. It can also silence remorse and corrective self-exploration. Psychosis and depression, then, can be defined as a person's surrender of active relating or as a retreat into projectively identified relationships. Paranoid and narcissistic relationships, then, have at least two intrinsic functions: 1) They displace the originally disappointing relationships into the internal world of needed accusation; 2) They periodically reexternalize the internal world onto third persons, frequently onto their mate or even onto their children. Consider the situation of a man who has earned destructive entitlement from a frustrating and rejecting relationship with his mother.

His deep disappointment is first channelled into a wishful idealization of women. Then it is transformed into a process of hurting and abandoning them without any experience of remorse at the point of making his decision. By now, his wife of long duration (and mother of his children) is counted among the women who have failed him and whom he can rebuff and reject without experiencing feelings of guilt or remorse. At the same time, the new woman in his life seems "different" and irresistible for the moment, a motivating factor in his life that he expects his wife to accept and understand.

The real tragedy in a retreat into internal relating is linked to the fact that it always blocks a genuine, responsible investment in interpersonal dialogue. This loss is compounded by the protagonist's destructive entitlement which blocks insight and redress from her own destructiveness. Should the man in our story begin to feel remorse, it would probably signal an increase in trustability. Here remorse can be defined as a self-correcting device. For it automatically serves to counteract motivations for exploiting an innocent third party.

Blocking the Retreat

In its effort to block the retreat into a person's internal relational world, psychoanalytic therapy has traditionally oscillated between two foci: insight as cognitive mastery and offers of a corrective emotional experience as empathic fueling. Corrective emotional experiences involve a client's transference attitudes to the therapist, therapeutic empathy and sensitivity. An active search for ways to repair relationships with one's family of origin is characteristically discouraged. In contrast, classical family therapy emphasizes the restorative effects of direct experience between people who are currently significant to each other. Open communication, experiencing a person's presence, and finding an opportuntiy for immediate response are all component parts of this process.

Contextual therapy offers additional options. Its emphasis falls on helping family members respond to each other in ways that give due credit where credit is due. Its chief consideration is extended to intergenerational relationships even when parents are alleged to be negative, inactive or dead. Its aim is not necessarily directed to revitalizing relationships with parents who, in any case, may or may not be able to respond or cooperate. The aim is rather the liberating effects of earned entitlement. The demand here has less to do with the offspring's renewed attempts at care than with how resentful he or she may become at the likelihood that a parent will give little or nothing in return. Consider the man in his late forties who came for help with a lifelong struggle with marginal relationships.

He is gifted with outstanding intelligence and musical talent. Nevertheless, he is depressed and carries an onerous sense of failure. His parents live far away and have long given up on what they consider to be their defiant and rebellious son. It seems a fact that his mother, who may have been deeply disturbed, even forbade the mention of David's name in her presence.

The therapist listened to the gruesome details of David's childhood. He had constantly been torn between murderous hatred towards his parents and devastating guilt feelings interspersed with memories of allegedly severe rejection. "Given these feelings and realities, were there still ways in which David could consider dealing more directly with them?" the therapist asked. David was massively resistant to the suggestion. The therapist responded to David's resistance with heightened partiality towards him and all that he had suffered for so long. He also continued to raise the question of what David thought he could actually do about the situation.

Eventually David raised the possibility of writing his parents an explanatory letter. Here the therapist made repeated efforts to remind him of the likelihood of not receiving a reply. In fact, he asked David not to write until he thought he could tolerate the possibility of his parents' not responding. The real issue was whether David could make peace with his own resolve to reach out. Could he appreciate and gain from the integrity of his own intervention independently of his parents' capacities? Could he simply draw satisfaction out of his own initiative? David finally sent his letter. Several weeks later, he indirectly heard that his father had died. He may never learn whether or not his father read his letter or if his father wanted to respond, and how.

There are therapists, for example, those with a psychoanalytic orientation, who would not have encouraged David to send a letter. At best, it could be reasoned, little would be resolved. At worst, he exposed himself to still another experience of rejection. Conversely, it can be argued that David's decision developed into a unique asset. He had taken the chance to initiate dialogue with his parents before his father died, a chance that no longer exists. He earned entitlement for himself through the actual fact of a renewed expression of concern. And he would be strengthened by the fact that he had found the courage to face and act on a now unrepeatable risk.

The change that started to take place through David's efforts signifies a shift from a destructive to a constructive coalescence between internal and external patterns of relating. David's hostile avoidance of his parents coincided with his rigidly held, internally "bad" object, and both were reinforced by the destructive entitlement that parent and child alike had earned in their respective upbringings. In addition, his parents' actual rejecting behavior coalesced with the preceding dynamics. But as David began to mobilize enough courage and concern to reach out in a caring way, he activated his side of the dialogue and began to earn constructive entitlement. His own interests were served by taking the initiative despite the fact of his historic injuries. In contextual work either a parent or a child is at liberty to try to activate a dialogue through self-validating moves. Most often it is the offspring who initiates.

Unfortunately, many schools of psychotherapy endorse the conventional attitude that simply asserts the factuality of a "bad" parent-child relationship. The "fact" itself suggests that the status of the relationship can neither be directly challenged nor changed. In addition, the operating premise seems to be that any effort in the direction of a reworked relationship is never worth the emotional costs. It might be implicitly assumed that here the son is victim and, as such, is entitled to abandon his "monster" parents whatever their age or needs. This general attitude probably reflects the anxiety and trepidation with which modern society has come to regard the binds of parent-child relationships. Another common attitude pictures parent-child distance at any cost as evidence of the success of "separation."

The therapeutic philosophy that gives permission to abandon parent-child relationships has evoked a tremendous cost in defective trust, most notably in the offspring's capacity to make commitments beyond his or her family of origin. This failure of commitment includes generative stagnation and self-destructive patterns of living that include periodic suicidal inclinations. It is close to tragic that the prospect for earning constructive entitlement in parent-child relating has not just diminished in frequency; it has nearly come to a total impasse. The option of life has yielded too much room to the option of relational death.

The universal laws of human behavior underscore the realism of filial efforts to risk and to explore new options for relating with aging parents. It may indeed be true that, historically, the parent generation was more responsible for the impasse than their children's generation. On the other hand, it is also the parent generation which carried the responsibility of shaping the nature of the early relationship. It was initially up to the parents to validate themselves as responsibly caring partners in a dialogue with unmatched partners (phase II). At the same time, the child's task was essentially to delineate himself throughout the relationship (phase I). This balance necessarily changed by the time the child reached his maturity. By then, the parents had become more vulnerable by virtue of age. At this stage offspring always stand to gain by choosing the option of validating themselves. At this point, offers of due care are in order even when parents have failed to earn sufficient credit. Should a grown son or daughter opt out and finally give up, they are in danger of losing too.

In sum, the most effective way to diminish and replace a reliance on the reality of internal relating comes from a balanced commitment to the realities of interpersonal relating. This includes the existential realities of dialogue which include genuine caring for the self (phase I) as well as for others (phase II). A person's care and commitment can obviously be displaced onto others, including the therapist. But to choose to leave parents out of one's care and concern always amounts to a serious and costly omission.

THE INTRINSIC TRIBUNAL ASPECT OF RELATIONSHIPS

Parent-child relationships provide the fundamental paradigm for all of the built-in conflicts, collisions and rivalries of existence. How people respond in these primal relationships shapes how they are likely to respond to all conflicts, collisions and rivalries. Conflicting needs, interests and investments are obviously inevitable in relationships and difficult to overcome. They can be kept in check only by mutual care over the fair and due distribution of burdens and benefits among all relating partners. Paradoxically, perhaps, the process of mutual care is linked to a function of close relationship that can best be described as an intrinsic "tribunal" (Boszormenyi-Nagy, 1983).

In brief the tribunal-like function in relationships is inherent and operates as first one partner and then another claim credit and need someone to receive their claims. Put in other terms, they both can acknowledge the rivalrous or adversary aspect of their relationship without using a third party as judge or referee. Typically, one person makes her plea and expects her partner to weigh its worth in the manner of a judge who can listen with dispassion. Her partner, however, is not dispassionate. To the contrary, he is invested in the opposite side of the matter at hand. Moreover, if he chooses to hear the legitimacy of his partner's claims solely on her terms, he might have to concede his own claims and might even strengthen hers at the same time.

These assumptions presuppose a dyadic structure: Here I am with my needs and there you are as a prospectively disappointing source of gratification for me. Or here you are as the complainer and I am the likely culprit. The dilemma here is the presence of a third party, often imaginary, who is supposed to hear and decide the issue between you and me. And so a triad is "born." If a triadic structure is squeezed into a dyadic relationship, partners tend to parentify each other. This longed-for tribunal function is not just constricted to a parent-like adult role; it is supposed to stand over and above the quarreling adults. Take the example of an 11-year-old obliged to listen to his mother say, "Your father is always late with his checks for child support." Here the boy is used as a tribunal of justice for his parents. In addition, he is supposed to absorb his mother's anger and to deal with his own frustration over not getting an allowance which his mother has withheld. Obviously, an 11-year-old ought not be asked to sit in judgment of a parent. Just as obviously, mother needs to find a way to hold her former husband accountable in a more direct and immediate dyadic exchange.

Like family members, therapists are also assigned a tribunal function. This function is rarely therapeutic, however, and can best be circumvented through the skillful use of the method of multidirected partiality. The therapist can address each partner's quest for an inherent tribunal through having them advocate for themselves as well as insisting that they listen to each other. The therapist can confirm each person's merit in searching for fair answers and resolutions, but he or she is obliged to decline the role of referee. Therapists are free to address people's intrinsic tribunal but not to become that tribunal. They can help family members learn how to activate the tribunal-like function between them through a catalytic use of the therapeutic role. Consider the situation of a father and two of his married daughters in their first therapeutic interview.

Christine, 35, the mother of two small children, is on the brink of divorce. Father initially described her sister, Edith, 32, as the easy, compliant daughter. Christine suggested that her parents had many marital problems. But father painted a picture of himself as a strong and benevolent spouse, one who always gave room to his wife because of her difficult childhood experiences.

The therapist was in no position to draw conclusions from what anyone said, especially in mother's absence. However, the tribunal aspect of the family's relationships was at work in the session. For the first time in her life, Edith was moved out of her silence into a statement about her parents' marriage. "Father," she said, "my most painful childhood memory is the picture of you at the dining room table letting mother tear you and us to pieces. How could you let her be so cruel and unfair?" The truth of Edith's words evoked father's truth as well. "Yes, you're right," he replied, "but, you see, I had to choose between my daughters and my wife. It is with her, not with you, that I have to spend the latter years of my life."

The common experience of these family members was inaccessible to the therapist. Any judgment he might have made would have lacked direction and integrity. So would any attempt to referee or mitigate the family's hard truths. On the other hand, his encouragement of each person's quest for fair exchange precipitated the tribunal function inherent in their relationships.

CHAPTER 12

Resistances: Obstacles to Therapeutic Progress

Therapeutic progress occurs in many different ways. So do obstacles to progress. These obstacles can be grouped into contextual dimensions for organized and comprehensive understanding. We have chosen to designate a conglomerate of resistances. In doing so, we keep in mind the limiting, individually confined connotations of the word "resistance." In its original meaning, resistance means the client's partly unconscious opposition to therapeutic intrusion into his or her inner balances of motivational forces. Once we consider obstacles to the therapeutic progress of several relating persons, we begin to deal with an interplay of internal balances, *and* external balances *between* persons as well.

DIMENSION I: FACTUAL OBSTACLES

A lack of healthy childhood experiences is chief among the factual resistances to therapeutic progress. Lasting psychological damage to young human beings, just as to young animals, results from a lack of parental input, empathy and care (Harlow, 1962; Spitz, 1946). The failure of input may result in lasting impoverishment from underdeveloped skills and borderline experiences of fair relating. Overwhelming circumstances like serious illness (brain damage or diabetes) are also factual obstacles to therapeutic improvement. They are sources of resistance that affect the victim directly and can have massive, if indirect, effects on the victim's family members.

Detrimental childhood experiences are a further factual obstacle, especially in terms of damage to the development of early trust. Exploitation and aggressive or sexual use of a child are especially significant antecedents that can limit people's capacity for realigning relationships. So are shameful circumstances that form a cloud over a person's family of origin. The issue of family shame is often a particularly profound source of resistance made even more problematic by psychotherapy's frequent failure to touch the topic. To compound the problem, a client's fear of disloyalty often prevents him or her from ever mentioning real shame. For example, a person is likely to be unable to reveal (betray?) a parent's incestuous behavior, and certainly not before she has developed considerable confidence in her therapist's capacity to be partial to everyone, including the parent in question. The therapist usually has to schedule private sessions for the offspring, sessions that may even exclude the client's spouse.

Psychosomatic symptoms may be partly caused by relational factors. Their physical consequences, though, may also be characterized as a factual obstacle to therapeutic progress.

DIMENSION II: PSYCHOLOGICAL OBSTACLES TO THERAPEUTIC PROGRESS

Good feelings themselves can be a psychological obstacle to therapeutic progress. Paradoxically, feelings of security can evolve from damaging relational situations. People often choose to adhere to destructive internal patterns of relating for secondary gain. They may value a "bad" relationship with the internal parent, even cling to it because of the feeling it can produce. Consider the situation of the daughter whose mother placed her in a foster home before the girl was two. Now the daughter is grown and has a young son. "My mother abandoned me," daughter now reports. "She was selfish, centered only on herself. I never could expect anything of her. But look at me. My son is past two and, unlike my mother, I've kept him with me." Unstated is her struggle with child abuse, and the authorities' threat to remove her son if he is beaten once more. Here her mother is a "bad" internal object for daughter who, despite other options, maintains that her mother is bad. She gains feelings of self-worth, even superiority, through this perception of her mother.

Familiar patterns of behavior can also retard the development of therapeutic progress. Relating partners as individuals or as groups often feel more comfortable with habitual, conditioned behavior. In turn, the force of habit mitigates against new attitudes and behaviors. An insistence on clinging to old ways of doing things is analogous to Freud's notion of a "repetition compulsion," a similar though more specific consideration. Clinging to customary ways of relating is also likely to be motivated by a person's fear of losing a relational partner. This fear of loss leads to individual and "collective postponement of mourning" (Boszormenyi-Nagy, 1965b). People can be consciously or inadvertently loyal to each other without a full awareness of their loyalty. Relationships may be maintained at any cost in order to deflect the reality and consequences of loss for those immediately affected and for others who may "need" to be protected. The longing to defer or avoid the consequences of loss is another stumbling block to therapeutic progress.

A fear of losing a source of gratification and thus losing gratification itself is analogous to the more general fear of losing a relational partner. Parentification is one method of mitigating anxiety over anticipated loss and, in fact, of delaying it. In a way, parentification originates from a parentifying person's failure to give up habitual patterns of dependent relating in order to consider another person's side. It embodies a reluctance to face into the mourning process so loss can become an accepted fact. More basically, fears of loss can be allayed through destructive entitlement.

A reliance on destructive entitlement is obviously a sad and guilt-inducing way of life. Nevertheless, it can satisfy a deep personal need for making things right and just. At the same time, it inflicts new injuries and injustices and, in some cases, creates psychological guilt as well. Destructive entitlement with its ethical dynamics can combine with the psychological consequences of persistent, internal "bad" relating. This combination may then be coupled with a selective pattern of interpersonal relating, e.g., a woman consistently picks "inadequate" men for companions and so repeatedly enters relationships that are doomed to fail.

Destructive delegations constitute another obstacle for people's freedom to improve. Heavy, intergenerational delegations presume that an "as if" position is of an ethically valid nature. The mother who "commits her son to God" (and thus to the ministry) at birth, as if it were her own life rather than someone else's, has set up conditions that produce both guilt and resentment. The success of intergenerational conditioning, whether too little or too much, depends on the degree to which the injunction is embedded in the offspring's propensities for guilt feelings. The therapeutic task of differentiating delegations from valid legacies is made even more difficult by intergenerational impositions of destructive delegations.

DIMENSION III: TRANSACTIONAL OBSTACLES TO THERAPEUTIC PROGRESS

People who comply with the counterproductive behavioral patterns of other family members are caught in a "clinch," an impasse, or in pathological complementarity. A case in point is the person whose anxiously, curious attitude about a family situation may be a legitimate point of view. On the other hand, his overarching tendency to be anxiously curious about other people's welfare may evoke a protective, cover-up attitude on the part of other family members, e.g., "Your worrying makes me sick."

Power coalitions also function as obstacles to therapeutic progress in their provocation of confrontations, defeats, victories, and vendettas. The question of who is allied with whom misrepresents the dialogic nature of close relationships even though it may convey an essence of closeness. In one transactional sequence, mother may seem to be allied with the children against father. In another sequence, these parents may jointly criticize one of their daughters and undermine her marriage. Each of these game-like configurations refers to "subsystems" from a transactional perspective. Yet the underlying patterns have to do with intrinsically parentified children who are exploited by their parents rather than simply with repetitive, transactional patterns and their feedback structure.

Therapeutic progress is also stymied by myths about children that make them ideal or hopeless, selfish or all-caring, inherently redeeming or essentially destructive, good or bad, needy or self-abnegating. Another undermining myth has to do with illusory, transactional truths and conclusions about a family's circumstances. For example, parents may say, "We used to argue but we're fine now. Our children are grown up and we've become three separate families. We don't have any conflicts because we no longer have to deal with each other close up." Facts about transactions? Perhaps, but bereft of any concern about trustworthiness or an apparent ability to credit people for their past care.

DIMENSION IV: ETHICAL OBSTACLES

Resistance to the ethical dimension of relationship is traditionally so heavy that much of the therapeutic profession has chosen not to raise it at all. It is not only family members who are hesitant to enter into a process that will expose a family's deep-rooted truths and lies; therapists are also reluctant, especially with clients who may be older than they. Moreover, the complexity of family dynamics is often overwhelming and sometimes seems to warn everyone away. It may simply seem easier, initially, to raise questions about a delinquent child than to ask if this youngster is somehow carrying the burdens of his parents' marriage.

The implied contradictions in selfish or altruistic views are also a stumbling block to progress. A demonstrably giving mother, for example, may be exploiting her child in subtle and nuanced ways. However, the situation may be protected against exposure, simultaneously by mother's narcissistic vulnerability and by her youngster's loyalty to her.

Destructive entitlement is a major obstacle to therapeutic improvement. Credits and rights earned in a person's childhood may paralyze her current capacity to offer due concern to others. Her inability to respond is substitutive, retributive and unfair. The injuries that she incurred remain unfaced and help to protect her from remorse, regardless of the injustices she has caused.

Intergenerational expectations can also get in the way of healing. Divorced parents who actively delegate children to mediate their unfinished battles with each other actively retard everyone's therapeutic chances to improve. A child may be rendered incapable of ever resolving the conflict linked to two mutually warring parents who insist on posing two mutually exclusive sets of claims for filial loyalty.

SIGNS OF THERAPEUTIC PROGRESS

Psychodynamic psychotherapy has looked to individual criteria for signs of health and therapeutic progress. Fairbairn (1952, p. 156) writes of the "salvation from bondage to one's internal bad objects." Erikson (1959) emphasized maturation within each stage of the life cycle. And Rado (1925) compared "working through" with the work of mourning. Traditional, individual psychotherapy has not invested itself in working with its clients' relationship nor has it included healing for a person's partner as a primary or immediate goal. This stance presents some dilemmas. At the very least, if a person makes individual gains, her progress will be out of step with her partner's life cycle adjustments. A partner's salvation from his own internal objects or from a stagnant mourning process may be equally crucial determinants of a client's well-being. A failure to be decisively involved with a client's partner, then, may inadvertently undercut significantly held relationships. In our experience, it is simply more efficacious and productive to incorporate an active concern about a client's relationships, whether or not these people are physically incorporated in the therapy sessions.

In contextual work therapeutic progress is confirmed when a client can respond to encouragement to take some actual steps. Therapeutic seeds are planted and begin to take root in one family member. He uses whatever therapeutic moratorium is available to him and then may take one of several options. He may invite his parents to a session or write them a letter, or he may reopen contact with a long cutoff brother. What is central here is that an important chain reaction is being set in motion: One person gains enough trust and courage to activate his part in facing his relational panorama without any guarantee of positive returns. In the doing, he risks shifting the balance between his own internal relating and his interpersonal relationships.

A person's willingness to attempt to progress also jeopardizes the equilibrium of his partner's stagnant relationships. For example, a man's efforts to get close to his mother after she has consistently scapegoated him over time may pose a serious threat to her. Until now she has managed her destructive entitlement by cutting off her son, and he has complied. Now he is asking for something different in his attempts to convert his own destructive behavior into opportunities to earn constructive entitlement. He is challenging the family's collusive postponement of mourning and, in the process, taking new options for himself and offering them to others. Everyone here will need new supplies of energy to complete the mourning process. That energy is likely to evolve from a well-founded hope for new ways of developing trustworthy give-and-take and of earning new entitlement.

It is true that new demands are placed on all relating partners whenever one of them progresses. It is also true that as an individual attains new therapeutic gains he or she injects new levels of courage, trust and risk-taking into the entire context. The very effort to investigate where and how acknowledgements and credits are due is *ipso facto* a trustworthy move. It *invites* people into dialogue and addresses the inherent tribunal function of significant relationships. The dialogue becomes increasingly trustworthy as each partner can come to perceive the other as a caregiver (phase II) as well as a one-sided taker (phase I). As perceptions continue to shift, people can begin to relinquish their excessive reliance on internal relationships. They will simultaneously be able to diminish their exploitation of the relationship as well as their reliance on power manipulations.

As people risk new levels of commitment to their relationships, they take responsibility for their own input. Taking risks and responsibility helps people become more defined as individuals. For example, a parent may be able to admit how he tends to place the children in the middle instead of dealing directly with his wife. A woman may decide to talk for the first time about her father's incestuous relationships with her and her mother's abuse of her. Or a terminally ill, perpetually bitter and distant parent who has long been resented by his children may unexpectedly be able to acknowledge their lifelong devotion to him.

REWARDS OF THERAPEUTIC PROGRESS

As family members rejoin and deepen the dialogue, their give-and-take inevitably becomes more rewarding for everyone. The liberation that evolves from earning entitlement is one of the major driving forces undergirding therapeutic progress. In the first instance it is neither "good" nor "moral" behavior that sustains or motivates therapeutic work, but the spontaneous outburst of a sense of inner freedom.

Therapeutic progress produces numberless signs of liberation. For example:

- After several months of resistance, a young woman brings her long-resented mother to a therapy session and talks with her in a trusting way. Shortly afterwards, for the first time since her wedding night, her persistent frigidity disappears.
- After two years of cutoffs, a single woman relinquishes her resistance to resuming contact with her parents. A short time later, she plans a trip with a friend, her first vacation in seven years. She simultaneously decides to give up the habitual drinking which has dominated her life for so long.
- The mother of a psychotic teenager takes her terminally ill mother into her home. She has decided to nurse her mother despite abiding re sentment towards her. Subsequently there is an unexpected improvement in her marriage and in her daughter's function.
- A woman decides to reconnect her adopted children to their families of origin. To her surprise, she finds herself liberated rather than deprived in her relationships with them. She also feels free to begin to examine the ghosts of her past.
- A man comes into therapy on the verge of divorce and involved with another woman. He has long abandoned the relationship with his parents about whom he is ambivalent and resentful. He decides to explore what, if anything, he can offer them in terms of fresh concern. In the process he receives unexpected help from his wife. She has apparently been the victim of his invisible filial loyalty. As a result of his work in therapy, their marriage finally gets a real chance for consideration, and their children visibly benefit from their parents' renewed relationship.

In sum, as people learn to rely on the self-sustaining spiral of earning constructive entitlement, they earn increasing amounts of freedom for some of the following functions.

- Facing the consequences of their own responsibility rather than resorting to blame. Their ability to face and be responsible diminishes tendencies to scapegoat and inclinations for projective identification of a destructive kind.
- Exonerating their parents, a process that leads to liberation from the ghosts of the past and improves a person's potential for relinquishing repetitious relational patterns from the past.
- Developing increased mutuality in offering care to posterity. This is the freedom of spouses to help each other repay their parents through due concern and so to improve their capacity for peer relating and parenting.

V. THERAPEUTIC METHODS

CHAPTER 13

A Case Illustration

It is sometimes difficult to convey the therapeutic agenda of contextual work. Its scope and goals are rooted in the complex considerations of its four dimensions of reality and extend well beyond the limits of symptom corrections and techniques. On the other hand, live demonstrations readily show how, through the leverages of Dimension IV, family members can be reached at a deep level in the early moments of their first therapy session. Despite the undisclosed complexity in and between family members, it is relatively easy to surface every person's fundamental longings, claims, disappointments, and discouragement with their lives together, as well as to surface their inevitable hopes for a better way.

It is relatively easy to elucidate the relational realities of closely relating partners. It is to be noted here that the emphasis is on the balances of fairness between *individual members in their close relatedness* rather than on "the family." It is also relatively easy to demonstrate how to activate their residual or unutilized resources for commitment. Contextual therapy proceeds on the premise that people's commitment to each other is the essence of relational reality.

Intermember behavior is secondary to the reality of their fundamental commitments. The origin of commitment is the *fact* of people's existential relatedness and the family members' desire to get something from that relatedness. Commitments obviously exist whether or not they are viable. The viability of commitments always depends on the relating partners finding ways towards fairness in the balances of give-and-take between them (Dimension IV)—time and time again. Consider the situation of the mother and her adult daughter and son whose respective outward behavior seemed dutiful, if rote. Twenty minutes into their first therapy session together was time enough to surface dynamics among them that none of them had ever addressed. The presenting issue was the superficiality of their exchanges and transactions. The underlying issues all had their roots in intergenerational injuries and injustices that motivate ethical disengagement.

The following excerpts illustrate the nature of some of the contextual interventions that can take place in the space of a few sessions. The daughter, already doing contextual work, invited her mother and brother in from out of town to attend some sessions with her. Therapy, like life, is never a short-term process. On the other hand, though, the period of intervention is not necessarily long. Contextual therapy, through its focus on Dimension IV, is immediately relevant to clients at deep levels of their existence. It takes time to learn how to be a competent therapist, of course, and it takes an even longer time to become a competent, short-term therapist.

At the beginning of therapy, Sarah presented herself as a hardworking, overburdened, frequently unappreciated person who was deeply committed to social and religious concerns. She sometimes suffered from insomnia and occasionally from suicidal thoughts. She also felt exploited by males. She had been married for a brief time in her early twenties. At some levels, she felt inferior to her mother who had been able to sustain the marriage to Sarah's father, now dead.

Sarah was often guarded and suspicious of close relationships with men. She was wary of another marriage, though sometimes she regretted never having had a child. On the other hand, she was dubious over whether or not she would have offered good parenting "material." In essence, she was highly defensive, if not paralyzed, in many areas of personal relating.

Sarah's picture of her brother Will was one of a successful businessman who knew what he wanted from women even when it seemed difficult to get what he wanted. She was impressed with the courage it took for him to risk marriage for the third time. She longed for a closer relationship with him, but felt unable to reach out to Will in any significant way. Sarah also realized her own success and competence in her profession. In fact, her work as a helping agent provided her with her major source of deep satisfaction.

The therapist worked on preparing Sarah for the meetings with her mother and brother in earlier, individual sessions, conveying the importance of each family member taking a courageous stance. For Sarah to face and express her own needs was likely to serve her own and her relatives' best interests in the long run. She had initially sounded all too eager to

GENOGRAM OF THE L FAMILY

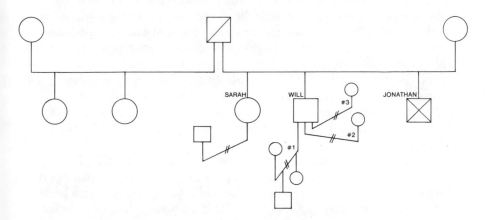

excuse her parents and could see very little of how her hurt feelings had originated from her relationship with them.

Sarah was concerned about her mother's drinking. She remembered mother's suicidal gestures and her past psychiatric hospitalizations. Recently, she had also begun to worry about Will's increasing emotional isolation. He seemed emotionally remote from his children and his relationship with his daughter was especially angry and estranged.

Failing in outside relationships is usually the tip of the iceberg, characterized by stagnation over using dialogic resources, i.e., the capacity for reciprocal commitments to fair relating in significant relationships. Patterns of overgiving are often used as a substitute for a dialogue of reciprocal commitments. In the beginning, patterns of overgiving may seem to be an effective means of binding people. Yet it is likely that they originated from the fact that a person has been a parentified, exploitatively depleted child forced into a pattern of self-denial. The pattern of self-denial then develops from a child's ambivalence over giving, while, *at the same time*, he or she fears being exploited by the very person he is giving to. The exploited overgiver is likely to develop destructive entitlement which is bound to surface in and poison later relationships.

Contextual therapy holds that overgiving relationships can often be reshaped through work on the interpersonal dialogue of fair balances. Overgiving can actually improve the quality of a person's giving if, simultaneously, he or she can honestly claim his due (self-delineation), *and* his partner can validate herself through learning to acknowledge how she benefits from a more open exchange. First, however, the frustrated overgiver has to learn to credit the fact that, indeed, he was unfairly victimized.

Only then is he genuinely ready to exonerate the exploitative parent.

The contextual therapist knows that a child is most destructively parentified when he is caught in the obligation to service the failing, mistrustful relationship between his parents. The more subtle the mistrust between spouses, the less manageable it is for their youngster. The covert collusiveness of extractive, dependent parents may make matters even worse. Their apparent, joint disregard for the child's genuine needs will ultimately force him into becoming an even more desperate giver. By comparison, honest, parental quarrels are a much more tolerable filial burden than this hidden bind of severe parentification, with all of its subtle, guilt-laden implications.

Sarah brought her mother, Ms. L., and younger brother, Will, in from the Midwest for a series of four therapy sessions. The therapist opened the first session by asking Sarah if she had told her mother and brother her motives for bringing them together. Sarah said that her work as a lawyer underscored the significance of family relationships.

Daughter indicates her fear that family members will oppose the exploration of their relationships.

Sarah: At a conference last fall, someone said that it's really hypocritical to ask families to come and talk about each other if you haven't done it with your own family. There's an integrity issue. For example, when I suggest that a client might benefit from therapy, I always say, "I've had therapy and it's really changed my life." The other thing is if you see connections in your own family, you're more likely to see connections in other families too. But when I finally called, I found it was scary to ask my own family to come in.

Therapist: Well, my experience with my own relatives, as well as with clients, tells me that there's typically a lot of love and care that often get derailed in families. People get stuck in terms of what they can safely say to each other, what issues they can discuss, what reactions

Emphasizes hidden, relational resources. Implies courage to

face option for self-validation through extending concern about the humanity of the other (Dim. IV). Emphasizes positive resources *over* a search for pathology. Appeals to the deeper truth of the search for love among close relatives.

Makes explicit the inclusiveness of therapeutic care and partiality. Thereby begins to define the therapist's contractual attitude. Elicits daughter's spontaneity in choosing an area of obvious concern. Directs same partiality towards son as well.

Mother credits daughter's generosity in giving to people. Yet the childhood example she recalls raises the question of a familial pattern of sacrificial overgiving at the expense of legitimate efforts at self-delineation.

they expect. Each of us builds up a kind of family fiction and loses the humanity of the other person. The issue today is not to emphasize anything negative —all families have negative aspects—but to gently nudge the caring so that some of the harder issues among you can get conveyed. That way you have a chance of getting closer. The problem is that people can love each other and still be distant from them.

I guess, for me, the people in this room today include the three of you, plus Mr. L and your other son, Johnny. I hope they get incorporated in the discussion because, in many ways, they are here; there's no way it could be otherwise. Beyond that, Sarah, where would you like to start? It may be one of the areas that you would like to change between you, for example, the anxiety you carry when you want to raise a difficult question. And you might have parallel issues, Will.

Mrs. L: I'm very proud of what she's doing, helping people. As a little one she always wanted to do that. My husband didn't like to go to things at school. She was president of some organization, so I said, "Come on now. This is a dinner and she's down on the program three times." We went but she didn't say a word the whole time we were there, and my husband wanted to know why I had brought him. I asked Sarah why she didn't speak if her name was on the program. "Oh," she said, "I had friends who felt terrible because they weren't included in the program. So I told them to take the time allotted to me." She's always helped other people.

Therapist: From whom did she get that, Ms. L?

Ms. L: My father was a Methodist minister and I think she may have gotten that from him.

Sarah: But you've always done a lot for people. Don't you think so?

Ms. L: Well, I don't know.

Sarah: I think you gave a lot of parties for people, and for us. You know, I guess what I always think about a lot is when you sold your piano when Johnny died. I sort of feel like you sold your song. You know, the one thing I remember that mother did with us a lot—and I'm curious if you remember it too, Will— was play the piano. Remember, "The snake is going to come and get you."

Will: I remember that. It's the only thing I remember her playing.

Ms. L: I hadn't thought of that for years.

Sarah: Whenever there was a party, you played the piano and Johnny played the piano. And Johnny used to go out in the

---

Inquiry into the origins of the pattern and the question of whether giving to people binds them into undue obligations.

The parentified daughter intervenes on her mother's behalf.

Pattern is connected with self-denial and with the grief over the death of a family member. Acknowledges mother's giving.

Further acknowledging.

kitchen and say, "How many years has she taken lessons?" You played the piano so beautifully. Johnny played the piano so beautifully, and I guess I. . . .

Ms. L: You just ditched it with your teacher. Sarah thought her teacher was wonderful. They had great visits but I don't know that she ever played the piano.

Sarah: But I think the reason I did that, Mother, was that I really didn't feel very gifted and I didn't work at it very much.

Ms. L: No, you didn't.

Offers open, honest talk as a giving relational resource.

Sarah: So my way of trying to get around that was to entertain people. But to get back to you, I think that sometimes you and I can talk so much at such a deep level, like that time in the hospital. And there have been other times, not all of them happy, when you've gotten pissed at me and I've gotten pissed at you.

Ms. L: That's right.

Credits mother with same.

Sarah: I also remember a time when you said that you were proud that we worked at our relationship so much. Wouldn't you say that we have?

Ms. L: Yes, we have.

Opens up the search for greater spontaneity in parent-child relating.

Sarah: I guess, sometimes, that I don't know how to get to you in terms of more than just talking about pleasant things.

Ms. L: Could be.

Partial to mother via expectation of spontaneity and commitment to open dialogue.

Therapist: Do you know what Sarah needs from you, Ms. L?

Cautious response. Mother may be asking for a moratorium.

Ms. L: No, I don't know whether it's encouragement; I really don't think she needs anything from me. She gets along beautifully.

Tries to emphasize positive resources. Credits mother's merits.

Therapist: Maybe not as much as you think. Maybe you're so proud of her that she's bigger than life to you. Maybe you're unaware that she has some needs that only you can address.

Ms. L: I think you're right.

Partial to mother through suggesting ways for her self-validation through helping daughter with her self-delineation.

Therapist: Have you ever been able to say to Sarah, "What do you need?, or "I need you."? Maybe you need to come in at this point too, Will.

Ms. L: No, I don't think I've ever said that.

Explores pattern (Dim. III).

Therapist: Is that hard to do in your family?

Ms. L: Well, I guess it must be. I never thought about it.

Therapist: Why would that be, Ms. L?

Ms. L: I don't know.

Is the pattern a renunciation of efforts at self-delineation?

Therapist: How about with other people in your life, like your husband, for example? Were you able to tell him what you needed?

Ms. L: Yes.

Explores nature of parental marriage vis-à-vis fairness of give and take.

Therapist: Was he able to give you what you needed?

Ms. L: Yes.

Extends partiality to mother.

Therapist: And what happened when he couldn't?

Ms. L: When he was ill? Well, there wasn't anything to do except to realize that he was awfully sick and dying.

Explores capacity for dealing with interpersonal conflicts of interests. Were the children placed in the predicament of split loyalty?

Therapist: What happened before he was sick, when you simply had differences of opinions or quarrels? How did you handle that?

Ms. L: We talked things out. We didn't always agree.

Explores the state of mother's mourning work as a widow.

Therapist: Do you have some leftover feelings from your marriage?

Ms. L: I don't think so. I think I had a very good marriage.

Sarah: But I remember one time. You took us to a movie to see Hamlet with Laurence Olivier and you cried. Do you remember that? You were crying and saying that you were thinking of leaving Dad, that it was just a real hard time. And last summer I asked if you might have gotten a divorce if it had been as easy to get one then as it is now. You said, "No," because Dad was pretty dependent on you and had taken the money you had hidden and saved.

Daughter remembers having been placed in a confidante role between father and mother. The dilemma of split loyalty appears: Was father a contemptible exploiter of mother? Does this circumstance burden the children with a legacy of having to undo parental shame and having to exonerate a parent?

Ms. L: Yes.

Turns partiality to mother: She has the option of self-validation via assuming self-critical responsibility.

Therapist: Do you have some regrets, not so much about your husband, but about your own behavior in your marriage? I know these are hard questions.

Ms. L: I don't believe I do. I think we always felt we were pretty lucky. Don't you think Dad and I felt we were pretty lucky? We had disagreements. I remember when Sarah was at Northwestern. She was to be in something and didn't know it. They called us and told us it would be nice if we'd come. My husband had a plane and loved to fly but I wanted to drive or go by train. He said, "No," and we argued and argued. Finally Will called from his bedroom. "Why don't the two of you stop acting like children and remember you're going up there to see Sarah?"

Example of how the parents' bickering parentified Will—a smaller burden than implications of contemptuous behavior on the parents' part.

Sarah: I never heard that story. Do you remember that?

Will: I remember so many of them.

Sarah: But I remember that one area you were very gutsy about, very very gutsy about, was Dad flying. She would go every place with him. We always knew we were in trouble when we were in the back seat and my mother would take her newspaper out and start to read . . . because she was terrified.

Mrs. L: That made him so annoyed. He'd say, "You can read that when we get there. Look at the scenery now." Oh, he just thought that was terrible and I guess you do, too, Will. When I've flown with you, I'm in the back and you're up there where you can't see what I'm doing.

Will: All I care about is that you relax and have a good time.

Shares personal fears and acknowledges mother's courage.

Therapist: I feel anxious about planes too, Ms. L. You're pretty courageous. You'll do things you're frightened of.

Mrs. L: Yes, I've tried.

Sarah: I think you were always a rebel. She just told me a couple of years ago that, when she was at De Pauw University, she'd gone down to smoke at the railroad track and then she'd gone to a bar. . . .

Gives credit to mother; but it is as if Sarah were the parent.

Mrs. L: No, we went to a dance at Terrahove.

Sarah: De Pauw was so religious and rigid that they didn't let her graduate.

Mrs. L: I got my diploma two years later.

Sarah: Because she was then the head of the English department at this little high school and the head of the Board called and said this was ridiculous. Did you know that?

Will: No.

Sarah: Isn't that outrageous?

Will: That's where I get all my bad traits, I guess.

Therapist scans the relational context regarding the dialogue of reciprocal availability and sensitivity to each other's needs. Also extends concern to the next generation of offspring regardless of the fact that they are absent from the session.

Explores apparent reserve between family members (Dim. II–III).

Request for an example is likely to bring in concreteness and a multilateral, relational perspective.

Further elaboration on the pattern of distance via manipulating a partner through self-denial ("helper" complex). Does this indicate attempts to control the other through a guilt bind?

Therapist: I want to suggest that I'm presuming a lot of resources among the three of you. So I want to ask two related questions which are more demanding than the level on which we're talking at the moment. One has to do with the question of how you meet each others' needs and reach into each others' lives instead of wondering and outguessing each other. The other has to do with your children, Will. I know that Sarah has a real affection for them. So they're the other people in this crowded room. The other question has to do with the protectiveness I see in how you relate. I suspect that it's hard for you to cut across your imagination and really pull the other person into your lives, but that's only a guess.

Will: Very true, though.

Therapist: Could you give an example, then, of how and why you see it happening?

Will: If I have to. It's very difficult for me to be emotional; I suppress my emotions. I guess I don't feel that I've been very good at it. I've been married and divorced three times and I have the same helper complex that they do. I feel friends are extremely important. I guess somewhere along the line I got hurt and I can bring people in to a point. To the wall, so to speak. And then nobody gets beyond the wall. Nobody! Kids, sister, nobody!

Offers partiality for son's past victimization.

Is he free to point his finger at the sources of split loyalty? Or at his father's shame?

Begins to test motherly readiness and openness to hear.

Does not encourage intergenerational exploration.

Offers partiality to both son and parents by suggesting the self-validating option of the openness to search for truth.

Mrs. L: I think your son and his wife are just as close to you as anybody could be.

Therapist: But Will is saying that he limits his accessibility to people.

Will: Yes. Very definitely.

Therapist: Where did the hurt come from, Will?

Will: I have no idea. It came a long way back.

Therapist: Could you say it if you knew it, or are you protecting people?

Will: I actually think I would like to know. I'm not sure if it was a relationships with a girl in high school, or if it was the relationship with my parents.

Mrs. L: Or if it was Jeannie, your first wife.

Therapist: Can you allow yourself to pursue the question, even if it involves your mother? Obviously there's no raising children without hurting them in some way or degree. The gift is when parents and adult children can reconnect and say, "What did you do, and why did you do it?" How much time have you put into considering where you feel cheated or what you missed in your upbringing?

Will: Yes. To give you an idea of where that's at, I've always

Refrains from a critical review of his parents, but is mildly critical of their distance from their children.

Encourages search.

Seems inclined to overcredit his parents first. Only then does he imply the children's deprivation of parental love, a factor in parentifying children.

Again asks for an example. Tightens the son's proposition.

Father could not give on the son's terms. As is often the case with parentified children, Will had to give first in order to get his father's attention.

Makes parentification issue explicit.

The parentified child's giving is soaked up by the parents, but

had the opinion that my parents had one of the best marriages that I've ever been connected with. But we children weren't totally connected. There was a great love between my mother and my father. . . .

Therapist: . . . Which excluded the children in some way?

Will: Which excluded me. I never was concerned about whether they loved me. I never had any doubts or anything. I felt we were all equally treated. But I just felt that the love was so much stronger between the parents than it was between the parents and the children.

Therapist: Could you pursue that? Give a specific incident in which you were somehow extruded from that inner circle of love?

Will: Well, this thing about father going to Sarah's events or his attending my athletic events which he didn't have time for. I grew up with the feeling that my dad cared about me but he was too busy doing things that he wanted to do. If I wanted to be a son to him, I had to learn to play golf.

Therapist: So his terms were paramount, and your terms really didn't quite ever measure up to his.

Will: Right. I tried to please him all my life and, I've been told, when I finally got to the point

acknowledgment is not forthcoming.

Protects father. Silences son?

Gives illustration.

Persists on theme.

Is his repeating father's pattern
mere learning, or is it the revolving slate of substitutive revenge through withholding?

Again son was the parent who
broached the subject of affection.
Father uses his first wife as an
excuse to cover up his own
limits or inability to give to his
children.

where he was very proud of
me, he couldn't communicate
that to me. What's worse, I was
never able to believe it.

Mrs. L: Now I didn't know that.

Will: Well, you may not remember. But I think that I had
told you about that one time.
There were so many things I
was trying to excel in. I was
never an outstanding athlete but
I participated. And nothing
could have meant more to me
than for him to come to the
bench and that sort of thing.
But he just was not that way.
He apparently couldn't do it.

Therapist: Do you know why
he couldn't do it?

Will: My feeling is that I should
understand it. It's possible that
I feel the same way. I try to be
just the opposite but I just can't
release it.

Mrs. L: I think he was interested
in making money.

Will: Well there's no question
about that. But I had an inter-
esting conversation with Dad
one time. I said to him, "You
know, we've never been like
brothers or close or in a hugging
type situation or anything like
that." He said, "That comes
from my first marriage. All of a
sudden I was involved in a
divorce with two children and
she was from a fairly well-to-do
family. All of a sudden, I came
to the realization that she could

Will is still eager to excuse his father; but true exoneration of a parent first requires the offspring to face his own pain and victimization.

Explores intimations of split loyalty through parental mistrust.

Challenges mother's evasive pattern (Dim. III).

Inadequacy (Dim. II–III)

The deprived son is glad to credit his parents. The demand for parentification was rooted in the missing parental dialogue of fairness, not in the fear of divorce.

take those children anywhere she wanted to go and there wasn't a goddamn thing anybody, including me, could do about it." He evidently got hurt very badly because she did take the children and leave. He said, "I made up my mind that I would not let anybody, namely my children, get that close to me that I would be that hurt again. I don't want that pain again." And I can understand that but it doesn't mean I didn't want it.

Therapist: So you're saying your father feared your mother leaving him.

Sarah: Yes, we talked about that.

Therapist: You know, Mrs. L, when it comes to making money, especially for men, it can be a way of avoiding intimate relationships. It's a way of hedging yourself in and not having to face the fact that your son wants you. Even more, a man might not know how to be a father to his child.

Will, who could get close to your father? Who could reach out to him, kiss him, hug him? Just your mother? Was it ever you?

Will: That's strange, because I never had the feeling that Dad was concerned about mother leaving. I don't know how many people I've told this to, but there was a really unique thing about my parents' marriage: No matter what my mother would be doing at 4:45 in the afternoon, if she were in the middle of preparing dinner or whatever, she'd stop, go up to wash her face and put on her makeup. No matter what was going on, when he walked in the back door she stopped, went over, kissed him and said, "Hi, I'm glad you're home." And that's always been the neatest thing I've ever seen in my life. That really impressed me.

The deceased father gets the therapist's partiality: His emotions are understood (Dim. II) and his own past victimization credited (Dim. IV).

Therapist: Earlier you talked about the shock that your father experienced over the dissolution of his first marriage and his wife's decision to walk off with the children. It's easy to imagine that he expected to be abandoned in this marriage and that your mother knew it.

Son continues to credit mother for her patterns of action (Dim. III), character (Dim. II) and capacity for generosity (IV?).

Will: Yes, but I still think that my mother was truly a unique person in that matter. I've never seen it in any other marriage. I've heard a couple of people like that; but she made an extra special effort in that sort of thing, the kind that appeals to a man. You know, if I had to say what I would like in a wife, that would probably be the neatest thing in the world. It's only two minutes a day but people just don't think about it. To me what this lady did for my dad was something really special.

Sister is partial to brother. She also points out the possibility of a revolving slate: He may protect his parents through taking revenge on his spouse.

Sarah: I've heard you say that so many times and that, in your marriages, you just didn't get what you needed. You were so disappointed, something always went wrong.

The parentification is credited.

Gives mother an option to make revealing statements about her side and role in her team relationship and partnership with father.

Father's insensitivity as a parent may indicate the depth of his own destructive entitlement emerging from his own deprivation.

Makes mother accountable for her own position-taking.

Tightens demand.

Ambiguous answer.

Asks mother about her integrity as a parent.

A typical answer in defense of the practice of parentifying children.

Therapist: I'd guess that the two things connect, Will. Maybe you're tired of never being number one, sometimes, even with your parents.

Mrs. L, how do you interpret the fact that you and your husband seemed so deeply devoted to each other but that he was apparently unavailable to the kids? You opened the meeting today by saying that he resisted going to their school events.

Ms. L: He always said, "It's you and I. If we don't have enough money to buy the kids clothes or send them to college, it's alright. You and I are the important ones."

Therapist: I don't want to assume that father was the headmaster here. What happened to you in all this?

Mrs. L: Lots of times he didn't go.

Therapist: What did that do to you?

Mrs. L: I don't think it bothered me. I just went anyway and was awfully annoyed that he didn't go.

Therapist: Did it worry you that the children didn't have their father on some of these occasions, or that they needed them?

Mrs. L: I don't think I thought that they needed him. I think I just thought that they understood.

Therapist: Did you talk to them about this situation?

Tightens demand.

Mrs. L: No, I don't think we ever mentioned anything.

Honest admission.

Therapist: How would they understand it, then? I guess all children need something of both of their parents. Did you explain their father's side to them?

Tightens emphasis. Partial to the children's rights. Partial to mother through making her accountable as a member of the parental team.

Mrs. L: I don't know. I suppose I told them several times, "Your father is interested in making money so that he can leave money for you people, for all of us."

Money as an excuse; also, as a valid contribution on father's part.

Sarah: Maybe some of the frustration in our family has to do with the fact that none of us knows very much about how to ask for what we need. Maybe it's the same thing as what you describe as a kind of wall. You know, Will and I have a memory of something that Dad did. Either he did it or we heard a story about his standing at the foot of the steps, it was on Arcadia Court, and telling one of us to jump. Do you remember that? What happened?

Daughter seeks for formula that exonerates parents, not knowing how to ask.

Will: I landed on the floor and he said, "See, never trust anybody!"

Father seems to discredit his own trustability as a parent.

Therapist: Maybe you're saying he built in mistrust. But Sarah's question is important for everyone in this family. You're a special lady, Mrs. L, who really does want to see things in their best light. But drinking has been something of an issue for

Therapist stands for honesty of discussion. Confronts evasive mother. Raises the issue of her drinking and makes her accountable for an explanation.

you. That often happens because alcohol can be a more reliable companion than the people around us. And it's a way of covering over pain.

Not ready for openness.

Mrs. L: Well, it could have been. I didn't realize I was trying to cover up anything.

Sarah: I just think about when you tried to kill yourself. You were at the hospital and the psychiatrist told Dad that some things were going to have to change.

Confronts mother with truth of the heaviness of mother's despair.

Supports disclosures. Lends her own courage in the face of discussion on suicide.

Therapist: What kind of things, Sarah?

Sarah: I never knew for sure. Part of it was that Dad had sort of let Mother take care of everybody and everything. After that, Dad started carrying things out to the kitchen and everybody would laugh because he had never done that before, because Mother had always carried that full load. Do you remember?

Remembers father's switch to a pattern of giving to mother in a personal manner.

Will reveals the family's lack of relatedness.

Will: Yeah, but you really shocked me when you said that Mother had tried to kill herself.

Seems like a simple denial.

Mrs. L: I don't know, I don't think I ever tried to kill myself.

Takes great courage to confront mother with the truth.

Sarah: Are you serious? Okay, let me tell you. When I was at seminary one night, I called. You were on one phone and Dad was on another. Dad said he was staying at home because you had found a gun.

Hardly believable.

Ms. L: I don't remember.

Father's remark was cold, non-caring. Or was this another invisibly collusive, parental maneuver to parentify the daughter? Daughter was left in a helpless position; yet she was expected to help.

Sarah: You had found a gun and you had gone in the bathtub to shoot yourself. Dad's words were, "She didn't have the guts to do it." You started crying and said, "You shouldn't have told her." Well, I was hysterical, obviously because I love you a lot. When I came home that Christmas, I had just started therapy. You were keeping your windows shut and your drapes drawn and you were obviously very depressed. Will was just leaving his wife for the first or second time.

Will: First.

Father refuses responsibility again.

Sarah: Okay. I think you said that my divorce and Will's divorce had made you very depressed. Dad told me, "Just because you're getting therapy doesn't mean everyone needs therapy and I don't have the money for it." That was always his answer when he didn't want to do something. He also said, "I don't want to leave her; I'm staying at home so she won't shoot herself." I said I didn't think that was enough. I sent a telegram saying that if he didn't hospitalize you, I was coming home to do it. The telegraph people showed up at your house, rang the bell, Dad apparently didn't hear it and you came to the door. You opened the telegram, read it, and said, "This is ridiculous. Sarah is not coming home for that. I'll take care of it myself." And you went over and hospitalized yourself.

The absent daughter tries to live up to her responsibility. She is willing to treat her parents as if they were children.

Credits mother.

Disconfirms daughter.

Mrs. L: I don't remember that at all. Do you?

	Will: I don't either.
	Sarah: Don't you remember?
Supports daughter.	**Therapist:** Were you hospitalized?
Evasive.	**Mrs. L:** Yes, I saw a psychiatrist.
Tightens query.	**Therapist:** Were you hospitalized?
	Mrs. L: Yes.
Helps to clarify.	**Therapist:** How did that happen? Do you have any idea of how you got to the hospital?
Helps mother avoid a response.	**Will:** I think Dad took her. I never saw the telegram.
Same.	**Sarah:** Well, that's what Dad told me. Either Dad or you told me.
Offers moratorium to mother.	**Therapist:** That's alright. It's hard to recapture that kind of truth. It's a hard, painful memory. An important question is whether you had to be there to make things work.
Another variation on the factual circumstances.	**Will:** I think that when you spent the time in Westlawn, it was explained to me that you had a minor stroke.
	Therapist: Who explained that to you, Will?
Vague.	**Will:** Probably my dad.
Partial to father.	**Therapist:** It could be argued that your dad may have had some sense of shame or guilt over it.
Glad to extend credit.	**Will:** Absolutely. A lot of people do.

Therapist: So there are unfaced myths circulating in this family.

Will: I knew absolutely nothing about this at all.

Mrs. L: I didn't either. I don't remember it at all.

Daughter could not rely on parents in her own pain.

Sarah: Isn't that fascinating? I wrote you a couple of letters at the time but just couldn't come home to visit you. I was in such pain, my own pain, and knew you were in pain too. I remember calling Dad at your house, Will, and asking how he was. "I'm fine," he said. I knew he wasn't fine, and that he was eating a lot of meals over your house. That was my sense of it, anyhow. You were seeing Dr. Wren, then, and Dad went to see him too. He told Dad, "You're going to lose your wife if you don't change some things." One of the things you told Dr. Wren was that you were afraid to keep secrets. He told you that everyone keeps secrets and you said, "You mean it's alright for me to have secrets from my husband?", and he said, "Of course." Do you remember that?

Will: Well, I can vaguely remember Dad explaining that he was going to change some things but he never said why.

Sarah: And you tried in some ways. Remember when you and Dad took a lot of green medicine?

Mrs. L: Yes. Dad and I had the flu and we had a nurse for him.

Parentification of the nurse through irresponsible behavior resembles parentification of the children.

I said, "Don't you let him have more than one dose of that medicine." The next day she said, "I'm sorry, Mrs. L, but nobody can do anything with your husband. He took six doses of that medicine and I couldn't do a thing about it."

Sarah: It was a nerve medicine that they took throughout their marriage.

Defends self and husband.

Mrs. L: There's nothing you can do about it. We both stopped taking it eventually.

In the face of mother's blatant disinclination to respond, the therapist offers her partiality by alluding to Mrs. L's childhood circumstances (3-generational leverage).

Therapist: I want to turn this around just a little bit, Mrs. L. What about your own mother and father? How did it go between you and them? Did you have siblings?

Describes rigidity of her parents.

Mrs. L: Well, they were so religious. I was having dates with a Catholic and he had to go to church with me on Sunday night or I couldn't have a date with him.

Therapist: What about brothers and sisters?

Mrs. L: I had a brother and sister; I was the youngest by 11 and 13 years.

Explores mother's ability to rely on her own mother.

Therapist: How was it between you and your mom? Did you get what you needed from her?

Reveals her own childhood deprivation.

Mrs. L: No, we weren't very close. My father and I were close but my mother and I were *never* very close.

Therapist: Why was that?

Another source of her inability to parent.

Mrs. L: I have no idea. She and my father had things they had to do all the time.

Tries to exonerate mother via her origins.

Sarah: It sounds like you and Dad, doesn't it?

Mrs. L: Yes it does, doesn't it?

Therapist: So mother took over and father went away?

Sarah: In fact, her mother used to hide money so she could send her kids to college. Grandpa would just give everything away.

Underscores needs that were not fulfilled for mother.

Mrs. L: When he'd call on people, he'd come home and say, "Amy called today and said they needed coal. So I called up and had them send coal." She had to pay for all those things. Ministers were not paid much in those days. But my mother made sure they could send three kids through college.

Affectionate ties explored (Dim. II).

Therapist: How come you were so close to your father, then, if your mother did so much?

Mrs. L: I don't know. When I was little, I used to go with him to make calls.

Therapist: Do you think you were your father's favorite child?

Mrs. L: Yes, because I was the youngest, I think.

Further exploration of affection and triangular (oedipal) situation.

Therapist: Maybe it was easy to transfer that closeness from your father to your husband to make him the center of your life. Did your mother ever feel angry with you for being so close to your father?

Ms. L: No.

(Dim. II).

Therapist: What did you want from your mother that you didn't get, Mrs. L?

Not ready to delineate her needs.

Mrs. L: I don't think I ever wanted anything. If I did, I don't know what it was.

Presses for information.

Therapist: What would have made you closer?

Evasiveness.

Mrs. L: I don't know. She was an excellent cook and a good manager with money.

Humor and persistence offered.

Therapist: Was she a good manager of hugs and kisses?

No affection remembered.

Mrs. L: No, we didn't do that in our family. Not sisters and brothers or mother or father. We never did any of that.

Therapist: How about in this family?

Mrs. L: Well, we don't do that a whole lot.

Therapist: How come?

Mrs. L: I don't know why.

Will: I'm kind of uncomfortable with it.

Connects consequences.

Therapist: Your family background teaches you to be uncomfortable with it.

Introduces posterity's entitle-

Will: That's a funny thing. I have really worked hard at try-

ment. The deprived generation owes the next generation a legacy that gives proportionately more, precisely in the area of starvation and deprivation that they have had to experience.

ing to do that with my kids. I like to do it and I continue to do it. Yet I have to force myself to do it; it doesn't get easier. I don't really understand that. When my son comes over and gives me a hug, I absolutely love it but I feel funny.

Are Will's children beginning to act parentified? Do they know how to delineate their own needs and rights (3 generational leverage)?

Therapist: Do your kids pursue you, Will?

Mrs. L: Yes.

Will: Karl more than Lee.

Therapist: Why is that?

The revolving slate of extracting from children through frustrating them continues.

Will: I guess Lee doesn't pursue me because I don't do what she wants me to do. She's always been a rebel, like me.

Therapist: Were you a rebel?

Will: Oh yes, black sheep number one. It was my striving for attention, that type of thing. I feel better and more comfortable about the way I've raised my kids than the way I was raised. But I still don't feel as if I've been very good at it.

Displays sensitivity to the legacy of parental accountability.

Almost from the beginning of this segment, the therapist operates from a stance of multidirected partiality to try to establish a contract with these three family members. Her goal is to induce everyone to start work on their self-delineation via intermember dialogue. The dialogue of fair give-and-take is, of course, the main vehicle for the constructive reorientation of family relationships and for everyone's individuation. This process involves,

- Facing and dealing with hard, conflictual issues;
- Facing the offspring's past, destructive parentification as the basis of their destructive entitlement;

- Piercing certain family myths;
- Opening up new ways of offering due credit;
- Facing anger which leads to facing one another's denied justifications;
- Facing the full extent of our own victimization before turning to exonerate a victimizing parent;
- Facing the ways in which we victimize innocent others in order to spare members of our family of origin (revolving slate).

Despite these advantages, a powerful obstacle to dialogue lies in the destructive entitlement of each family member. The therapist thus has to explore resources for converting a client's reliance on destructive entitlement into a reliance on self-validation.

Methodologically, the issues in the L family can obviously find redress through the valid and effective techniques of all therapeutic schools. Contextual therapy is more than eclectic though. Whatever the other methods used for intervention, its primary guidelines are provided by the ethical dimension of relational reality. The specifics of contextual therapy are summarized in these guidelines. Dimension IV obligates a family to a fair consideration of all of the members who are affected. And it obligates the therapist to help family members towards this goal. The question of *either* an individual approach *or* a systemic approach loses its meaning under the ethical umbrella. A comprehensive consideration of relational reality implies the totality of individual and systemic angles alike.

Though the ethical dimension is the guiding consideration of contextual therapy, the other three dimensions contribute their share of methodological guidelines. The factual dimension may require medication. The psychological dimension may require help with a developmental impasse or with neurotic guilt feelings. The transactional dimension may require immediate, prescriptive restructuring of openly destructive behavior.

CHAPTER 14

Balance in Motion: Crediting

Contextual work invests itself in that fundamental core of relating in which all relationships are in a state of dynamic equilibrium or "balance in motion" (van Heusden & van den Eerenbeemt, 1983). This core is where the lived reality of all relationships meets and intertwines. This is where relational reality encompasses more than any one individual, one family or one human group. Accountability for the future is the fundamental anchor point of this relational core. Like contamination of the water or air, it cuts across religious, racial and ethnic groups of every kind. No one is excused from the responsibility of investing in it. Even a failing parent can eventually become a giving grandparent.

Caring about posterity subordinates all the strategic goals of contextual therapy. Consider the therapist's mandate in the case of the youngster with intensely destructive behavior.

A contextual therapist will always explore the prospect of adult responsibility and care for a child regardless of the degree of negativity in his or her behavior. In point of fact, many youngsters function as captive referees of their parents' controversies. Divorce typically heightens the parents' inability to cooperate in raising small children notwithstanding the fact that they continue to share parental responsibility. In addition, adults frequently lack sensitivity to a child's caring gestures or are unreceptive toward his offerings.

A contextual therapist explores the interface of all these possibilities. This process of exploration is conducted in a manner that is partial to parents and children alike. Multidirected partiality is initially a demand on the adults who are usually there "to have Johnny cured." On the other hand, helping mother and father rethink what is happening to Johnny serves to mobilize their residual, untapped resources. Helping parents actualize their responsible mandate for posterity is ultimately the greatest source of leverage for everyone's therapeutic progress.

Contextual therapy is based on the dormant resources of family relationships, then, rather than on therapeutic transference. Here people may inquire if contextual work is actually psychotherapy. Our answer, of course, is unequivocal. The ethics of relational responsibility are more meaningful to people's lives than the usages of psychology. All therapists need to be sensitive to their clients' psychological clues. But more significantly, they need to focus their work on where people invest themselves, day by day, over extensive periods of time. To be involved in Dimension IV means therapeutic concern for the fluctuating balances of merit. The therapist sensitively credits merit where family members deem it belongs.

One resource to be developed here is to free brother-sister relating from its stagnant, isolated reliance on distancing based on destructive entitlement. In the ensuing segment, the therapist attempts to develop this resource through fighting against the self-destructive features of an offspring's inclination to relate through offers of self-sacrifice, i.e., the offer to be parentified. The method is eliciting the siblings' options for mobilizing resources for reciprocal give-and-take rather than a singular focus on insight or simple behavior modification.

Questioning the psychology of feeling wanted (Dim. II), the therapist begins to look into the balance of fairness of give and take (Dim. IV).	**Therapist:** I guess I'm wondering, Will, where in your life you feel that someone actively wanted you.
Lack of a sense of fair give-and-take is coupled with lack of trust.	**Will:** You know, it's very difficult for me to accept gifts although it's easy to do things for people. It's not easy for me to understand why anyone would want to do something for me.
Diversionary attempt.	**Mrs. L:** Well, his wife . . .
	Therapist: Let's put off talking about Will's wife for the moment.
	Will: It's too big a subject.
	Therapist: It seems like you've been too little a subject, Will. It sounds as if you've gotten ad-

The risks of receiving are explored and manifested in the patterns of overgiving (Dim. III), feeling rejected (Dim. II), not going by the principle of fairness (Dim. IV).

dicted to giving because you're doubtful of an alternative. To receive from people is a risk. Once it happens, you might want something from them again. If it doesn't happen, you might feel rejected or abandoned. So receiving is a very risky business. Sometimes it seems easier to keep giving. But a person gets worn down that way, and resentful and angry. And that's as good a reason for shedding mates as any other.

Will: It just seems that everybody I know, with marital problems or whatever, uses me for their counselor. I do an awful lot of it. Sometimes I just get tired and don't want to be around anyone. I just need some space. I want to be myself.

Continues to offer himself as the parentifiable partner. The exploitation of Will's availability is being described.

Therapist: You seem to be carrying a lot, Will. First your family background and your view that your parents were so much there for each other and not enough there for you. When you get worn down, to whom do you turn for consolation. Who's there just for you?

Acknowledges Will's burden. Partial to him in his lonely lack of a dialogue of due consideration.

Will: Just me.

Therapist: I'm not sure that's good enough. None of us can make it indefinitely without someone there sometime.

Empathic partiality is again being offered.

Will: I understand that. There's always the dream that you'll find that super-someone.

Will's model is the parentifying relationship.

Therapist: But you've pulled in for now. Is that what you're saying?

Relational resources are under-developed.

Will: Oh yes. I've probably been ''in'' for most of my life. The fact is that our family wasn't close. So I grew up with the idea that if something were going to get done, I had to do it myself.

Tries to elicit the resource of concrete mother-son relating.

Therapist: But what if you're feeling really sad and needy? Can you turn to your mom and have her hear you—on your terms?

No trust in family relating.

Will: Probably not. I have a couple of friends, one in particular, with whom I could sit down and cry.

Is there a relational resource in the sister who is present?

Therapist: How about Sarah?

Cautious denial.

Will: No.

Reinforces query.

Therapist: How come?

Excuse offered.

Will: If she lived nearby, yes. But she's too far away.

Persistence.

Therapist: There's always the phone.

Excuse offered again.

Will: That's not good enough. There's also the fact that I like to expedite these things, get rid of them. She has no idea of the background of what's going on. We lead two separate lives.

Persistence.

Therapist: Isn't that a choice?

Hiding behind simple facts.

Will: It's circumstances. I don't know if it's a choice or beyond our control. She chooses to be out here and I have to be where I am.

Partial to his feelings.

Therapist: Is that a source of tension for you?

Begins to respond in a more genuine way. Brother-sister relating may be freer of the burden of exploitative parentification.

Will: I don't know if it's a source of tension but I'd like her to be home. I realize that what she's doing here is very important to her, and her happiness is very important to me. But if nothing else counted and I could have it my way, I would rather have my family close to me; we're not a big family. It hasn't happened that way and I don't know that it could be.

Partiality redirected. Sarah's spontaneity is invited.

Therapist: You haven't done much talking, Sarah, mainly because I haven't let you. Do you have a direction that you want to pursue, or shall I pursue my own direction?

Sarah: I do feel I need to be here, and I do feel that sometimes both of you are annoyed that I'm here and not there. Lots of times I feel you call when you're disturbed about things. I would really love it if you would call more, sometimes with happy news. I guess I don't do that with you either. You are both really so important to me. So many times I feel that you are the only brother and you are the only mother I have and that. . . . What I've found is that you might talk if I come to your house, Will. But if we're at your house the television goes on.

Sarah is able to invite give-and-take.

Acknowledges her need for family ties.

Sarah's courage for commitment and the trustful initiative to relate is increasing.

One of the reasons I wanted us to have these sessions is that I so much long for more intimacy between us. I would like to be more for both of you and for us to battle things out. My hunch is that if we could be close to each other, we could be close to other people. If we can't. . . .

These four hours are more important to me than any other. I'm really happy that you've come here to see me accept the award, but talking at another level is even more important to me. I would so like it to be more, and I don't know how to do it.

Suggests a concrete option for initiative.

Therapist: Have you ever pursued Will to go on a vacation together, for example?

Acknowledges brother.

Sarah: That's a wonderful idea. Will took me to the Bahamas for a couple of days in '68. He did say that when I arrived, it started to rain and when I left, it stopped.

Mrs. L: He took you to Florida.

Credits brother for his initiative.

Sarah: And then about a year and a half ago, I was overloaded with work. Will called and said that this guy with whom he usually roomed wasn't going to be there and could I come. It was really a Godsend. But he was busy the whole time.

Partial to both. Credits Will and urges Sarah on.

Therapist: Well, Sarah, you seem to be saying that Will has taken you on trips. When have you invited him?

Sarah: I don't think I have ever taken him on vacation.

Therapist: Or any place?

Will: She brought me here.

Sarah: Except that you paid!

Will: I'm curious. Are you aware

Discredits himself.	of the fact that when the emotional break started, I went right out the door?
	Therapist: But there's a lot of caring here. Can you come back through the door, Will?
Acknowledges brother-sister relating.	
Parentifies therapist.	**Will:** Yes, but that showing of emotions. Boy! Whew!
	Therapist: Well, men are often frightened of crying women, and women are often frightened of angry men. Whether Sarah cries or not is really beside the point. Both of you want more from each other.
Partial to both. Gives empathy and crediting.	
Continues to parentify therapist.	**Will:** When somebody starts saying, "I want to be that close," I say, "Hey, wait a minute!" I would like to have it that way but it just scares the hell out of me. It opens you to an emotional pain which I ain't having any of, thanks.
Fair reciprocity is raised as consideration and as an option for every family member (Dim. IV).	**Therapist:** My guess is you're at least willing to try or you wouldn't be here. Maybe, Sarah, you and your mom both need to look at your failure of initiative towards Will. The two of you may be experiencing an abandonment that was never intended, and Will may be experiencing the same thing. Why should he, as a male, be the only one in pursuit?
Describes features of the balance of fairness.	**Sarah:** In fairness to me, though, I'm the one who usually calls him about what's going on in his life.
	Therapist: Maybe that needs to be reversed. You may need to

Suggests reciprocal giving between brother and sister.

keep after him to reach out to you. But Will's already said that he's pretty boxed in and scared as hell. It may be that you have to stop asking him how he is and start saying, "How about meeting me in New York and we'll spend a couple of days just having a good time."

Suggests active claiming and asking.

I'm not suggesting that everything has to be heavy or a replay of the past. I am suggesting that each of you develop the aggressiveness to make a claim on each other. You each seem pretty vulnerable. My guess is that none of you, including your Dad, has a baseline of experience that entitles you to reach out and say, "Come on, let's enjoy each other." It's that kind of initiative that I'm talking about; one that's actively inviting, not solicitous or maternal. Most men can live without one more maternal intervention.

Risk of initiative-taking.

Begins to reveal his own needs for personal relatedness on his own terms.

Will: I guess there's a little anger about when you've gone to California on vacations. You didn't stop either going or coming. You just went right on ahead. I never thought about that until we started talking about this thing. Then I thought, hmmm. . . . She'd rather do that than be with me. You know, there have been a couple of times that I've asked you to go to Vegas with me and you've said you were too busy.

Raises his issues of fairness of reciprocity in initiating.

Fair acknowledgment of brother's terms offered.

Sarah: Well, you're right. I guess you've stopped asking me because I never do it.

Is there an invisible loyalty to the parents that results in brother-sister distancing?

Therapist plants seed of initiative for closeness.

Evasive remark, perhaps in father's manner.

Partial to Will through placing a demand on him.

Therapist: It's important stuff that you folks are putting out here. I hear several things. As you phrase it, Will, "I wasn't significant enough for you to take time," or "I can't compete with your business." It sounds like your attention to business is somewhat akin to your father's, Sarah. However unintentionally, you might be caught in an unreworked loyalty bind, trapped in a way of evading intimacy through work. After all, good works have no limits. You can drown in them. It sounds like an important pattern on which you might want to reflect. Maybe Vegas is not the kind of place you'd choose to visit, Sarah. On the other hand, if you and your brother are trying to build some life in common, it doesn't matter if you're in Gomorrah.

Will: One of the things I've discussed with her is the fact that I'm not a fan of Philadelphia. I hate it. I've told Sarah on many occasions, your profession can be practiced anywhere. You could work in Dallas, New Orleans, Denver, Los Angeles. You go there and I'll come see you all the time. The East, with its little, tiny, narrow streets and that sort of thing, makes me feel boxed in. And I travel all over the country for a living.

Therapist: What about some flexibility on your part, Will?

Will: I'm unsure of myself here, but I wonder if I'm really cutting

| Gives honesty as an offering to the family. | Philadelphia or am I saying, ''I ain't coming to see you!'' I don't feel that way but now you've got me wondering. |

The therapist sows seeds for the prospect of a trustworthy brother-sister relationship through the multidirected crediting of one family member after the other. Here the prospect of fair reciprocity (Dimension IV) alleviates the fear of closeness (Dimension II). The therapist places high creditability on the courageous initiative that overcomes mistrust. As a result, brother-sister relating can turn into a model of reciprocal self-validation instead of self-justification via destructive entitlement.

A choice to respond to a relating partner with care and consideration is the essence of dialogue. The capacity to do so is rooted in the fair and reliable exchanges that have actually taken place between people rather than in the psychology of experiencing pleasurable closeness. Genuine dialogue suggests autonomy and spontaneity. It suggests self-delineation rather than fusion. The goals of physical ''togetherness,'' inclinations to avoid separate directions or permanent subordination of one generation to another, are never implied.

Contextual methodology is based on the reality of the relating partners, on the resources that reside in the interface of all their relationships, and on the consequences that flow from their connectedness towards posterity. The therapist's activity is geared towards these aspects of ''the between'' and are more catalytic than substantive or prescriptive. A therapist's input during the therapy hour is only worthwhile if it can mobilize the family members' own momentum towards progress.

Consider the example of the adult offspring whose mother is approaching the terminal stage of illness. The mother's legacy to her child is characterized by cutoffs, abandonments and resentment. The contextual therapist is aware of how ''monsterlike'' the mother seems in her son's view. Still he will ask, ''In five or ten years from now, what do you imagine that you'd want to have done at this point?'' The question itself is enough to plant the seeds of dialogue. There is no prescription for what should be done. The question is not a premeditated paradox intended to manipulate coalitions. The therapist's response is not based on any particular family member. His is a stance that bears the risk that he might sound judgmental or be disliked or unpopular. Still, his task is to inject the courage to explore a previously stagnant relationship.

In the first instance, the offspring's attempts to break the relational stagnation between him and his mother have to be motivated by his wish to obtain significant gains for himself and his other relationships. Attempts to do so to comply with a therapeutic design for restructuring behavioral patterns which, for example, are superficial and unlikely to endure. There are certain personal gains in everyone's life that are tied to caring about others. An improved quality of care in relating functions as a means, a goal, and a way.

CHAPTER 15
Starting Therapy

INITIAL STEPS IN THERAPY

The Referral Call

People who find their way to contextual therapists will reflect the diversity of individual notions of therapy in their initial calls. In their responses, contextual therapists may describe their work in terms that range across the spectrum between classical individual therapy and classical family therapy. It is helpful to indicate to prospective clients that what distinguishes contextual work is 1) its expectation that interrelating family members can help each other heal even if it seems that only one of them is in trouble, and 2) its emphasis on action rather than on insight.

The Contract

Contextual therapy obligates its workers to offer a professional helping contract that cares about their interventions' impact on everyone who potentially may be affected. To begin, a therapist does well to suggest that all family members be asked to attend the first interview or one of the early sessions during the initial assessment period. It is counterproductive to insist on it, however, or to convert the request into an absolute condition.

The person calling to set up an appointment may have his or her reasons for wanting to be seen alone. He may be ready to disclose aspects of his life that have been secret up until now. It may be less of an emotional cost to try them out on a stranger than to implicate himself with his relatives. He may also want to test out how trustworthy the therapist seems to be. The therapist will, of course, evaluate the nature of the client's concerns and then try to help him decide whether or not his insistence on privacy is constructive or destructive to the therapeutic process, and why.

Taking a History

Assessing a client's life and context incorporates history-taking though it goes beyond a simple, individual history. Both the assessment and the history are full of therapeutic implications. The burdens that a person carries, with all their residue of resentment and guilt, are quickly connectable to his or her injuries and hurts. In helping people develop a plan to redistribute burdens and benefits, the therapist uncovers the prospect of resources and learns who holds what advantages. He also learns whether family members tend to credit each other for their contributions to each other or whether they tend to withhold.

Evaluating Emergencies

Some initial complaints represent emergencies and require immediate intervention to prevent further or more serious damage. On the other hand, there are some initial complaints that are simply conveyed as emergencies. After 18 months of severe marital problems, for example, a professional woman in her forties decided to contact a therapist and set up an appointment. She characterized her situation as an emergency and registered her demands accordingly. She was ready to look at her situation and wanted to do it NOW. Hurrying in to see an overdemanding client, a therapist is often faced with the fact that he is the only one present who is working on an emergency basis.

On the other hand, real emergencies are typically characterized by the degree of threat to life or health. Whatever their nature, emergencies are always best addressed by the therapist's insistence on involving whatever relational resources are available to the threatened person. Threats of murder or suicide require special attention and sometimes institutionalization. Serious, violent or sexual child abuse requires immediate intervention. So does serious violence between adults. Recently divorced people, with volatile, unresolved issues between them, can so escalate their personal vendettas against each other that the consequences to their children or even to each other may represent a clear and present danger.

A Basic Attitude

Contextual therapy's basic attitude to clients is a fundamental consideration for doing successful work. Contextual work is concerned with helping people who are suffering, incapacitated or handicapped. Its aim is to help closely related family members help each other. Its notion of health and a wholesome quality of life is founded on a balance between enlightened self-interest and due concern for the interests of others. More specifically, contextual therapy encourages steps toward both self-delineation and self-validation. It perceives life as inherently relational and sees the self as a primary figure over against others who provide the self's "ground." It recognizes the inevitability of conflicting interests between people. It also recognizes that most of them are potentially capable of mitigation. It assumes that human beings inherit the intrinsic right to survive and thrive, and to develop and grow. It acknowledges that posterity is vulnerable and cannot represent itself; thus it deserves everyone's concern and priority.

A Dialectic Context

Early in their contact with clients, contextual therapists try to convey how an individual and his or her relationships constitute an irreducible gestalt. The "self" or "I" of the individual is essentially unthinkable without the "you" of others. Even though an individual life is a biologically and psychologically defined entity that is unique, this gestalt cannot be reduced to its parts. On the one hand, an individual is more than a mere cogwheel in a relational system. On the other hand, people's commitments and interchanges cannot be reduced to any one participant's psychology or mental function.

A concern for relationships evolves from the knowledge that the self and the other are irrevocably set in a dialectic relationship. This knowledge requires that every contextual therapist be fully aware of the self and of others as individuals with a lifespan between conception and death. Every person inevitably experiences the frightening confrontations involved in presenting his own side in serious conflicts. Every person is passionately concerned with his or her own survival, health and prosperity. No one can be an honest partner or even a participant-observer in relationships if she denies the significance of her own individual interests and priorities. On the other hand, people can neither address reality as a whole nor function with ethical integrity without a capacity to care about the consequences to others of his or her own life strivings.

Contractual Ethics

Contextual therapy, then, is an integration of relational (family and marital) therapy and individual therapy. A therapist may actually meet with one person, a couple, a nuclear family, a multigenerational segment of an extended family, or with a network of complexly related people. Whatever the set, she considers the consequences of her work for all of the people potentially affected and contracts accordingly. From a contextual perspective, to do otherwise would distort relational reality and render it unethical.

There is obviously no way that a therapist can be made responsible for actually knowing all the consequences of her work. Still she can hold herself to account for caring about the entire self-other gestalt. At the very least, she is obliged to raise the question of how other people in the client's context can be considered. The complete exclusion of even one family member whose offensive behavior has created a mythical monster violates the operating principle of all-inclusive consideration, and undermines all multidirectional methods.

THE REAL LOCUS OF THERAPY

Physically, a therapist's work takes place in actual meetings with his or her clients—in an office, in a home or in a hospital setting. But the process of therapy and the outcome of therapeutic interventions belong to a person's and context's spontaneous and continuing existence. The process and outcomes belong to the meetings between people who are significant to each other, to the preface and aftermath of life-cycle rituals and special events, to the rest of the week following a therapy session, and to the unfolding years and circumstances that accompany them. They also belong to posterity. Absent family members are as dynamically significant as the people who are present in the therapy room.

Contextual therapists encourage face-to-face meetings between family members and themselves. But the design of their interventions and their decision-making are never limited to the people whose voices can actually be heard even in the face of geographical distance, the hardship of fiscal obligations, or the consequences of the choice to cut off. Therapists must take care never to sever the dynamic connectedness of people's significant, reciprocally-committed relationships, either inadvertently, by intent or by omission. A consistent regard for the fairness of the context and the balance in motion is contextual work's basic rule.

Eliciting Therapeutic Action

Contextual therapy eschews prescriptions and techniques that require therapeutic impositions of any kind. Instead it hews to methods that *elicit spontaneous options, actions and decision-making.* Fundamental to the method of eliciting is the practice of "planting seeds." Seed-planting includes teaching, evoking spontaneous motivations, and channeling transference dynamics. These elements are based on eliciting, catalyzing and influencing people and their motives rather than on direct manipulation. Here the question of indirect manipulation suggests itself. In contextual therapy, dialogue is always a goal in both its self-delineating and self-validating phases. Contextual therapists use every available technique to urge relating partners toward dialogue. Dialogue, in our sense, is inseparable from responsible position-taking by two or more relating parties. If a response is intrinsically manipulative, it focuses on only one person's expectations and definitions of both partners' accountability.

THE CHILD'S PLACE IN CONTEXTUAL THERAPY

One of the nuances of a multidirected methodology has to do with our conviction that even the very young child is to be viewed as a fully participating member of the therapy process, as one who deserves as much attention as the adults. Here therapists are expected to make every effort to involve a child in therapeutic encounter and exchange as soon as possible, to try to grasp the nature of a child's contributions to his family and world, *and* to credit him for them. A child's caring contributions may equal or exceed those of the adults around him even if his understanding and language abilities are limited. Ackerman (1958) has cited Freud's view of the child as a "pleasure-bent anarchist" (p. 28). By no means do we agree that the child can be regarded as an empty container waiting to be filled by adult attention.

In cases where parents fail to act with responsibility, three- and four-year-old children often carry adult concern. Recently we witnessed a four-year-old standing outside the office of a child-psychiatrist, begging his mother not to disclose his father's bad behavior. "It's important to me to talk to the doctor," the mother implored. "I won't blame your father. I'll just talk about his arrangements to visit you." 'Don't!" the boy begged, clutching his mother's leg. "I don't want Daddy to hurt." In our experience, children are not only naturally loyal; they are also naturally generous. Irresponsible adults exploit that natural generosity by extracting a child's truly adult-like creativity, without acknowledging it.

In the therapy room children are to be regarded with dignity and respect. The therapist discourages anyone's attempt to talk down to them in a pseudo-protective stance. Nor is anyone permitted to mock or laugh at their natural limitations. In no way do we intend to inhibit or prevent a youngster from taking appropriate responsibility for his elders. On the other hand, generational boundaries are given due consideration; so are all efforts to help keep the young intact. We do mean to make parents aware of the precocity of their children's concerns, and to help them grasp the nature of their prospective exploitation and its countertherapeutic consequences. Whenever possible, the therapist requires that parents 1) acknowledge the youngster for his investments of care, and 2) take steps towards a restoration of their responsibility. Crediting rightful devotion is always the first step to deparentification. Conversely, heaping blame on a child in the midst of his generous, self-depleting offers represents one of the most trust-demolishing forms of parentification.

As parents become capable of more responsibility, children will naturally take on more appropriate child-like responsibilities. At times, these attitudes may be of an attention-getting or disorganized nature. On occasion, the therapist may have to help a mother or father accept the fact that their child's behavior is a sign of his greater freedom to act his age. On the other hand, parents will sometimes have to cope with their child's resistance to giving up a controlling, if age-inappropriate, role. Yet this is a much less urgent task than the restoration of the parents' trustworthiness. Too much stress on restraining the child strikes us as inappropriate, overburdening parentification that results in implicit blame and the strong suggestion that the youngster retains super, grown-up power over adults. In fact, parents may simply have to endure a lag that can occur between the time that an adult takes on more parental behavior and a child registers the fact that he has to let go of his own efforts to exert inappropriate parent-like control.

Another dilemma of this nature has to do with a parent's tendency to appoint a child as the first one to speak in the therapy session, sometimes even at the first meeting. This expectation reinforces the destructive parentification already weighing the youngster down. It also stresses the probability of his being assigned the role of the family's exclusive "patient." Here it is always wiser for the therapist to invite and, if necessary, insist that adults begin the session. It is always preferable to hold parents accountable for making the session's initial, responsible statements. It is always more in keeping with parent-child dynamics to presume that father and mother pace the family and are the people who, out of their maturity, have led the family into a therapeutic contract.

The decision to elicit a response from parents first is helpful to the therapist in any case. It enables her to support parents when they require her adult concern. For instance, the therapist may concur with the parents' assessment that their son's patterns of action are undesirable. Her response can then join theirs on an adult-to-adult plane. "Yes, I'm a parent too, an adult who cannot endorse that type of behavior in my children either." A display of sensitive and due concern for parents also gains the therapist an opportunity to lessen their child's implicit disloyalty. For a youngster to report on his family in front of a stranger is always a highly disloyal act. To do so in front of a family therapist who is as concerned for his parents as she is for him is significantly less disloyal.

Shielding Filial Loyalties

If forced to choose between an adult's and child's culpability, in our experience therapists almost automatically tend to blame parents and side with the young. It seems characteristic of therapists and, perhaps, of people in general that, at the point of heated exchange, outsiders are likely to be able to be more partial to a youngster than her parents can manage to be. It may well be humanly impossible for parents to convey dissatisfactions with their offspring and manage to be empathic at the same time. This is one of the reasons, among others, that a therapist does well to indicate her partiality to parents before she turns it to the child. By acknowledging the parents' struggles first, the therapist intervenes at a preventive level. Her recognition of their disappointments and of their real and imagined injuries and injustices helps to derail therapeutic blame. It keeps the parents from turning against the therapist, and it allays the child's fears of being disloyal as well as the guilt that disloyalty brings.

Simple questions are an effective way to acknowledge parental merit: What have they tried to do about their problems up until now? Were they caught up in situations that were very demanding as children, or in demands "worse" than what their own child is now facing? On whom could they rely as they were growing up? Multidirectional questions beamed at parents not only diminish their antagonisms and free them to take a more searching look, but also free their child from an onerous sense of guilt over whether or not he has offered an accurate picture of the family's situation. Furthermore, the therapist's partiality to the parents reassures their child that at least this adult will not demand that he ally with her against his parents.

CHAPTER 16
Multidirected Partiality

A therapist's ability to acknowledge one person's merit, terms and claims and also to acknowledge another's teaches him how to utilize the inherent resources in people's relationships. It also frees him from the sometimes compelling tendency to be the guarantor of everyone's improvement. Here the premise is that the therapist is a catalyst whose primary functions are to elicit and to lend courage instead of functioning as the ultimate source of energy. In this construct, the therapist is not bound to offer "unconditional positive regard" (Rogers, 1951). Instead his task is to induce all family members to claim the merit due to their respective sides of conflicting life interests.

It may be said that contextual therapy operates out of a paradigm of "conditional regard;" out of the regard that relating partners offer each other; out of regard that depends on the credibility of each person's willingness to take a position of caring responsibility. Regard for family members coming from the therapist may have integrity; it may also be defined as model behavior. But, at best, it is always secondary to the efforts of family members. At a methodological level, it can best be understood to serve to induce fair intermember consideration and crediting. The therapist's regard is not a therapeutic result *per se*.

In order to discover their clients' relational reality, therapists need to proceed methodically, moving from the known to the unknown. For example, if a person says, "My father was never satisfied with anything I ever did," a therapist might wonder aloud whether or not there were specific patterns of behavior or action that evoked parental criticism. It is always logical and methodologically well-founded for the therapist to ask both the person making the statement *and* parents or other relatives about their respective sides. Under the circumstances, a therapist may seem to be interjecting himself into a family in a tribunal-like way. In reality, he refrains from anything like a juridical role save for his expectation that the family members hear and respond to each other. The therapist's role is not analogous to that of the judge who decides the merit of other people's contributions.

One last return to the L family may help to demonstrate how a therapist can proceed from the known to the unknown, with beneficial consequences to a family. In this instance, she helps everyone make connections between Will's concern for the health of a close friend and its relevance to the family's long delayed and unaddressed issues of mourning, loss and grief.

One of the aspects of persistent family myths is based on the family members' collusive postponement of mourning. The pattern of myths is often delegated by one or both of the parents, through overt or covert injunctions. This form of relational stagnation coincides with the members' lack of individuation, a lack of self-polarizing, genuine dialogue. Stagnation, of course, affects subsequent relationships outside the nuclear family.

The pattern of an impaired capacity to give affects every member's grief process. In fact, the most painful aspect of mourning has to do with not ever again being able to give to the person who has been lost. This permanent limitation is further aggravated by a family member's defective capacity for giving. Giving in the form of offering the self to be parentified is identical with destructive overgiving—essentially a monologue characterized by a person's martyrlike invitation to the world to exploit him or her. The implicit, parentifying delegation is sustained by a mutual self-victimization of each family member.

As a constructive alternative to self-immolating parentification, the therapist helps family members explore prospects for self-validation through exonerating a deceased parent, for example. Exoneration remains an avenue that is still available to offer solidarity to a family member who believes he has failed to offer care to a relative while there was still time to do so. Here it can be hoped that efforts at exoneration can eventually mitigate the destructive entitlement of family members and rework their substitutive victimization of any more, innocent people. Before a person can exonerate anyone, however, he has to delineate his own legitimate needs and entitlements. On a larger scale, the therapist multi-directionally addresses everybody's side.

| Introduces her concern about her brother. | **Sarah:** I don't want to speak for Will but he's had a hard time since we were last here. |

Gives facts.

Will: My friend had open heart surgery, a triple bypass. He had gone in for tests before I left, and I couldn't find anything out until this morning. He came through it fine, as far as I know, I've talked to the hospital and. . . .

Injects her own anxiety.

Mrs. L: They said he's in serious condition. I don't see how you can say he's come through it fine. Maybe the hospital always says that.

Offers empathy.

Therapist: So you're carrying a lot. Is he a long-term friend, Will?

Appears ready to reveal his deeper feeling reactions.

Will: Twenty years or so, but we've become, I guess, very close in the last two years. I had a real bad feeling about it. You know the crazy things that go through your mind.

Persists.

Therapist: What crazy things?

Will's fear of closeness mixes here with his fear of losing a friend. The implications of unworked-through aspects of Will's mourning over his father's death seem to emerge.

Describes fear of having to face emotions (Dim. II).

Will: I had finally found somebody that I could really let it all hang out with. Why was he going to be taken away from me now? That type of thing. I seem to be entering into a period of opening up my emotional life. It's always been blocked out before and it's coming from 15 different directions at once. I'm very interested in it and I'm absolutely terrified. I've always been a very controlled person. This seems awfully big, like there's an emotional monster inside of me that all of a sudden is screaming to get out. And I just don't quite know what to do about it.

Forcefully injects the issue of fairness (Dim. IV).

Emphasizes the ubiquitous need for trustability in relating (Dim. IV) as a condition for responding in dialogue.

Therapist: There's another way to look at it, Will. I doubt that there's an emotional monster in there. My guess is that there's a man there instead, one with all the capacities for emotion that are given to any human being. I think the issue's one of fairness. You can afford to let your emotions out if you can somehow trust that there's someone to hear you, and not judge or undercut you. Someone who can just stand there by your side. It's like you're saying about your friend: "I found someone with whom I can be an emotional, logical, full human being, and I need that in order to let all of who I am emerge. You're saying it powerfully and you're surfacing everybody's fear: Can we afford to be emotional or logical or successful or a failure—all of those things—and just be received for who we are? And hell, most of us have concluded in one way or another, "No. It's just too scary to try."

Is this the first relationship in which Will did not have to offer himself as the parentifiable one?

Will: Well, that's the way I've been for years but my curiosity is working on me. I've had a few friends but the relationship I've established with this gentleman has really been super. It's been neat. He's the first person with whom I don't feel guilty. If I want to talk to him at two o'clock in the morning, I pick up the phone and call him. I've always been willing to have anyone call me. I'm always available, but I just never had anybody that I felt that close to before.

There may be transferred attributions of similarity (Dim. II).

Will may be voicing a deeper wish for a more parent-like father.

Describes friend's dependence (Dim. II).

Shares own experience.

Revolving slate implied.

Therapist offers partiality through identification.

Therapist: No qualities like your dad?

Will: The only similar quality is that he's a big man, and I always felt my dad was a big man in terms of stature even though I ended up being taller and bigger than he was. He just always seemed to be a big man. No. They're about as far apart as anything you could imagine.

Therapist: Could you say how?

Will: Well, my dad was very successful, very programmed and did things well. Though he's the greatest friend in the world, Mike has trouble tying his shoes. He goes from job to job but that doesn't seem to make any difference. For years he's just attracted people. People love him for what he is no matter what he does. He's gone through bankruptcy for the second time and all the guys that are in the bankruptcy hearing are in there laughing and joking because they love him.

Therapist: You know, Will, I spent an awful lot of time looking for a replacement for my father. He seemed so withholding and cold. The more I knew about other men, the angrier I got. Who they were made my father seem even more remote and further away from meeting my needs. On the other hand, the more I knew about other men, the more I could see how my father desperately wanted to talk in terms of affection rather than money. But no one ever taught him how to change his language.

Uses a 3-generational perspective and expresses partiality to Will, his father and his children.

We're not that different from one another, Will. So maybe, over time, you might begin to tease out of your head and heart what different gestures in your father's life might have represented an invitation to love that he couldn't verbalize. If you can do that, you may find that you'll be able to take another look at how it is between you and your kids as well. Kids always misrepresent their parents because parents usually look bigger than life to them.

Mrs. L: Well, his kids are crazy about him.

Therapist: Then maybe this is a God-given moment. It could be a way of restoring your father and you to a more balanced relationship. I suspect you need that. You can't afford to stay outside of the scheme of your father's love indefinitely and keep interpreting it in negative terms.

Hopes the 3-generational leverage will serve to help exonerate Will's father.

Self-delineation effort combined with a sense of unrelatedness.

Will: I don't think I could describe my father's love. I don't know that I ever knew what it was or how he was doing it.

Mother validates self through lending validation to the deceased father. Helps with exoneration of father's image.

Mrs. L: He adored Will. I gave birth to Will without getting into the delivery room. Then the doctor arrived. They started to take Will out to bathe him and Dad said, ''Don't you take that boy out of this room. You do everything right here. Take his footprints here; he is not to go out of this room.''

Elicits more of the same.

Therapist: How else did your husband show love for Will?

This kind of behavior may co-exist with father's inability to give to his children.

Ms. L: He bragged about him to our friends all the time. He adored the kids.

Will: He couldn't communicate with me though. He would try to do that through Mother.

Persists.

Therapist: That sounds important Will. You said that you couldn't describe your father's love. Can you describe it Mrs. L?

Ms. L: Yes. By everything he said. He'd say, "my" children; or "We can't afford this, we have to save for the children." I guess it was just in words that he showed his love and pride for you.

Intends to help Will exonerate their father.

Sarah: He spent time with Will too. I remember their wrestling together. In fact you and I were talking, Will, about how you remember more about how Dad held you more than mother did. Mostly we remember Mother and Dad holding and hugging each other. It's been hard on us. It's probably why I love my church so much; the people hug each other.

Will credits father.

Will: He used to put me on his shoulders when I was going to bed. I remember more from 10 years old on. . . .

Injects a painful truth in siding with Will.

Sarah: You were sent away to military school in seventh grade.

Attempts to place decision on teachers.

Ms. L: His teachers said he had to go to a military school; he was causing trouble in the school system there.

Challenges mother's statement.

Will: I've always had the feeling that kids went to camp for a week or two when their parents loved them; they went for eight weeks when their parents wanted to get rid of them.

Therapist: Did your parents want to get rid of you?

Places all responsibility for this decision on others: father and teachers.

Mrs. L: No. My husband wanted the best. He graduated from good schools and he wanted the same thing for Will. Will was just playing in school and we thought that military school would give him a chance. Didn't you realize that?

Father consistently seems to give on his own rather than on his son's terms.

Will: No. I think where my father and I miscommunicated was that he wanted the best of material things for me, and I wanted more emotion. What he did was fine; it cost him a lot of money. It just wasn't what I needed or really wanted.

Therapist helps exoneration of father through exploring the possibility of his victimization.

Therapist: How was it between your father and his father?

Will: My grandfather passed away before I was born.

Father grew up with parents who lived in marital mistrust.

Mrs. L: His father was a chaser. Ken was crazy about his mother. She overheard lots of hurtful things between her husband and other women. That's really all hearsay. His father was senile when I knew him.

Sarah: Didn't Dad have a nervous breakdown?

Ms. L: He had to stay out of college for a year.

Brings attentions to the deceased, youngest child of the family.

Therapist: We've talked a lot about fathers and sons. Jon must fit in here too. Maybe you had to be pretty noisy to get the attention you were due. It sounds like you had to scream to be heard.

Ms. L: I think that's true.

Asserts herself through honesty.

Sarah: You had to play piano to be heard in your family.

Gives credit to parents before voicing his frustration.

Will: I guess I would say that my parents were very fortunate to have a very unique marriage and that we were also a part of that. But this man and wife were the main boat and the kids were kind of an also-ran.

Attempts to be partial to everyone by putting a contextual landscape together. Tries to explore the roots of the parents' needs for parentifying their children.

Therapist: One day you may decide to pull down your idealized notion of your parents' marriage, Will, and replace it with something closer to reality. I suspect it was a refuge for two scared people who didn't know how to parent their children more helpfully. It would help if you could get a better hold of what their marriage really represented to them, and why they were so closed and attentive to each other—in rigid, inflexible ways that locked other people out. If you can do that, you may ask less of yourself and learn to appreciate yourself more. You may also ask less of women. Your mother lost a lot trying to please your father without ever surfacing her own needs.

Points out parents' pattern of fusion instead of dialogue with reciprocal polarization. As invisible loyalty to parents yields to more human caring about their shortcomings, the offspring's expectations from partners and children will become more realistic.

They didn't know how else to relate. Maybe they couldn't teach you how to come closer.

They seemed to handle their relationships with distancing and structure rather than through availability, accessibility or process.

It looks like a closed world rooted in a fear of abandonment. Love seemed to be there but everybody lost.

The parentified child describes the sources of her bondage: Realistic worries about both parents. Parental drinking places the child in a lonely, overresponsible role.

Protects mother.

Sarah: Dad did a lot of drinking that used to worry us all. When I came home, mother, you seemed to have a problem too.

Will: I don't know that Mother drank a great deal. She could have one and a half drinks and catch up with people who had a two-hour start.

Sarah: I want to bring Jon in here. When I came home from China, you had had your service. Dad kind of said, "We've grieved; you grieve on your own. I'd really be proud of you if you didn't cry." You sold the piano then and it was a very hard time for all of us. And then Dad told about that experience in his airplane when he thought Jon had come for him. We were all bottled up; we just always did what Dad said was the L. family way.

Again tries to be partial to living family members: Offers options for validating themselves via giving fair consideration to their father.

Therapist: My guess is that your father was not in touch with his demanding ways. Who would have told him? It may be that he lived and died with deep-felt vulnerability.

Will: One of the best things

Picture of husband being parentified by wife: Protectiveness (Dim. III). Generosity (Dim. IV).

about Dad that always amazed me was whenever Mother had a washout after her bridge club, he would get her tea and take her up to bed. It would never irritate him. He would never say, "I wish she wouldn't drink like that." Instead he said, "That's the way she is and I'll get her bedded down." Maybe he was burned up inside but he never let it show.

Defends her posture as a responsible adult.

Mrs. L: I would call and invite the husbands over for dinner and he would say, "I get so tired of seeing the same people. Let's go out instead."

Partial to mother.

Therapist: Do you remember many moments of discontent? It sounds like you'd rather have had things different and weren't able to pull it off.

Mrs. L: That's right. I guess I never made the effort; it never seemed that important to me.

Is the renouncement of due self-delineation connected with an inability to face mourning over loss of a son?

Therapist: It seems like none of you knew how to ask for what you wanted for yourselves—though your husband looked as if he could. It makes me wonder how the four of you, the three of you now, ever talked about Jon? What did the loss of your son do to you, Ms. L?

Mrs. L: We were crushed.

Wants to help through facing issues of grief over loss.

Therapist: Let's just talk about you.

Mrs. L: I used to be annoyed. On Christmas vacations my husband would say, "You pack

Mother may be describing her inability to give to the children, using the excuse of hating to pack on short notice.

the clothes and be ready to go to Florida tomorrow.'' We'd take the kids. Remember, Jon sat in there and we'd go bumpity, bump which he thought was wonderful. But that business of my having to pack the clothes and go to Florida! I'd say, ''We have plans,'' but that didn't make any difference. One year he said, ''I want to see my friends so I won't go.'' So I stayed home. . . .

Therapist: How old was Jonathan when he died?

Mrs. L: He would have been fifteen in a week.

Therapist: What happened?

Mrs. L: I was crushed. We had just had lunch at the kitchen table at noon. My brother was in the hospital. I went to pick up a gal that he dated and we went to the hospital together. I couldn't believe it when I got home. We had had this terrible storm and Ken and a couple of the neighbors were standing out in front and I waved. I had gerania all the way around in the shrubs and I wanted to see what the storm had done. They yelled to me to come back but I paid no attention. When I got around the corner, Ken called, ''You come back.'' So I backed up. I don't know why I didn't think it was queer that he was home early in the day, but I didn't.

Seems to appreciate therapist's interest in factual circumstances (Dim. I).

Therapist: And what happened?

Mrs. L: I was crushed, just crushed.

Therapist: Who helped you?

Explores capacity for relying on people.

Mrs. L: My friends, I think. People came in. Remember the Whites came out right away. The Lindquists wanted to go to the funeral parlor with us to pick out a casket. Sarah wasn't there.

Therapist: What happened to your husband?

Mrs. L: He was just crushed.

Therapist: How did he show it?

Mrs. L: He just didn't talk.

Therapist: Did you talk?

Did they mourn as children who lost their parent in a parentified child?

Mrs. L: No, I don't think either of us talked. When we'd go to bed though we'd both cry ourselves to sleep.

Therapist: Did you help Will?

The son who showed appropriate emotion is pictured as the one with a problem.

Mrs. L: No. When we buried Jon, some friends were there. Poor Will. When they buried Jon, he burst into tears. Remember that, Will? And Jack Ronsted said, "Will, there's nothing we can do about it. We just have to make the best of it."

Can mother acknowledge realistic, helpful availability?

Therapist: Do you remember who held Will or comforted or guided him?

Will: I think Jack Ronsted did. When we were standing at the graveside, I turned and ran. When I was a sophomore in high school, a schoolmate had gone to Tennessee and drowned during a flood when he tried to help someone. A bunch of us went to the funeral. We weren't terribly close but we went. After the service was completed, while everyone was standing around, they lowered the casket into the ground. We were standing there at graveside and, all of a sudden, it occurred to me that they were going to do that to Jon. I couldn't handle it so I turned and ran. Jack chased me down and helped me through that. I basically got through Jon's death by taking care of my parents. It was easier to concentrate on helping them than by concentrating on my own grief.

Mrs. L: I think he helped a lot.

Describes lack of dialogue between brothers.

Will: Jonny was five years younger than I was and, in my feelings, he was almost another family. I was not a kisser and hugger with him because he was a little brat. He had his own circle of friends and he operated more or less independently. I guess that's not so unusual in families where children are five years apart. Sarah and I are only 18 months apart and we fought like hell. It was always her fault, of course. Jon made good grades and played the piano and did all those things I really wasn't into. I just felt that this was an easy way out for me, that I could deal with my grief better by taking care of my mom and dad.

The parentified child is again ready to give his concern to the parents.

I've always felt it had to be 10 times as hard on a parent than on a brother or sister. I've laid in bed at night and worried about something happening to my own two kids. You can worry yourself right into the zoo, doing that sort of thing. I've literally had to grab myself and pull myself up and say, "Get off of this or you're going to twist your tail." I happened to be down at Indiana University when this happened and it was a terrible experience. It's a terrible thing to watch your parents go through. I needed time to get things squared away and not worry about how I felt.

Asks about the most painful part of grief. His regrets over missed opportunities to give to the lost one.

Therapist: Did you have leftover feelings about Jon, Will? Regrets?

Will: Sure. A couple of days before, Jon was getting to the point where he wanted to do the driving. He wanted to back the car out of the driveway and I would say, "No, it's not that time yet." So I blamed myself for little things I should have done. If I had only known; you know, those sort of things.

Recalls an occasion where he could have given more.

Therapist: Were you resentful that Sarah wasn't available?

Will: No. She just chooses not to be in town when these things happen.

Jon sounds like a desperately demanding child here. Why is

Ms. L: At that age, Jon used to say "I'm going to have a birthday party and I'm going to have 150 people here. That way I'll get loads of gifts," and I would

mother perceiving him like that? Was he really the counterpart to the two, parentified, older children?

Admits to the serious problems caused by her unfinished grief.

Hesitates to connect grief and lack of good school performance.

Inserts seed of joint mourning work as a relational resource.

say "I just can't handle that." Jon's response was, "You had that many for Sarah and Will so I want a big party like they had." I didn't know what we were going to do; he just kept demanding it and I never said yes or no.

Sarah: Do you think it was hard in the fall? I know I got sick and came home and never put it together. It was the only time I had to drop a course and I know it was because of all of this. And you quit school before Christmas, Will.

Will: Well I couldn't lay it on that. I just wasn't cut out to be a student. I kept myself in a pretty tight rein. I wasn't really sure I belonged in a fraternity. I joined it and got out of it. I had bad times when I would sit around and cry. I don't know what caused it. That kind of grief would just creep up and grab you. Maybe it was because you fell downstairs or flunked a test. Who knows? When you have that kind of grief in you, it doesn't take much to punch the clock. I just suppressed it.

Therapist: But would you agree that there was some connection?

Will: Yes.

Therapist: Sarah, are there things you still need to surface with your mother and brother? Have the three of you ever been to Jonny's grave together?

Sarah: Not the three of us. Will

and I went out a year ago Christmas.

Will: I remember that vaguely. I remember you said that you'd like to go out there because you had never been. That shocked me. I didn't realize that Dad or Mom had never gone out there with you.

Therapist: Had you been out there, Will?

Admits deep emotional needs.

Will: Oh yeah. At the funeral, and then I tried to go once a year. I'd go out and talk to him.

Mrs. L: I used to take flowers out and my husband went one time and. . . .

Openly speaks of how mother and son are relating.

Therapist: Your son is crying, Mrs. L. He's upset.

His grief is described as halfway between facing and denying the loss of his father and brother.

Will: I've always had the feeling that he was right here, he and Dad both now that they're gone. Probably not true. I guess it's a fantasy of mine. I just felt that there were times when I wanted to go out and tell him what was going on. I may seem silly but it felt good to communicate.

Sarah: I didn't know you did that. When we went out that day, I got teary and you said, "Well, it's over now." So I thought, well, I really can't share that pain with him because he's done his grieving.

Delicate observation about the possibility of resources in deep, emotional sharing.

Will: You start to avoid it and then you quit. I once had a counselor tell me, "Sometime

The grief of the parentified child includes craving for a parental parent.

Here again the son was parentified by a frightened parent.

Describes depth of need for someone like a parent.

you're going to have to accept the fact that your father is dead. I don't think you've done that yet." That was probably true. I care a great deal for him and I really didn't want to let go. As I got older there were a lot of times when he was a big help to me. We really did get to know each other more.

After I was married, the two of us would take trips and play golf or something we had never done. We went to Vegas and that's when I found out how terrified he was of going broke. He wouldn't put a nickel in the slot machine. He and I put some money together and we played baccarat and won. He just stood at the rail and watched. "I'm terrified of gambling and going broke," he said, "and that's never going to end." He loved to play gin rummy; it was just professional gambling. He was just terrified of becoming a professional gambler and decided not to start. I really made a lot of progess in the last 10 years of his life.

Mrs. L: I think you did, too.

Will: There was a totally unquenchable thirst on my part for that.

The therapist's method of moving from the known to the unknown has led from Will's open concern for a friend who in "no way reflected" his father to profound disclosure of the limitless facets of the burdens and benefits of his long-term relationship to his brother and father—and how they intersected with the entire family's past.

The series of three sessions ended in apparent harmony. Brother and sister eagerly agreed to continue their newfound closeness and exchange.

Mother seemed pleasant, if less communicative. A few weeks later, though, new concerns surfaced. Mother failed to answer Sarah's letters and was cold and evasive with both of her children. The fear that she might increase her drinking or act on suicidal impulses haunted both of them, but especially Sarah who expected to be blamed for instigating a new definition of family relationships.

There was a new resource in the family, however. Sarah and Will could now reassure each other through the ways they pursued important issues with directness and vigor. They were able to persist in their concern about mother's day-to-day living. On the therapist's suggestion, they were also able to follow up on an almost lost clue: Mother had a half-sister with whom she had cut off relationships for decades. Reasons for the cutoff were associated with hurt pride and the implication of shame regarding the half-sister's allegedly "illegitimate" origins. Will and Sarah were willing to explore the situation.

It took real detective work to discover that Aunt Vera was living in California. The information came via a distant cousin. Vera, a matriarch and widow of a wealthy banker, was surprised and deeply pleased by the interest expressed by long-forgotten relatives. She seemed remarkably free of any resentment over the fact that her relatives had previously ostracised her, despite Mrs. L's major part in cutting ties between Vera and the family.

As Sarah and Will began to explore their mother's feelings about Vera, they found that her response was a mixture of curiosity and guilt. As she learned more about the circumstances of her mother's humiliation and the issues of family pride and shame that surrounded it, Sarah's own curiosity began to stir. But much more was involved. Mrs. L's lonely alienation, underlined by her drinking and preoccupation with suicide, had been challenged by the prospect of discovering a long-lost family connection. She was excited at the chance to learn something about her parents' early life circumstances. She was being given an opportunity to explore and so exonerate the harshly rejecting attitudes she had encountered from both her mother and other family members. This was in addition to the fact that Vera seemed to appear from nowhere, an unexpected gift of life. She was lively, resourceful, warm, and capable of offering friendship.

Sarah's tendencies for self-blame gradually turned into newfound security. She found confirmation for her loyal, filial intentions that were well received by her mother. Sarah's and Will's shared efforts to give to their mother on her own terms had begun to pay off. As if she were less in need of the invisible loyalties that resulted in self-damage, Sarah showed a renewed capacity to turn to the real issues of her own social life. She started to face the fact that she was entitled to invest her energy and creativity in her own pleasure and plans for her own future, that she could be concerned for her work and her friends but also invested in herself in increasingly more liberated ways.

At the same time, Sarah was successful in convincing Will to begin therapy with his own family. Will soon learned how many areas of the relationships with his children were in need of his attention and nurturant care. He and his children began to diminish the emotional cost of their relationship with each other by discovering new options for receiving through giving. In the process, they also learned how to validate themselves and, eventually, to forgo patterns of self-denying, isolated relating.

Multidirected partiality might be likened to a situation in which several chess games are simultaneously being played. Each time one of the players makes a move, it has to be included into a new and revised short-term and long-term plan. As each step unfolds, the therapist has to offer due credit for the merits of each person's constructive intentions and care. His capacity to credit each family member in turn reinforces the demand on all of them to do the same, that is, to intensify each person's self-exploration *and* willingness to respond to others with consideration and care. It is precisely through his efforts to address and explore the balances of fairness in a family that the therapist forms and seals the therapeutic contract with family members in a very profound way. In so doing, he also enables them to tap trust resources and to invest themselves in the process of earning constructive entitlement.

REJUNCTION

As family members engage in these simultaneous chess games with each other and with the therapist, they begin to join or rejoin each other's lives in newly creative and healing ways (Boszormenyi-Nagy & Ulrich, 1981). Family members have already taken the frightening risk and experienced the pain of facing up to their own responsibility for unfair actions and behaviors. Now they can begin to explore where in their relationships unactualized trustworthiness still resides.

Paradoxically, residual trustworthiness can exist in the very midst of seeming hopelessness. The prospect of trust-building is typically elicited out of chaos, hostility, rejection, abandonment, and all forms of exploitation. Their negative presence in people's lives may slow the trust-building process but need not necessarily unseat it. The fragments of residual trustworthiness can survive the rubble of destructive entitlement and cutoffs born of an earlier day. These fragments grow off the reality of a blood relatedness and/or the fact of a long-term ledger of merits.

Rejunction, then, is to be understood as a reconnection with resources from the past which can be oriented to the future with posterity in mind. Obviously, despite one's fondest longings, rejunction can never restore what was missed in the circumstances of the past. For better and for worse, the consequences of earned entitlement, constructive and destructive, are timeless. However, a family's ability to account for them always has a creative outcome; the fate of the future is always implicit in people's willingness to take responsibility for the past.

The rejunctive process always proceeds on the force provided by the family members' intrinsic motives and resources. The therapist invites the family into an active search and concern for responsibility for relational consequences. He never imposes his own criteria for responsibility nor himself determines the consequences of everyone's position-taking. Neither does he measure the family's situation through the glass of his own moral preoccupations or concerns. People struggling with the problems of relationship naturally tend to be attuned to questions of fairness, injustice and exploitation. Consequently, therapists need only learn how to turn to all family members in sequence and require them to voice their own discrete positions about the issues that are being raised.

Family members naturally use each other in the rejunctive process. Here again the question is one of fairness. For example, when parents require their 13-year-old to take care of younger children on a frequent and continuing basis, do they acknowledge his availability as a contribution or do they take it for granted as something they're owed? When do parental expectations become unilateral demands and begin to crush a youngster's individuation and emancipation? And when are they reasonable requests for efforts at mutual care? What specific criteria count as a fair return to parents at any given time? The questions are complex, the answers even more so. But even raising these questions has beneficent consequences for family members. Improved and improving balances of give-and-take show themselves in numerous ways: in increased and spontaneous age-appropriate autonomy in children, adolescents, and young adult family members; in a diminishing burdensomeness of parenting; in increasing mutuality in marriage; and in a growing capacity to exonerate aging parents.

ASPECTS OF MULTIDIRECTED PARTIALITY

In one-on-one therapy, the therapist's unilateral partiality to his patient is established by contract and by counter-transference. Here partiality is used in the narrowest sense of the word, to single out the patient from all the other people in his life. However significant to the primary client, everyone else in his relational world is more or less excluded from help by the therapeutic contract. In contextual work, partiality can be more specifically defined as a therapist's commitment to help everyone in his client's relational world who is likely to be affected by therapeutic intervention. It operates with a minimum of three people, of whom the client is one.

Empathy

Empathy is an aspect of partiality, that is, a therapist's openness to imagining the feeling mode of each family member as he or she proceeds to describe personal perspectives and conflicted interests. The therapist's own natural feelings and reactions towards particular family members are reined in by his efforts to be partial. One family member may evoke resentment in him, another may evoke contempt. For example, a father who has sexually abused his little child may evoke feelings of revulsion at such monstrous behavior. But finally, no one is a meritless monster. At the very least a therapist has to find room in his feelings to imagine how the offending person has himself suffered as a childhood victim.

Crediting

Crediting is another aspect of partiality, a more clearly contextual one. Obviously the task of giving credit most appropriately falls to family members rather than to the realm of the therapist. It is the tribunal-like function of close relationships that lets people call each other to account for their balance of credits and debits. It is also the tribunal-like function of family relationships that allows its members to establish criteria for fairness among them. However, the therapist can use the fairness of his own relational context as a measure and guide. In that regard, he is just a member of humanity. His own circumstances can function as analogies to the family's situation and evoke the same "jury" function from the family members.

Expectation

A therapist's expectation that family members *care* and *do* for one another is still another aspect of partiality. The therapist who expects a relative to explore ways to exonerate the family's monster-member is being partial to both of them. The person doing the exonerating can relinquish negative behavior patterns and earn new options for earning entitlement. He may harbor resentment toward the therapist for maintaining her expectations. Still, over time, he comes face-to-face with the consequent benefits of his own efforts. For her part, the alleged monster-member may finally get the chance to explain herself. She may also be able to find new, more constructive options for relating to family members who can then rework their reliance on the behavior of the "culprit."

Inclusiveness

Inclusiveness is still another aspect of multidirected partiality. It places a demand on the therapist that requires him to offer every family member a fair chance, even the chronic "wrongdoer." Whatever the pulls toward one or another person, the therapist cannot consistently side with one clique of family members against another member or clique and still be multidirectional. It is to be noted here that the term "partiality" is meant to describe a serious professional commitment to benefitting every family member rather than to convey a technical "siding" with a strategically selected member. Multidirected partiality is the only conceivable method for insuring that the justice factor in every person's life is taken into account.

Timing

Timing is another important aspect of multidirected partiality. The process of the therapist's turning in sequence to various family members is governed by his timing. In this process, the therapist has to determine the order of his priorities: To whom is he to be partial next? As a general rule, a priority of consideration is most effectively assigned to the most decisively wounded person. It makes little sense to expect someone who is bitterly hurt to offer generous concern to a partner who has been unfair. The therapist's task may include 1) searching out the circumstances of the alleged injury, 2) crediting its unfairness to the injured party *and* its mitigating circumstances, 3) possibly having family members credit it, too, and 4) eventually suggesting that the current victim make some efforts to exonerate the people who are the source of his hurts at a time that he is most ready to do so.

Here a combination of efforts is at work: first a call for due consideration, then a seed planted that may yield exonerative work at a later time. It is the realistic quality of this combination that makes it a powerful strategy for therapeutic intervention. Persistent goal-setting combined with the offer of a moratorium is a strong therapeutic position, one that is hard to resist.

The therapist elicits accountable action in sequences from family members. Through the process, he helps them (re)engage in dialogue, now by acts of self-delineation and now by acts of self-validation. The first stage offers options for self-assertion, for overcoming self-fragmentation, inhibitions and other like obstacles. The second stage offers options for earning merit. This stage requires due consideration of a partner's burdens, of the price paid by a partner who is being used, and examination of how, indeed, one person is unilaterally exploiting his or her partner. Successful efforts at self-validation reduce a person's need to rely on destructive entitlement or, simultaneously, on a set of internal relating to ''bad'' objects. As people rework this reliance, they can suffer a loss of self-delineation, at least temporarily. The therapist tries to provide specific aid to each person according to his or her requirements in each stage.

Multidirected partiality can eventually lead to a redistribution of intermember burdens and benefits, to a shift in transactions and roles, and, usually, to more responsive parental and marital care. It is a methodology which draws its leverage from an underlying dialogue of trustworthiness that resides among family members. This dialogue, based on actual mutuality of commitment, is forward-thrusting in nature. It cannot be equated with a simple deviation amplification or with a reduction process that results from a correction of the cybernetic (feedback) regulations of ''control.'' In the dialogue, all partners may be liberated by entitlement earned through due consideration and fair contributions to each other's wellbeing. It does not lead to one person's inherent control of another. One partner's active contribution to the other inevitably results in a benefit to the self.

Trustworthy dialogue leads to the kind of relating that invites candid confrontation of conflicting interests, an inevitable circumstance in relationship that requires recognition and work. Trustworthy dialogue produces a self-motivating process in each relating partner, not a pretty set of relationship patterns. Rejunctive efforts and their consequences ultimately yield some beneficial returns for all.

A therapist can facilitate dialogue among family members but she does well to remember that it is not hers to create. She also does well to note that dialogue is an inevitable facet of interpersonal relating and not a set of criteria for communication or transactions. Intergenerational relationships, in particular, cannot be measured by the quality of parent-child conversation. For it is especially in the intergenerational realm that dialogue springs from the simple fact of being and becoming. Offspring receive from parents and give to parents. This mutuality of reliance represents a life-giving existential dialogue even if communicational and transactional patterns between parent and child are undeveloped, overtly destructive or apparently at a dead-end.

The inexorable nature of intergenerational connectedness is often evident in situations in which, posthumously, people struggle to exonerate ambivalently held parents. Efforts to ''reconstruct'' relationships with dead family members can take many forms, including discussions with surviving relatives, the use of photographs to share memories, and a search of whatever correspondence remains. The very attempt to reconstruct a relationship is a measure of this work's success. So is the liberation that comes from earning entitlement through exonerating parents even after their death.

Surviving offspring may try to ignore their dead parent out of a felt helplessness. Or they may remain inactive vis-à-vis dead parents for fear of intensifying unfaced hurts. Conversely, surviving children often try to ignore the legacies left them by a parent who was "bad." However, their inactivity toward the dead parent by whom they have been hurt is counterproductive. Memories of a "bad" deceased parent are likely to haunt the offspring-in-flight. The offspring's other relationships may also suffer from his failure to commit to them in ways that are also fitting to the dead.

There are many ways to address family members that can further the goals of multidirected partiality. Exploratory questions that are open-ended can be the most direct and the least frightening methodology:

- Can you describe your side of the conflict?
- What might happen if things don't improve?
- Who first raised the issue of divorce?
- Have you told the children about the essence of your struggle?
- Do you think that anyone is desperate enough to be considering suicide?
- Is someone's physical health affected? How?
- How is your sleep?
- What is there for you to live for?
- Did you protect your parents the way your son/daughter seems to protect you?
- Do your children know just how you were victimized as a child?
- Who was there for you then? How?
- Are your children torn between you and your mate?
- Do your children criticize one parent in order to protect the other?

There is no limit to the "down-home" kind of questions that can be asked. Clients are frequently freed up by a therapist's ability to penetrate to the heart of their situation in immediate, direct and relatively unthreatening ways.

MULTIDIRECTED PARTIALITY AS A GUIDE
TO GIVE-AND-TAKE

To focus on the entitled rather than destructive aspect of the person acting under destructive entitlement can be seen as paradoxical. A person's friends or acquaintances may try to address the destructive element: "Look, why not consider how lucky you are to have these wonderful kids?

Why do you have to act like this?'' This kind of attitude is usually offered in the spirit of customary, "reality oriented" comments on the part of a parent, a sister or spouse.

To all appearances, it is paradoxical to tell a "hysterically" destructive person that he or she is obviously entitled to be vindictive, given the facts that he never received reassuring parenting and that his oldest child died of leukemia at age seven. Yet a contextual therapist does not choose simply to be paradoxical by focusing on the entitled side of a victimizing person. Instead, the therapist means to come closer to the deeper personal truth of his client. That is, the therapist takes care to consider the injustice of his client's destiny (compared with an average parent's lot) rather than, for instance, assuming the authority to therapeutically prescribe pathological behavior: "I want you to continue your hysterical outbursts." Strategic manipulation reinforces dependent complacency on the client's part. The search for a client's personal trust opens up a dialogue of respect via separateness.

In the matter of dialogue, contextual theorists take a radically different view from traditional psychodynamic theory. We do not judge the parenting generation as the primary source of dialogic failure. Instead, we assign responsibility for dialogue to the members of all of the generations in a family. Existentially, parents are neither innately more or less endowed to take the risks of dialogue than their offspring. Still parents *are* responsible as are their adult children. Offspring, like parents, have the right and potential to initiate dialogue and to begin the process of rejunction. An adult child's prospects for actively offering responsible care is a major relational resource in itself; at the very least, he himself benefits from efforts to initiate.

A person's move to exonerate his parents who are now grandparents, too, can be a crucial step through which everyone stands to gain. Such steps may be spontaneous though not momentary. Impulsive efforts to reconnect with parents are understandable but not efficacious. A failure to follow through with some continuity once a flag has been raised may lead to confusion and cynicism as well as to deepened stagnation. It is here that people can look to guidelines previously conveyed and clarified by their therapist and offered without pressure of time. Initiating intergenerational dialogue may be demanding and complex. In our therapeutic experience, though, no single occurrence in a family's life ever signals a greater promise of improvement than an adult offspring's move to exonerate his or her parents.

Intergenerational dialogue with its will to mutual responsibility is an interhuman absolute assumed by contextual therapy. Children, by inclination, are practitioners of the trust-building process. It is in their vested interests to gain and extend trust to parenting adults. Gaining trust is a more fundamental and pervasive therapeutic goal than elaborating the intricacies of matters like sexual identify formation, pleasure economy and useful sublimation patterns. As people proceed toward new dialogic input, they will inevitably undergo stages of regression, sublimation, new insight, and a new integrative level of function on the way. Even in the midst of these stages, it is the criterion of caring, channeled into new patterns of action, that counts.

Intergenerational dialogue relies as much on the actual existential needs of all relating partners as it does on the superego psychology of inner standards. These needs are made concrete when the therapist asks for a description of specific examples of how family members attend to each other by actually offering care. For example, the therapist may ask a mother, "Can you cite an instance of how Paul, despite his so-called delinquent behavior, shows his concern for you? Can you recall how he acts when you're unhappy?" If mother claims that she can remember no such occasion, the therapist may ask Paul what he does when his mother is crying. Statements like, "I stay close to her" or "I say things that cheer her up" are almost invariable responses from the young. Whether or not a child can be concrete or specific, these responses indicate his or her innately generous, loyal, caring, and giving inclinations toward parents.

In instances in which reports from a parent and child subtly or blatantly diverge, the therapist does well never to pit their statements against each other and certainly never to use the child's words as testimony against his parent. Were the therapist to commit such an error, the child would immediately be cast into a loyalty conflict between his parent and the therapist. And the parent would be humiliated to say nothing of becoming demotivated and disinclined to offer the child acknowledgment or his fair due. All in all, it would be a conflict that no one could win.

In such instances, the therapist can always take refuge in a multidirected stance. She can choose to acknowledge the child in a manner that reinforces the future promise of his relationship with his parent. For example, "Maybe when you and your mom go home, you can have some fun trying to remember how you help each other when she cries." Or the therapist can choose to inquire into an analogous example in mother's life like, "How was it for you when *your* mother cried?" and then, "Can you tell Paul what you used to do then?" Or the therapist can choose to acknowledge the child in a manner that acknowledges mother, too: "It must be hard for you to cry in front of Paul when you want to be able to comfort him as much as he wants to comfort you." The buildup of dialogic trust benefits parents and children alike. Giving mother a chance to exonerate herself strengthens the therapeutic relationship. But more significantly, it diminishes her felt isolation, lessens the adversary nature of her relationship to Paul, and allows trust to creep into the parent-child relationship.

The trustworthiness that does develop in the dialogue between Paul and his mother will not evolve from equitable returns. Nor can it build on claims of altruism and sacrifice or, conversely, on accusations of selfishness. It will develop from accumulated merit, actual and internal. It is to be noted that earned merit accumulates most decisively on the side of a parent whose offerings are bound by the fewest possible strings. On the other hand, a parent's investment in dialogic trustworthiness with her child is sure to bring a liberating inner reward, even when it fails to bring immediate joy or satisfaction from the child himself.

UNUTILIZED INCLINATIONS TO GIVE: A RESOURCE

A real loss occurs in therapy when practitioners focus entirely on pathology without reference to its resource side. For pathology in individuals often relates to the unutilized or underutilized inclinations in people to give to one another. Consider the following situation, for example.

> A divorced mother, 42, is bitter and chronically depressed. She cites two incidents to document her failure as a mother. In the first incident, Debbie, 12, was reported to have destroyed her brother Ronny's glasses. Ronny, 10, was then forced to wear his sports glasses in school. Debbie is afraid that their mother will report what she did to her father. Her father, remarried, is allegedly strict and punitive toward his children. To help Debbie avert her father's anger mother has offered to help pay for a new pair of glasses for Ronny. On the other hand, she blames herself for Debbie's poorly controlled rage.
> In the second incident, mother reports that a little girl hit or pushed Debbie at the swimming pool. Debbie retaliated. She scratched the girl down the full length of her back and made her bleed profusely. Mother's report to the therapist made Debbie very anxious; she threatened not to talk to either of them.

The therapist insisted that the story be told but changed its focus. He shifted away from the apparent pathology of this very depleted woman and her depleted children to concentrate on the residual resources that he knew had to still lie between them. He elected to draw on a comment that Ronny had made to their mother who was displeased with her appearance and her struggle with her weight. "You're not mommy when you're fat," he said. Here the therapist heard the boy's desperate attempt to praise his mother. He recognized that this terribly depleted family was constantly frustrated by a lack of opportunity to give to each other and to gain the acceptance that comes of giving. So he turned to Debbie and referred to the kernel of information that was hidden in Ronny's remark.

"Do you hear Ronny trying to make your mother feel good?" he asked. Debbie relaxed. "Yes," she replied with relief. "And it makes me feel happy too."

However meager a family's intermember resources, the therapist can rely on their existence and can draw on their reserves. He can also draw on the likelihood that among the family members there is probably an unutilized desire to give. Here multidirected partiality not only acknowledges people's longings to affirm each other, but helps them support that inclination in each other. Simply put, it gives them the "space" or the "room" they each need to develop responsible positions toward their relationships with each other.

Crediting Relational Reality

Contextual therapy rests heavily on the elicitory technique which often takes the form of crediting. It is sometimes difficult, though, to credit the family's "monster-member," or even its "acting-out" child. It is plain hard work, for example, to credit a delinquent adolescent for his captive if subtle demonstrations of devotion to his family. Whatever its difficulties, in contextual work crediting always takes place on an appropriate ethical basis, that is, on a recognition of people's genuine efforts at fair exchange. Crediting in contextual work does not follow the random patterns of "positive connotation" or "relabeling" that are used in transactional family therapy. Crediting here is geared to change the behavioral system. In contextual therapy, crediting is meant to acknowledge a family's legitimate efforts to redistribute its members' benefits and burdens.

The therapist has to be able to advance credibility to intermember inclinations to build trustworthy relationships. He can do so only by forwarding the processes of responsible dialogue which have to develop among the family members themselves. Again it is their relational reality rather than his values, interests or personal preferences that matters in therapy. It follows, then, that his crediting has to occur along lines that are existentially relevant and ethically sound in the family's context. Crediting is meant to acknowledge the merit and hence the legitimacy in every family member's terms, and so to unleash the reserve potential of their impending dialogue.

Partiality and Affect: Two Sides of the Dialogue

A person's involvement and investment in a relationship always includes a concern for affect, her partner's as well as her own. She, like the rest of us, will probably draw gratification and frustration from her relational situation. She and her partner will invariably express their affect in verbal and nonverbal communications. They will communicate their current emotional state and data about how to channel their need gratification. In part, needs are contained in the emotional tensions themselves. In the long run, though, needs originate from the demands for survival, from reproducing and supporting children, from having to become a functioning member of society, and from demands for room for personal action and striving. Survival itself requires people to act in ways and patterns that serve a person's needs and interests.

In addition to his personal relationships, the therapist's work engages him in a dialogue of affects. The members of a family will have attitudes and behaviors that will please or frustrate him. Whatever the particulars, it is crucial that the therapist stay in touch with his feeling reactions. His emotions are important indicators of what is going on in his client's fundamental attitudes. Attitudes, of course, are oriented to affect as well as to action. Ultimately, therapy's goal lies in inducing attitudes and in discovering action patterns that maximize the positive potential of the clients' relationships with people. Confidence in relationships have the secondary effect of good feelings about oneself as well. In any case, the therapist is better served to base his interventions on existential concern and ethical relevance than on emotionally warm expressions that can be used to obscure his indifference.

Literature in the field has a lot to say about the therapist's exchange of affect with his clients. Freud, among others, has cautioned against the dangerous forces of the therapist's own emotional needs. Countertransference can destroy the exquisite balance that therapy requires. Kohut talks about the compensatory use of therapeutic empathy that, he says, can partly make up for a lack of parental input. Whitaker claims that the therapist's experiential participation with his client is a requirement of therapeutic engagement. Bowen sometimes sounds as if he is declaiming the value of affective guidelines when he equates "emotional systems" with pathology. Metaposition theory provides guidelines for keeping therapists emotionally detached. Contextual theory argues that a therapist's emotions are best channelled into a mode of alternating, inclusive partiality that can provide guidelines for how family members might credit each other.

Therapists engaged in multidirected partiality are bound to become emotionally involved in issues of fairness in the family. That involvement carries a special poignancy when it stems from a situation in which adult sophistication and cunning are pitted against a young child in exploitative and abandoning ways. Adults can always be critical and destructive toward a child. But destructiveness carries an even more bitter edge when parents mock a youngster's trust and take what they can without any show of commitment in return. The mother who hates her own mother, for example, expects her son to parent her. She and his father are recently divorced.

When her son leaves for college, she taunts him with accusations of his indifference to her over the years. When he gets to school, she harasses him with upwards of five calls a day. When he comes back to vacation at his father's house, she refuses to see him and fails to acknowledge the seven years in which the boy literally tended to her and her needs, e.g., prepared meals, driving younger siblings to after-school activities, locking up the house at night, consoling her in her depression and manic outbursts of hate.

No therapist can finally protect herself from feelings of anger in situations like this.

On occasion, it may be of value for therapists to openly express their angry feelings. Some even suggest it as a model. That may or may not be helpful. But if the burden of work has to do with ethical exchange within the client's context, then there is at least some doubt about the merit of suddenly shifting the emphasis from intermember dialogue to what is occurring between the therapist and a given individual vis-à-vis affect. That is not to suggest that the therapist is never entitled to be angry. It is to suggest that he might acknowledge his anger but use it in alternative ways. A family worker's display of anger may be of therapeutic value in some cases, but it is never a major item in the therapy process. For us the main issue has to do with how a therapist's feelings might most creatively and efficaciously be channelled into therapeutic action.

If parents can begin to take better care of their child, the reasons behind the therapist's anger will certainly diminish. If a therapist can effectively hold parents to account, he will have channelled his affects into action. After all, his angry frustration is more likely to originate from helplessness and ineffectiveness in moving clients away from their unfair actions, and less likely to originate from a personal conflict between him and the people he is treating. Family members may indeed resist his moves. Still the therapist's best use of affect is its investment in a courageous and forceful exploration of options for reworking deep-rooted patterns of unfairness. Regardless of outcome, a therapist's work is eventually vindicated by the degree to which he can 1) monitor his tendencies toward unilateral partiality, 2) muster the courage to channel his emotions into a creative therapeutic process, and 3) invest his convictions and skill in helping people face into the justice of their order of being human.

THE THERAPIST'S SIDE

It should be amply evident by now that the driving force of multidirected partiality flows from the therapist toward the family members, and is intended to increase pressure on them for increased courage and integrity in their responses. Initially, it is the therapist who takes the risk of addressing the issue of intermember responsibility. Gradually, though, family members usually grow less fearful and inhibited and move away from their status of participant-observers. As one member's growing integrity results in his or her increased participation, pressure builds for matching efforts on the part of other family members. The role of affect is generally secondary in this sequence. People come into therapy hurt, resentful, guilt-stricken and enraged. The therapist always has to acknowledge the suffering that gives rise to a family member's emotions without finally allowing her interventions to be unduly swayed by them.

In initiating the quest for trustworthiness, the therapist has to deal with his own emotions too. Obviously, his decision to help people pursue the latent sources of trust comes from the therapist's own experience with both his own personal relationships and with the restorative consequences of the work. His affective sensitivity functions as an important guideline and clue for sensing his clients' motivational states. But his strategy cannot finally depend on his emotions. If his emotions do manage to dominate his strategies, a therapist does well to readdress the unfinished work in his own context. It is true that clients may distort or rebuff his therapeutic work, and may leave him feeling dissatisfied and angry. Even so, his therapeutic agenda has plenty of avenues for channeling his feelings into an effort at renewal that carries its own validation, whether or not his clients can invest themselves immediately. Contextual work always proceeds on the therapist's *prior evidence* that the seed of responsible dialogue invariably produces a nurturing yield.

CHAPTER 17

Contextual Work with Marriage

Marriage, like other long-term, symmetrical relationships, operates out of expectations that characteristically contrast with the level of expectations that exist between parent and offspring. In symmetrical relationship, peers, mates, lovers or friends expect equitable give-and-take. Peer relationships stay viable only as long as people can manage to achieve a balance of relatively reciprocal contributions between them. Otherwise their relationship becomes one-sided and exploitative, and cannot be maintained.

Balances between peers are composed of complex considerations. The following factors stand high among those that contribute to the viability (or unviability) of peer relationships, and require careful balancing.

- The existence of a romantic period of intensive infatuation;
- A genetic match between a man and woman who plan to have children;
- The past accumulation of merit vis-à-vis friendship and trustworthy attachments and care;
- Family of origin loyalties, family legacies, how a marriage was arranged, the circumstances surrounding the decision to marry;
- Shared responsibility for children and grandchildren, functioning as a parenting team;
- A constructive coalescence between merited entitlement and internal object relating;
- Business and material interests and values;
- Racial, religious and ethnic considerations;
- Ongoing sexual options up to and including old age;

- Concerns about health and aging;
- The degree of dependent exploitation between partners.

Over the long run, people have to accommodate to each other and delineate themselves as well. Finding ways to balance their colliding interests becomes a significant and relation-long task. In order to create fair balances, though, peers have to build on factors that are fundamental to each other's past and future as well as to their present.

The manifestations of marital and other peer relationships vary. They include lack of communication, violent quarrels, sexual avoidance, limits on sexual freedom, a preference for other people, loss of affection, affairs, substance abuse, and struggles with parents and in-laws. Spouses have frequently exhausted their resources by the time they come for marriage counselling. Often, efforts to save their relationship amount to a *pro forma* try. If the couple is responsible, the existence of their small children will naturally provide a significant consideration in helping them keep the family intact. At minimum, ex-spouses can work on constructive, post-divorce, parental team collaboration.

The decision to mend their marriage belongs to the couple alone. In the process of deciding whether or not even to try, one or both partners often parentify the therapist. People's tendency to cast therapists into a deciding role is a common one that often carries a negative sense. The push to defy an authority figure becomes a dynamic of its own. In any case, it is always questionable if not plain undesirable, for the therapist to allow himself to get caught in a position of primary responsibility for healing a marriage as a product of his work.

The therapist is surely entitled to his biases in the matter if he identifies them as such. He may say, for example, that he is neither a marriage therapist nor a divorce therapist. Instead, he is someone who might help two people assess what, if anything, is left on which to rebuild their relationship. He may even say that, when possible, there is probably a lot of merit for a couple to consider reworking their marriage instead of presuming that somewhere out there is an ideal woman or man.

Many therapists are afraid to encourage parental responsibility in their clients for fear of alienating them. In our experience the opposite seems to be true. It is fairly rare for a couple in trouble to have somewhere to turn. Their pastor? Perhaps. But even here, too often, they feel that they are supposed to act in a certain kind of way. Most clients see the merit in a challenge to be responsible, whatever they finally do.

A therapist who helps people think through how they might prevent damage to their young children, for example, is doing the couple a favor. This is especially true in circumstances in which both parties' natural tendencies are to use parenting issues as weapons in their quarrels with each other. In all likelihood, they have already exposed their children to a predicament of split loyalties, and the therapist always runs the danger of reinforcing its consequences. As a baseline, then, a contextual therapist will help a couple explore options that will best avoid unnecessary damage to children, whether or not they choose to stay together. This baseline establishes a foundation that is essentially without challenge, this in a stormy world of emotions where nothing is absolute or objective.

Except where there is a clear and present danger to children or to one of the mates, the contextual therapist first attends to the spouses' complaints about their marriage. She will listen for indications of unfairness and exploitation, for ways in which one partner is taken for granted by the other. And she will watch for patterns of how the partners interact and communicate. She will also try to identify the means by which one person uses the other person's guilt feelings to control the relationship, e.g., violent outbursts that spill out of the guilt-laden partner's helpless fury. Overgiving can be a piece of early learned behavior. Overgiving aimed at holding the other captive through guilt, even if inadvertent, is a masterful double bind.

The therapist uses her skill and experience to help the couple face into the issues related to the marital conflict. She elicits each partner's potential for responsible concern and care through a multidirected approach, and helps them shape a more trustworthy atmosphere in which caring might take root. In the first instance, marriage partners, in trouble or not, need the kind of relationship that can draw on every resource they have. Marriage may be society's most vulnerable institution. Strengthening it can never be confined to a matter of solving problems. It depends, instead, on everyone's ongoing options for a dialogue of fair concern.

Marriages founder because of imbalances between the two people most involved (horizontal). They also founder because of vertical imbalances. A contextual therapist understands the massive impact of intergenerational conflicts and tries to help a couple explore them. He can identify just how one spouse's invisible loyalty to her family of origin can undercut the marriage's potential, e.g., through a chronically supercritical attitude. Punishing your mate in order to be loyal to your parents is a commonplace phenomenon. A man may be indifferent and cold to his parents when he sees them, and still maintain indirect loyalty to them. From our perspective, underlying invisible loyalty to parents may well prove to be the major cause of most early marital difficulties and a continuing cause of trouble in longer-term marriages too. A combination of vertical and horizontal loyalty conflicts may finally block any chance that partners might give to their marriage, or to other closely committed, loyalty-based relationships.

It is therapeutically important to uncover the dynamic source of abandonment in each partner's family of origin, as well as to uncover factors behind rejected peer relationships. Helping clients face into intergenerational cutoffs is not done to foster insight into the displacement mechanism in hopes that the insight will correct the spouse's detrimental behavior. It is done to identify options that can help a victimizing mate discover ways to make direct loyalty payments to his parents. An offspring's cutoff from his family may be well-founded but it always signifies a defeat of his personal ability to validate himself through earning entitlement.

Its insistence on exploring the sources of early injury and pain may be one of the more controversial aspects of contextual theory and practice. "Why go to all that trouble?" is frequently the first response. Why glorify parents who behaved so objectionably, and probably still do? Why expose my mate to old issues that will make her feel rejected again? These questions carry an inherent logic that is valid in many ways. For us, though, the impact of destructive entitlement and its consequences override this rationale, and make it irrelevant to therapeutic planning.

Whenever destructive entitlement is at play, it exacts a high price from everyone regardless of intent. The victimized offspring pays through his indirect loyalty to his parents, and his parents pay through the failure of their son's marriage, e.g., the abuse of his spouse. Exploring the failures of destructive entitlement can take many forms, including psychophysiological consequences, e.g., a woman gets pregnant after years of fruitless attempts, or a person finds sexual satisfaction of a kind that has long eluded him after they begin, with great reluctance, to invest positive energy in their families of origin.

Overriding all objections to contextual therapy's rejunctive demands is the powerful impact that comes from the moment a person can enter the process of exonerating his parents. Suddenly he can break loose from ways of relating in which he has been caught. He is free to choose new options for relating and is freed from actions that he would hate were his children to treat him in kind. Suddenly he is presented with options that were previously blocked but now open up avenues through which to earn entitlement and gain new degrees of integrity. Suddenly, reliance on destructive entitlement, with all its abuse, is no longer his only alternative; no longer does he face a future colored mainly by chronic inability to offer fair treatment to others, an inhibition growing out of a person's incapacity to treat his parents well.

THE USE OF MORATORIA

A therapist's efforts to help people rejoin their families of origin always have to be tempered by her willingness to use the mechanism of a moratorium. Here the word "moratorium" is meant to convey a period of time in which a client can delay working toward a therapeutic goal that he embraces but is too fearful or resourceless to implement. For example, if a spouse is currently reluctant to rework a cutoff relationship with his parent(s), he can defer it without losing the interim benefits of therapy. During this period, the therapist will work from alternative, if temporary, resources for trust-building. She will acknowledge her client's suffering and the degree of his victimization. And she will continue to affirm her own conviction that sooner or later, given the toll that they continue to exact, conflicts with his family of origin will have to be addressed, though not before the client is willing to do so.

Under the conditions of a moratorium, the therapist will encourage her client to explore his issues with his parents in thoughtful anticipation of how he might proceed: Is there an easier rather than more difficult approach to them, e.g., an initial discussion that might address their unexplored involvement with his child (their grandchild)? How might they respond? Are there realistic dilemmas in surfacing hard issues? What might they be? Might his parents' current needs regarding health and aging facilitate genuine dialogue? What might the chief source of their resistance to hearing him be? Obviously, the therapist has to help her client attend to the question of how allegedly unreceptive older parents can be helped to be more receptive and affirming of their offspring's anticipated offers of care. Consider the situation of Peter, 26, who temporarily dropped out of medical school to reassess his situation (Krasner, 1986):

> Peter initially resisted the idea of bringing his mother and father into therapy. He just wasn't ready to "take off his clothes" in front of them. He simply was not prepared for an abrupt disclosure or announcement of his struggle with his sexual identity. The therapist assured him of his right to privacy. She also stressed his right to decide the therapeutic agenda should his parents agree to attend. If either of them was to be invited, he was clear that it was easier to begin with his father. Peter was reluctant to address both of his parents together. Somehow, facing his father was less frightening than taking on his mother right now. . . . Besides, since his older sister's death, he has conceived of his mother as an aging and dying parent about whom he has to care without expecting much of a return. With his father, he felt, he might have more to gain.

For several weeks Peter had struggled with the dilemma of addressing his parents face-to-face in the therapy room. His reluctance seemed deep-rooted, even intractable, until he was able to surface the source of his strongest fear, his sexual identity. Did he have to choose between telling his parents everything or telling them nothing? He had also had to rework his comprehension of therapy. Did attaining his own freedom really depend on letting his parents know how they concern him and aggravate him too? Peter has questions, concerns, challenges of the therapist. She accepted them and assured him that the pace of the therapeutic process depended on his relative readiness.

Here, as always, the moratorium period completed the contextual process of eliciting the client's terms for dialogue. The process works to induce individuation rather than either to teach or prescribe it. Its catalytic potential is reinforced by the therapist's conviction of the hidden and unutilized resources that lie dormant between closely relating family members.

During the moratorium, the therapist helps her client explore other compelling issues, especially his potential for teamwork with his wife or peers. Are they always driven apart by their family loyalties? Can they sometimes help each other or simply support each other in coming to the best possible terms of relating to their own parents? Can they be helpful to each other even in light of the fact that their respective in-laws disapprove of their marriage? Marriages always stand to gain when conflicting loyalties can be resolved. Marriages also benefit from the couple's team effort to remove loyalty conflicts. In addition, each of the partners earns entitlement from the fact of their actualized concern for each other's future and for their children's future as well. Their decision to try to work as a team can ease the burden of split loyalty for their children. The conflicting loyalties of mates always reflect themselves in the split loyalty of their children. The two are inexorably linked.

FUSION VS. DIFFERENTIATION

The following terms have too often been used to describe the dynamics that are at work in the families of disturbed individuals: fusion, enmeshment, symbiosis, pseudomutuality, and undifferentiated ego mass. In our experience, these descriptive criteria fall short of explaining the causal or sustaining factors of the underlying process. Therapists can treat these symptomatic configurations with a variety of interventions, all of them akin to treating fever with aspirin. The interventions may range the spectrum of options from restructuring prescriptions and behavior manipulations on the one hand to attempts at promoting visible differentiation and individuation on the other.

Fusion may take the form of blurred individual identities whose outward appearance may express itself in isolation and alienation between family members. The essence of fusion, however, is *blurred individual responsibility* rather than cognitive identity. People who lack trust in relational give-and-take tend to retreat to avoidance, manipulation and withheld communications. Paradoxically, perhaps, their defensive reliance on power-based relating tends to undermine trustworthiness even further.

The substrate of chronic untrustworthiness consists of an apparent lack of options for earning constructive entitlement. When parents and eventually their children rely heavily on destructive entitlement over time, they eventually become "enmeshed" too. A brief return to Peter and his family can help elucidate. Mother's life, as she saw it, was in everyone's hands but hers. She felt particularly defined by her husband of whom she sometimes still managed to speak with humor and grace: "My husband can best be described as a modern, old-world man," she said.

> On the one hand, he has to be head of the family. On the other hand, he's always been ready to accept the responsibilities of a father. In fact he accepted them too well. He would play with Tim (now 30) and call him endearing names like "brown bear," and he would take long walks with Peter. He would tell the kids how much he loved them, and I always felt left out.
>
> I'm schizophrenic when it comes to my husband. For example, I can go out with the girls (friends) and have a wonderful time. They let me know that I'm fun and tell me that I'm bright. They treat me with respect and sometimes ask for my advice. Then I come home to him and never know what to expect. So I slink down and act moody and unhappy. It's like I'm two separate people. I don't know if I want to try anymore. How many times can you risk being hurt? (Krasner, 1986).

Mother's responses, when it came to her children, were appreciative, competitive, regretful. "Tim and Peter were the only two I really had time for; there were five of them you know. Peter was so beautiful, too beautiful to be a boy. He should have been the daughter; Anne, his older sister, should have been the son. She played softball, watched football with her father, and knew how to talk to him."

Peter had brought his mother to the meeting, anxious to tell her his side. He had obviously heard her statements before but this time he chose to respond.

> I don't like hearing that I should have been a girl. I've heard it all my life. How much, I wonder, has that added to all my trouble in learning how to be a man? I don't like being defined by you. There's no way anyone can replace all that you've done for me. But it makes me angry when you try to keep me from other people. "I would never do that," mother interrupted but Peter went on. "I always felt forced to choose between you and Anne. You demanded to know who I loved more, her or you. That wasn't a fair thing to do to a ten year old kid." "But I felt she was taking over you and Tim," Mother protested. "The only way to win with Anne was to make her leave the house. Even then she'd write to your father at work. I know how hard I've tried with Anne." "It's not Anne that's the

problem," Peter argued back. "Look at what happened whenever we brought people into the house. If Carl or Tim brought women home, you were always incredibly jealous. What were we supposed to do?" (Krasner, 1986)

Mother's own deprivation from her family of origin played itself out on her husband and children. Her destructive entitlement eventually allowed her to take what she could from the family no matter what form it took. Everyone, including mother, lacked real trust in the option of relational give-and-take. Each of them withdrew into himself or herself and became alienated from each other. It is true that their identities were blurred. It is also true, and more significant perhaps, that their isolation and alienation gathered force as they grew and forced each of the family members into a crisis of responsibility. If they could not offer each other care and concern and get something back in return, what options were open besides fusion and enmeshment?

Dialogue as a therapeutic goal is the antithesis of enmeshment. In its self-delineating phase, dialogue provides an opportunity for assertion, differentiation, separation. In its self-validating state, it provides the chance to earn increased freedom through offers of empathy, consideration and care. Enmeshed families sometimes test therapists sorely. They often respond to multidirected efforts with chaos and confusion. They insist on ample demonstrations of the therapist's trustability. They lean heavily on the therapist in a press for substitutive parenting. They are frequently reluctant to disclose themselves or inquire into other people's sides. They are slow to take initiatives to redistribute the family members' benefits and burdens. They are reluctant to enter the process of mourning that will let them work through their losses and put them behind them. In brief, they are stuck in patterns of being that support unaccountability as a way of relating.

UTILIZING TRANSGENERATIONAL LEVERAGES

Some of therapy's most powerful leverages issue from the dynamic resources that exist between and across the generations. It is a step backwards, therefore, when either the current generation of offspring or therapists can identify the parent generation only by its parenting status. For obviously, parents themselves were once vulnerable children, too, and their feelings and ways of relating often stay stuck in a childhood clime. Nevertheless, therapists frequently find it difficult to ally themselves with a young client's mother or father who seems callous and destructive, or to try to support a responsible parental attitude in her or him. Here a therapist's subtle tendencies to be judgmental can block a client's growth.

On the other hand, a therapist can break through to a client whose defensive displacement protects him from insight and whose destructive entitlement protects him from remorse. Here, a therapist's most promising hope lies in her use of multidirected partiality. Here, the most effective intervention in her client's stagnation lies in her ability to turn to the offending parent and be partial to *his* or *her* past childhood victimization. It is precisely the moment in which there is real question and implicit blame over whether or not parents have given their children adequate concern that therapeutic intervention can be most constructive. It is precisely this moment in which parents are closest to their own need for vindication of their own side of justice issues that is most suitable for the therapist's empathic partiality.

Psychologically, the maneuver breaks into the faulty alignment between a parent's needed internal "bad" partner and his attitude toward his child. The shift in focus from father's bad behavior to his own early suffering and misuse over time usually permits him to identify with his exploited child. The obvious parallel between the two generations is likely to induce the parent to reassess the unjust characteristics of his behavior, i.e., his insensitivity to the retributive, if substitutive, victimization of his son. The therapist's capacity to offer credit where it is due allows father to become increasingly partial to his child's analogous lot. Members of two generations may find an ability to meet exactly at the point at which their respective identity formations are built on destructive entitlement with its consequences of vindictive character development.

Partiality to a parent's own childhood victimization also slows down the spin of the revolving slate (Boszormenyi-Nagy & Spark, 1973). In the process of facing into the facets of his own unjust parenting, father moves one step closer to exonerating his own parents. The chance to exonerate *per se* lowers a parent's intense need to resent his own parents. It also diminishes his ambivalent protectiveness toward his parents and his need to avoid them (or memories of them). As a parent comes to terms with his own mother and father, he has an ever-lessening need to victimize his child in order to "defend" his parents. He earns constructive entitlement in this process and diminishes his reliance on displaced retribution and destructive entitlement alike. He is slowly freed, then, from his compelling need to "get back" at either generation. When intergenerational stagnation is loosened, it gives way to options for restoring intergenerational dialogue.

Later, the therapist will ask father to consider still another step. By now he has invested a lot of thought in his parents. Can he find the courage to face them and convey his concerns directly to them? What concrete steps might he take to let them know that he cares, and so manage to build his store of earned entitlement even further? There is really no substitute for direct loyalty payments. A person's ability to bring himself to face his parents with fresh offers of consideration and due care *always* diminishes the need for indirect and invisible forms of loyalty that can eventually play themselves out at the expense of a person's future relationships.

"SEED-PLANTING" PRINCIPLES

The utilization of transgenerational leverages under discussion in the last paragraph depends on two principles: 1) Resources have to be seeded, that is, adults have to find ways to come closer to being responsible for fair consideration of their parents. They have to discover what contributions they can make to their parents' current well-being; 2) Resources are made available through the very process of seeding. For example, a multi-directed stance can increase trustworthiness: A therapist presses a parent to explore options for offering her own mother care. In the process, she becomes more accessible to finding new options for caring about her own child. Up until now she has, in effect, victimized her son, i.e., she has kept him away from all contact with other children his age out of her fears that he might catch infections.

The secret of seed planting is buried in the fertile soil of dormant relational resources with their hidden prospects for trustworthy dialogue. These unutilized prospects for relational integrity, grounded in the realm of the between, lie dormant and await people's initiative and courage to take new risks. The energy to stimulate new growth and trust is inherent in the creative potential of relationship itself. Self-sustaining growth evolves out of the inherent potential of dialogue, that interaction between the self-delineation and self-validation processes of everyone involved. When these resources dry up and harden, stagnation takes place, resources wither and, weedlike, symptoms and pathology emerge.

The concept of planting seeds naturally converges with the concept of a moratorium. Seeds need time to grow. People have to move on their own initiative and timing. Therapists have to honor the fact that it is not they, but family members who create the energy for raising health and trust. The therapist's capacity to accept a need for timing, without abandoning therapeutic conviction, strengthens his message rather than weakens it. Moreover, life's influence over therapy is characteristically more penetrating and decisive than therapy's influence over life. The following questions are fundamental to the contextual work of seed planting:

- Was your childhood happier than that of your children?
- Is your marriage similar to your parent's marriage?
- How does your marriage and the consequences of your parents' marriage affect your children?

- On whom can you rely?
- With whom can you speak openly?
- How do your children contribute to your well-being other than through chores?
- How do you acknowledge their contributions?
- Which parent is more vulnerable? How?
- Do the children protect their more vulnerable parent? How?
- Which parent can the children criticize more safely?
- What do your children know about the hardships of your childhood?
- Where is your relationship with your children hopeful? Where is it cause for discouragement and despair?
- Are your experiences as a child a source of your tendency to blame your children?
- Do your children ever see you cry?
- What does your (un)willingness to let them see you in pain say about the trust level between you and them?
- Is there anyone to live for rather than to drink for?
- Have grandparents ever expressed a wish for grandchildren?
- Were you a wanted child?
- If your parents were to suddenly die, what would you wish to have said or done for them earlier?
- Do you ever tell your children anything positive about your ex-spouse?

Answers to questions like these are not to be found solely in the intellect. To be most clinically effective, answers need to be documented by parable or example. They are the kind of questions that are fraught with individual and interpersonal complexities that are best clarified by specificity and brought into consciousness slowly and through the interplay of time.

To elicit responsible spontaneity of participation in each family member, the contextual therapist will heavily rely on the leverages of Dimension IV., i.e., the ethics of relational responsibility. For example, in trying to mobilize a parent's spontaneous resources in the face of his alcoholic habits, the therapist may choose to address father's residual concern about his child's right to a good image of his parent. In many instances this argument is stronger than an appeal to the threat his drinking is bound to pose to his liver.

Eventually the process of planting seeds yields intergenerational dialogue which, in turn, takes root and grows through questions that are inherently multidirectionally partial. These questions and the answers that flow from them induce and maintain continuing buildups of trust. The main effect of multilateral exchange is associated with its capacity to use family members' simultaneous quests for trustworthiness, channelling them away from stagnation and toward constructive actions, e.g., a new basis for family solidarity, and learning how to give space to each other's needs for growth.

As a method, multidirected partiality also addresses other problems, among them: how to structure behavior; communication patterns, e.g., how to listen, how to define one's own positions, how to use metaphors. The method also address questions associated with psychic configurations, expression of affect, trust needs, transference-based displacements, deferred mourning, projective identification, object relatedness, and defensive distortions.

OVERCOMING OBSTACLES TO A MULTIDIRECTED STANCE

A number of obstacles, including resistances from family members, make it difficult to apply multidirected partiality. People's pursuit of multilateral fairness in intermember dialogue runs into several difficulties. First of all, partners have to overcome their self-serving, exclusively unilateral perspectives on their relationships. Their effort is helped by the lure and inherent merit of genuine dialogue that can ultimately help overcome the relational stagnation rooted in alienation.

We have already discussed just how the existence of acquired destructive entitlement in one family member interferes with everyone's capacity to develop attitudes that are multilaterally fair. In addition, despair and alienation from the possibility of genuine dialogue can drive people into relational habits that are difficult to overcome. Beyond the family, community mistrust can be linked to patterns of criminal behavior, as well as to addiction and other forms of self-abuse.

HERE AND NOW PATHS TO DESTRUCTIVE ENTITLEMENT

Contextual goals include the immediate relief of current suffering. They also span the generations. The present generation relates to posterity through being of consequence to it, not merely by making it an object of their needs and affection. In fact, the future is created by the generations that precede it. Posterity is bound to be enriched by the past or exploited by it, whether or not it is a love object. For example, whatever its good intent, the present generation's environmental exploitation may irreversibly damage the future.

Whatever our parents' good intent, most of us were left hungry for trustworthy dialogue. Many of us seem helpless to do anything constructive about initiating it. Massive numbers of people simply cannot risk investing in trustful giving nor can they acknowledge or credit the initiative of others. Under these circumstances, residual trust reserves stay untapped. The self-propelling, healing forces of transgenerational dialogue cannot be put into motion.

Destructive entitlement is the alternative to dialogue. If the grandparent and parent generations are unable to convey how to take hold of balanced give-and-take, dialogue automatically surrenders to monologue and constructive entitlement automatically yields its sway. Destructive entitlement lies at the heart of pathogenic relating. It is a disruption of the natural connections between a person's receiving and then finding the inclination and conviction needed to give to others in return. Only so is one generation able to initiate new dialogue and convey it to another.

Family therapists usually see badly injured offspring in conjunction with parents who can no longer give or whose giving is solely self-referred. The family's original complaints may describe a delinquent, "acting-out" adolescent or a child who is failing at school. In either case, the parent and child generations wound each other time after time and escalate their behavior with little sign of remorse. Consider Sue's situation.

Sue's behavior at private school was jeopardizing her situation there. Not only did her classmates resent her for her lack of cooperation in class, but she was in danger of failing her senior year. Reports from home indicated that she would share no responsibilities there either. When she arrived from school, she went straight to her room. On the other hand, her older sister Barbara, 21, runs the house. Father and mother are in the midst of an acrimonious divorce. "Mother is so desperate over it," Barbara says, "that all she can do is cry. She leaves no room for our grief; she doesn't seem to realize that we're losing a family too. Worse still, both she and Sue leave everything to me. I want to find an apartment as fast as I can. There's no family anymore. I feel like I'm running a hotel. Everyone has their own therapist but I can't see what difference it makes." As for Sue, she finally broke down in tears. "You keep saying the family's breaking up, Mother, but I can't see it. I define family as a group. We're still a group; you have your four daughters. We love you very much. Why can't you be satisfied with that?"

In situations like this, the parents' marital difficulties may or may not have surfaced into view. Under these circumstances, a contextual therapist has first to overcome his negative reactions or even repulsion at the behavior of a retributive parent or child; then he will search for the redeeming characteristics of each of the family members. His partiality will extend to people's past hurts and victimizations even if he cannot embrace their victimizing side. Sue's mother, for example, is close to paralyzed. Her mother died when she was five. When she was 16, her father remarried and soon moved away. She was raised by maids and made her own way from the time of her early teens. Her whole life has been spent in creating a family life she never knew and now she is seeing it disintegrate.

Eventually the therapist has to establish a solid base for building therapeutic trust through multidirectional techniques. His capacity to identify signs of destructive entitlement in each family member and, nonetheless, simultaneously find past and present behaviors to credit furthers the work of reconstructing trust. It is also a source of relief to the therapist when he can discover a person's redeeming features at times when the process of therapy perforce focuses its bright beam on that same person's detrimental parenting. Having his side credited and acknowledged, the destructively entitled person will be more inclined to be accountable for his behavior towards others.

Destructive entitlement is both a motivating force and a pattern that is transactionally reinforced. As such, it is often difficult to alter its essence. It is also hard to alter because the natural self-corrective motivator, remorse over doing harm to others, is no longer operational. To be sure, current symptomatic behavior in a person may nonetheless be changed. Prescriptive, directive and manipulative therapeutic interventions may all produce symptomatic relief. But the partners themselves are characteristically paralyzed by frustration, ambivalence, despair, hate, and helplessness over unfair legacies of loss.

LOSS AS BROKEN DIALOGUE

Contextual therapy redefines the very notion of loss. For example, a parent-child relationship can be lost because it failed to develop into a trustworthy dialogue of care. Should the dialogue between a parent and child exist, though, even physical death is not likely to interrupt its trustworthy impact. For death itself is not the ultimate arbiter of dialogue. Instead, it is a stage which seals out the chance for another intergenerational try at care.

In sum, the essence of dialogue lies in a mutuality of commitment, that is, in a forum in which relating partners can earn merit and receive direct benefit from the merit earned by others. This process begins when a child is born and becomes loyal to his or her parents. When a child is burdened by a predicament of split loyalty, however, dialogue suffers a grievous blow. For the child cannot find a way to be simultaneously loyal to mutually mistrusting parents. To the contrary, he learns that trusting one cancels out the option of trusting the other.

As a result, no basic trust is attained. Inadvertently or not, as a team (system) these parents have chosen to be fully self-directed, destructive and "narcissistic." They impose age-inappropriate and exploitative demands on their children and in the process effectively manage to get in the way of the development of a parent-child dialogue. Instead, they produce ambivalence in parent and child alike. They produce mixed feelings in which hostile, contemptuous and rejecting attitudes dominate and prevail.

The loss here is neither an existential given nor, like death, an irreversible fact. Rather it is an undeveloped potential, a wasted life option for several family members at once. Its psychological sequelae include frustration, contempt, pain, sadness, displaced revenge-seeking, self-destructive motives, fragmented self-development, depression, psychosomatic damage, incomplete mourning, alienation, and an inability to relate, in addition to other forms of pathology. Frequently, both parents and child are paralyzed by mistrust, unable to act in order to repair the loss. By the time he becomes an adolescent, a youngster's self-destructive and destructive motives may propel him toward actual rejection of the offending parents. The loss then escalates. Missed opportunities for trustworthy relating between parents and their young child telescope into later life and magnify physical separation as if distance itself were a devastating and tragic loss.

In traditional psychodynamic work, a child's long-term injury is typically regarded as irreversible, mainly intrapsychic (ever since Freud abandoned his earlier seduction theory), passively endured by a child, and anachronistic, that is, maintained by fixation and by repetition compulsion. It follows, then, that a child refrains from efforts to alter the relationship with her actual parent(s) and simply considers them a bad debt. If she cannot regain what she deserved as a young child, the reasoning goes, it can only be painful and pointless to try again. The implied uselessness of turning to her parents left her with the alternative of turning to her therapist. It was his benevolent concern, skill and availability—in contrast to her parents presumed malevolent intent, incompetence and resourcelessness—that could help her "work" on her psychic wounds. It was in the bosom of therapeutic wisdom rather than in the vise of parental ties that she could hope to face her losses via the transference process. Eventually, she would work her way through, once she was capable of relinquishing the transference relationship.

DEPARENTIFICATION

Deparentification is a term applied to the goal of helping everyone in a family involved in the parentification process. Contextual therapists see parentification as a destructive reliance on a captive person, usually a child. Intervention is thus first aimed at the exploitation process and later at its transactional-behavioral manifestations. In other terms, untrustworthy, exploitative attitudes and behaviors have to be reworked, reversed and replaced by trustworthy ones. A contextual therapist initially tries to help parentifying family members acknowledge the benefits that they extract from the person they parentify. The line of questioning might proceed like this: "Mrs. K, how come you ask Charles to close up at night, lock the doors, check the garage? Were you aware before he said so today how frightened he is to do that?"

At best mother might say she was unaware of her 11-year-old's fears and fantasies. Yes, she did expect him to close up. "Since his father left, he's the man of the house and it makes me feel more secure." Seeing her son's side more clearly and acknowledging the value of his actions for her helps mother become more trustworthy in the eyes of the parentified child. It also helps the parentifying adult earn constructive entitlement. Yes, she might reason, I have made mistakes. I do feel like a little girl sometimes and use my son to comfort me in ways unhelpful to him. But I am his mother and I want to be a good one. So I'll work on seeing what that means.

Efforts to help the parentifying adult become more independent is another part of the deparentification process. Parentification always implies one person's dependent clinging to an unmatched partner. Our criteria for parentification are more penetrating than a description of surface behavior, however. For example, a parent's tendency to infantilize a growing child probably represents the most damaging form of parentification through overt failure. Drug addiction, for example, is a way that one 18-year-old could stay at home to tend to his parents' failing marriage.

The parentification process often takes the form of binding the offspring into a prematurely adultlike parental role. In this case, the emergence of more spontaneous, childlike behavior will occur as one of the results of the successful deparentification process. Here the youngster's behavior will sometimes be playful, sometimes careless, and sometimes annoyingly boisterous. In cases where infantilization or self-destructive behavior has been the manifest expression of the parentifying process, the parentified youngster will gradually begin to act increasingly grown-up and more positively purposeful. The period in which the process of deparentification is taking hold can be a difficult one for parentifying adults who will sorely need the therapist's partiality to make up for their loss of a secure, if misbegotten, source of self-confidence. Their losses may include,

- Actual reliance on their young whom, until now, they have viewed as a personal possession of a quasi-parent nature;
- Reliance on a securely dependable mode of relating, i.e., on a rather dependent personal stance;
- The cover-up role of parentification. Its loss leaves people alone to face their own early childhood deprivations and victimization for which parentification became a substitute.

Parentifying adults, like parentified children, hurt, and they are entitled to therapeutic partiality during times of their greatest stress. The therapist's queries about their own childhood suffering and his ability to credit them provide a mechanism that can often build a path from exploitation to merited entitlement.

Deparentification is intimately connected with people's capacity to surface their legacies, and sort them out from delegations. Parentification occurs through delegation as well as through transactional binding. As noted, delegations are specific injunctions imposed on offspring by parents or by forebears through specifically binding ways, e.g., through the use of guilt-reinforcing leverages. By contrast, legacies offer options which are subject to choice, decision-making and negotiation.

Parentification and the deparentifying process take place between adult and adult too. The most apparent difference here is the premise that adults are relatively matched and thus less open to the unilateral exploitation that might occur in relationships between adult and child.

The dynamics of parentification are abundantly evident in the adult world. At base, parentification is one person's imposition of his or her own needs on a second person who is thereby expected to assume responsibility for meeting the needs so delegated. The parentifying person takes the partner's position for granted and essentially requires tha partner to function *in loco parentis*. It is true that the parentified person is not unquestionably obligated to assume responsibility for someone else's agenda. But even when a person colludes and is willing to accept parentification in the name of rescuing a needy person, the process inevitably results in disappointment, resentment and blame.

Perhaps the most excessively destructive parentification is perpetrated by unfairly blaming the victim. Heaping a sense of guilt on a helplessly captive child can escalate the damage already done to him; it also serves to keep him captive. On the other hand, if acknowledgment of the youngster's merit and real contribution to his family can be elicited, the acknowledgment *per se* will actually counteract the blaming process.

Clearly, then, whatever its expressions, parentification can serve only to undermine the fundamental premise of the dialogic process, that is, that people can still hope to bridge the chasm that exists between them and their (legacies) without having to relinquish their (personal) integrity (and their capacity to be fair). There is no place for parentification in a process that relies on direct address, reliable exchanges of fairness and the merited trust that (can still be) actualized between person and person.

SUMMARY

Contextual therapy insists on trying to explore the resources that are buried in abandoned, cutoff relationships. This insistence is a theoretical criterion and a technical requirement, but is not limited to that. Clinical examples bear out the soundness of this insistence after months of initial resistance. For example, ''I stayed with you because you kept pushing me to deal with my folks even though I gave you hell for it.'' Or consider the woman who used to attack the therapist for what she termed ''siding with my rotten father.'' One day, after therapy's end, she called to thank the therapist for his unyielding insistence. ''My father is dead now,'' she reported. ''I can never repay you for the good visits that I had with him before he died. It was too hard to let you know about them while I was still in therapy with you. But it's not fair not to tell you now.''

Contextual therapy appeals to people for a lot of different reasons. The social dynamic of justice, at the core of its therapeutic rationale, is one of them. The notion of applied justice, so to speak, has wide appeal. The approach's insistent concern for all generations and all family members is more basic to the common needs of diverse groups than to their differences. Sophisticated and simple people, poor and wealthy people, third world and first world people, and people of diverse religious, racial and ethnic groups are drawn to the fact that who they are and how they live are considered from within their own contexts and not from the perspective of the therapist's predilections. The same truth applies to families whose members are immigrants of minority status or victims of discrimination.

People are drawn to contextual work because of its emphasis on trust and justice. There is danger here, though. Words like fairness and trustworthiness are easily misunderstood. An overready acceptance of the approach may evolve out of a person's wish for an island of justice that is automatically guaranteed. Such a wish is fantasy, of course. Any evidence that the world is composed of wholly good and just people on the one hand and wholly evil and unjust people on the other can only be a paranoid scheme in which black hats and white hats are at war all of the time in a holy jihad or crusade. To the contrary.

Contextual therapy has firm criteria for its work, particularly its demand that each family member overcome his or her unilateral considerations of relationship. Each person is presumed to have merit just as he or she is also presumed to be accountable for instances of being unfair. All demands for fairness are simultaneously placed on all relating partners. But these demands are eventually rewarded by the returns of earned merit. The validation of contextual work comes from relational reality. Its aims are practical and concrete and in no way to be confused with moralistic or value-oriented concepts and abstractions. As a result of successful therapy, people grow freer, more autonomous and more spontaneous.

VI. APPLICATIONS AND GUIDELINES

The following section offers a selection of specific situations in which contextual principles and methods are demonstrated and applied. Marriage, divorce and custody, remarriage, adoption, parenting problems, the flight from parenting, foster home placement, child protection, child abuse and sexual misuse, teen-age parenthood, pregnancy counseling and abortion, terminal illness, mental illness, depression, therapy with psychotics, mental retardation, issues of suicide, addiction, sexual identity and function, school problems, and incest are all areas of direct and immediate concern to contextual therapists.

Our intention is a broadscale demonstration of the impact of contextual work in adverse spheres of human existence and endeavor rather than a comprehensive or exhaustive survey of all the circumstances in which the approach can be applied. It is our hope that these essays will lend themselves to deepening the reader's grasp of contextual methods and techniques, along with the orientation and spirit of contextual therapy.

Contextual applications are characterized by a future-oriented inclusiveness. Goal criteria incorporate a concern for posterity's well-being into the health goals of the current adult generation. Contextual therapy's bent to support each generation's concern for succeeding generations comports with the natural order of the family as conservator. Its effort to extend direct consideration to posterity helps the present generation towards its immediate goal of self-gain. Thus, the health of the present becomes essentially inseparable from preventive interest in the future.

The specific methods of intervention have to be assessed in each case, of course. What constitutes health and what constitutes intervention remain complex questions for all applied therapy. On the other hand, contextual therapy maintains its concern for the consequences of therapy on all affected participants, a given never contraindicated whatever the particular circumstances.

CHAPTER 18

The Evolving Face of Marriage

Marriage is the foundation of the nuclear family and precursor of a stable parenting team. It is probably society's most vulnerable institution. It is also the most important of all *optional* human relationships—optional in most of Western society, at least, since its shift from arranged marriage selections to self-selections. Whatever its limits, marital life functions as modern history's most steadfast and reliable forum, the place in which people most readily invest their efforts in trying to reach tolerable and sometimes creative balances between individual freedom and fulfillment on the one hand *and* long-term comfort and security on the other.

It is readily apparent that ancient societies expected to support and control the institution of marriage. Their expectation of control not only extended to the mating instincts of individuals but also to the circumstances surrounding birth, nurturance and bringing up the young. The conditions, attitudes and laws of ancient societies joined marriage to issues of property ownership. When two families were joined by the marriage of their offspring, survival itself depended on answers to such questions as how much property is to be designated for the new family and its offspring, and whether designations should be made via male or female lineage. Material goods like land, dwellings, livestock, precious stones, and utensils always constituted valuable and scarce commodities which were automatically conveyed from the old to the new generation. The problems of inheritance are amply conveyed in ancient literature (Gen.27:32-39). Nevertheless, the parent generation was bound to pass on what it knew and what it had. In return, offspring owed obedience, respect and law-abiding behavior.

The emphasis of traditional societies more often fell on children's obligations than on their rights. A disobedient offspring could be subject to harsh retributive measures, even death. On the other hand, child-rearing tasks were structured and supported by the entire extended family. Members of this large coterie supervised young parents and taught them how to raise and educate their children. The couple's general behavior and sexual commitment were ensured and monitored by law, religion, surveillance, and a lack of mobility and private space. Family and community life was also protected by real and enforced insularity. Travel was inhibited by limited methods of mobility and unidentified outsiders had to deal with the xenophobia of local residents.

Only the industrial revolution and large scale migration to North America could eventually shake the rigid patterns of earlier European marriage customs. Prior to those developments, marriage was alterable only by suicide or, among the highly privileged, by scandalous behavior. Industrial mobility and emigration to distant lands surely loosened the hold of family sanctions and rigid marriage customs, and contributed to the eventual emergence of divorce as a tolerable solution to marital conflict and dissatisfaction. In the process, religious loyalties were also altered. The church's resistance to divorce, rooted in Biblical mandate and patristic literature, softened in the face of changes in society.

Societal fluidity always yields changes in sexual mores. New life-styles and living arrangements as well as wide-scale extramarital sex are generally condoned, and confused with individual freedom. Sexual relations are increasingly viewed as a temporary, if crucial, aspect of friendship or, alternately, as an entertainment commodity. New sexual arrangements open up new options for patterns of open marriage, complex remarriage, single parent families, and communal life-styles. This welter of new options may or may not "work" for individual adults. In any case, it is their choice for their personal life. Individual choice has consequences, however. Among them is the devaluation of traditional marriage and long-term commitment, and the challenge to the viability of the nuclear family or even to the commitment to parenthood.

MARRIAGE FROM A FOUR-DIMENSIONAL VIEW

Marriage is obviously just one more institution that is subject to change. The healing quality of change is only half a story, though. The other part of the story always requires responsible people to ask, "Change for what?" Like any other area of consideration in contextual therapy, marital relationships are subject to comprehensive evaluation from the vantage point of all four relational dimensions: facts, psychology, transactions and communications, and the ethics of responsible give-and-take.

From a factual vantage point, part of the legacy impinging on marriage evolves from the prospect of reproduction and long-range childcare and support. It is difficult to challenge the conclusions that reproduction is the key foundation for relationship in human and animal life and that it requires long-range consideration spanning a child's life from birth to maturity. These realities converge with still another fact about marriage, that is, the relative age, strength, health, and genetic traits of each partner. Obviously, if a man, 25, marries a woman, 55, these factors offer little significance, at least for the future of children. On the other hand, a woman, 30, who is pregnant by a man, 65, does well to ponder the consequences of these facts.

Economics are also pertinent here and represent another factual aspect of marriage. When two people with strength and courage enough can clarify how individual and common money and property are to be handled and used, they usually gain a toehold on trust. On the other hand, premarital financial agreements can shatter the romantic aura and promise of marriage and, at worst, put the partners on notice that they may very well get duped. One couple came within a $10,000 difference in agreeing how they were willing to arrange their financial affairs with each other. After marriage, they got stuck and put the money in escrow. The matter stayed unresolved for four years and was finally settled in a court of divorce.

From the vantage point of individual psychology, marriage draws on the sex and affection that exist between partners. The romantic aspect of love represents one of the most intensely absorbing emotional conditions in a person's life. It is founded on both the biological imperative of mate selection and on the individual's need for warmth, intimacy, affection, and sex.

Much has been written about marriage and couples. Discussions on need complementation and communication patterns, transactions, fair fighting, dependency configurations, and *quid pro quo* fill the pages of psychological literature. Therapeutic strategies based on techniques for paradoxical shifts of overt patterns of exchange abound. But few, if any, incorporate the basic human phenomenon of trustworthiness.

Little children on the playground talk a lot about what is and isn't fair. When they grow up and marry, they are still talking about whom they can trust to be fair. Traditional psychotherapy can ignore or diminish the trust-based foundation that is the core factor in the fiber of close relating, but cannot eradicate it. The consequences of fair or unfair relating are the most decisive component of the marital bond, and the major source of the next generation's factual reality. Marriages founder or succeed on the question of whether or not two people can develop the capacity to be responsible for the consequences of fairness and trust.

On the face of things, marriage is two people's conscious choice to pursue a life in common. It is a process of a man and a woman learning to accommodate each other's needs. Yet marriage is always informed by the prospect of procreation even when a choice has been made against it. Consider the situation of Ann, a teacher in her early thirties, who had married for the first time.

> Her husband, married once before, had had two children and then divorced. The agreement between Bruce and Ann was very clear: no children in common. In any case, he had had a vasectomy and was reluctant to try to have it reversed. Over the next three years, Ann struggled in her relationships with her stepchildren. She also began to struggle with the consequences of her part of the decision to forgo children; it seemed more important now. Her husband and his children were close in a way that she just couldn't touch. She began to wonder if mates could match that kind of intimacy.
>
> Her mother, who had been ill for many years, died when Ann was 12. In ways of which she was still unaware, Ann had protected herself against any more loss by withdrawing into herself. Her life was difficult after her mother died, but it was even worse when her father remarried. She hates her stepmother to this day, but remembers how hard her father tried to make up for his new wife's behavior. Maybe that was it. She can't remember much about her parents' marriage. She can remember being special to both parents. Maybe Bruce feels that his kids are special too. More special than she can ever be? How come she didn't consider all this stuff before she agreed with Bruce about not having children together?

The question of whether or not to have children remains a priority for people whatever the current shifts in "acceptable living arrangements." It may even be that cohabitation outside of marriage and the ready accessibility of divorce have compelled people to be ever more aware of what they want to do about having children. Compounded, all of these factors may also be lifting up marriage as the most viable context for reproduction and childcare.

MARRIAGE, PARENTS AND PROGRESS

However parents choose to live, the reality of a child's life remains unchanged: He or she is born of two biological parents and benefits from their joint availability as resources. The relative loss of the traditional extended family and its supportive network has underscored the need for parental availability with a special truth and poignancy. If not parents, who else will be available to offer children concern and care? This reality is a starting point for contextual therapists in their work.

From an ethical vantage point, it is unjust for a therapist to advocate for parents in quest of freedom if their freedom is to be gained at a prohibitive cost to their children. On the other hand, any attempt to advocate for children over against their parents would be reductionistic, ill-advised and an oversimplification of the deep and complex layers of the parent-child bond. Yet, when all is conceptually said and done, society's growing acceptance of diverse life-styles can be a serious test of a therapist's professional integrity. Can therapists manage to advocate for adults in their pursuit of new options, help them discover new ways to live their lives, and still fight for the kind of parental planning that continuously includes a child's vested interests?

However central its significance, the couple's parenting investments are only one facet of the overall marital context. Families of origin are another significant, sometimes overwhelming, demand on mates. Dynamics that seem linked to personal, emotional or even sexual incompatibility often primarily have to do with the couple's loyalty to their respective parents and siblings. It is probably true that the prospect of loyalty conflict between families of origin and peer relationships always exists whenever adolescents and young adults try to make new commitments. This prospect of conflict is a common element in friendships, love relationships and marriage. Ideally, in each case a balance is to be found, e.g., a young bride can find options to spend some time with her parents, even though her husband is begrudging. In fact, balances usually require massive amounts of awareness, energy, patience, and time.

Many situations also exist in which balances cannot be found. The difficulty is compounded when a daughter or son has no overt commitment or expressed loyalty to his or her parent(s). "Who my parents are," a person may argue, "what they do and what they want are of no consequence to me. However, whenever my husband wants sex, I wonder why I should be close or warm to *him* when I never give *them* a thing." The ambivalent offspring who persistently avoids, denies or distances from his or her parents usually finds ways to be loyal to them. In these cases, filial loyalty may take the form of direct or indirect rejection of one's marriage or mate.

In part or in fact, a couple's sexual difficulties, lack of interest in intimacy, frigidity, impotence, and the prospect of extramarital affairs may be ways of expressing indirect loyalty to one or both families of origin. The couple may alternate between distancing on the one hand and scapegoating on the other. In either case, the peer commitment is forced to pay

for the unrequited requirements of dormant filial loyalty. Such loyalty conflicts in marriage may show up rapidly or surface over the years. Were
the couple aware of how they were indeed caught, they might find alternatives to sacrificing their marriage. They might also be able to identify
the degree to which their loyalties are exaggerated, either by parental
"delegation" of unrealistic expectations or by their own internalized inclinations toward guilt. It is to be noted here that there is no valid justification for filial loyalty whose consequences require disloyalty to an offspring's own dependent child.

Extramarital affairs characteristically represent a complicated set of interlocking, invisible loyalties and disloyalties. The affair is disloyal to the
marriage. The marriage may be disloyal to the family of origin. The affair may, therefore, appear to be justified because it allows a person to
be indirectly loyal to his or her family of origin. "See, Dad, I never meant
to hurt you by my marriage. We're in agreement that my wife has been
a bitch." There are other factors in affairs, of course. On a peer level, extramarital relations are often an attempt to rebalance the couple's own
ledger of fairness. "You've nagged, you've been distant, in essence you've
always had things your way. I haven't gotten from you, so now I'm taking my turn."

Typically one partner has taken more and given less, and a long-term
impasse based on fairness has found its way to the surface. "She's taken
all her life," a weeping man said of his wife who was still grieving over
the loss of her mother. "My mother-in-law was the one who used to give
us emotional support; it was never my wife. Now it's her turn. I'd like
to see what she can do now that her mother's gone." Fairness here has
to do with a variety of factors, including the husband's unfaced ledger with
his own parents which, in part, he has displaced on his mother-in-law.
It has to do with an equitable balance of give-and-take. It also has to do
with the matter of distributive justice, that is, when one marriage partner quantitatively claims entitlement to more emotional satisfaction than
the other person wants or requires. Nevertheless, the undemanding mate
can be left with a sense of unfairness even though she makes fewer claims.

Contextual work proceeds on the premise that lasting marriages finally
succeed on the basis of their long-term resources rather than on the basis
of short-term behavioral patterns. In young marriages, an important trust-
building period usually follows the initial phase of romantic infatuation.
Its capacity to facilitate lasting attachments can be understood in two ways:
1) as a mutuality of commitment, and 2) as a lack of consistent exploitation of each other. Frequently, in therapy, a mate with a foot out of the
door of marriage is deeply wounded by her husband's lack of interest in
complementarity or in pursuing her. She is unwilling to reassess her part
in the breakdown of responsible consideration between them. She is

already in flight. But she still wants a sign of his commitment to her. The term "exploitation" puts more stress on psychological and, obviously, physical abuse than on actual material advantage. In other words, one or both marital partners may use the other mainly for projective identification, for attributions of badness, or to vindicate past injuries. It is impossible for partners to avoid some degree of psychological "use" of each other. However, consistent, unilateral usage evolves into parentification.

In marital therapy, the couple's insights about their situation may have a clarifying, if not corrective, effect. The therapist's skill and experience may also function to break up detrimental relational patterns. But the lion's share of therapeutic resources is anchored in the trust formation that comes of each partner's attempts to earn entitlement. Merited entitlement may be an impossible goal to reach, though, until each person can face his or her own patterns of destructive entitlement and make progress in reworking them. Consider the 40-year-old woman, for example, who was apparently centered on religious studies and "devotion":

> She suspected that her husband was having an extramarital affair. She was willing to tolerate the situation while she could focus on her husband's depression and the possibility that he would commit suicide. Under these circumstances, he could be defined as ill and misguided—and she as martyred, needed and in control. When she was asked to consider her contribution to the breakdown of their marriage, however, she panicked. When she was asked to what degree her emotional investment in her classmates took precedence over relating to her husband, she fled.

Despite her designated "contributions" to her husband, the woman's behavior blocked her option of earning merited entitlement. Caught in long-held patterns of evasion and denial, she used theology to exonerate her stance and psychology to explain away her husband's behavior. She chose for feelings of self-righteousness and labelled her husband "sick" to avoid the obligation of facing her own patterns of destructive entitlement, let alone work on them.

Reworking patterns of destructive entitlement is a preface to earning constructive entitlement in marriage, as in other significant relationships. This process is furthered by the couple's willingness to become an effective parenting team as well as a considerate marital pair. The tendency to misuse children in the midst of marital discord is destructive for the marriage and for parenting alike. Establishing new criteria for parenting is as significant a basis for reparative work in marriage as any more direct intervention on the marriage's behalf.

The couple's respective legacies also represent an important aspect of earned entitlement. Family legacies differ significantly from parental delegations and prejudicial injunctions that are inherited. Legacies, by definition, are to be conserved as well as changed. They are a valuable element of racial, religious, ethnic or family heritage that can benefit posterity. Each generation is faced with the task of selecting out what is of underlying, universal value in their legacies, i.e., beneficial to the next generation, as well as what elements are to be defined as possessive, rigid or prejudicial ancestral injunctions.

Basically, marriage partners always come from differing backgrounds by virtue of their two particular families of origin. But comparatively, the differences can be more or less, e.g., mixed marriages can have partners of radically different racial, religious or ethnic backgrounds which can make their loyalty issues more pointed and complex. As one man put it, "I became more aware of my Protestant identity when I married a Jewish woman; and she became more aware of her Jewish background, too. Now we also have to represent *our kind* to the members of each other's family." The move from personal identity to representative identity is fraught with problems. People may "forgive" an individual for his or her personal background, but representative identities are always potential targets of prejudicial suspicions. The stronger the prejudice that a person comes up against, the more he is likely to be driven back to being loyal to his original group. By definition, in a mixed marriage, there is increased potential for loyalty conflicts between a person's loyalty to the marriage partner and to his or her own origins.

COPING WITH LOYALTY CONFLICTS

Couples who are facing loyalty conflicts have a number of options for reworking them. The most obvious one is for them to move towards each other and become a bulwark of strength, a solid team that can function as a buffer *against* both families of origin. Yet filial loyalty is formidable in its depth; denial may strengthen rather than diminish its force. Furthermore, it is a fact that two people come from separate life contexts which can neither be fused nor treated as a common opponent. A case in point is the situation in which one partner, after being away from his faith for a long time, decided to return to his synagogue—"Only for the music," he said, "and only for one time." His wife responded with feelings of betrayal and an accusation that he persistently avoided going to mass. On the other hand, partners from similar backgrounds but diverse customs can evoke powerful loyalty conflicts too. One spouse working to protect the other against her family's "malignant influences" is another option for reworking loyalty conflicts. However, his attempts to save his wife from her own family may be counterproductive. A man who views his wife as her parents' victim may reinforce her visible and invisible loyalties to them. In addition, his efforts on his wife's behalf effectively prevent her from investing in her own struggle for autonomy from them. Paradoxically, a husband's misguided efforts on his mate's behalf may have the opposite effect of what he intends. It may push her to reunite with her family in order to justify them. Then, she and the members of her family of origin may join forces and turn against her protector, who now becomes their common enemy.

Another way of coping is for a spouse to join with his family against his wife and her family, and vice versa. The two original loyalty contexts from two overtly warring camps vilify each other's intentions and effectively ensure that a marriage never really takes place.

The most effective coping option lies in the couple's giving each other sufficient room to work on their respective agendas with their own families of origin. One of them may be rejected by the other's family, but even here it is in both parties' vested interests to struggle towards a team relationship that can reinforce each one's efforts to develop the best possible relationship with his or her own family. This solution serves to decrease invisible loyalties rather than to exaggerate them. A case in point is the situation of a couple who married within the same religious tradition but from opposite sides of the spectrum of religious observance.

The wife's failure to be more ritually committed created resentment in her father-in-law. The tension between them increased when father-in-law announced to his son, her husband, that he would have preferred a mixed marriage to one in which his daughter-in-law fell so very short of his expectations.

No love was lost between the daughter-in-law and father-in-law over the years, a fact that put her husband (who is his parents' only surviving child) into a constant loyalty conflict. In time, however, the woman reworked her attitude towards her husband's loyalty bonds. She never came to like his father but realized the validity of her husband's offers of care towards his parent. Eventually, father and son came to spend time together and even managed to travel abroad with each other. In effect, when it came to her husband's father, the wife had learned to get out of her husband's way. But it was no altruistic act on her part, for she gained too. She earned entitlement for herself in giving her husband room, and she saw the positive transformation in her husband's relationship with their son.

In sum, a couple's alleged inability to be close may be anchored as much in their invisible filial loyalties as in a personal deficiency from early deprivation, in a systematic error in current communications, or in skewed patterns of interpersonal behavior.

THERAPEUTIC GUIDELINES

A contextual therapist's contract in marriage work is neither simply to reinforce a failing marriage nor to hasten to divorce. The therapist does well not to allow his competence to be measured by the outcome of his clients' decisions. His basic mandate in marriage, as well as in all other aspects of his work, is to be partial to both mates and to expect each of them to take responsible dialogic positions. His contractual obligations are essentially met when he touches all bases—factually, psychologically, transactionally, and ethically—on each of their behalves. On the other hand, a therapist may be sufficiently parentified by his clients to make him feel personally responsible for their decisions. If he allows their parentification to stand as a measure of his work, he is automatically transformed into a referee charged with watching the ball and calling the count.

Here experience reaffirms the wisdom and advantage of a therapeutic agreement whose terms involve only one contractual commitment—to nudge people to assume responsibility for making their own choices and, if there are young children, to assume responsibility on behalf of benefiting them. If a therapist adheres to these fundamentals, he is always on safe ground, even if he feels profoundly sad when a couple whose marriage he had hoped to "save" has decided to divorce. No parent is forever obliged to stay in an untenable marriage to make it right for their children. What they do owe their children is an honest attempt to consider and safeguard their interests. Even in the midst of the heat and stress of an ugly separation, parents do well to keep their eye on the prize. An ongoing investment in jointly parenting their children may help a divorcing couple rechannel their pain and refocus on one of their key realities.

Therapists are especially accountable for helping a couple take responsible positions when small children are involved. In this way, clients are given their due: They are treated like the adults they are. Here the therapist resists the temptation to lure people into a childlike role vis-à-vis his own magic-like authority. He refrains from prescribing specific behavioral structures and helps the couple seek out their own options instead. His self-defined function, conveyed to clients early on, is a courage-lender and a catalytic agent who helps people take responsible and spontaneously autonomous positions.

In marriage work, a couple also needs to explore the ledger that exists between them; to address the issue of how fair the distribution of burdens and benefits among them and other family members is. In this process, each person is helped to see both sides of the balance, as well as to take an individual stance. One or both may suppress the major configurations of items to be balanced. For example, a husband may have carried a chronic illness into his marriage and not want to talk about it. A wife may have "imported" children by another man. Both of them were aware of these factors when they married, but now they are growing sources of resentment and fatigue. Instead of dealing with these matters, it may be easier for a couple to argue over who left the dishes in the sink or who forgot to lock the door after coming home very late.

Bickering over small, everyday issues is usually easier than handling large, global matters that are essentially unalterable burdens on the relationship. In the long run, though, it may be of lasting benefit for them to face the ethical implications of these burdens, and to acknowledge and credit those family members who are carrying the bulk of the weight. The outcome of facing hard realities can be especially healing if fair crediting can spread to include other areas in need of balancing.

Many areas of the marriage relationship can be explored if the partners' anxiety and resistance can be allayed. For example, is one of them overlooking the other's genuine contribution? Is someone being taken for granted? Are a person's relational strengths responsibly used? Is someone acting out of destructive entitlement, ignoring how he or she hurts and humiliates others? Is someone being exploited through destructive parentification? Is one of them actively undermining the other's attempts to be a responsible parent or caring in-law? How valid is the wife's claim that she can be more giving to her husband now that she has a lesbian lover? The therapist retains an abiding interest in questions like these. She patiently explores the family's suffering, couple and children alike, and tries to lend courage to each member.

Contextual therapists are not essentially interested in secrets *per se*. Secrets can clearly be a part of needed privacy and so have their own legitimacy. Early on, family therapists naively wanted to reveal every secret in their clients' lives. Total candor and openness were presumed to make families function better. Secrecy, however, is more complex than that; other principles also prevail. For example, who will benefit from disclosing a secret, and how? On balance, does the secret result in everybody's gain? Or is there more gain to more people if the secret is broken? Mother knows that father is not Junior's natural parent. Will it help if Junior knows? Rita has just discovered that she was born out of wedlock. What is the benefit in telling her brothers and sisters? These questions are hard to answer in any absolute sense. But they deserve discreet consideration in the context in which a family's secrets have occurred.

The evaluation of complex relational conflicts is always most effectively governed by the issue of whether or not people care about the distribution of a family's benefits and burdens. Can the husband agree with his wife's claim that, since her lesbian relationship began, she can love him more? Can the wife agree that her husband has become a more giving father since he has openly "come out" about his weekly needs for a homosexual affair? Can affairs or open marriages take place without damaging anyone's interests, especially the children's? In contextual therapy, a general principle is at work. No child should be victimized in consequence of his or her parents' quest for freedom or openness in adult sexuality. Conversely, a consideration of their children's interests always helps parents earn entitlement to increased varieties of freedom in their adult pursuits. Consider the case of a family who originally came into treatment with complaints about their 12-year-old daughter.

> The husband is deeply hurt by his mother-in-law's insinuations, so the wife finds herself in the middle of a loyalty conflict hidden thus far in Lisa's scapegoated role. The unsettled mother-grandmother ledger is playing itself out in a revolving slate and is currently threatening mother's second marriage as it had helped to sink her first.
>
> This time though, mother is taking a harder look. She has begun to discover the links between her unsuccessful marriages and her indirect loyalty to her parents. In the process, she is being helped to reexamine her own unfairness, particularly the chronic blame of her current husband for the noxious state of family affairs. It is true that his attitude towards Lisa is less than fatherly, but he is, after all, "only" Lisa's stepparent. On the other hand, his is a long-term effort to accept another man's child and try to make her a member of his own household and family.

From this point on in the process, therapy turned in the direction of a four-generational exploration. Both marriage partners were gradually able to face their respective parents' destructive entitlements. Throughout the complexity of this case, the therapist was able to be partial to both spouses. He was also able to be partial to Lisa, her mother and her grandmother. The burden of his work was guided by the fact of his chief consideration, given to the couple's children whose future was being distorted by their parents' revolving slates.

CHAPTER 19
Divorce and Remarriage

Divorce, in a contextual view, is always a regrettable, if necessary, event that represents more than the vicissitudes of adult life. For children it always means the end of continuity in a nuclear family. Even in cases where parents can manage to be a cooperative parenting team, divorce shatters the underpinnings of the security of a child's world. At least in the interim, there is no way that a child can act on his own vested interests when his parents are involved in going their own separate ways. There is no way for him to emulate their actions, i.e., to choose one of them over the other in a divorce-like manner, too. A parent-child divorce is dynamically inconceivable, of course, for the bond is essentially unbreakable. Its uniqueness is irreplaceable and persists throughout a person's lifetime. The tenacity of the parent-child bond is endurable and thousands of times older than humankind's experiment with the nuclear family itself.

THERAPEUTIC GUIDELINES IN THE DIVORCE PROCESS

Therapy in the midst of divorce proceeds on some specific principles and guidelines of its own. First of all, it is unlikely that two adults can manage to stay in a marriage solely for their children's sake, whatever the expectations of their extended family and community might be. Even were they to try, they could not get around the fact that it is their chronic mistrust of each other that is the chief source of harm to their children, not the issue of whether or not they live together under the same roof. Therapy with couples in the midst of divorce thus has many facets and aims.

Therapists are obliged to help couples begin to close off the past, walk through their pain, work through feelings of rage, helplessness and the trauma of loss, negotiate as fairly as the circumstances will permit, tentatively lean less on the legal system for establishing their terms and goals or settling their affairs and more on their capacity to argue for what is fair, identify new directions for their lives, and reenter a long dormant social world of "singles." The work unloosed by the process of separation and the divorce event itself is usually massive and typically involves all kinds of unfaced issues flowing from the past, like trustworthiness, autonomy, unrealistic expectations, collisions with parents, judgmental friends, retributive in-laws, social and communal displacement, the introduction of lovers, and the children's behavior and future, including custody, visits, vacations, and all of the consequences thereof.

In contextual work with divorce, multidirectional partiality remains the guiding principle and method with both adults. Where young, dependent children are involved, the safeguard of their interests is therapy's primary goal. Eventually, this goal also serves the best interests of the parents as well. For example, no divorce can take place without the children's being parentified to some extent. At the very least, their parents are likely to count on their capacity to be concerned, caring and benevolent observers. In these circumstances, parents typically lean heavily on their children's good faith which, in fact, far outweighs the young's capacity to actually help their parents.

At worst, youngsters in all their helplessness function as insular sources of trustworthiness in a blatantly untrustworthy and manipulative adult world. Hurt, puzzled and resentful parents almost always feel compelled to use their children as a forum in which to vent their contempt, hatred and mistrust. Here a therapist can alert parents to their often inadvertent misuse of a child. A therapist can also help parents see how they use their child as referee. "Would you like to spend Sunday with Daddy or me?" is the kind of question that burdens children, sometimes to profound withdrawal or some other breaking point. Parents are best helped by learning to surface what each of them wants on a given day, to settle issues between each other, and, then, to negotiate with their child.

The parents' ability to identify their own terms is central to whether or not they are eventually compelled to make the legal system into a kind of superparent. Can they indicate what they want and argue for it with each other? Or will they be more at ease to let lawyers and the court do it for them? The choice is a difficult one. On the one hand, if people could negotiate their differences, they might not be getting a divorce. On the other hand, leaning on lawyers is often like leaning on physicians. In both cases, a person is often forced to regress into an unwanted dependency stance. But can a lay person really expect to have the competence to walk through the maze of medical or legal esoterica? The answer is usually "yes" and "no." A lay person can know, for example, what a lawyer might characteristically ignore, that is, the less that parents resort to legal battle, the better it is for their children.

Whether in legal or in general terms, the parents' vilification of each other always hurts and shames their child. A belligerently adversarial divorce injures the residual trust resources that the family will have to build on after the process is done. In any case, any legal move that lends itself to all-out war between divorcing adults always counters the best interests of a child. All-out legal warfare also runs the risk of deepening the estrangement among the members of each party's family of origin, with potential loss of contact for the children. Especially at times of unwanted separation and loss, any child can benefit from being in touch with *all* of his or her grandparents, uncles, aunts, and cousins. A youngster never gains a thing if the legal process pits his father's set of relatives against his mother's. Contextual therapy's emphasis on multilateral concern among family members, even in the midst of divorce, is the precursor to divorce mediation which, in essence, is contextual.

CHILD CUSTODY

Ideally, child custody is shared between the divorced spouses and characterized by each person's marked willingness to cooperate with each other vis-à-vis their child. Whether the child sleeps under one or both parent's roof is of secondary importance. The real issue is whether parents can make an honest effort to work together in their children's interests. The effort is a demanding one at best, one that can keep open ugly aspects of the past, getting in the way of current living arrangements, sometimes evoking jealousy, envy and unanticipated emotions of every kind, forcing the adults to wonder what might have been, and creating awkward circumstances like obligatory meetings at graduations, special birthday celebrations, weddings, and times of illness, to say nothing about questions of where a youngster should stay during vacation times from school. Still, the alternatives are few.

The matter of visiting is a case in point. If adults can find the energy and take the time to set up a precise schedule for visiting on which their children can rely—and then adhere to it—they are essentially offering a gift of respect for their children's rights and dignity. A visiting schedule, of course, is meant to function as a baseline, a roster for unanticipated events and expectations, if you will. It gives newly-shaken family life a ground and a direction. It is meant to protect everyone from the excesses of rigid, compulsive lack of spontaneity, on the one hand, and from overspontaneous "liberties" on the other. For all the inconvenience, visiting schedules allow members of the family to plan collaboratively. On the other hand, visiting times can be used as weapons and bludgeons. Consider the situation of the 13-year-old girl whose parents had gone through an acrimonious divorce five years earlier.

Visitation rights included a plan for Mary to stay with her father six weeks of every summer. Other issues obviously impinge, e.g., split loyalties and parental preferences involve mother's bias towards her daughters and father's bias towards his son. Still, the last summer that she was to visit father, Mary had to negotiate with him. Six weeks seemed too long; what about four? She had friends and activities in her neighborhood. Could she find a way to fit them in? Anyhow, even when she visited her father, he spent all of his time with her brother and she spent all of her time with her stepmother who was very nice but. . . . Could something be done about that? Father could only respond by saying that Mary was influenced by her mother and that's why she made things so hard.

Unable to hear Mary or credit her side in any way, father remained distant from his daughter and suffered all of the expectable consequences. He felt abandoned, accused and accusing. He felt helpless in the face of what he experienced as his daughter's rebuffs. He felt furious at his former wife. He felt that his older daughter had set a precedent against the girls' spending time with him. And he felt even more proprietary of his son than he had before.

Mother grew depressed. After five years, shouldn't something else be happening? Mary's older sister felt guilt-stricken. Had she set a harmful precedent by refusing to visit her father? Mary's younger brother felt trapped. How could he ever have time for himself if he were the only one to visit his father? Mary felt guilt-stricken and resentful. She also felt bereft. She had tried to reason with her father. She had offered alternatives. He had refused them. Either things were to be done his way or obviously not done at all. Mary felt that she had not only lost her father, maybe for good, but had also lost the image of what it meant to have a father at all. So she wrote him a letter.

DAD, FATHER

When I hear that word, I always stop and think. What does "Father" mean to me? I see what "Father" means to most of my friends, and it bothers me that the word "Father" will never mean this to me.

A Father to me, in my life, means tension, pressure, hurt, anger, upsetment, frustration, and so much more. Is that what a Dad means to my friends? I don't think so. Dad probably means love, understanding, kindness, compassion, and so much more to them. Why are our definitions so extremely opposite? Maybe because we've all experienced many different people. This probably doesn't make much sense to you because I am writing it with a confused mind.

Sometimes I think "Father" could mean the same to me as it does to my friends (that is, in a stupid, lovely, fantasy world I place myself in frequently). But in reality I know it isn't true *or it never seems possible*. Sometimes I hate the word "Father" because it brings such happiness to so many others and none to me. When I was a child I loved my Dad. I love him in my own way now—but it's different.

I began to grow, and he wanted me to stop. I began to be my own person which made him unhappy because I didn't want exactly what he wanted. I wanted to work through *our* problems and, maybe in doing that, strengthen our relationship. I wanted compromise—he wanted "*ALL or NOTHING.*" It was either all or nothing, nothing in between. He made himself clear—the rest was up to me. He either wanted me to sacrifice myself *completely* or forget everything. In the beginning, he didn't even talk to me about our problems, or maybe we would talk, but he wouldn't hear what I was saying. He didn't want me to bring my own person.

I felt myself as being an "extension" of my Father; like an arm, I do what I am told or ordered to do—I have no personality. Is that the kind of relationship I wanted with my Father? This was the hardest decision I ever made in my whole life. Maybe the decision was right and maybe it wasn't but I had to make a choice and then I had to live with it.

Mary never sent the letter. She couldn't imagine an answer that wouldn't bring still more pain. She no longer visits her father though she has sent him a couple of notes and a gift. Nothing is ever enough though, so there is less and less reason to try. Mary and her brother don't speak much these days; they argue whenever they try. He screams at her all of the time, she complains. Family members are all stuck in positions they never seemed to choose. Ostensibly, all of this is over the issue of visiting and a family's seeming inability to set up a workable plan.

A lot of self-defeating effort used to be invested in defining criteria for the "good" custodial parent. Setting parents against each other to measure their good qualities resulted, among other things, in the further disintegration of trustworthiness in the family. Professional advice typically aggravated the situation even more. In the best known effort of its type, Goldstein, Freud and Solnit (1973) argued that a child benefits most from a custody arrangement in which one parent holds exclusive custody—to the point where he or she can even prohibit contact with the noncustodial parent. This argument flies in the face of family theory and therapy which show that a child's relationship with both parents is permanent and indissoluble. Consider Bruce's situation.

Bruce, who is potentially suicidal, is the middle child of three children whose parents are involved in a brutally contested divorce. The youngest child in this family is a girl, 7, who is content to live with her mom. The eldest is John, 14, who has seemingly opted for his dad. But Bruce is 9 and in the middle in every conceivable way. He misses John and Dad whom Mom regularly calls a son-of-a-bitch in front of the kids, and repeats just how much she wants to vomit whenever she sees his face.

From his side, Father is trying to prove that his behavior is considerate and appropriate, and entitles him to custody of Bruce. He was shocked, he said, when the judge told him she hoped he could prove his charges of child-abuse against his wife. "I thought I'd only have to demonstrate that I'm a better parent," he complained. "I wasn't out to prove abuse."

Bruce is discouraged, confused and depressed. He is visibly torn and counting on May 5, the hearing date, to decide that he can live with his dad. In an evaluation session, he repeated again and again how frightened he is to go to court. He is afraid of his younger sister for fear she will betray him to their *mother* by telling her what he says. His mother tells Bruce she will never, never forgive him if he abandons her for his dad. On the other hand, he says, she screams and curses at him a lot. She calls him a dog and, should he drop any food on the floor, allegedly insists that he eat it off of the rug.

Does Bruce ever have a good time with his mom? Yes, he admits reluctantly. "She holds me sometimes and tells me stories. And sometimes we go for a walk." Whatever the truth, here, Bruce is 9 years old and he seems to feel totally trapped.

Under the circumstances, forced separation between a youngster and his or her parent not only deprives the child in and of itself. In the child's eye, it also undermines the trustworthiness and credibility of the custodial parent and even of his siblings.

Recently, a number of states in the United States have established a notion of custodial fitness that argues for the child's right to access to both of his or her parents, a trend started by the state of California in 1980 (California, 1980). Boszormenyi-Nagy was responsible for the following recommendation to the courts: "In determining parental competence, the court should seriously consider the comparative willingness of the two contestants to provide the child with access to the other parent, to siblings, grandparents and other relatives" (GAP, 1980). A child's right to accessibility to closely related others has an intrinsic wisdom of its own. It preserves and maintains a child's natural resources instead of withholding them or cutting them off. The courts naturally have a right to expect evidence of parental cooperation. Failing that, they act in the child's best interests if they mandate therapeutic intervention in appropriate situations.

Parents frequently recognize their own limits vis-à-vis their former spouses and their children-in-common, and so seek therapy. One woman could define her dilemma very explicitly.

> I want my children to know their father, to love and depend on him and to find ways to enjoy him. But I'm also afraid they'll like him better than they like me. He gives them whatever they want and takes them wherever they want to go. If he keeps that up—and I'm always the one to tell them what they can't have or have to do, he'll turn out to be the good guy; and you know who that makes me.

The dependent children of divorced parents usually benefit from the continued availability of a therapist even when parents can't or won't agree to talk to each other without the presence of their lawyers. Even under these conditions, a contextual therapist can sometimes help sufficiently for the parents to become a working team where their children are concerned. Consider the situation of a woman who left her home for a homosexual love affair.

> Her husband was alternately outraged and convinced that his wife would eventually come home. For her part, his wife had enough of men: An abandoning, judgmental father; a withholding, manipulative husband; and an absent, disinterested brother. She was tired of answering to people and wanted to be left alone.
>
> Both parents, however, were receptive to how their struggles were affecting the children. The tension between them was so high that the therapist advised them to stay away from each other in order to regain some balance and direction in their separate worlds. One of the children was suffering from migraines; the other had gone back to sucking her thumb. Still, even in the middle of volatile emotions and punitive behavior, these parents were each willing to try to do something that could bring relief to their young.

In this and other cases, the therapist is able to alternate her modes of seeing family members. She can see the children with their mother in one session and then with their father in another. It may even be beneficial to see the children as a group without either parent, perhaps to explore how they can work as a better team in the face of the lack of adult reason.

REMARRIAGE

Once their mother and father divorce, many children face the possibility that one or both of their parents will remarry. Remarriages evoke all kinds of emotions for good and for bad. They also create a complexly interwoven network of old and new loyalty expectations. Remarried families in the United States are increasingly common and are becoming so in Europe. Obviously it is a pattern that follows from high divorce rates. It is also a testimony to people's needs for creating a family context.

Remarriage is often used in compensatory ways. Adults understandably expect it to undo the painful aftermath of divorce, to soften loneliness, to insure financial security, to offer another chance for family life and, perhaps, for romantic involvement. Adults also frequently hope or even take for granted that their children will be reassured to have a home again in which there are two parents. Sometimes parents naively hope that their children will automatically find a friend in their new step-parent, perhaps even a replacement for their divorced and absent natural parent.

"I don't expect to bump into any trouble with them," said the never-before-married stepmother-in-waiting. "I know they'll love her," said the father of the step-children-to be. "They haven't met her yet but I've told them all about her. I can't wait until they meet." A hope? A fiction. Adults remarry on a wide spectrum of terms, including notions about their children's receptivity. Whatever their terms, it is unrealistic for them to expect their children to be emotionally prepared to accept their new situation without the adults having to invest a lot of parental sensitivity and attention to the young's persistent loyalty bonds with both natural parents.

A storm may begin to gather, for example, when a stepmother begins to take over the kitchen and replace the children's divorced, even lacking natural mother. On the one hand, the stepmother may be acting in perfectly good faith. On the other hand, the fact that she took over without careful preparation sets her up to invite her step-children to be disloyal to their mother. The same could be said about the father who makes genuine if overquick efforts to befriend his new step-sons whose natural father is dead. Their first reaction is to blame their mother for marrying again. Both the natural parent and the step-parent experience a lot of pain at the children's apparent rejection. So do the children. Yet such incidents are just about impossible to avoid.

Holidays are often particularly painful moments in the early years of divorce, and the dynamics often subtle. One father told his adult children not to come to his newly established home at Christmas time until they can be comfortable and act from their hearts. So they opted not to come. His unrealistic expectations of them, issued in frustration—as well as his need to protect his new wife, threatened to negate early therapeutic efforts to help them reconnect. One twenty-seven year old, five years after her parent's divorce, still agonized at having to leave her mother's home at holiday time and arrive at her father's, only to be greeted by the outstretched arms of her stepmother. "She means well, I know," she said.

"But it's pure anguish to leave my mother's arms and then be held in hers."

Young children, like older ones, are deeply invested in a concern for both of their parents. The more needy the parent, the more anxious and worried a child will be. By the time their parents enter a process of separation and divorce, children are already likely to be heavily parentified. Perhaps their parents expected them to act as go-betweens. The children are likely to have taken on the task of helping their parents' marriage. Up until the present, they may have avoided assigning blame for the divorce to either of their parents. But now the parent who stays single is more an object of their sympathetic concern; the parent who remarries now seems less in need of them and their worry.

The new step-parent is readily viewed as a culprit and usurper, someone who has undeservedly taken over the role of the same-sex, natural parent. He or she is never initially entitled to the stepchild's loyalty. In most cases, the step-parent's best option is to give respectful room to the stepchild's enduring loyalty to the absent parent. In return, the youngster can eventually find ways to safely commit him or her self to the step-parent with respect and devotion.

Whatever happens between youngsters and their step-parents, the children retain the prospect of parentification in the new family. First of all, they are likely to absorb a great deal of tension between their natural parents. Financial matters and shifts in role among other factors create an atmosphere of suspicion. They are likely to work hard to spare their parents from needing to be suspicious. They may be anxious about their father's paramour, for example, and protect their mother from learning of his romantic involvement. They may suffer trauma from criticism of their absent parent and have to absorb their own anger, sadness or shame. Even when children are themselves critical of the parent, the parent's absence almost automatically guarantees loyal devotion on the child's part. In addition, a youngster may work hard to protect her parents from being jealous of each other.

When a parent and step-parent have a child-in-common, a son or daughter from a previous marriage almost automatically becomes a second class citizen. The youngster is likely to become a hostage or whipping boy who is supposed to secure civil behavior between parent and step-parent: "If he hadn't been making all that noise, the baby would still be asleep. Why can't you make him behave?" The child of a previous marriage is usually disenfranchised through no fault of his or her own. Regardless of intentions, a parent's commitment to his natural child existentially preempts analogous commitment to a stepchild. Given this reality, the child by a previous marriage is likely to reinforce his loyalty to the parent who has been "left behind," by idealizing him or her or his previous family life. Fidelity to his own loyalties predisposes the youngster to a role of disloyal, ungrateful traitor in the remarried family.

It is difficult for a child to give up the idealized image of his or her natural family of origin. Hence the inevitable need that children develop some rationale or explanation of their parents' divorce. Which of them caused it? Which of them refused to work at making things better? Why? A youngster's preoccupation with the reasons behind the divorce is an inevitable outcome of his or her original loyalty to both parents. The child's dual loyalty may be his own legitimate response. It may also have been expected of him by the family before the parents' divorce.

Complex triangular jealousies abound in the remarried family. The new spouse's marital role is an immediate source of rivalry and competition with the former spouse regardless of people's good intentions. Here the child's stance is precarious at best; at worst he can be used as a pawn. For example, he may be tolerated by his step-parent if only his natural parent will behave. Consider the example of the five year-old whose ethnic, racial and religious background was simply an offense to the woman that her father married. To compound the problem, father traveled extensively in his job and was away from home at least sixty percent of the time.

> When father left, the little girl stopped talking. At best she grunted in response. By the time her new husband returned, his wife was in emotional turmoil feeling rebuffed, enraged and full of regret. For father, the pressure was on. No one had anticipated his daughter's behavior nor faced how her background might offend his wife. The pressure grew when the couple had children of their own. Eventually father could no longer be in a room when both his daughter and wife were present. He would have to do something about his daughter's behavior, his wife insisted: "After all I've done over the years," she went on, "she owes me something more."

Here, as in other situations, unfaced issues in remarried families can float through the years; the child can be scapegoated in large ways and small; and neither of the adults need openly take responsibility for his or her side of the family's dilemma.

In parallel ways, a romantically or passionately hostile relationship between divorced "partners" can persist for years and years. The biggest danger in this situation is that their child may be delegated to carry covert messages between them. A therapist can help the parents understand the weight of their actions and offer them alternative options to the misuse of their child. She may point out that however inadvertent, this kind of behavior can only force divorced parents to deepen the split in their youngster's loyalty to them, with problematic consequences including threats of suicide. The same danger exists when either a child's stepparent or one of her biological parents presses her to "forget about" her other natural parent. Here a child's loyalty to the absent parent typically deepens, but now its hold is tinged with feelings of helplessness and entrapment.

CHAPTER 20
Parenting Problems

The option of parenting is supposed to present adults with their most satisfying source of gratification. Yet it is also the most demanding test of adult responsibility. Contemporary parenting seems to be suffering from a lack of direction and support. Life in our grandparents' society, for example, was structured by generally sanctioned values and codes of behavior, certainly more than in ours. Today's hurried and fragmented existence lends itself to few guidelines, let alone *dicta* about what is right or wrong. Contemporary adolescents and children sometimes are so deeply submerged in peer culture that they seem to reject parental guidance out of hand. For all of this, it is very clear that, if anything, leadership from parents remains an undiminished social need.

The criteria for parenting in the contemporary world are under heated discussion. Today's family has to create its own stability. Not many families are left who can reasonably rely on the ready availability of grandparents, aunts, uncles, and other relatives. And in the nuclear family itself, marriage is often unstable. New forms of parenting, e.g., divorce, single parenting and remarriage, all create new challenges to continuity and security. Given the fluidity, it seems inevitable that parenting suffer an inversion: Children themselves have become the most reliable resources available to reinforce family stability—with varying results. A child can grow and develop from offering resources of care, loyalty and availability if they are well utilized. Even very young children can contribute to family life, especially in emergencies, and can do so without understanding the adult world and its specific problems.

Thoughtful utilization of a child's care requires adults to recognize an offspring's contributions rather than belittle them. Children who are ac-knowledged for their caring intentions become trustworthy and gain a sense of worth and self-esteem. In particular, feuding or separating parents do well to protect their children from conflicting demands that eventually impose a predicament of split loyalty. A child's functioning as a perma-nent referee to his parents' battles is not only an ungrateful and impossi-ble task; it has devastating consequences to the child.

Situations of split loyalty often develop out of unsuccessful parental attempts to solve in-law problems as a team. In most cases of this kind, each person is likely to target the other one's parents as the culprit. And each person is likely to have to retreat to a defensive position vis-à-vis his or her own families of origin. The more one partner attacks the other part-ner's family, the more both of them will question or doubt their allegiance to each other. The loyalty conflicts between the two of them are eventually converted into a predicament of split loyalty and conveyed to the next generation.

Fortunately, there are ways to retard the development of loyalty con-flict. Consider the time in which a couple faces the fact that one of their in-laws is simply intractable in his resentment and rejection of their mar-riage. In fact, it takes very little to set him off; the slightest reason provides a basis for fault-finding. The injured partner, the daughter-in-law, may choose to do battle. "One of these days," she says to her husband, "you're going to have to make a choice between me and your parents." The sharper her demands, the more forcefully will her husband be pushed into conflicting loyalties. However, another option exists.

Her husband may approach her with a new proposal for understand-ing their situation and acting in more helpful ways. He may have realized that it is in everyone's interests if the two of them can establish a trust base and become a trustworthy team. "Let's face it," he may say. "You're stuck with your parents and I'm stuck with mine. I'd like to be able to see them, and take the baby to see them, sometimes, without the feeling that I'm hurting you. Maybe you can do the same thing with your parents. Instead of Sunday dinner together all of the time, it may be easier to visit our parents separately. I can fish with Dad and sometimes have lunch with Mom. It feels funny to think this way, but it may help us out of a trap."

In the first instance, one of the partners can think through his options or, if the situation can tolerate it, think them through jointly with his mate. They can discuss the alternatives and gradually, if not immediately, im-plement them. They can develop a situation in which they eventually rely on each other's trust resources. The couple can then minimize the damage done to a marriage by the partners' split and colliding behavior. Their new approach and plans are also in the best interests of their children who can hardly benefit from numberless quarrels or loss of contact with any of their grandparents. The grandparents may, in fact, protest and try to use the situation to escalate the estrangement. Their reactions, however, are secondary in importance to the fact that their children have found new options for offering them ongoing consideration and care.

Therapeutic interventions that support trust-based teamwork between adults and their parents benefit the children, too. The development of parental trust and joint decision-making always has preventive consequences for the young. On the other hand, a family world based on entrenched mistrust and unfairness, specifically between adults and their own parents, gives little hope to children or adolescents, and certainly offers no basis for a future model. School phobia and frequent school absences, delinquency, substance misuse and abuse, teen pregnancy, depression, and suicidal inclinations are all potential outcomes of a predicament of split loyalty and the mistrust and unfairness it engenders.

TRENDS OF FLIGHT FROM PARENTAL RESPONSIBILITY

Traditionally, women have been tied to parental responsibility both by pregnancy and by society's expectations of their availability to small children. Just so, traditionally, men have been able to opt out of direct responsibility for parenting. It follows that courts have tended to give women custody of small children in legal battles between two parents. More recently, the scene has changed and in an increasing number of cases neither parent wants the child.

The trend towards renunciation of parental responsibility seems to coincide with the kind of technical progress that enables one woman to have another woman carry her fertilized ovum. Given the developing possibility of biological manipulation, it becomes increasingly possible to separate the commitment to parent a child from the decision to carry a fetus by calling on one or even two paid outsiders to provide the biological roles related to conception and pregnancy. This kind of development is usually a two-edged sword. On the one hand, it offers new prospects for pregnancy to women who, for reasons of illness, injury or surgery, cannot sustain pregnancy. On the other hand, it opens up frightening options for further fragmentation of parental responsibility and family trustworthiness.

The absence of biological ties compounds the complexity and developmental burdens of adoptive parent-child relationships. There are increasing instances in which adults are turning to disadoption when the going gets too rough, especially in their children's adolescence. Will the disavowal of conception or insemination become an analogue to disadoption 15 years from now? And who, then, will rightfully be identified as this given child's parents? Will carrier pregnancies serve to destroy the remaining vestiges of the traditional bonds that make parent-child relating unique and irreplaceable? How will the fact of babies born of another woman's womb or conceived *in vitro* affect the quality of family relations at every level? However inadvertently, will this radical shift of the locus of conception and/or pregnancy diminish human dignity, respect and entitlement for everyone involved?

Inclinations to abandon parental responsibility are not a new phenomenon. What is new is the absence of a kinship system that might protect the members of a family when its nuclear structure begins to break up. If a parent is without family members who can provide a backup when she or he and their child are in serious need, parent and child alike are in jeopardy—the parent from helplessness born of isolation and the child from telescoping parentification. As a parent's life becomes increasingly chaotic, a child is forced to become the responsible party in the midst of an irresponsible adult world. The young pay when adult freedom and convenience are achieved at the expense of a child's security and entitlement. There are always direct consequences attached to the need for children to provide the glue that bonds adults to responsibility for parenting.

Here it is important to note the sharp differences in approach between structural family therapy approaches and contextual therapy. In traditional family therapy, the parentified child is defined as a satisfied beneficiary of his power position who should be therapeutically retrained. In contrast with this implicit "therapeutic parentification" of the child, contextual therapy argues that the father and mother who parentify their children nonstop are not only exploitative and manipulative; they also actively deplete and drain their offspring's energy and resources. This existential loss for the child outweighs any gain he might draw from a power-laden position.

In our experience, children need to be acknowledged for their sacrifical contributions to family life so they can be extricated from the trap of parentification. A parentified child requires help in dealing with the guilt-laden insinuations that his parents have used to keep him in an over-performing stance. In order to effectively liberate their child from the bondage of parentification, parents require help in learning how to acknowledge what he or she has actually given to them. If parents can manage to credit their child, they will also have met the first requirement of more responsible adult performance.

FOSTER CARE PLACEMENT

It is unfair to expect young children to fend for themselves as if they were mature adults. They need and deserve adult care and commitment preferably from their natural parents. In times of emergency, when their parents can neither provide nor function, someone else has to move in. If no family member can take over, representative community agencies are obliged to provide children with a caretaking environment.

However, ample literature describes how a failure of adult commitment puts children at jeopardy even when their material needs are well met. The problem is compounded when the young are placed in foster care and shifted from home to home, from stranger to stranger. Constant movement and shifts are essentially unjustifiable in our view unless a child is known to be in a home that endangers him. Ideally, a single childcare authority might function as a fixed anchor point that could most effectively assess and respond to a family's situation. The agents of this kind of authority would be more likely to offer a greater potential for a degree of adult reliability and interpersonal continuity that is currently absent from the foster care scene. Functioning as a fixed point, a single childcare authority could also take responsibility for recognizing the young's profound investment in family solidarity, with all of its developmental consequences.

There are many indications for the emergency foster care placement of children: Violence or sexual abuse, grave and intentional parental neglect and deprivation, and the loss of parents by death, crippling illness or abandonment are chief among them. In these cases and others like them, the courts and service agencies are mandated to initiate foster care action that will serve the best interests of the child. The best interests of the child are also served initially by careful planning that includes short-range and long-range consideration of effective principles and guidelines for foster care placement.

A delicate balance of considerations usually exists within the decision-making process itself. On the one hand, a family's current circumstances may be severe enough to warrant an immediate decision to remove a child from his or her parents' care. On the other hand, it is always questionable to proceed on the automatic assumption that the effects of placing a child in a foster home will necessarily have essentially redeeming characteristics. To weigh the advantages and disadvantages of foster care over what the natural family can offer is always a task in itself, a task in which black and white solutions are seldom helpful or effective.

Professional experts are often used to consult and advise the court of the feasibility of foster care. But the goals and directions of a lot of professional help may themselves be ill-advised. No professional consultant can answer questions about the fitness of the parental home with accuracy or reliability. Professional answers to questions of this kind imply a magic knowledge of the future. The capacity for parenting cannot be scientifically predicted by experts in human engineering in ways that mechanical engineers might employ to estimate the load capacity of a bridge.

In our view, courts would be better served to inquire into what potential impact therapy might have on the prospects of future parenting. For example, do a parent's own neediness, despair and destructive entitlement play themselves out in child abuse and neglect? The victimization of children is often a distress signal on the parent's part, an indirect call for help. Parents can often respond to interventions that recognize the sources of their destructive entitlement and that help them address their behavior. Their motivation to parent their children can increase in direct proportion to the parenting which they can be helped to identify and claim for themselves.

As a practical step, courts might order mandatory family therapy to establish a sound basis on which to evaluate a family's fitness and potential to care for their children. All parties to the decision-making process might also benefit from a trial period of, say, approximately six months to a year. Therapeutic efforts can be supported by concurrent, family-shelter, living arrangements. If therapy fails to indicate appreciable improvement in the parents' capacity to deliver care, plans for foster care arrangements or long-term institutionalization can then proceed.

ADOPTION

In adoption one couple or individual takes a child who biologically belongs to another couple. The adoptive family commits itself to raise the child to the best of its members' ability, i.e., with real consideration for the youngster's self-interests as well as for their own. Whether directly acknowledged or not, the adoptive parents expect a return. Their adoptive child is to offer them allegiance and loyalty comparable though perhaps not equal to what a natural child might owe them. This expectation might be easy to meet if the child were not bound to his biological and adoptive parents alike. The loyalty dilemmas of adoptive children fester and deepen in direct proportion to the split they intuit between the natural and adoptive families. The greater the barrier of contempt between them, the more vulnerable and exposed the child becomes. One of the hopes on the horizon is the promise of open adoption. Accessibility to both sets of parents is the fundamentally new option here, an option that can decisively help to diminish the destructive aspects of an adoptive child's loyalty and entitlement.

In adoption, natural parents give up their child and, in the process, decide to abrogate commitment to their child. Nevertheless, the natural mother has invested a significant amount of her life and energy in bearing the child. She carries the fetus through pregnancy and goes through childbirth. She may have been ashamed of the process, afraid of it, or even physically vulnerable to it. In some cases there seem to be few justifications for a person's decision to give up her baby. Even so, she has expended herself and is due a certain degree of consideration and concern. In situations where a woman suffers massive anguish over her decision to adopt her baby out, even more consideration may be due. Consider the following statement written by a biological mother who adopted her child out.

I am a birthparent who gave up her son four days after his birth. The memory of his birth is burned into the scar tissue of my heart and it is with the voice of grief and longing that I try to formulate this dialogue into the void of unknowing.

I had given my son his last feeding. We had been together for four days because the nurses had failed to realize that I was giving him up and so brought him to me as they would bring any infant to their mother's waiting arms. I had been overjoyed at this unexpected turn of events as I thought my sin so great that I deserved nothing at all. The nurses bathed and dressed him. The social worker was with him when they brought him back for one final kiss, one last embrace. I saw the gold medal pinned to his clothes which my mother had thought to buy for him. I remember thinking that something from us would be going with him to his new surroundings.

After they left with him, the ground of my being shifted to compensate for the void that his departure had created. Over the years I would have to silently and desperately try to determine what was real from what was not. Boundaries would dissolve unexpectedly around me and the only solid and ever present factor would be my fear. No one knew how to speak with me about my loss and so grief transformed itself into anxiety and depression.

Sixteen years later, the silence presses in more forcefully as the consequences of my actions take on new and ever more complex meaning. But now I am trying to push back the silence with the only thing left for me to use—my word. It had always been difficult for me to refer to this child as "my son." I colluded once with my family to leave home so that I could carry him in solitude and shame, and again by agreeing not to tell my son's father of his child's existence.

I decided to break the collusion by informing my husband and children about the baby. But Charles' reality means little to my husband and remains a question and a predicament for my children. Still, I am willing to open the dialogue for those who wish to participate, realizing that each of us will bring a different word.

It was about 5 years ago that I decided with great anxiety to pierce the silence. I gathered what courage I still had and retraced my steps to the agency I had originally contracted with to handle my son's adoption. I learned to my horror that my son was not adopted until the age of 7. His had been a "difficult" placement, not because he was a difficult child, as the social worker assured me, but because his biracial background made him hard to place.

He had spent the first two years of his life with the family who took him from the hospital. The next four years he spent with a family who couldn't decide whether or not to adopt him. The social worker told me that Charles saw the other foster children who lived in that home having visits with their parents and he wondered constantly when his parents were going to come for him. For a while, he maintained the fantasy that his father and I would appear and take him home to live with us. During his stay, the foster parents decided to adopt one of their foster children. He was not the chosen one.

When I hear these things about my son's early life, I turn more deeply against myself. I struggle against the urge (and the need) to despair that my selfishness and immaturity have caused him to experience so much pain at so young an age. For the sake of the children whom I have since borne, I have tried to forgive myself and not to yield to despair. But the effort can only be balanced by the hope that he too could (or would) forgive me. Futility and frustration must be overcome again and again and again.

My son finally found a home with people who possessed sufficient courage to overcome their own doubts about raising a child who had already been through so much and who would doubtless face many more trials throughout his life, given his mixed racial background. With the scant but precious bits of information that I was able to glean from the placing agency, I have pictured the adoptive parents as being benevolent, caring, generous people to whom I am indebted (Miros, 1983).

Filial consideration of a father's just due in the decision to give up a baby may be significantly different from what is owed a mother. The natural father may not even know that he is the parent of a child. If he does know, his contribution is infinitely less comparable to what his female counterpart has made. He may have been indifferent to the pregnancy; he may have objected to the baby's being given up; he may even have fought it and lost.

From the offspring's perspective, it is usually difficult to find a sufficient excuse for the parents who gave him or her away: "What could have made them renounce that helpless baby who was me?" an adopted child might ask. A biological child is inherently loyal to his natural mother whether he knows her or not. He, in turn, is owed consideration (at least from a therapist) for his inherent loyalty to her. How, then, can this child's inborn right to his natural parents best be served? How can this adopted child be helped to prevent the spillover of the consequences from a damaging legacy of split loyalty? Consider the ongoing loyalty struggle of an adopted person who is now in his mid-twenties.

My (adoptive) mother and father are the richest resources that I have in my life and much of what I am is the result of the foundation they have given me. My family life is no *Leave It to Beaver* but of the families that R (his natural mother) could have chosen for me, the one she chose was the very best.

I have never talked to either of my parents about how I came to live with them and I only assume that they never talked about it to me because they wanted to protect me. This is a matter I must resolve but I am more apprehensive calling them into account than I was in talking to R. Although I knew I was claiming what is rightfully mine in talking to R, I felt an existential disloyalty to my (adopted) parents. I just don't know if I can deal with them thinking that I'm not satisfied with their parenting or that they fell short in any way. They didn't.

I refuse to hurt them on this matter. Understanding the circumstances that surround my coming to be with them is important to me but not more important than the present relationship I have with them. This is a loose end in my life but I'm not willing to exchange my courage for their pain.

What, if anything, can this young man do for his adoptive parents to mitigate the likelihood of their jealousy or contempt?

Adoptive parents are usually vulnerable to the issue of their child's colliding loyalties. In any case, their child has the theoretical option to seek out his natural origins. In the past, the adoption records were permanently sealed; few people could use them to trace the whereabouts of their natural parents. Sometimes, adoptive parents used this requirement for secrecy to their own advantage. In many instances, they felt that the less their adopted child knew about her original family, especially their positive attributes, the more loyal she would stay to her adoptive family (Fisher, 1981). To reinforce this rationale, adoptive parents might use only negative hues with which to paint the picture of their child's natural mother.

Contextual theorists argue that everyone benefits when adoptive parents can convey the positive as well as negative aspects of their child's natural parents. Everyone also benefits if they can encourage their child's questions and eventually find the resources to answer them as fully as they can. This open-ended stance is usually difficult to muster and maintain. Proprietary interests clash with common sense. "Look what we've done for you," may be the predominant, if involuntary, thought. "Why bring them into the picture so late in the game? It will only complicate life." Nevertheless, adoptive parents do well to struggle towards the kind of open attitude that can assure their child's right to explore his or her origins. A case in point is a couple living on the East coast with their three adoptive children.

They planned a trip to the adoption agency on the West coast that placed the children with them. There they tried to secure whatever information was available about each child's natural parents. Though they were only moderately successful in their efforts, their eldest child was ecstatic. He had seen his birth certificate. His footprint and time of birth were on it. So was his mother's name. The adoptive parents had very little information but what they had, they shared: The natural parents' race and age, and the reasons they offered for "giving their son away." The boy kept inquiring about the information, repeating it, nuancing it. And his adoptive parents helped in whatever ways they could.

This kind of courageous advocacy for adopted youngsters is emotionally costly but ethically fruitful. It not only frees a child to claim his right to his origins, but also safeguards the interests of the adoptive family's harmonious development.

Biological children automatically gain access to information about their family of origin by virtue of their birth. Adoptive children are immediately placed at a disadvantage concerning the reality of their natural family ties. An adopted child belongs to a family that he can only partly claim as his family of origin. His biological parents are potentially objects of suspicion or censure, so what he actually receives of them may be discouraging and disconfirming. Some adoptive children claim disinterest in knowing their roots but most insist on their right (and obligation?) to know. As far as we can tell, when adoptive children discover that their natural parents are in dire straits, they are likely to feel they owe these parents even more.

An adoptive child earns entitlement and freedom from offering his or her natural parents concern, even if those parents are eventually rejecting. The gain comes from transforming invisible loyalties into visible ones and therefore preventing the likelihood of future destructiveness that may bring harm to the youngster as well as to others. Loyalty obligations are met at the very moment that a child begins to search out his natural mother, and eventually inquire into her well-being. In any case, all of these efforts can best come about through the adoptive parents' permission.

Adoptive parents are often reluctant to let their child explore his or her natural relationships on several counts: Their biggest fear may be that the youngster will be less loyal to them once she meets her natural parents. Here they do well to ask how much room for loyalty is engendered in a child by secrecy or by overt and covert condemnation of her natural parents. Loyalty is always founded on merit rather than on a power base. Adoptive parents may have the power to withhold information that their adolescent child wants. Naturally they are entitled to use discretion. "At what age?" and "How much or what kind of information?" are appropriate questions to ask.

Still, what the youngster is requesting is more relevant and consequential to his existence than to his adoptive parents' lives. "They know where they come from; how come they won't tell me where I come from?" Clearly, adoptive parents can do more to evoke their child's enduring loyalty if they nudge him towards his natural parents than if they operate out of power-based restraint. The same dynamics are at work vis-à-vis an adopted child's natural father and mother. Mother's claim to loyalty from her child is automatically valid by virtue of pregnancy and birth. Father, on the other hand, has to earn his right to his child's loyalty through proven evidence of his efforts to be a parent.

Destructive entitlement can be another root of insensitivity in adopted parents' attitudes toward their child. In adoptive parenting as in biological parenting, there are many situations in which the child becomes an object of his mother's or father's destructive entitlement, and an innocent victim of their revolving slate. In certain families, it may even be that an adopted child, like other "outsiders" of differing genetic origins, is a prime prospect of substitutive vindication. Faced with the problems of an adopted child in his congregation, a clergyman was heard to say, "Well, his original parents were of a different faith. That's probably why he doesn't behave well. Just poor genetic material."

Whether the clergyman was reflecting the adoptive parents' view is unknown. Still, the point remains. An adopted child's behavior may be totally discredited by members of his own family or community despite the fact that it is his parents who take his concerns and turn them into destructive parentification. Unfortunately, his parents' vindictive tendencies may converge with the adopted child's own natural destructive entitlement. The less legitimate his place in the adoptive family, the greater the adopted child's destructive entitlement, e.g., when natural children are born to the adoptive couple and preempt the adopted child's place.

PRINCIPLES OF CHILD PROTECTION

Whenever possible, family and community efforts should be aimed at supporting and salvaging the relational resources of the endangered child. Child protective agencies do well to reassess the operating principle that automatically or overquickly prods them to substitute foster care for a natural family's care. Foster placement neither breaks the hold that failing parents have on their children nor does it guarantee something better to a child. To the contrary. Authorities place extra burdens on children by taking a simple "surgical" route, i.e., by cutting the young off from their natural relational resources. Cutoffs not only deprive children of their natural investments in family loyalty; they also reinforce their ethical imperative to salvage and redeem their parents—NOW, apparently, against the will of society or at least in opposition to the placement agency. These conditions tend to channel a youngster's visible, filial loyalty into invisible, destructive forms.

In essence, it is always preferable to base efforts at child protection on a foundation that makes allowances for the presence of indissoluble family loyalties in children than to produce solutions that ignore the basic phenonenon. It would be paradoxical if child protection agencies finally ignored the child's intrinsic right to be protected against the powerful consequences of destructive entitlement. In situations in which therapists are individually involved with a child, their contract might well be founded on the search to discover "how you and I can help your parents." A therapist has to acknowledge a child's right to resentment at his or her parents whenever it is due. On the other hand, she does well to guide children towards an active investment in their parents' well-being, a condition for earning freedom for themselves.

THE VIOLENT AND SEXUAL ABUSE OF CHILDREN

Ours is a time in which the protective structures that used to surround the nuclear family are diminishing. Deprived by this phenomenon themselves, contemporary parents turn towards their children and use them as primary sources of relational security and support. The hungrier, lonelier, more deprived, and more insecure the adult, the more destructive the parentification and the more likely a violent outburst or sexual misuse. The use of children as objects and outlets for violent or sexual impulses is grossly exploitative, of course, and requires decisive and immediate intervention. However, the definition of violence and sexual misuse is not always clear.

It would be an error to assume that all physical discipline can be interpreted as child abuse or even as necessarily damaging. In some families and cultures, physical punishment is a legitimate vehicle of parental concern and corrective inclinations. Alternatives to physical discipline certainly exist and can also be used to influence a child. It can also be argued that well-meaning, moderate use of physical punishment can be less harmful to a child than the consequences of neglectful inaction, seductive permissiveness or sophisticated, guilt-based inducements.

The incestuous use of children invariably places a heavy demand on society and on the professional as well. Overt sexual relating between a child and his or her parent or grandparent, or between siblings for that matter, violates the important taboos of most civilizations. Moreover, the control of sexual rights and transgressions is a matter of great emotional significance for all concerned. Western civilization is significantly influenced by the ascetic codes and antisexual bent of early Christianity, with its stress on the sinfulness of pleasure. It may be, however, that this early Christian bias stemmed in part from the fluidity and excesses of an era not so unlike our own. Contemporary society is engaged in removing limits from many forms of previously prohibited sexual behavior. In the process, we seem to be testing the feasibility of alternatives to the time-honored sexual proscriptions of family life. We seem to be forcing the question of whether behavior of any type is eventually acceptable just because there is evidence of common or frequent practice.

Contextual theory addresses the sexual use of young children from a relational rather than an individual point of view. If one person's code or criteria for sexual gratification affects no one but him or herself, e.g., masturbation, then the issue rests in the domain of private morality or personal wisdom about how to live life. The same line of reasoning applies to forms of sexual expression chosen by consenting adults. On the other hand, relational ethics function as the essential guideline for assessing the consequences of one person's decisions on another. From this perspective, adults have an enormous ethical responsibility for how they relate to children, and for the consequences of how they act.

A child may willingly participate in adult sexuality. Later on, though, that child may have to account to society for his or her behavior and, in so doing, pay an exorbitant price. Cases in point include the woman who, through her early teens, had sex relations with her father's friend; the man who at 16 often had anal sex with an older man; the woman who, from age 12 on, had incestuous relations with her father; the woman who, throughout her adolescence, had a love relationship with her older brother. Trust is the first casualty of adult-to-child sex: The child's trust in the world in general and in prospective mates in particular may take on negative hues. Or a youngster may try to protect the incestuous adult and justify his actions by early promiscuity, for example.

No single factor is likely to be the cause of incest. But parentification is always a concomitant element. Needless to say, it is in the interest of restoring every one's trust if a family can enter into open exploration of the incestuous situation. But it is more usual than not for father to forget or to deny his acts, and for mother to overlook her own part in sexually denying her husband or in rejecting the significance of either parent's behavior towards their child. The parents' hidden or open collusion in incest may aggravate their loss of trustability. Still, trust-building is the major therapeutic task in cases of parent-child incest. The issue here has less to do with the actual incestuous experience or even with trauma. Nor are learned patterns of behavior the major part of the intergenerational spread of parent-child violence and sex. The overriding significance lies in the intergenerational conveyance of destructive entitlement, that is, in the adult "right" to exploit the young. Without therapeutic intervention, subsequent generations are likely to develop ever-deepening layers of insensitivity towards their children.

ABORTION AND PREGNANCY COUNSELING

For generations, women have struggled with the social consequences of their body functions and for their right to have a say over whether or not to continue a pregnancy to term. Family planning, contraception, abortion, and career development are all examples of areas of decision-making which many contemporary women claim are exclusively theirs. Whether or not that is a fair stance is still being debated. Nevertheless, it is true that human reproduction would come to a standstill without women who were willing and able to conceive and be pregnant. Most women view reproduction as a personal gain and so invest in it willingly. On the other hand, the process itself can be risky. Its physical and emotional costs constitute a unique contribution on the part of women and their entitlement vis-à-vis their male partners. Reproductive options are intrinsically asymmetrical in their processes. But men can convert the asymmetry into relative reciprocity by investing in a caring parental and marital partnership for the benefit of offspring as well as for themselves. It remains to be seen how new techniques that offer the option of "carrier" pregnancy will affect the balance of reproductive entitlements between men and women.

From an ethical perspective, contextual theory always assigns top priority to children. So, in matters of reproduction, the most fundamental question is how a youngster's prospects for survival and quality existence can best be secured. Should a baby be born, it will need someone's solid commitment of care for a long time to come—devoted parents, a supportive network of other relatives, food, shelter, clothes, medical care, and education. At the very minimum, at least in traditional terms, an infant requires the care of a concerned, available mother.

All higher animals depend on a devoted mother and, in some cases, father. On the other hand, human mothers suffer from emotional options. They can be discouraged, resentful and rejecting of their offspring. The more burdened, the more isolated, the less supported the mother, the less likely she is to invest and devote herself to childrearing and the more destructively entitled she is likely to be. Childrearing is a job most effectively done by generatively competent parents and by a generously giving parenting network. Yet it is a fact that many mothers-to-be are essentially alone if not abandoned.

Whatever the circumstances of the baby's conception in terms of their own or their partners' lack of responsibility, it is women who end up holding the bag for themselves, for their child and, so to speak, for society. Under the circumstances, there are pregnant women who consider their pregnancy a trap and their baby a symbol of male irresponsibility and abandonment. Furthermore, a woman's future chances to relate to another man may be seriously hampered by the mere existence of her child. From another perspective, a newborn may represent financial security, borderline though it may be. The birth of a baby may constitute guaranteed "pay" to a welfare recipient.

If there is a lack of adult commitment to parenting or if the commitment is grossly insufficient, whence stems the pressure for salvaging every opportunity for reproduction? Put in other terms, does the fetus have the right to remain unborn? Like all other species, human beings are also devoted to securing their own survival. The high premium on successful survival is understandable in the light of the high risks of infant mortality, hunger, disease, war, and natural enemies that have decimated people at high rates throughout most of human existence. In some ways, this situation seems to have been reversed. It is now overpopulation rather than underpopulation that is threatening human resources and survival. The very conditions that have led to overpopulation are now altering the significance of sheer numbers of surviving humanity.

Increased rates of divorce, increasing rates of addiction and crime, pollution of environment, overcrowding in cities, all lead to the hypothesis of a diminishing quality of human life. There is evidence to indicate that the escalation of negative human qualities is based in part on a decline of parental availability and investment, e.g., the disintegrating circumstances of extended families, nuclear families and marriage. If this assessment is at all accurate, then it is *quality parenting of fewer children* rather than scattersite parenting of ever more children that is at a premium. What is to be gained by an unremitting production of ambivalently-held or unwanted children whose fundamental entitlement to a caring welcome is violated from the outset? If it can be argued that the fetus too has rights, can it be asked whether it is *more* or *less* fair to be born unwanted, abused, exploited, and rejected?

By nature, children are detrimentally parentified in their own biological families. Their chances of being thus parentified are likely to increase in adoptive, foster care and group home situations. In response to the lack of a trustworthy parenting environment, the young themselves become mistrustful as well as deprived and narcissistically isolated. Ultimately, they also become extractive and untrustworthy future parents to their own children. In any case, answers are never crystal clear. Whatever the course, there is always a risk. Still, there is no way to circumvent the question: If these are the risks, is adoptive or institutional care really more desirable than giving up a pregnancy?

Contextual theory is far from indifferent to the charges of murder vis-à-vis the implications of abortion or even of contraception. There is no question about the fact that nature intended every animal and therefore every germ cell to unite with its counterpart and develop into a new entity. Interference with that process amounts to an interruption of life's self-propagating potential and is hence akin to death or even murder. Yet the absolutes of a biological ethic that argue for survival under any circumstances are tempered and contradicted by an ethic that focuses on the quality of life. In an ideal world both goals might be equally attainable. But ours is less than an ideal world.

A choice for abortion may or may not be an act of responsibility towards posterity. Producing a new life without parental willingness or ability to care for it amounts to a choice against adult accountability. The choice to reproduce without intention to parent, compounded by a heritage of unaccountability, sets up a predictable pattern of destructive entitlement for the offspring *and* the likelihood that he or she will repeat the pattern. Whether or not a pregnancy is welcome at a feeling level is not the primary question here. Under discussion is a level of intergenerational victimization and exploitation of a prospective mother or father that has rendered them indifferent to the welfare of another human being. Intergenerational victimization and exploitation desperately need to be addressed in its prevailing form; but why at the cost of still unborn generations?

Contextual concern is always directed at interventions that can create a responsible context around every child. Its goals are no different here (Cotroneo & Krasner, 1977). Consider the woman whose struggle to make a decision about her unwanted pregnancy involved complex issues that outweighed her anxieties about abortion. The therapeutic process was focused on the issue of fair and responsible consideration for the fetus as well as for the host of other actors in the cast:

Julia, 29, is pregnant and is in the process of getting divorced. She has a two-year-old daughter but previous to that pregnancy, she had had an abortion. Even five years ago, she wasn't sure if she could stay married to John who always drank more than he could handle. She's living with Bob now, and he drinks a lot, too. What is worse, he is a medical resident and has access to drugs. She is afraid he will wind up like his father, a pharmacist and alcoholic who takes a lot of drugs as well. Julia's parents divorced about 12 years ago. Her mother got tired of being abused and just decided to leave. After that, her father broke down and spent six months in a mental hospital. He lives a couple of blocks away with her younger brother now, but Julia never visits them. Men confuse her; she does not know what they want. Besides, her father remarried and has two daughters by that wife. He treats them better than he ever treated her. He does not curse them all the time or threaten to throw them out of the house. As far as she is concerned, he is "a typical wino," and she has decided to write him off. On the other hand Bob is a typical "Italian prince." Isn't there anything in between?

Julia is very close to her mom but thinks that she is much more like her dad. He always had trouble finding a job. She has trouble with that, too. She wants to be an actress but that is such "an impractical goal." Right now she is a waitress on a night shift. She has a baby sitter for Meg; Bob takes care of her the rest of the time. How would she take care of another baby? She can hardly take care of Meg. Bob is threatening to leave her if she has an abortion. He will not come into therapy: "He says the problem is with me". He also says that his parents will raise the baby if Julia does not want it: "But I couldn't bear that," she insists. "What would that mean for my life- and the baby's? He wouldn't really have a mother, and they would raise him the same way they raised Bob."

When Julia came into therapy, she wanted help in deciding what to do about her life. She was sorry she was pregnant and reluctant to have another abortion. She suffered with the questions of whether fetuses have a soul and whether God could forgive her act. An even more pressing question seemed to be whether she could expect a man to have a soul.

There was little question of resources in this family. While her financial circumstances were very limited, Julia had welfare as an option as well as Bob's support. She had also decided to confide in her mother and her mother's male friend. Her mother had helped her through her other pregnancies and would, Julia was sure, be helpful now. At an overt level, Julia had few illusions about what her options were and little self-deceit: If she chose for abortion, she was going to "take a life." She already suffered because she could not take the sacraments at church. Did she want to see an understanding priest? Yes, she thought that would help. Could she consider the thought of a forgiving God? Yes, she would like to think that was so. But she knew she would carry guilt. "That happened the last time, too, and the only thing that had helped that guilt was giving birth to Meg."

For Julia, the two pressing issues in her life were Meg and men. On the one hand, her mother felt that Julia could make it with another child "like the rest of us did." But did not Julia owe Meg something more? Did Meg have to grow up like Julia, always second to everyone else's needs? If, in 15 years from now, it was Meg who was pregnant, Julia would tell her to do what was good for her; she wanted the best for her kid. Who wanted the best for Julia?

And then there was the question of men. Her father obviously did not care for her even in little ways. John and Bob always seemed to want to live life on their terms, never on hers. Sometimes she thought that they were both kids themselves, and she was supposed to be their mother. She was in constant mourning over being abandoned; but did she have to abandon herself in order to keep a man? Couldn't she ever have things her way for a change? Wasn't she worth anything just the way she was? What did a relationship with a man really require of a woman? Was having a child the only thing that really counted for them? And *what* if the baby was a boy? She was not ready for that!

Julia eventually decided to have an abortion. Was the decision self-validating? Was she opting to give priority to her two-year-old who had precious little of her mother's time and energy as it now stood? Was she protecting the fetus against future indifference, insufficient care or even abuse? To what degree was she acting out of destructive entitlement? To what extent was the fetus a victim of the exploitation and indifference with which Julia had been treated by men? For that matter, to what degree did Julia use pregnancy as a way of getting back at men?

Here, as elsewhere, the intricacies of the situation were both delicate and demanding for the therapist. Here, as elsewhere, it was not the therapist's bias or prediction of what was best for Julia that would be at play. It was the therapist's capacity to be multidirectional that could help Julia make a decision that might eventually be healing and life-giving: mother, father, brothers, half-sisters, stepmother, ex-husband, paramour, in-laws, her previous abortion, church, Meg, the fetus, and Julia were all significant actors here. Consciously, Julia knew that becoming pregnant when she didn't want to raise any more children was detrimental to her own best interests. She also knew that she wanted a trusting relationship with a man. Whether or not Julia can find the courage and energy to invest in building trust with a man remains an open question. She left therapy the week she was to try to open dialogue with her father.

It is a multidirectional assessment of resources, not powers of prophecy, that is being called for here. Latent or belated decisions for responsible parenting may always be evoked. Helping a prospective mother or father face into a fetus' best interests is a way of holding parents accountable. What alternative options exist in cases like the one in which a woman and her paramour are involved in a court action against them by the Children's Aid Society?

Her husband-to-be has admitted to putting her child in an oven and in a bathtub with water so hot that the little boy's skin simply stripped away. The man has asked not to be left in charge of the child but the boy's mother insists on going to church to sing in the choir at least three times a week. Now she is pregnant by this man. She takes no responsibility for her part in leaving him in charge of her child. She has no plans to change her own nightly agenda. She is furious, however, at the Children's Aid Society and at the court-mandated therapist who, she says, are trying to take her baby away.

In instances like these, a therapist is duty-bound to ask if it is in the fetus' interests to exist at all. Is it only the parent's need or wish that deserves consideration? Similar questions may be asked when hereditary illnesses are in a parent's background, e.g., Huntington's disease. Is it fair to produce children whose predisposition to a devastating illness is estimated at fifty percent? Conversely, is it fair for potential parents to have to refrain from having children? Does existence itself entitle adults to the right, however destructive, to dismiss crucial issues that have an impact on their child's destiny?

CHAPTER 21

Other Applications of Contextual Therapy

TERMINAL ILLNESS

Terminal illness is a precursor of death, a conclusive separation between the generations. It is an occasion for mourning and for anticipated grief. It is also an opportunity to tap the resources of everyone involved. The prospect of loss through death can be converted into a stimulus for reassessment and reconnections between people who, up until now, have been stuck in relationships marked by cutoffs and resentment.

In its classical sense, the process of mourning deals with a person's anger and frustration over the loss of a relationship. Here the term "loss" encompasses separation from the dying or dead person and from the relational context and patterns connected to that person. Of course, life itself is marked by constant losses defined by lesser separations. In this sense, a person's mastery over mourning lost relationships from infancy to life's end represents psychic growth. Freud suggested that the road to emotional maturity leads through a graveyard of abandoned relationships. Relational loss occurs right from the beginning when a baby is weaned from the mother—the price of independence.

The prospect of dying alters people's relational routines and usually opens them up to different patterns of give-and-take. It attunes them to the fact that certain options for giving will close permanently, e.g., exploring the childhood circumstances of the dying person. It forces an awareness that now is the time to do what will otherwise remain undone. In contextual work, that translates into an evaluation of what possibilities still exist for balancing certain ledgers and for trust-building, that is, for healing. There may yet be time for offspring to learn about their parent's childhood victimization, to establish a basis to understand and exonerate her from whatever destructive images are still there. Offers of care and consideration to a dying person ease the grief work of the surviving person and diminish his or her tendencies towards experiencing guilt, and more.

> In some cases, a dying parent's children discover a new chance to explore their own ledgers with each other. A brother and sister made separate attempts to settle their accounts with their dying father. The two siblings had not talked to each other for several years. However, in the process of tending to their father, they uncovered their linkages to each other, and began to connect again. In another situation, a 48-year-old man suddenly suffered paralysis in his right arm, symptom of a rapidly growing, inoperable cancer. He lost interest in his business and clung to the meaning brought to his life by his two sons, 11 and 8. The man and his wife had been divorced for some time. Still there was talk of his going "home" to die. His former wife chose against that option, though, citing the severity of his condition and the demanding nursing procedures.
> The children were horrified. They wanted to do something for their father. The therapist asked if there were any ways in which the children could help. For example, were their mother to take her former husband in, could she enlist the children in nursing him? Her boys immediately enumerated all the things they might do. Could their mother reconsider bringing their father home? In one session, family members could help each other surface their deepest longings and conflicts, find an option, and bring some relief to the dying man. They prepared to bring him home. In the meantime, he took a turn for the worse and lost consciousness. The actual reunion never took place. But his sons had actually offered him care, and so had their mother.

The family's offers of care earned all of their members entitlement and eased the pangs of their mourning on a lasting basis.

The early death of a parent represents a definitive loss to a child. It is a serious deprivation but should not be defined as a "betrayal" on the part of the dying parent. At best, this kind of formulation can only be described as a psychological metaphor. In reality, no one dies to deprive his child. In any case, the young may suffer the loss of their parent's trustworthiness as well as the loss of the parent herself. In addition, he may have to endure a change in his surviving parent's personality and attitudes. Visible loyalty to his dead parent may turn invisible, and show in an overt or covert rejection of the surviving parent or, later, stepparent.

The youngster's guilt feelings play a big part in the mourning task, so preventive interventions are the most effective strategy. A child's active contributions to a dying parent always diminish guilt and ease the process of grief work.

The terminally ill child stands at the opposite end of the spectrum from the terminally ill parent. Here is young potential, unfulfilled and unfulfillable, and bringing trauma to parents who didn't bring children into the world to have them die. Still, the terminally ill child, like other dying people, needs to *give* to others as well as receive from them. Ordinarily, it is assumed that the adult world is indebted to a sick child who is the rightful recipient of her parents' love and care. But what parents are less depleted than the terminally ill child herself? What if her resources for trust and life are more available than her parents'? Death has prematurely descended on the family in which parents are too worn down to give, while an ill child is forbidden to give. On the other hand, the youngster might be invited to express his concern and care for his parents at precisely the point where their pain will wound and drain him.

Distance can never do the work of dialogue and with a dying child or adult there simply will not be another chance. Like the rest of us, the terminally ill need the option to earn entitlement and the freedom and dignity that come of offering other people care.

MENTAL HEALTH AND ILLNESS

Since its inception, family therapy has stressed the relational nature of mental health and illness rather than its individual quality. The sharp ''either-or'' stance between the individual and relational systems points of view is unwarranted, though, and really requires a more balanced stance. None of us is in a position to make scientific statements about causation. None of us knows to what degree psychosis is caused by biological factors. No therapist can afford to omit relational leverages for helping individuals who are labeled mentally ill. This broad relational guideline for mental health incorporates individually defined principles as well. A healthy, well-functioning person is capable of emotional expression and social achievement as well as of self-actualization. It is the socially self-isolating person who suffers from symptoms of feeling observed or persecuted, or tends to hear voices.

Resources for helping lie in a trustworthy, responsible investigation into the sources of harm and detriment suffered by any family member. Harm and detriment, in our view, evolve from intergenerational destinies as well as from an individual's psychic structures and from here-and-now relational transactions. Furthermore, a person's mental health is inseparable

from his or her responsibility for how posterity is affected by the consequences of the actions of preceding generations. Any overt or covert form
of the present generation's serious exploitation of posterity's children can
never be classified as evidence of mental health. To the contrary. A lack
of remorse over harming innocent people signals destructive entitlement
rather than mental health and is a major source of pathological behavior.
On the other hand, people's constructive capacity to earn entitlement
stands at the heart of transgenerational solidarity. It is the relational basis
of mentally healthy individuals and of humanity as a whole.

Depression

Depression is one of the classical diagnostic-nosological entities of psychiatry. Its essence is a depressed, lowered state of mood combined with
an inclination for feelings of hopelessness, failure and self-blame. It represents a phase of defective, narcissistic personality development with a
characteristic inclination towards a lack of empathy for the feelings of
others.

From a contextual vantage point, the syndrome of depression resembles
a lowered *sense* of entitlement. By definition, rigid attitudes of self-blame,
held in the face of contrary evidence, signal an inadequate sense of entitlement. So do a sense of worthlessness and corresponding suicidal ideas.
In a similar vein, a person's inability to enjoy life's pleasures often coincides with the belief that he or she doesn't deserve any enjoyment.

A depressed person sinks ever deeper into narcissistic preoccupation
with his own pain and helplessness, losing the capacity to duly consider
other people's suffering. The failure to care for anyone but himself actually
disentitles him, rendering him unable to validate himself and disinclined
to earn constructive entitlement. How is he to accumulate merit or to be
credited, then, if he makes no investment in any relationship?

From a contextual vantage point, the development of a state of disentitlement is easily linked to a long-term pattern of narcissistic, self-centered
character formation. A narcissistic person, callous, remorseless and without empathy, is likely to rely on previously earned destructive entitlement
in any case. Overentitlement even deprives him of the urge or inclination
to try to earn entitlement in a constructive way. Small wonder, then, that
his behavior is unilateral and exploitative in all of his relationships, and
that he finds himself disentitled.

Depression occurs at the point of imbalance, that is, at the moment that
the ledger of a person's own past victimization tilts and slides under the
impact of the injustices that he is now inscribing into the ledgers of
his current relationships. In simpler terms, once he was chiefly a victim;
now he is chiefly a victimizer. How can he accept his victimizing self?

From a therapeutic perspective, destructively entitled people require two basic interventions: 1) fair acknowledgement of their own past victimization, and 2) a demand that they give due regard and consideration to how their patterns of relating exploit and victimize other people. Point two dovetails with the traditional, clinical observation that a depressed person is helped more by expectations that he apply himself to redeeming tasks than by consoling or pampering him. This therapeutic plan is difficult to implement in the face of adamant resistance and tough challenges to the therapist's persistence. Nevertheless, therapeutic efforts to nudge a depressed person towards the task of earning entitlement may lessen the risk of suicide even when they do not lead to any positive, behavioral change.

Relational Work with Psychotic Family Members: A Rationale

The meaning of the word "psychosis" has lost much of its initial, fatal connotation. It has moved closer to being a synonym for schizophrenia even though terms like psychotic depression and organic psychosis survive and prevail. In its generic sense, psychosis amounts to faulty reality testing, thought disorders, delusions, and hallucinations, as well as to regressed, disorganized, irresponsible, and irrational behavior.

Psychotic patterns of behavior were found to fit family role patterns and often to caricature them. It would be a gross misrepresentation, though, to view psychosis as some kind of game or transactional ploy. There is an aspect of psychosis that is primary and involuntary, whether on a biological or characterological basis. The beginning therapist does well to refrain from manipulative, "therapeutic" strategies here. He is dealing with a deeply hurt human being who is also endowed with profound if residual humanity despite apparently bizarre behavior. Game playing that risks a therapist's trustability may lead to a worsening condition of the psychotic's mistrust and, in certain cases, to suicide.

The psychotic (schizophrenic) person represents more than a failure in human adaptation. He or she may reflect the absurd, intrinsically contradictory and unavoidably exploitative aspects of life. He or she is also hungry for trustworthiness, a universal human need. A psychotic person may use power advantages, hatred and ruthless, insensitive competition to reflect how victimized he has been. Yet he may also be in quest of human solidarity. At times, the psychotic may be a self-destructively overloyal family member or a naive seeker of truth. Outwardly, he may be unable to trust anyone; inwardly he may long for a fair and rewarding exchange. Whatever the situation, a psychotic person does poorly if tested through tricks. Therapists who specialize in the treatment of schizophrenia insist that a psychotic person's trust inclinations are never to be betrayed.

The psychotic person's weak ego lacks the trust reserves on which he might rely in the face of dishonest manipulations. Therapists do well to vent their frustration, disappointment or despair directly and candidly to their patients rather than try to manipulate them.

From a psychological vantage point (Dimension II), the therapist who treats psychotics faces two difficult tiers of consideration:

- Fragility of self-structures, fragmented self-experience, unpredictable swings of emotions, perforated self-boundaries, defensive splitting and denial mechanisms, e.g., projections, projective identifications and inappropriate affect among others. These signs of severe injury are indications that psychotics are poor candidates for insight-based therapy.
- Rigid internal patterns of relating that have substituted for interpersonal relating. Object relations theories (Fairbairn, 1952; Guntrip, 1961) are highly relevant to understanding psychotics. Internal relationships may manifest themselves as paranoid delusion, hallucinated internal voices and experiences of being influenced, among other expressions. Psychotics themselves may attest to the value of these relationships. For example, "I like my voices; I can count on them when I need them" (Hollender & Boszormenyi-Nagy, 1958).

The relational formulations of the object relations theorists seemed to offer a new perspective for helping schizophrenics. No striking breakthrough has occurred. Still, it can be argued that the family relations approach is more promising than any other form of help to schizophrenics. It was the application of the object relations perspective to the therapy of schizophrenics that originally led Boszormenyi-Nagy to develop a family therapy approach in the late 1950s.

The classical era of individual therapy for psychotics yielded invaluable clues. Several therapists recognized that their patients needed nurturant love, trustworthiness and consistent guidance (Fromm-Reichmann, 1948; Sullivan, 1947; Sechehaye, 1956; Will, 1958). Their therapeutic guidelines resembled those of Kohut (1977) who advised therapists to offer to self-fragmented, narcissistic clients the empathy that they should have received from their parents in early childhood. Like Kohut, Rogers (1951) thought that therapists owed their clients substitutive parenting in the form of "unconditional, positive regard." In our view, however, it is questionable to presume that therapists are privy to such vast supplies or reserves of empathic giving, nurturing attitudes and offerings.

One of the premises of classical Freudian therapy is cure by resolution of transference to the therapist. This premise was rooted in assumptions that all neurotic pathology (including unrealistic relating patterns) hinge on archaic, regressive, intrapsychic configurations and attachments (cathexis). These archaic internal patterns, usually hidden in unconscious trends, fantasies and avoidance maneuvers, interfere with realistic interpersonal relating. The therapist is able to bring these relational patterns to the client's attention as they repeat themselves in transference. If a patient has sufficient ego strength for self-reflection, he or she will eventually face and presumably revise the repetitious internal patterning. It is clear that Freud's transference model of therapy was based on an artificial recreation of the family relational context. It is also clear that it was safer for the client (and for the therapist?) to address these patterns by means of transference to the therapist, a safe partner with whom to experiment, than to directly address his or her family members. Yet this process is a difficult one, even in the neurotic or nonpsychotic patient.

All people are not suitable for the analytic process. The suitable candidate has an ego strong enough to be led to confront his outdated and anachronistic infantile patterns. Even so, he is reluctant to let his need formula be converted to the wave lengths of mature and adultlike relationships. Attempts to work through insight are met with a barrage of resistances. Indeed, the demands of working through have been compared with the work of mourning; adopting a desirable change requires the renunciation of the long-held relationships with the internal partner. To give up the archaic pattern resembles the loss of a loved one through death. These considerations apply to neurotics. For whatever reasons psychotic people seem to be even more rigidly conservative about internal patterns than neurotics and other people.

Contextual theory and therapy began its evolution as a challenge to the classical, individual therapeutic approach to schizophrenics. The nucleus resided in the newly discovered force of intrinsic family solidarity. It became apparent that family members struggle with more than their own resistances in their efforts to change their relational patterns. They also tend to protect each other from the pain of losing the old pattern and exchanging it for the new. This "collusive postponement of mourning" (Boszormenyi-Nagy, 1965b) eventually led to the discovery of significant dynamics of invisible loyalties between family members (Boszormenyi-Nagy, 1972; Boszormenyi & Spark, 1973).

It became increasingly obvious that the shift from working with individuals to working with family members provided new resources for the treatment of psychotics. For one thing, it was now easier to develop the trust base for a therapeutic alliance, and the rigidity of persistent "pathology" obviously yielded more, and more easily. What could be a more natural arena for facing archaically formative, infantile relationship patterns than the family, especially as people mix with more mature person-to person patterns. In addition, family sessions *per se* often incorporate both the self and the original partner of the self's internal and external relationship. What could be more natural and effective than for them to jointly relive and validate each other's archaic self-object (Kohut, 1977) patterns of relating, and to help one another gradually work out new patterns? Here the threshold for mourning work has been lowered: First of all, the original partners are available to each other and hence only the patterns have to be changed. Then, the transference operates primarily among family members who can be guided by a therapist.

Therapy with Psychotic Persons

Individually-oriented therapists tried to modify Freudian therapeutic principles and apply them to psychotic patients. The recognition that direct reliance on the psychotic client's ego strength was unproductive led therapists to empathic, nurturant and sometimes patronizing approaches. Therapists now had to offer something in advance to draw their clients out of hibernation. Direct, linear efforts at "individuating" the psychotic turned out to be inadvisable and too risky. It is counterproductive to try to emancipate the young adult or adolescent psychotic forcibly without regard to his invisible loyalties to the family, or to turn them against their parents as if their parents were in fact their enemies. It is also counterproductive simply to condition the psychotic patient to drop his annoying symptom(s) so that he can be declared cured, and so terminated.

In sum, our experience shows that over one-third of psychotic clients react favorably to relationally-based therapy. Others reach a balance between their passion for truth and justice, and their ongoing destructive entitlement. If they are talented, some may turn into creative artists or intellectuals. Others simply continue their day-to-day struggle in a fragile compromise between sharp insights and shyness.

How much the psychotic personality can be liberated and isolated from its malfunctioning side depends on the individual case. Frequently, psychotic people turn out to be better parents than their overall performance would suggest. A partially recovered psychotic mother may not be able to offer her children too much in the way of mature care. She will probably need assistance and supervision on crucial points in reality. On the other hand, she may be sensitive to any injustice that may threaten to victimize her young.

In work with psychotics as well as with other people, a key practical question about relational therapy based on a resource orientation has to do with how genuine the family members' commitment to therapy may be. Can the therapist motivate them to invest the necessary effort and good faith in a joint enterprise? Obviously, the enterprise needs to be shaped to fit everyone's goals. All participating members need help with the process, and all must be made aware of how they will benefit in exchange for their commitment to doing therapeutic work. They might be encouraged to see that, at minimum, their contributions to the needy psychotic member will earn them their own entitlement.

Therapy usually has to overcome family resistance. Family members are often invested in the notion that one person's illness has nothing to do with the condition of the rest of the family. This obstacle can frequently be overcome by the therapist's assurance that the goal of family-based therapy is not intended to judge, fault or blame anyone. The purpose of therapy is to locate effective joint leverages rather than to fix causal responsibility. A source of further resistance may then be the psychotic person's renewed insistence on his or her destructive entitlement.

In essence, therapeutic work with psychotics has to rely on existing pockets of residual trustability. Therapists utilize these pockets but do not have to create them. They originate from our common humanity, from the gain that each of us receives from due consideration of another person's needs. Erikson (1959) stated that adults are motivated to fulfill the criteria of generativity to meet their own developmental needs. Thus, at a certain stage of maturation, a person benefits from offering care and is ready for the task of parenting. It follows that an individual personally gains more if he does something for a needy, troubled relative than if he does nothing at all. It may be that the success of early family therapy was rooted in this human propensity. If so, it defies the linear logic that people gain through a callous disregard for those in trouble. The dialectic of receiving through giving transcends a simple, self-serving, unilateral possessiveness.

Pockets of a psychotic person's residual trustability may gradually unfold in the process of therapy. A person may continue to be destructively entitled, but the therapist may still be able to identify and credit his invisible loyalty and care, such as:

- His devotion and concern for his sick father;
- His deep longing to establish a loving, caring relationship;
- His devoted availability to his needy or anxious mother;
- His parentlike care of his depressed father at bedtime;
- His invisible loyalty that protects other family members via his symptomatic role.

We suggest that the language of relational integrity and fairness offers the best chance of breaking through psychotic obstacles to communication; it is most likely to be heard by the withdrawn schizophrenic. He may stop using his bizarre language, at least for a brief period of time. He may hear how he was parentified as a child and how available he has been to other family members in their times of need—and he may respond. For their part, family members may discover options for a new distribution of their own benefits and burdens. They may become more open to voicing their convictions and become freer to consult with each other.

The issue of psychotropic drugs raises many additional questions here. On balance, our view is that they are clearly worth trying. If a tranquilizer can allay a psychotic person's anxieties, it makes sense to use it. On the other hand, a constant use of drugs can result in prolonged reliance. Other psychotic clients claim they derive no benefit from tranquilizers. It is their sense, instead, that the drugs bind their minds like a rope or make them feel unnatural or unlike themselves. In some cases, people develop deep resentments over having to take these medications. In any case, definitive evidence does not yet exist. Some people can work in therapy under medication; some people gain little or no help from it.

MENTAL RETARDATION

Individually-oriented psychotherapists traditionally have had little motivation to work in the area of mental retardation. It is a condition whose essence is often anchored in physiological changes in the brain or on structural or chemical brain damage that makes it inaccessible to psychotherapy. From a relational vantage point, some creative possibilities exist despite one person's decisive limits. Here the retarded person is viewed as a resource, as well as a burden, for the caretaking relatives. In fact, he or she represents a classical illustration of the redemptive potential of earned entitlement.

The seriously retarded person is effectively in a deadend. His own prospect for a rewarding future is constricted and his prospects for parenting are virtually nonexistent. His parents are in a continuing state of mourning, their dreams for their living child's future as obliterated as if he were dead. His very presence is a reminder of their own "failure" and prolongs the mourning process which is unending.

His family is usually frustrated by the task of caring for the retarded child's needs. Nevertheless, he remains a source of relational benefits since he is often warmly devoted to his family members and wants to help and contribute to them. Family members may fail to recognize this aspect of the retarded child's personality and may even discourage it through their anger, shame, irritation, and impatience. They may also be bound by guilt. After all, who is really responsible for the care of the retarded member? By a process of elimination, the task usually falls to mother. If this is the case, the rest of the family continuously operates under the challenge of mustering good team cooperation. At the very least, can the parents cooperate? Can siblings sometimes subordinate their own need for support and convert themselves into assistant parents?

The rest of the family is at psychological risk; they carry a high likelihood of turning angry and resentful. They are also liable to accumulate destructive entitlement. Yet, taking their feelings out *on* the retarded member carries a very high price. The injustice of this kind of choice undermines the perpetrator's actual entitlement. Taking one's feelings out can be an act of dumping accumulated impulses on a helpless, retarded sibling, a cruel and subtle means of destructively parentifying him. It is also a damaging way of parentifying the family member who tries to protect the family underdog. On the other hand, family members can help each other earn entitlement through cooperative and effective teamwork on behalf of the retarded child.

Even when family members get a return on their concern for their retarded member, it is unlikely to be symmetrical. But the very asymmetry of the situation is what makes it especially suited for earning entitlement. Learning to rely on constructive rather than destructive entitlement in difficult situations is also in the vested interests of every family member. In addition to undeniable self-validation, it can be defined as preparation for generative activity in their future parenting.

SCHOOL-RELATED PROBLEMS

A child's poor school performance commonly motivates a family to seek therapy. Its causes are numerous, of course, and need to be explored in terms of the many loyalty conflicts that can underlie learning or behavioral problems at school. School usually constitutes a small child's first commitment outside of the family. To that point, no one but the family normally has had jurisdiction over a child. Now a teacher steps in and lays a claim for obedience and trust.

Sometimes parents have overt and specific objections to a school's leadership or policies. These may have to do with class, racial, ethnic, or religious prejudice. Parental objections may have an element of reality in some instances, but they may also be based on parental rivalry. The more possessively inclined the parents, the more they will experience the school's invasion of the child's life as competitive. Overtly or covertly, the child gets caught in the middle. For example, the parents may be critical of teachers and make open comments within a youngster's earshot, while the teachers may imply that the child has been misguided at home. In the midst of these collisions, the child will cling to his ultimate priority, i.e., loyalty to her family, but may evidence how caught she is through failing school and misbehaving while in it.

School phobia is a condition that frequently occurs in conscientious, scholastically capable students. Efforts to force a fearful child to go to and stay in school can lead to hostile, belligerent outbursts which are generally linked to the parents' relational mistrust and despair. Here the child is implicitly parentified and invisibly loyal to his parents' caveats against trusting or investing in ANYONE. School phobia can last for years. Whenever it is presented in therapy, it constitutes an emergency by virtue of its irreversible waste of valuable options for learning. Paradoxically, if a therapist is forceful enough to mobilize the parents and help them decide on a cooperative plan of action, the child can usually return to school to stay within a week or two. This can be so even in cases of many years' duration. On the hand, the condition requires prolonged, family-based therapy to help the parents rework their own serious problems.

Extreme, provocative behavior at school most frequently constitutes a child's signal for help. Total rejection of the teacher's authority, or violent or sexual acts committed in public can indicate rather dangerous conditions in the youngster's family. The parents' lives together may be totally stagnant through mutual fear. They may threaten each other with serious violence, or incest may be a family secret. One parent may protect the child against the other. Or the youngster may be used as a weapon in the struggle between his parents. Whatever the manifestations of danger, a courageous therapeutic exploration is in order. Searching out the inner patterns of a family's life is the first step towards deparentifying the child.

It is unwise to see school-phobic children alone. Their parents' participation is an important aspect of treatment just because their parentification of their child and the child's signal behavior converge. Therapy is designed to explore the situations in which the child is caught in the adults' conflicts and mistrustful attitudes. In addition, the therapist can offer to be helpful to school personnel. She can facilitate helpful communication between school principals, administrators, counselors, teachers, and the parents.

SUICIDE PREVENTION

Suicide is caused by many factors. There are times that life realities genuinely justify a person's surrender of his or her will to live, e.g., progressive, incurable pain and debilitating disease. On the other hand, the connection between depression and suicide is less clear. There is no known way to predict the likelihood of suicide in a person. A therapist may suspect her client's suicidal inclinations, however. She does well to ask him about it rather than to gloss over the possibility, especially since a sense of isolation and abandonment are concomitants to despair. It is always safer to err on the side of unnecessary caution than to seem ignorant, indifferent or timid. Furthermore, relational exploration is always a potential resource for the suicidally endangered person. To treat him on a totally individual basis, as if the therapist were his sole resource, amounts to malpractice.

Suicide in a child or adolescent is usually linked to his sense of being trapped in an unsolvable riddle. This entrapment is characterized by both a growing sense of disentitlement and by destructive overentitlement. Consider the case of the eldest of five children.

Paul's parents were in their forties and financially well off. But they had long been at war with each other. Father was away a lot and it was common family knowledge that he was involved in an affair. Mother cried often and turned to Paul for consolation. He was a perfect boy, she said, always there for her. He sometimes wished that his father would talk to him. But he knew that silence was his father's way. He also knew that father had suffered a lot in his own family of origin where no one ever talked about their struggles either.

Like any youngster caught in a predicament of split loyalty, Paul was placed in the role of compensating for his parents' failure to build a trust base between them. At 16, he was faced with an urgent but unmanageable task. He tried one thing after another, improving on his own designs; yet every one of them was a hopeless failure. Neither parent budged. His manifest, one-sided loyalty to his mother cancelled out the immediate possibility of establishing a trustworthy relationship with his father. Inevitably, Paul felt his parents' disapproval and, at times, their insinuated blame for not being able to right the situation. Finally he took some pills prescribed for him by his father's psychiatrist, and left this suicide note:

Dear Mom,
    Yes, you are right. I am far from perfect. But I have found the solution.
                                      Love, Paul

Paul was wedged between his feuding parents. He functioned as his mother's confidant and, until his death, repeatedly made desperate attempts to heal the mistrust between his parents.

ADDICTIONS

Excessive reliance on alcohol or other chemically addictive substances usually has a basis in destructive entitlement. The addicted person seems to be insensitive or immune to feelings of remorse over harming himself or others. A capacity to establish trustworthy relationships is replaced by reliance on chemical stimuli and by negative relationship patterns. Substance abuse resembles suicide in many ways, and can also evolve from a heritage of split loyalty and the user's attempts to restore trust to his parents' relationship.

An addicted person may have a cynical or callous response to therapeutic efforts. But even the most destructively entitled addict was once a devoted, giving person until she reached the critical point of depletion and despair. Under these circumstances, a therapist's most effective option is to reach back to the past, acknowledge the addictive person's contributions to his or her family, and so take a first step towards establishing a therapeutic contract. The therapist's next step may be to help the addict's family members acknowledge something positive in the past at least, if not in the present.

In cases in which an addict is a parent of young children, still another leverage is open to the therapist: She may address the addict at the level of his concern for the future, even if that concern is presently dormant. A chronic drunk who cares little about his liver may still want to spare the feelings of his little son. The last therapeutic resource may lie in the dialectic of a person's willingness to earn entitlement through caring for his child.

CHRONIC PHYSICAL ILLNESS

Chronic illness always tests the trustworthiness of family relationships. The sick member tends to feel as if she is an innocent victim who is inflicting inconvenience on others as well. She is also likely to feel that she has been committed to an "unjust" fate and has no one to blame. Therefore, she is entitled to be destructive. On the other hand, she desperately needs other people's helpful consideration. It would be completely unfair, then, for her to take her resentment out on the very people she needs to help her.

Transactional-systemic family therapists are rightfully concerned with the "power of helplessness," that is, the nature and extent of the sick person's manipulative leverages. This manipulative leverage is also an issue for contextual therapists who primarily focus on the ethical rather than the transactional dimension. Here, manipulation is linked to the chronically ill person's actual helplessness that then gives rise to destructive entitlement.

The chronically ill child, suffering from hereditary conditions, diabetes, epilepsy, or tumor, may even be more destructively entitled than the sick adult. Healthy children discriminate against him; he is left out of activities that other kids pursue and he has to follow unwelcome diet and medication régimes. The illness itself may further parentify the sick child by its demand for discipline, e.g., the need to watch his blood or urinary sugar levels and take appropriate measures. He is not only frustrated and deprived but expected to display adult responsibility and discipline. From the vantage point of distributive justice, destiny has dealt him a rotten hand.

Contextual work will help the family explore their ledgers with the member who is ill. A therapist will encourage family members to credit each other where credit is due. He will help the well members take hold of the fact that supporting the sick person is also a way of validating themselves. Finding ways to care about the needs and problems of the rest of the family will also help the chronically ill person earn his own entitlement. It will serve to prevent a chronic state of disentitlement from developing in the sick person.

SEXUAL IDENTITY AND FUNCTION

From a psychological vantage point, sexual identity is an important part of the overall identity and strength of the self. Sexual function is usually influenced by the nature of the person's felt sexual identity. Yet gender identity is also relationally determined. Heterosexual partners aid each other's gender identity by their perceptions and appreciation of mutual difference. The nature of this perception may vary. Men, for example, may rely more on visual clues, women on evidence of male attentiveness or caring. Gender identity and the vicissitudes of sexual function become important determinants of a person's reproductive prospects.

The prospects of reproduction are strongly determined by a person's intergenerational relationships. Intergenerational relating is a continuing dialogue whose consequences intertwine with the offspring's dialogues with his or her peers. Powerful injunctions about sexual identity and function issue forth from our families of origin. Some of them are overt or the outcome of direct parental delegation. Others are embodied in the offspring's invisible loyalty. A woman whose mother is lacking affect and is cold may turn out to be sexually frigid or incompetent. On the other hand, a seriously ambivalent relationship between mother and daughter that is steeped in resentment may be expressed by the daughter's reluctance to have sex with her husband even though she is estranged from her mother.

A peer-related commitment is implicitly competitive with a person's commitment to his family of origin and therefore may be deemed to be intrinsically disloyal. This conclusion applies to sexuality as well as to any other relational realm. A therapist always needs to examine the degree to which sexual commitment is regulated by a loyalty dynamic. Paradoxically, since heterosexual relationship in marriage is the most socially supported form of peer commitment, it can also be the major source of covertly alleged, filial disloyalty.

Invisible filial loyalty that eschews peer commitments is characterized by the following phenomena, among others. They appear in a descending order of reproductive competence:

- Sexual difficulties in marriage;
- Separation and divorce;
- Remaining childless;
- Failure to marry but maintaining heterosexual friendships;
- Bisexuality;
- Homosexuality;
- Asexuality.

Invisible filial loyalty that inhibits parenthood is characteristically less than a constructive goal. It usually fails to command a genuine, legacy-based option for earning entitlement. It can also combine with a lowered sense of entitlement.

In cases in which invisibly loyal offspring have children, it is helpful for them to understand their options for earning entitlement through accountable parenting. They also need to explore options for exonerating their parent rather than blindly continuing to protect him or her. Only so can therapeutic interventions begin to reverse the trend set by the young who are constructing their sexual identity and function at an ever more apparently inhibited pace.

SURVIVORS

The modern era has found no way to eliminate the catastrophes of attempted genocide and widespread human carnage. The Nazi holocaust, Stalin's large-scale efforts at extermination, and the massacre of up to 50 percent of the Cambodian population are but three examples that are difficult to forget or ignore. The survivors of human carnage and eventually their descendants inherit weighty legacies that impose different burdens on different generations.

The survivors themselves have paid an enormous price in suffering and life's lost opportunities. Despite the enormity of the cost, most manage to make a new start. They may have established a new family and raised children, apparently like every one else. But survivors *are* usually overentitled both because of their actual suffering and because of their extraordinary efforts to overcome difficulties that are larger than life-size. On the other hand, they suffer feelings of indebtedness to those who were unjustly killed even though the fact that people perished is obviously not their fault.

Appropriate or not, survivors characteristically feel more obligated than people who have lesser claims to entitlement in life. There are often inescapable feelings of indebtedness to:

- Those who have perished;
- Their group for its future survival;
- Posterity, through the survivors' efforts not to burden their young with manifestations of destructive entitlement;
- Humanity, through a continuing personal witness to the horrors and realities of the carnage.

Often, the parent who survives does not want to burden the offspring with knowledge of his or her experience. Therapists may too quickly or easily take this disinclination to be a neurotic or defensive symptom and urge the survivor to talk. "It is better for you to surface your feelings" is a natural line for intervening. This kind of approach may be a futile and naive, if well-meaning, effort on the part of the therapist. It is difficult to say whether people who carry such an inhuman, experiential load can really be unburdened simply by talking to people who have not shared their experience.

The survivor's children may be spared the pain of hearing details of their parents' past misery, but they are burdened by their parents' actual overentitlement. Even if they accomplish the highest ordinary goals of life, these offspring can never live up to the superhuman achievement of the survivor parent. This fact automatically imposes a legacy with basic obligations, including:

- To excel;
- To help unburden their parents;
- To actively support the survival of their ethnic, racial or religious group;
- To give the "right" message to humanity;

Here, as always, legacy considerations are our guide to therapeutic goals. The legacy of survivorship demands appropriate action commitments that may help humankind prevent the occurrence of similar mass murders.

VII. THERAPISTS IN CONTEXT

CHAPTER 22

The Making of a Contextual Therapist

THE THERAPIST

The therapist and the client meet in the midst of the latter's misery and need. The therapist's mandate, like that of the traditional physician of Hippocrates' time, is to be worthy of the client's confidence: trustable enough to receive secrets, reliable enough for the client to reveal himself and show his wounds. The therapist invests genuine care, competence, skill and confidentiality in return for the client's implicit investment of trust in the person of the therapist. Reciprocity stands at the very core of their contract and is ample but never symmetrical. The therapist meets his client and reveals himself as a fellow human being. But he neither reveals his own wounds to the same degree as the client nor depends on him for a cure. The therapist-client relationship falls short of the symmetry of friendship, for example. Therapy may provide moments of genuine meeting between two people. Still the degree of investment and the level of expectations between them are alway uneven.

In many ways, a therapist's role is one of a concerned caretaker. As caretaker, he is selectively partial to his client's pain and cause. This selective partiality provides a contrast with the physician who has a simpler, more straightforward role. His partiality to the patient is unconditional. He sides with him against disease and the debilitating forces of nature. This kind of clear and unfettered side-taking is a luxury to the psychotherapist whose partiality *for* one person inevitably makes him temporarily choose *against* another, at least in the short run. For example, when he sides with his client against her marriage, he takes a stand against her husband. When he is partial to a grandfather who is guilt-ridden over incest, he is simultaneously obliged to be partial to the best interests of the grandchildren who have been violated. Whether he sees individuals, couples or families, the psychotherapist is always stuck in the midst of conflicting interests. Under the circumstances, can he really follow the ancient principle that is the baseline of ethical medicine: *nil nocere*—do no harm to anyone?

The nature of therapy's professional ethics is linked to a definition of the therapist's personal qualifications. The therapist as person is always a part of psychotherapy's technology. The therapist is a variable, though, that is the least quantifiable or operational aspect of therapy. The literature of individual therapy is replete with requirements for the therapist's personal maturity. In a contextual view, the test of maturity is measured by a person's individual responsibility for defining her own terms and a fair concern for her partner's terms. The contextually competent therapist is able to convey a profound concern for clients vis-à-vis lived reciprocity—a goal that can be reached only through an improved multilateral stance.

THE THERAPIST'S PERSONAL INPUT

The person of the therapist is his or her principle tool. At the very least, he is a needed authority to whom to talk, a wished for anchor point for security and stability, and a reservoir of trust. A good technician can do his job whether or not he has his client's trust. Not so for the therapist who either earns a trustworthy position or has only a limited and short-lived effect. A therapist offers responsibility, skill, care, and the willingness to open up controversial, painful, shameful, and trying issues, earning trustability in the process. In exchange, he is offered a person's serious investment and monetary recompense for himself or for his agency.

Part of a therapist's usefulness has to do with nonspecific supportive help. This kind of help might also be gained through a sympathetic family member, a caring neighbor, an interested colleague, a bartender, or a member of a support group. But two characteristics differentiate therapeutic support from peer concern and help.

- Clients are able to develop a dependable reliance on therapists who offer security, compassion and competence. This professional relationship is akin to purchased friendship. Inevitably the therapist is parentified in accordance with the specific, idiosyncratic, dependency needs of each participating family member. Part of a client's dependence on a helping agent is an unavoidable practicality; part of it is transferred from unresolved, prior, relational needs.

- Therapists are able to suggest suitable patterns of behavior and so can offer a model for restructuring among family members. In addition a therapist can notice when children are malfunctioning as a result of overburdening adult demands—for example, when parental responsibility is slipping; when marriage partners are so overresponsible that they are deprived of their own pleasures and satisfactions; when medical-pharmacological help needs to be explored through a physician; or when destructive behavior endangers a person or his relatives and requires immediate intervention.

THE THERAPIST'S SPECIFIC INPUT

A therapist's specific, active input is the determining factor of the particular kind of contribution made by any school of psychotherapy. The traditional emphasis on a "psychological" framework in psychotherapy has stressed the therapist's empathic sensitivity and her freedom to experience and recognize affect in herself as well as in her clients. This orientation converges with the psychodynamic hypothesis that therapy's major mechanism is to bring unconscious, emotionally significant configurations to the surface. In other words, the lack of consciousness over these configurations is the most significant stumbling block in a client's maturation. It is also true that a therapist has to be able to pay attention to her client's affective manifestations.

Therapy would be a mistaken occupation if a person were insensitive to other people's suffering. Expressing empathy for people's feelings is an important part of caring, but is a method rather than a goal. Helping to surface a client's pain, frustration, anxiety, and depression is always a significant intervention. But affect is only a clue, an indicator of relational configurations, actions and plans. Consider the following situation which is prototypical of a therapist's early efforts to assess a client's situation:

> From the beginning moments of their work together, the therapist acknowledged Peter's long-term care and concern for his family *and* surfaced evidence of their long-term concern and care for him. She acknowledged the crippling effects of his felt depletion and injuries, and the realities of his loneliness and felt isolation. Early on, she also indicated that Peter stood at a crossroad. Sooner or later he would have to make a choice about how to interpret his feelings. Would they eventually be used to validate *only his* injuries and pain? Or would they also be used as valid indicators of real and perceived injustices that exist between him and the people to whom he remains loyally attached?
> Will Peter use his feelings to justify his estrangement from his

family, i.e., to underwrite his disappointments in who his parents are? Will his sense of being overwhelmed by his family's neediness freeze into a permanent state of injuries and injustice, and solidify into an inflexible rationale for ethical disengagement? Will he choose to protect himself from the sources of his injuries and, in so doing, cut himself off from the sources of his healing? Will he trap himself in the self-pitying confines of self-imposed monologue and so lose the validation he can have confirmed only in the dialogic process? Buffered from the merit of their valid truths and trust, will he unilaterally impute causes, motives and blame to his family—and victimize them as he feels they have victimized him? Will his self-protectiveness ultimately reify into the keystone of a lifetime's solipsistic stance?

Will Peter's secondary, if currently intense, loyalties to the therapist, an accidental relationship at best, serve to undercut legitimate options for dialogue with the people still committed to him and to whom he remains committed—in spite of his anger and frustration? Can he recognize the built-in limits of the therapeutic relationship— that, regardless of caring feelings, the therapist's ledger with the client existentially can never be ethically analogous to that of his family's; that, perforce, her investment in Peter excludes a mandate of long-term commitment? Will his evolving dialogue with the therapist triangulate his family, however unintentionally, and serve to rob its members of the chance to articulate *their* valid claims and sides? Or, conversely, can Peter use therapy to help him find the trust and courage to test his world from the perspective of a dialogic stance? Can he eventually afford to read his feelings as manifestations of injustice rather than as indictments of someone else's limits? Or will he finally choose to consign himself to a world in which feelings are used as ends in themselves (Krasner, 1986).

A therapist's proven capacity to hear and sense the affective tone of the relational process is one of the first requirements of his or her trustability. A therapist's faithful interpretation of affect and its meaning in her client's life and context is another.

Emotional processes are involved in the development of a trusting therapist-client relationship, so emotional entanglement between the two is always a possibility. In psychodynamic or psychoanalytic terms, part of this entanglement is termed transference and is regarded as a prerequisite for therapy. Freud's description of transference and its therapeutic use obviously has much merit. Nevertheless, emotional entanglement is also the substrate of a client's real dependence on a therapist.

Here a cautionary note is in order in terms of trust and the psychologically adept therapist. Many, if not most, people are easily influenced by the condition of their emotional states. They find it easy to lean on a soothing caretaker whether or not he is contributing to the healing process. A therapist may learn to speak the language of concern without being able to maintain a genuine concern for how his interventions affect *all* of the people involved in a given context. In this sense, the therapist's apparent trustworthiness can be inversely related to his capacity for slick, manipulative skills or persuasive suggestiveness—all squarely set on his knowledge of people's emotional nature. In any case, emotion is always a two-edged sword and can function as a catchword for therapy whether or not therapy is really taking place.

Contextual therapists acknowledge the value of emotional maturity and openness but step beyond them into the realm of commitment. Here the goal is to help people gain an attitude that will free them for a quest for multilateral balances of fairness in relationships. The word quest is meant to suggest an active, open curiosity and inquiry into reality. Part of reality is an inevitable struggle between the conflicting interests of two relating partners. The question of fairness between them is always a matter of equity, though not necessarily of equality. And it always has to do with space, availability, benefits, and burdens.

Contextual therapists carry the special burden of having to be actively partial to one family member after another. Detached indifference, neutrality or impartiality, the basis of therapeutic interventions in other modalities, simply cannot do the work of multidirectional partiality. The barrier here is that life tends to condition people to be unilateral, prejudiced on behalf of our own kind *and* against others and other kinds. It may even be that in a persons' own emotionally involved struggles it is difficult, if not impossible, to be sufficiently multilateral. At base, each person has to be committed to his or her own side and acknowledge that necessity for other people as well.

To develop the vision of a stance that is multilaterally concerned is a special accomplishment that requires a special kind of guidance and a special kind of guide. Contextual workers are concerned about the factual reality of therapy's impact and consequences for all of the involved family members and even for their descendants. They are aware of the personal costs of sequential, selective side-taking. They also know that the method's eventual payoff can far exceed its short-term costs. Their choice of a multidirected approach is more than an intellectual preference or an emotional option; it is based on factual data.

Structural, strategic and behavioral family therapists focus on producing behavioral change among people. This change is often equated with a client's behavioral patterns in the therapist's office at the present moment. Other times, room is given to gradual change ouside the office and beyond the here-and-now. In this kind of work, therapy moves outward from the therapist to his or her client. The therapist's strength is viewed as direct, linear and influential, so it is no surprise that the therapeutic process is often depicted as power-based. The assumption, here, is that the therapist's conviction of what is good for family members is the crucial criterion. If he begins from his *own* convictions, the therapist can easily make judgments about what relationship patterns are desirable. That and the hypothesis that behavioral patterns are the fundamental source of breakdown and conflict provide the floor from which the therapist then proceeds to structure, label, unsettle, paradox, and, in general, manipulate people's behavior and lives.

Techniques, though, fail to provide a basis for trust. Only multidirected partiality can establish the kind of structure that provides the safety for exploring, identifying, mobilizing, and earning residual trust. To achieve this therapeutic attitude, a therapist needs personal freedom, conviction, courage, knowledge and skills, a capacity for empathy, and an ability to claim his or her own private existence:

Freedom

Therapists need freedom and minds that are open to the vantage points of others whose lives can be affected by therapeutic action. To attain this in the therapy room, they have to be able to attain it in their relationships with their own families of origin, with their children, mates, peers, colleagues, and others with whom they share a mutuality of commitment.

Conviction

- Existential guilt or disentitlement *can* be the basis of profound inhibitions in a person's life and context;
- People can be liberated from existential guilt through earned entitlement;
- People can unlearn excessive reliance on destructive entitlement, and discover how to earn constructive entitlement as a road to freedom and satisfaction;
- People benefit from distinguishing between the meaning of their real legacies and the missions and injunctions that originate from parental delegation and force of custom;
- Therapists as professionals gain entitlement through benefiting their clients.

Courage

Therapeutic courage, a prerequiste of therapeutic helpfulness, is involved in the following ways:

- Helping a family face its real issues of hurt, shame, pain and embarrassment;

- Confronting family members with frightening issues, e.g., incest or suicide;
- Taking the risk of being mislabeled by colleagues or clients for striving to clarify issues of a family's balances of fairness;
- Challenging pseudoadversariness that is defensive and protectively reinforced in the process of helping people sort out the real issues of person-to-person conflicts of interest;
- Facing the heavy existential and emotional impact of interpersonal conflicts of interest;
- Facing and interrupting exploitative business-like schemes between family members that destroy interpersonal trustworthiness;
- Risking the directness and persistence that help clients define and represent honest relational positions and convictions.

Knowledge and Skills

- A capacity to recognize the transcultural universals of existential merit and obligation, regardless of learned value preferences;
- A capacity to help people face the balances of fairness among them. And a parallel capacity to identify how family members use their moral and intellectual development and sophistication as weapons against each other;
- A capacity to recognize the factual issues of life that create deep interpersonal struggles., e.g., a woman's hysterectomy, a parent's early loss of his or her father;
- A capacity to acknowledge the genuinely differing vantage points that people may naturally and validly hold, e.g., male and female perspectives.

A Capacity for Empathy and Claims for a Private Existence

- A capacity for empathic partiality for *all* family members discharges a therapist's obligations towards clients and earns him or her the entitlement to detach from work and turn to personal relationships.

There are many ways in which the therapist's personal life interests and professional work intertwine. A subtle barrier may exist in terms of what therapists can accomplish in their own relationships and what they can expect to do in their relationships with clients. People tend to assess a therapist's personal limitations and, at least at first, react accordingly. If the therapist is a determined single woman or single parent, for example, clients may intrinsically challenge her guidance. For whatever valid or invalid reasons, people tend to be less intrusive on a male therapist's mode of living than on a female's. It may also be difficult for a woman to elicit a more involved relational commitment from clients than her own limitations signal. In another area, it may be difficult for heterosexual therapists to develop real sensitivity to issues of concern to homosexual clients.

THE THERAPIST'S OWN STRENGTHS AND SATISFACTIONS

A therapist's professional satisfaction evolves from self-interest as well as from good work with clients. Performing well and receiving fair payment contribute to any worker's deep-felt self-esteem. The significance of doing an adequate job is a central factor in the human services field. Here an orientation towards profit alone is even more self-defeating than in business circles. A therapist's knowledge that his or her work is worthless exacts a high price in personal integrity for a long time to come.

The core of the therapist-client dialogue hinges on the meeting that takes place between them. "Healing through meeting" (Trüb, 1952; Freidman, 1985), the essence of the therapeutic exchange, is not an emotional cathexis based on mutual stimulation or even on a hope for dependence. Like caring parents, therapists want to be fully connected with their charges. But the real sign of care is demonstrated in a therapist's ability to let clients go, free of dependence even on the therapeutic relationship. Real meeting is in responsible care, that is, in a therapist's and a client's regard for the well-being and success of each other. It is this responsible consideration, rather than feelings of attraction, approval, affection, or liking and being liked, that constitutes the essence of the therapeutic meeting.

The principle of self-gain that comes from earned entitlement applies to the therapist-client relationship as it does to any other. What is different here is the asymmetry of expectations. The therapist is not an equal actor in the client's attempts to rebalance fairness and earn entitlement in his or her family. The ledger between therapist and client is separate from a family ledger, if sometimes analogous in intensity. But the one can never merge into the other. A client's attempts to straighten out or sustain fair family ledgers is only one aspect of the therapist-client relationship, of course. Still, his or her capacity to care about multilaterally fair balances gratifies the professional needs of a contextual therapist. So do behavioral changes that take place on the client's own terms, a genuine capacity for trustworthy relating, and the improved patterns of manifest behavior among family members.

The therapist-client relationship functions as a working team in which the therapist helps to surface options, but the client alone chooses them. This stance surfaces the question of what constitutes therapeutic activity. Does it lie in a power confrontation in which a therapist controls clients? Is it a question of superior manipulative skill and cunning? Is it a test of the therapist's competence and skill to create change, regardless of the client's motivations? Can the quality of a person's life improve if his or her own life goals are out of range of the therapist's suggestions for change? Contextual therapists answer these questions through their attempts to help clients find their own autonomous, mutually freeing aggregate of motivations. Here, therapeutic activity lies in provoking spontaneity in clients rather than in overpowering them. The therapist retains the right to assert him or herself in active ways, however. Dialogue, not passivity, is the therapist's most effective tool.

Contextual theory exposes itself to charges of optimism. It expects its therapists to build on a premise of resources in family contexts, as well as on the positive strength of the process of earning entitlement. It also expects its therapists to operate on the conviction that due consideration of others results in an outcome of self-gain. The therapist's baseline function is to lend courage and to plant seeds of resourcefulness and trustworthiness. His gain comes from a family's growing capacity for dialogue. Consider Vera, for example:

> Vera brought her mother into therapy after several sessions alone. The therapist acknowledged mother's suffering, struggle and claims as he did those of his primary client. Mother was startled by his concern. "I'm better understood here than I've been before by any of Vera's other therapists. All three of them challenged me, blamed me, put me down. Now I can understand my own mistakes better. I guess I didn't take Vera's side after I separated from her father. I also realize that she doesn't have to love Gary (mother's common-law husband), or even like him." Vera responded: "I feel great that I don't have to like Gary. Otherwise you might blame yourself for separating from Dad!"

Or consider the exchange between a brother and a sister:

> Joan was frustrated by her brother. "I love you, Hank," she said. "But I really don't like the way you are. You talk down to people; you don't listen; you never help with the dishes; you always expect to be served. You're divorcing Wendy after just a year of marriage, and you haven't even tried to work things out with her." Hank was equally frustrated with Joan. "Can't you see," he asked, "how hard it is to use the court against a woman I used to love and maybe still do?"
>
> The therapist turned to Hank. "Can you get beyond Joan's criticism and nagging and see her care for you?" Hank didn't respond and the battle of words continued. But as the two of them left the room, Hank turned toward Joan. "Thanks for trying to help," he said. "I guess I can see some of the love you have for me in some of what you said."

In both instances, the therapist's position was one of openness and respect for the clients' own relationships with each other. This kind of therapeutic stance is a much less personally possessive one than the position referred to by Carl Rogers in his dialogue with Martin Buber, for example. The exchange that Rogers describes is on a one-to-one basis. He talks about "acceptance," a therapeutic stance characterized by some of the following, self-described elements:

> . . . I'm willing for him to possess the feelings he possesses, to hold the attitudes he holds, to be the person he is. . . . I am able to sense with a good deal of clarity the way his experience seems to him, really viewing it from within him, and yet without losing my own personhood, or separateness in that . . . there is a real, experiential meeting of persons in which each of us is changed. (Buber, 1966, p. 170).

Many of these observations obviously have merit for any therapeutic stance. These moments of dialogic exchange are clearly significant. Still, the therapist can undercut his client's significant relationships by competing with them. The healing moment incorporates a transcendence of the therapist-client dialogue for the sake of an involvement in a more fully responsible dialogue between the client and his family members. Even so, clients still give precious confirmation to a therapist when they offer their trust and risk a search for help.

One of the dilemmas facing the profession is whether or not therapists are expected to have more effective and trustworthy personal relationships than their clients, as well as superior knowledge and skills. This is a frightening and sometimes embarrassing question to many therapists, e.g., those who, single and/or without children, treat married people and parents, and those who are divorced and afraid that their competence in marriage work may be challenged. One of the mitigating factors here is the knowledge that the limits of relationships hinge on many elements, including legacies and partners, as well as on who the therapist is.

Like other people, contextual therapists carry covert or overt elements of destructive entitlement. If they can take personal responsibility for their unfair biases, however, and begin to work them through, then the course of destructive entitlement can be reversed. To the extent that any therapist can recognize his own dilemma over destructive entitlement and struggle with it, he can become increasingly competent in guiding other people who are mired in the pain of alienation and justifiable self-blame. In contextual work, therapists are obliged to start from the baseline of their own responsibility, as is everyone else. From there on, methodological questions may be raised. First and foremost among them is the question of whether inclusive multidirected partiality is a feasible goal. Can a therapist extend concern to all affected relating persons in the family, in community, in the whole human species? The therapist's answer is decisive here, for a major part of his personal and professional integrity rests on a capacity to make reasonable attempts at a multidirected stance.

The demand factor in multidirected partiality can be heavy in the short-run. It is clearly easier, for example, to be partial to the children who have been molested than to their molesting father. Conversely, it can be difficult to be partial to the father himself. Yet how is father to gain trust and courage from a therapist if his side is consistently treated as if it is bereft of any merit at all? It may be true that the therapist is obliged to give primary currency to the children whose futures may be at stake. Still a child's well-being and that of her father are never mutually exclusive. To the contrary. There is usually ample room to try to find a basis for understanding the elements that once victimized their father, too.

TRAINING THERAPISTS

The process of training contextual therapists is characterized by organic growth and heavy demands for openness towards the trainee's own relationships. The self-selection process in contextual training may be of greater significance than in other therapeutic approaches. All helping professionals self-select on the basis of deep commitment and practicality. Deep sympathy for other people's suffering probably connects the professional therapist with her own moments of helpless pain, despair and shame. Her alliance with a suffering person is thus likely to be real and honest. It would seem to follow, then, that an alliance *with* the victim implies an alliance *against* the victimizer.

Parents are the immediate and apparent symbols of people's backgrounds and so naturally represent real and alleged culpability for much of an offsprings's suffering. Just as naturally, most helping professionals tend to assign blame to the client's parents. That proclivity in therapists may help them avoid their own destructive entitlement. A therapist's destructive entitlement may coincide with his invisible loyalty toward his parents. In the case of such a coincidence, the therapist's revolving slate may be activated; and, in order to spare his own parents, he or she might channel retributive attitudes towards the client's parents.

Family therapists cannot maintain a one-sided advocacy for long, though. A therapist's prejudgment of a client's family members automatically precludes genuine commitment and trust-building efforts by family members. In fact, unlike individually-oriented therapists, family therapists view *any fixed* unidirectional partiality as essentially irrational and destructive to the process of building trust. A contextual therapist learns to anticipate his clients' early resistance to his multidirectional stance. He knows that his own unilateral tendencies to favor a given child, for example, can undermine the therapeutic process if the youngster feels that the therapist is prejudging either one of her parents. He knows not to delude himself with tunnel vision, i.e., the hope that the treatment of one person can effectively address his or her entire reality. He also knows that he cannot turn away from family members who are affected by an individual client's treatment.

Unlike most classical psychotherapists, contextual therapists have no theoretical framework to confine them to an illusion about the impact of their work on all the members of a family. Here, though, it can be noted that many experienced individual therapists often go beyond the boundaries of their theories and doctrines. Typically, however, they neither define nor publish their own version of how they circumvent the individual theory that falls short of addressing the relational aspects of suffering. Classical family therapists, like individually-oriented therapists, may also fail to find a way to responsible multidirectionality. There just seem to be too many byways through which to escape into the impersonality of the systems concept and its intellectual elaborations.

The process of growth for a contextual therapist has many byways, too, but all of them are geared towards building trust. First, the trainee has to learn to face her clients' relationships from a vantage point that is genuinely multidirectional. Then her work may induce some tingling doubts about her own terms and ways in analogous relationships. She may have avoided an exploration of her own relating, or find that she's done a superficial job of it. In either case, the therapist is in danger of preaching one thing and practicing another. At that point there may be an inner conflict over both her own exploitative tendencies and her attempts to spare others as well. If this conflict escalates, she may find that she has left the contextual approach, albeit partially or temporarily. Furthermore, she may be attracted to the concrete operational clarity of other approaches. Her unresolved personal conflicts may obscure her professional convictions; she may lose the guidelines for treatment, and her clients may intuit her ambivalence. It might suddenly seem as if contextual therapy, even if intellectually correct, cannot be technically applied. The therapist's departure from the approach may then be imminent and permanent.

Conversely, if a therapist has the courage to face his own exploitative use of closely-relating family members, he may steadily deepen his attachment to the approach and develop ever-increasing skill in implementing multidirected partiality. For example, can he examine how he is using his mother-in-law as a scapegoat for his invisible loyalty to his mother whom he resents and has cut off? Can he decide to work on his own relation-ships either by himself or with help from a friend or a therapist? *There is a nonnegotiable correlation between the degree to which a therapist invests energy into the fairness of his own relationships and the degree to which he can be free to risk courage and invest trust into a more inclusive therapeutic concern.* Therapist or not, a person's negation of relational multilaterality is never solely based on an inadequate intellectual grasp of his relationships. It is always linked to the residue of his or her destructive entitlement and im-poses a requirement on him and his family to seek therapeutic guidance as a requirement of training.

Endnote: On Meaning Between the Generations

My father's cardiac arrest and hospitalization are forcing me to consider what his death will mean to me. My thoughts focus on several questions, among them, Who was he? What will his loss mean to me? What will his death mean to my children? What parallels do I find in our lives as fathers? What did I receive from him? What did I give him?

WHO WAS MY FATHER?

My father was a man who felt he had been cheated by the world. Cheated because his mother would not let him study a musical instrument. Cheated because he was never able to get the formal education he would have liked to have had. Cheated because the father whom he loved died when he was 18 years old, leaving him with a domineering and controlling mother. Cheated because he lost two children, aged 11 months and 23 months. Cheated because he lost his home and two businesses during the depression. Cheated because he got a job sweeping a floor in a factory in which he felt he should have been part owner. Cheated because his first wife was an invalid for the last 19 years of her life. Cheated because he felt the constant outsider. Yet he also cheated himself. For he eventually drove away anybody who ever tried to get close to him.

WHAT WILL HIS LOSS MEAN TO ME?

I don't know for, in some ways, we were strangers to each other. It was difficult to communicate with him except on a narrow range of subjects. When I was young, we did many things together; we went for long walks and talked about the world. As I grew older, we began to part ways. There was a time when I would have been glad never to see him again. But encouraged by my wife, he and I travelled together, once more father and son. For the first time in our adult lives, we were able to begin the process of understanding each other's motives, of acting differently, of making peace with each other. We began to reconnect at a level of mutual interest and love. At present, it is very difficult to talk with him either over the phone or in person, to tell him what is happening to me and to the family. Will I miss him when I can no longer be with him or speak to him? Probably. There is still the child in me that wants him around.

WHAT WILL HIS DEATH MEAN TO MY CHILDREN?

Will my children think of him as their grandfather or as my father? Does it make a difference? I think it does. He is possibly doomed to the ultimate cheat: not passing his memory on to the next generation. If one can't pass on to subsequent generations something of who one was as a person, then what meaning is there to life?

WHAT PARALLELS DO I FIND AS A FATHER?

Given who my father is and was, my real question is: How will my children feel about me when I get older? Will I eventually alienate my children as my father has somehow managed to alienate the people around him, including me? I would hope not. Could I have been more understanding of him as I want my children to be understanding of me and my foibles?

WHAT DID I RECEIVE FROM HIM?

There were things that were uniquely his to give to me. He unequivocally cared for me, yet he could not see who I was because of his own neediness. He could be animated and tell fascinating stories, yet he drove people away with a misplaced word or phrase that conveyed meanings he never intended. He had a love of religious ritual, yet often confused it with dogma. He could immerse himself unstintingly in work, but this often functioned as a barrier to seeking pleasure for himself.

I'd like to think I can learn from him. I'd like to invest in my own life without running over other people's terms. I'd like to avoid offending with the misplaced phrase and the even more misplaced gesture or tone of voice. I would hope to enjoy ritual without using it as a bludgeon against others. I would like to immerse myself in work and still find room for some small, daily pleasures.

I am afraid of the loss of my father even as I anticipate it. For all of his talk about death and dying over the years, like everyone else he does not want to die. Contemplating the death of my father has forced me to reexamine the meaning of my own life (Krasner, 1983).

Glossary

ACCOUNTABILITY: Its first connotation is an ethical-existential one: Regardless of our psychic attitudes, we bear liability for the consequences of our action or inaction. Accountability keeps balance with entitlement (see below). Its second connotation is a psychological one: the person's willingness or ability to accept responsibility for dialogue (mutuality or commitment) in both its self-delineating and self-validating phases.

ACKNOWLEDGMENT (CREDITING): Acknowledgment or crediting is a factual truth. It involves one or more people's open, immediate and direct recognition of the merit that has accrued to a person from his or her offers of care and consideration, i.e., contributions that have earned the donor entitlement.

Acknowledgment is a response to actual contributions; it does not originate from psychic-emotional attitudes on the acknowledger's part, e.g., compassion, pity or empathy.

A difference is to be noted between family member acknowledgments and therapeutic acknowledgment. Acknowledgment between partners is a means of redressing their ledger or balance of fairness. Therapeutic acknowledgment is essentially didactic in nature—a behavioral option that can lead partners toward self-validation and earned entitlement.

CONFLICT (INTERPERSONAL) OF INTERESTS: Some conflicts of interests, needs and entitlements are inevitable between relating partners and are to be viewed as natural rather than pathological. Other interpersonal conflicts of interests are avoidable, however, and attempts to resolve *all* interpersonal conflicts of interests are unrealistic. A realistic therapeutic attitude is linked to working on inevitable conflicts (e.g., parent-child goals during adolescence) and avoiding conflicts that *can* be avoided (e.g., a capacity to tolerate real attitudinal differences—political, religious, social—that do not require joint decision-making).

In any case, efforts to work on a foundation of underlying trust resources is always a more realistic therapeutic goal than designing an attack on symptoms.

CONSEQUENCE: "Something that follows from a set of conditions" (Webster's, 1971). Consequences are an important aspect of relationship. All persons, linked through relatedness to each other, are subject to the consequences of their relationship. In the long run, these consequences constitute a more significant relational bond than do transactional or communicational patterns. Consequences may take a linear or circular path, but they differ from a purely random set of events.

Operationally, it may be difficult to describe the consequences of a mistrustful marriage on a couple's small children, for example. But it is unrealistic, irrational and hence irresponsible to deny the existence of such consequences.

The context of consequences holds both symmetrical and asymmetrical options. In the case of small children, options are typically more limited than for others; relational consequences are therefore more decisive and binding than for adults.

CONTEXT: The organic thread of giving and receiving that weaves the fabric of human reliance and interdependence. The human context extends into a person's current relationships as well as into the past and future. It constitutes the sum total of *all* the ledgers of fairness in which a person is involved. Its dynamic criterion is rooted in due consideration, not in a mutuality of give-and-take.

From an ethical and existential perspective, context is a more specific concept than the texture of a given environment. It is a matrix of motivations, options and rights. It is a syncretic notion of system rather than a particulate notion. It never loses its multicentered, consequential nature.

CONTEXTUAL THERAPY: A therapeutic approach based on the empirical knowledge that a person's fair consideration of his or her relational obligations can result in personal freedom to participate in life's activities, satisfactions and enjoyment. Due consideration is therefore a major relational resource, a wellspring of liberation from a false or inauthentic sense of obligation and from wasteful, inauthentic interpersonal conflicts.

Multidirected partiality, contextual therapy's chief methodology, allows for an inclusive scan of each person's entire context of essential relationships. The freedom to develop any one, specific relationship is assumed to be an indirect consequence of a person's capacity to responsibly face the whole context of his or her relating. Responsibility for asymmetrical relationships, i.e., for especially vulnerable parties, requires particular consideration. Solidarity with victimized or developmentally vulnerable offspring is a chief priority of therapeutic partiality.

Commitment rather than affect is the cornerstone of contextual therapy. Its major goal is to liberate each family member to spontaneously rely on earned entitlement, i.e., on the ethical process of self-validation that is linked to due consideration of significant others. The self-sustaining spiral of motivations helps people make optimal use of relational resources.

DELEGATION: A term initially introduced by Stierlin (1974). In contextual terms, it describes the transgenerational expectations imposed on offspring by parents' (or earlier forebears') personal demands. By contrast, other transgenerational expectations can constitute legacies, i.e., mandates for posterity. Sacrificing the quality of marriage, friendship or parenting to a parent's possessiveness, for example, represents delegation rather than legacy.

DESTRUCTIVE ENTITLEMENT: Tragically, internally contradictory overentitlement originates from a child's inherent right to be cared for or die. This intrinsic entitlement escalates into overentitlement in direct proportion to the degree to which the following factors accrue:

- The child fails to receive adequate nurturance;
- The child's own needs for trust, devotion and love are exploited;
- The child receives mistrust, deceit and mystification in return for his trust and devotion;
- The child is eventually blamed for adult, relational failures.

In consequence a child is justified in seeing the adult world as his debtor. He is in no position to make the world own up to its debt, however. Worse is any attempt the child might make at later, substitutive vindication of his rights. For here the child (or grown-up) becomes the source of new injustice.

DIALOGUE: In contextual therapy dialogue describes a dialectical rule of relational balance rooted in a mutuality of commitment. Here the term goes beyond the popular denotation of open, ongoing exchange between partners. For us, genuine dialogue goes beyond satisfying emotional expectations of fulfillment in relationship *to* a requirement of genuine equitability. That is, a person's "use" of her partner becomes equitable in direct proportion to her consideration of her partner's rights and needs.

The matter of equitability is more problematic in asymmetrical relationships, e.g., between a parent and small child, or between a person and his or her yet unknown descendants. If a person ends his substance abuse out of a concern for its genetic implications, he has potentially made a relational input into the life of a great grandchild. His return on this investment is unlikely to be direct. It most likely will be repaid through posterity's further consideration of future generations.

DIMENSION: The four dimensions of relational reality constitute clusters of the determinants of human behavior. These clusters, unlike levels, are not meant to order factors into higher or deeper positions. The four dimensions are interpenetrating and omnipresent in human relationships. A parent-child relationship, for example, is always influenced by facts, individual psychology, systems of transactional patterns, and the ethic of due consideration or merited trust.

DISJUNCTION (ALSO SEE REJUNCTION): A disengagement from fair or due consideration of relationships. Relationships based purely on power belong here. Disjunction may find expression in formulae which suggest that being considerate amounts to being stupid or that the manipulation of others is the only real justification for being pleasant to them.

ELICITING: Eliciting is a therapeutic method or mode that catalyzes people's spontaneous motives in a mutually beneficial and dialogic direction. It contrasts with a specific goal design. Rather than arbitrarily restructuring input, eliciting requires the therapeutic capacity to integrate the dimensions of fact, psychology, transactions, and due consideration—and help people face and rework the balances of entitlement and indebtedness in their contexts.

ENTITLEMENT: Entitlement is a key concept of contextual therapy. It is an ethical "guarantee" that can arise only within a relationship and which can accumulate merit on the side of a deserving contributor. Entitlement cannot be ethically transferred from the domain of one relationship to another. Nevertheless, a person who earns entitlement at a given time in a given relationship will function with greater freedom in other relationships, too.

No matter how overentitled a person may be or feel, he or she never moves beyond the requirement of having to care about earning more entitlement. Constructive entitlement, the result of *continuing to care* about earning entitlement, and destructive (or vindictive) entitlement, the result of *refusing to care* about earning entitlement, are two opposing kinds of clinical consequences. The ethical nature of entitlement sharply distinguishes it from the psychological phenomenon of a "sense of," "feeling of," or "attitude of" entitlement. A person's feelings of entitlement may or may not coincide with *being* entitled.

EXONERATION: Exoneration is a process of lifting the load of culpability off the shoulders of a given person whom heretofore we may have blamed. In our experience clinical improvement often coincides with the renewed capacity of parents to exonerate their own seemingly failing parents.

Exoneration differs from forgiveness. The act of forgiveness usually *retains* the assumption of guilt and extends the forgiver's generosity to the person who has injured her or him. Offering forgiveness, a person now refrains from holding the culprit accountable and from demanding punishment. In contrast, exoneration typically results from an adult reassessment of the failing parent's own past childhood victimization. It replaces a framework of blame with mature appreciation of a given person's (or situation's) past options, efforts and limits.

INTRINSIC RELATIONAL TRIBUNAL: This term represents a built-in juridical characteristic of close relating. The tribunal is unspoken and invisible, but it can execute its decrees. People who ignore the tribunal's requirements of due consideration eventually suffer from some form of negative relational outcome. Negative consequences may be psychosomatic and manifest themselves in insomnia, sexual inadequacy, self-destructive behavior, or patterns, guilt, and depression. Each relationship has its own juridical realm and criteria for equitable give-and-take. Any significant disregard for fairness in one relationship should be handled within its own jurisdictional realm rather than through "taking it out" on another relationship (see *revolving slate*).

INVISIBLE LOYALTY: Externally, invisible or indirect loyalty is manifested as indifference, avoidance or ambivalent indecisiveness vis-à-vis the object of loyalty. Overtly, it presents itself as a "pathological" force that blocks commitment to a current relationship, e.g., marriage. In fact, it is a current relationship that is usually victimized in a vicarious manner, an expression of substitutive requital related to a form of *revolving slate*. This phenomenon can be understood as a covert attempt to balance vertical relationships through overt interference with horizontal (or, at times, other vertical) relationships. In therapy, avenues will be sought to replace attitudes of invisible loyalty with acts of visible concern.

JUSTICE OR A BALANCE OF FAIRNESS: Relational justice or a balance of fairness is the dynamic foundation of viable, continuing, close relationships. At the very least, a periodic concern for monitoring the fairness of a relationship is required to keep a relationship trustworthy. A just state of relationship is not a possession, not a thing to be owned, of course. Rather it requires ongoing striving for a never fully attainable goal.

Contextual therapy regards justice as an ongoing challenge to existing balances of fairness. Every new act of give-and-take requires a new adjustment of the balance of retributive justice. Retributive justice emerges between relating persons. On the other hand, distributive justice hinges on the whim or coincidence characteristically imposed by destiny, e.g., the inheritance of a disease.

LEDGER OF MERITS: The ledger is a calculus concerned with the balance between the accumulating merits and debts of the two sides of any relationship. Just how much entitlement or indebtedness each party has at a given time depends on the fairness of give-and-take that exists between them.

The terms of give-and-take between people are shaped by the symmetry or asymmetry of a relationship. Symmetry and asymmetry pertain to the basic configuration of each partner's basic needs and entitlements within the relationship. In a symmetrical relationship, one peer owes the other approximately the same due consideration. In an asymmetrical relationship, the child is an unmatched partner who cannot be expected to fend for himself to an extent approximating what he is due. Fair balancing between parent and child requires equitable but not equal reciprocity. Clinically asymmetry regulates the fairness of mutual claims. The incestuous parent, for example, is involved in a gross disregard for asymmetry when he seeks an adult sexual partnership from a child. In general, no parent can realistically expect to be repaid in kind for what he or she has given to a child. Nor can an adult offspring expect an equal return for care extended to a terminally ill or impoverished parent.

LEGACY: A legacy (or transgenerational mandate) links the inherited endowments of the current generation to its obligation to posterity. The obligation to posterity is part of relational reality; it is not imposed by any particular value orientation or subculture.

All forms of higher animal life require an intrinsic commitment to the good of posterity for transgenerational survival. In this sense legacy is a positive, enabling input in the chain of the survival of the species.

Legacy is not an obligation to repeat errors of the past. For example, a "legacy of alcoholism" in a family does not suggest an obligation to perpetuate alcoholism on the future out of loyalty to the past. To the contrary. Legacy is an obligation to help free posterity from crippling habits, traditions and delegations of previous generations. Legacy is the present generation's ethical imperative to sort out what in life is beneficial for posterity's quality of survival. Each person owes the future consideration of both the mandates and missions of posterity.

LOYALTY: In contextual terms, loyalty is a preferential attachment to relational partners who are entitled to a priority of "bonding". At a minimum, loyalty is a triadic, relational configuration: the preferring one, the preferred one and the one who is not preferred. The definition of loyalty does not apply to one person's simple attachment to another person—unless the attachment is subject to a test of preference vis-à-vis another real or potential attachment. Loyalty and loyalty conflict are, therefore, difficult to separate. For loyalty conflict applies to a situation in which a person is caught between two explicitly competing loyalty objects. Picture the man who is in the middle of two competing forces—The claims to his loyalty on the part of both his wife and his mother. Both women have justifiable claims for priority of consideration in comparison to other women. (see *split loyalty*)

MORATORIUM: A step in a therapeutic method that tries to guide clients towards considering the benefits of a new relational attitude *and* utilizing the benefits of waiting until a person is spontaneously motivated toward that new relational attitude. A moratorium is an active therapeutic input: It retains a desirable, uncompromised goal without a disregard for the client's own timing. Put in other terms, it may be difficult for a client to ignore a therapist's message when it is a clear but not yet pressing priority for him. There may be merit in considering the message, the client is told, but it makes little sense to try until you are actually ready to act on it. A moratorium, then, includes and combines: 1) therapeutic insistence on a client's active accountability for seeking improvement, and 2) an offer to make room for the client to choose, depending on his readiness, when and how to implement aspects of his accountability.

MULTIDIRECTED PARTIALITY: Multidirected partiality (Boszormenyi-Nagy, 1966) is contextual therapy's chief therapeutic attitude and method. It consists of a set of principles and technical guidelines that require the therapist to be accountable to everybody who is potentially affected by his or her interventions. In the practice of contextual therapy, this principle of inclusiveness has to be linked to the therapist's determination to discover the humanity of every participant—even of the family's "monster member."

Methodologically, multidirected partiality takes the form of sequential siding *with* (and eventually *against*) member after family member. The therapist tries to empathize with and credit everyone on a basis that actually merits crediting. If a therapist cannot credit a person for his or her stance in a current issue, e.g., child abuse, he can at least credit a person in terms of past, childhood victimization.

MULTILATERALITY: Relationships are always characterized by two or more sides. Dynamically though, people tend to deny their partner's side and construct relationships on their own subjective, unilateral terms. This one-sided view is ingrained in individual survival and in every group's own prejudice toward other groups. A therapist's use of multidirected partiality enables a multilateral exploration of relationships. In response, clients can enter a dialogic realm which allows them to define their own terms (self-delineation) and respond to the terms of their partner (self-validation).

OBSTACLES (COLLUSIVE RESISTANCE): One of Freud's major contributions was his observation that people tend to actively resist a therapist's attempts to help them *and* their own progress toward cure. Much of this resistance has to do with the client's unconscious adherence to what Freud defined as "neurotic gain".

In family therapy literature, resistance is usually referred to as "family resistance." This term customarily suggests a collusive or collective purpose among family members to defeat therapeutic progress. Such phenomena have to be connected with each family member's own unconscious dynamics, of course. The term "resistance" was originally introduced to describe the functions of one mind. To avoid confusion over individual and relational usage of "resistance," we prefer to use the word "obstacle" to convey relational or collusive resistance to therapeutic progress.

PARENTIFICATION: The term originally described (Boszormenyi-Nagy, 1965a; Boszormenyi-Nagy & Spark, 1973) an adult's maneuver to turn a child (or adult) into a functional "elder," i.e., someone who takes more than age appropriate responsibility for a relationship. As a transactional shift of role boundaries, parentification is not necessarily detrimental to a child. In fact, it can be a child's appropriate adaptation to temporary family strain. In these situations, a youngster can benefit from learning about responsible role taking.

From a contextual perspective, parentification is destructive when it depletes a child's resources and trust reserves. This occurs when adults manipulate their offspring's innate tendency for trusting devotion. The predicament of split loyalty, for example, always parentifies a child in a systemic sense—even if each parent wishes to refrain from using the child.

POSTERITY: Posterity refers to future generations and includes the youngest living generation still subject to developmental vulnerability. Posterity is vulnerable to developmental, formative input and so merits priority in developing therapeutic plans. Thus, grown-ups look back at a formative past while posterity lives in a formative present and faces a formative future. Posterity is inherently entitled to due consideration. Offering due consideration is the present generation's primary way to repay the inherent generosity of its generative past.

REJUNCTION: A specific goal of contextual therapy, rejunction refers to the basic ethics of the process of relating, i.e., estranged family members benefit from rejoining each other in responsible dialogue. Disjunction is the opposite of rejunction, and means a divergence (or lack of integration) between self-service and altruism. Disjunction therefore suggests a depletion of relational trust reserves. It characterizes relationships in which family members have abandoned the process of ethically validating their own worth through offering due consideration to others (self-validation). Conversely, rejunction characterizes relationships in which family members choose to earn entitlement through self-validation.

RELATIONAL ETHICS: People use each other, are used by each other, and accept or fight against particular usages of each other. This is the essence of close relationships. Relationships can be trustworthy as long as the partners' use of each other is multilateral and equitable. The notion of ethics here is rooted in the ontology of the fundamental nature of all living creatures, i.e., life is received from forebears and conveyed to posterity. Life is a chain of interlocking consequences linked to the interdependence of the parent and child generations. In human beings, relational ethics require people to assume responsibility for consequences. But consequences *per se* constitute unavoidable, existential reality.

RELATIONAL CORRUPTION: Relational corruption refers to a subtle subversion of trustworthiness. When one person exploits another person's offer of care or consideration to himself or someone else, then a basic breach of trustworthy relating occurs. Examples include an adult's sexual use of a child, a choice that exploits the youngster's offer of care and concern for the adult, or a person's self-serving, destructive parentification of his mate when she tries to discipline their child. Relational corruption is usually a multigenerational pattern of flight, denial and evasion of responsibility for dialogue in both its self-delineating and self-validating phases.

REVOLVING SLATE: The revolving slate (Boszormenyi-Nagy & Spark, 1973) is a relational consequence in which a person's substitutive revenge against one person eventually creates a new victim. The term "slate" refers to a fixed account between people that ordinarily merits fair consideration. Instead, it gets turned against a substitute, an innocent target who is treated as if he or she were the original debtor.

RESOURCES (RELATIONAL): Relational resources are factual and fundamental means, options and opportunities in people and their relationships by which they can improve and help themselves and others. They are major avenues through which people can move toward healing the "discontinuity of self"

(Kohut, 1977) or strengthening the ego's mastery in the classical Freudian sense. The opposite of relational costs, relational resources provide the fuel by which fairness may be actualized.

Contextual therapy aims to catalyze positive relational resources rather than focusing on removing pathology, symptoms or problems.

SELF-DELINEATION: A person's capacity to define his or her individual, autonomous self. This is phase one in the dialogic process. Two or more people aid each other in the process of self-delineation. Delineating oneself is, therefore, a major resource offered by the relational process. On the other hand, the forms and facets of a child's initial, formative relationships determine the degree to which a self can be delineated.

The process of self-delineation includes boundary formation between the self and the not-self with which it enters into relationship. The self forms over against the ground of otherness. It encompasses the content of its own identity formation as well.

SELF-VALIDATION: A person's capacity to earn credit for relational integrity rather than simply defend power, prestige or self-esteem. This is phase two in the dialogic process. This process establishes and enhances the self's ethical worth.

Power gains are often inversely related to self-validation; manipulative self-gain can amount to a decrease in ethical self-worth. Self-validation is a step in the process of earning entitlement. It results, then, in the kind of freedom produced by earned entitlement.

SPLIT LOYALTY: The predicament of split loyalty occurs when a child is forced to choose one parent's love at the cost of betraying his or her other parent. This ominous condition surfaces when parents are deeply split by mutual mistrust and contempt. The manifestations of mistrust vary, but the more subtle its signs, the more unmanageable the predicament for the young. Attaining an attitude of basic trust toward the adult world is a fundamental need of the young. Only so can a child be capable of balancing realistic attitudes of basic mistrust. If trusting one parent inevitably evokes mistrust toward the other, though, trusting one *ipso facto* cancels out the option of trusting the other.

Split loyalty can be equally devastating if it develops out of a child's need to choose between his single mother and grandmother or sister, aunt or other significant adult. Over time, a child tries to create a trust base in any of these triangular predicaments. The trust-demolishing effects of split-loyalty create the basis for a child's destructive parentification and can lead to severe personality problems, as well as to suicide.

SPONTANEITY: Spontaneity represents a client's active and genuine commitment to his or her own life-goals. No therapy can be enduring or compatible without at least a degree of a client's own spontaneity.

Contextual therapy invests significant energy in guiding people in directions that are compatible with their own emerging spontaneous motivations. Chief among these is reliance on the self-motivating spiral of earned entitlement, i.e., the freedom earned by a person who offers fair consideration to significant people in his or her own life and context.

TRUSTWORTHINESS: Trustworthiness accrues on the side of the reliable, responsible, duly considerate partner in a relationship and is a characteristic of realistic, deserved trust. From a psychological perspective, the trust experienced by a trusting partner is no guarantee of the ethical worth of the trusted partner. A victim's naive trust in a con artist is no proof of the latter's trustworthiness. From an ethical perspective, trustworthiness is always earned over the long-term by balancing of the consequences of give-and-take between two relatively reliable partners.

References

Ackerman, N.W. *The Psychodynamics of Family Life: Diagnosis and Treatment of Family Relationships.* New York: Basic Books, 1958.

Bateson, G. *Mind and Nature.* New York: E.P. Dutton, 1979.

Bateson, G., Jackson, D.D., Haley, J., and Weakland, J.H. Toward a theory of schizophrenia. *Behav. Sci., 1,* 251–264, 1956.

Bateson, G., Jackson, D.D., Haley, J., and Weakland, J.H. A note on the Double Bind. *Family Process, 2,* 154–161, 1962.

Berne, E. *Games People Play.* New York: Grove Press, 1964.

Boszormenyi-Nagy, I. Family treatment in schizophrenia (Paper presented at the Annual Meeting of the American Psychological Assn., Chicago, 1960.

Boszormenyi-Nagy, I. The concept of schizophrenia from the point of view of family treatment. *Family Process, 1,* 103–113, 1962.

Boszormenyi-Nagy, I. A theory of relationships: Experience and transaction. In I. Boszormenyi-Nagy and J. L. Framo (Eds.), *Intensive Family Therapy.* New York: Brunner/Mazel, 1965a.

Boszormenyi-Nagy, I. The concept of change in conjoint family therapy. In A. S. Friedman, et al., *Psychotherapy for the Whole Family.* New York: Springer, 1965b.

Boszormenyi-Nagy, I. From family therapy to a psychology of relationships: Fictions of the individual and fictions of the family. *Comprehensive Psychiatry, 7,* 408–423, 1966.

Boszormenyi-Nagy, I. Relational modes and meaning. In G.H. Zuk and I. Boszormenyi-Nagy (Eds.), *Family Therapy and Disturbed Families.* Palo Alto: Science & Behavior Books, 1967.

Boszormenyi-Nagy, I. Loyalty implications of the transference model in psychotherapy. *AMA Archives of General Psychiatry, 27,* 374–380, 1972.

Boszormenyi-Nagy, I. Contextual therapy: Therapeutic leverages in mobilizing trust. Report 2 UNIT IV: *The American Family.* Philadelphia: The Continuing Education Service of Smith, Kline and French Laboratories, 1979. Reprinted in R.J. Green and J.L. Framo (Eds.), *Family Therapy: Major Contributions.* New York: International Universities Press, 1981, pp. 393–416.

Boszormenyi-Nagy, I. Contextual therapy: The realm of the individual: An interview with Margaret Markham. *Psychiatric News, XVI,* 20 and 21, 1981.

Boszormenyi-Nagy, I. The ethical dimension of the contextual approach: A presentation at the Harvard Medical School. Symposium on *Self-Esteem and Values,* Boston, September 14, 1983.

Boszormenyi-Nagy, I. and Framo, J.L. (Eds.), *Intensive Family Therapy.* New York: Brunner/Mazel, 1986. (Originally published 1965.)

Boszormenyi-Nagy, I. and Krasner, B.R.: Trust-based therapy; A contextual approach. *American Journal of Psychiatry, 137,* 767–775, 1980.

Boszormenyi-Nagy, I. and Spark, G.M. *Invisible Loyalties.* New York: Harper & Row, 1973; Brunner/Mazel, 1984.

Boszormenyi-Nagy, I. and Ulrich, D. Contextual family therapy. In A. Gurman and D.P. Kniskern (Eds.), *Handbook of Family Therapy.* New York: Brunner/Mazel, 1981.

Bowen, M. Family psychotherapy with schizophrenia in the hospital and in private practice. In I. Boszormenyi-Nagy and Framo, J.L. (Eds.), *Intensive Family Therapy.* New York: Brunner/Mazel, 1986. (Originally published 1965.)

Buber, M. Guilt and guilt feelings (1948). *Psychiatry 20,* 114–129, 1957.

Buber, M. *I and Thou.* (2nd rev. ed. with a postscript by author added. Trans. Smith R.G.) New York: Charles Scribner's Sons, 1958.

Buber, M. *The Knowledge of Man. A Philosophy of the Interhuman* (Trans. M.S. Friedman). New York: Harper and Row (Torchbooks), 1966.

California, Chapter 915, Family Law Reporter Reference File 305:0015–0016, 12, 12, 79. Bureau of National Affairs, 1980.

Cotroneo, M. and Krasner, B.R. Abortion and problems in decision making. *Journal of Marriage and Family Counseling, 3*(1), 69–76, 1977.

Cotroneo, M. and Krasner, B.R. A contextual approach to Jewish-Christian dialogue. *Journal of Ecumenical Studies, 18*:1, 41–62, Winter 1981.

Dell, P.F. Some irreverent thoughts on paradox. *Family Process, 20,* 37–51, 1981.

Erikson, E.H. Problem of ego identity. *Psychological Issues,* 1:1, 1959.

Fairbairn, W.R.D. *Psychoanalytic Studies of the Personality.* London: Tavistock, 1952.

Fairbairn, W.R.D. An *Object Relations Theory of the Personality.* New York, Basic Books, 1954.

Fisher, F. *The Search for Anna Fisher.* New York: Fawcett, 1981.

Fromm-Reichmann, F. Notes on the treatment of schizophrenia by psychoanalytic psychotherapy. *Psychiatry, 11,* 267–277, 1948.

Friedman, M. *The Healing Dialogue in Psychotherapy.* New York: J. Aronson, 1985.

GAP (Group for the Advancement of Psychiatry). *Divorce, Child Custody and the Family.* New York: Mental Health Materials Center, 1980.

Goldstein, J., Freud, A., and Solnit, A.J. *Beyond the Best Interests of the Child.* New York: The Free Press, 1973.

Guntrip, H. *Personality Structure and Human Interaction.* New York: International Universities Press, 1961.

Harlow, H.F. Development of affection in primates. In E.L. Bliss (Ed.) *Roots of Behavior.* New York: Hoeber, 1962.

Heusden, A. van and Eerenbeemt, E.P. van den. *Ivan Boszormenyi-Nagy en Zijn Visie op Individuele en Gezins Therapie.* Haarlem, the Netherlands: DeToorts, 1983.

Hoffman, L. *Foundations of Family Therapy.* New York: Basic Books, 1981.

Hollender, M. and Boszormenyi-Nagy, I. Hallucination as an ego experience. *A.M.A. Archives of Neurology and Psychiatry, 80,* 93–97, 1958.

Jackson, D.D. The questions of family homeostasis. *Psychiatric Quarterly (Suppl.)*, *31*, 79–90, 1957.

Jackson, D.D. and Weakland, J.H. Conjoint family therapy. *Psychiatry* 24 (Suppl. to No. 2), 222–248, 1961.

Jacobson, N. Expanding the range and applicability of behavioral marital therapy. *The Behavior Therapist, 6,* 189–191, 1983.

Johnson, A.M. and Szurek, S.A. The genesis of antisocial acting out in children and adults. *Psychoanal. Quart., 21,* 323–343, 1952.

Jonas, J. *Das Prinzip Verantwortung* (The Principle of Responsibility) Frankfurt (Germany): Insel, 1979.

Kaufmann, W. *Basic Writings of Nietzsche.* New York: Modern Library, 1968.

Klein, M. *Contributions to Psychoanalysis,* London: Hogarth, 1948.

Kohut, H. *The Restoration of the Self,* New York: International Universities Press, 1977.

Krasner, B.R. *Sublime Anthropomorphism: The Significance of Jewish Mysticism for Personal and Communal Existence.* Unpublished Dissertation, Temple Univ., 1975.

Krasner, B.R. Trustworthiness: The primal family resource. In Karpel, M. (Ed.), *Family Resources.* New York: Guilford Press, 1986.

Krasner, D. *Letter to My Children.* Unpublished, 1983.

Lederer, W.J. and Jackson, D.D. *The Mirages of Marriage.* New York: W.W. Norton, 1968.

Lidz, T., Fleck, S., and Cornelison, A. The intrafamilial environment of schizophrenic patients: II. Marital schism and marital skew. *American Journal of Psychiatry,* 114:241–248, 1957.

Lindsey, R. *The Falcon and the Snowman.* New York: Simon and Schuster, 1979.

Lorenz, K.Z. *The Foundations of Ethology.* New York/Wien: Springer Verlag, 1981.

Maslow, A.H. *Motivation and Personality.* New York: Harper & Row, 1954.

McCall, C. *Peoples Magazine.* Aug. 29, 1983, pp. 351–354.

Minuchin, S. *Families and Family Therapy.* Cambridge, MA: Harvard University Press, 1974.

Miros, M. *Through a Glass Darkly: Dialogue with an Unknown Person,* (unpublished), 1983.

Rado, S. The economic principle in psychoanalytic technique. *Internat. Journal of Psychoanalysis.* 6, 1925.

Reik, T. *Listening with the Third Ear.* New York: Farrar, Strauss, 1948.

Rogers, C.R. *Client Centered Therapy.* Boston: Houghton-Mifflin, 1951.

Sartre, J.P. *Being and Nothingness. Essay on Phenomenological Ontology.* New York: Philosophical Library, 1956.

Sechehaye, M.A. *A New Psychotherapy in Schizophrenia: Relief of Frustration by Symbolic Realization.* New York: Greene, 1956.

Selvini-Palazzoli, M. *Paradox and Counterparadox.* New York: Jason Aronson, 1978.

Spiegelberg, H. *The Phenomenological Movement: A Historical Introduction.* The Hague: Martinus Nijhoff, 1960.

Spitz, R.A. Hospitalism: A follow-up report. *Psychoanal. Study of the Child, 2,* 113–117, 1946.

Stierlin, H. *Separating Parents and Adolescents.* New York: Quadrangle, 1974.

Stirner, M. *The Ego and His Own.* London: Byington, 1913 (originally published 1845).

Sullivan, H.S. *Conceptions of Modern Psychiatry.* Washington, D.C. William Alanson White Psychiatric Foundation, 1947.

Trüb, H. *Heilung aus der Begegnung (Healing through meeting)*. Ed. E. Michel and
    A. Sborowitz. Stuttgart: Klett, 1952.
Webster's Third New International Dictionary of the English Language. Springfield; MA:
    G.C. Merriam, 1971.
Will, O.A. Psychotherapeutics and the schizophrenic reaction. *J. Nerv. Ment.
    Disease, 126,* 109–140, 1958.
Wilson, E.O. *Sociobiology*. The abridged edition. Cambridge, MA: The Belknap
    Press of Harvard University Press., 1980.
Winnicott, D.W. Ego distortion in terms of the true and false self. 1965 (quoted
    on p. 51 of Davis, M. and Wallbridge, D. *Boundary and Space*. New York: Brun-
    ner/Mazel, 1981).
Wynne, L.C., et al. Pseudo-mutuality in the family relations of schizophrenics.
    Psychiatry, 21, 205–220, 1958.
Zuk, G.H. and Boszormenyi-Nagy, I. *Family Therapy and Disturbed Families*. Palo
    Alto: Science & Behavior Books.

Index

Please note that page numbers in *italic* refer to the Glossary.